Svetlana Chmakova's
Nightschool
The Weirn Books

VOLUME FOUR

Yen Press

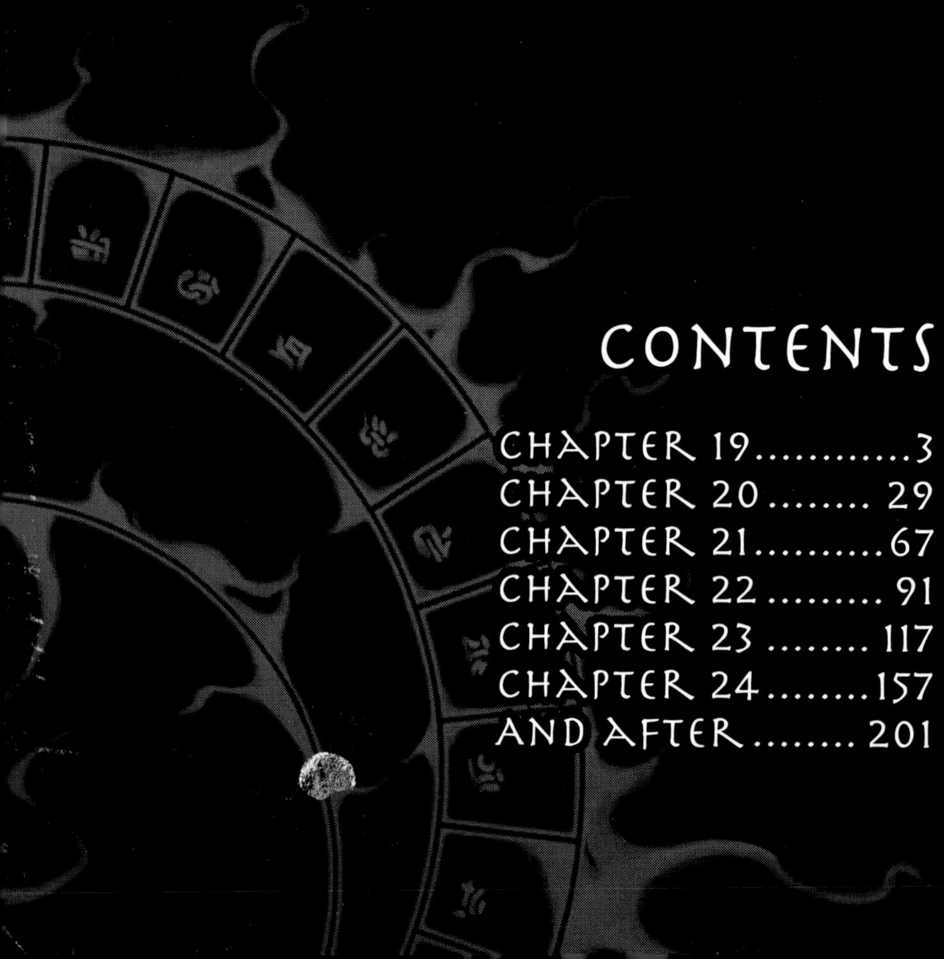

CONTENTS

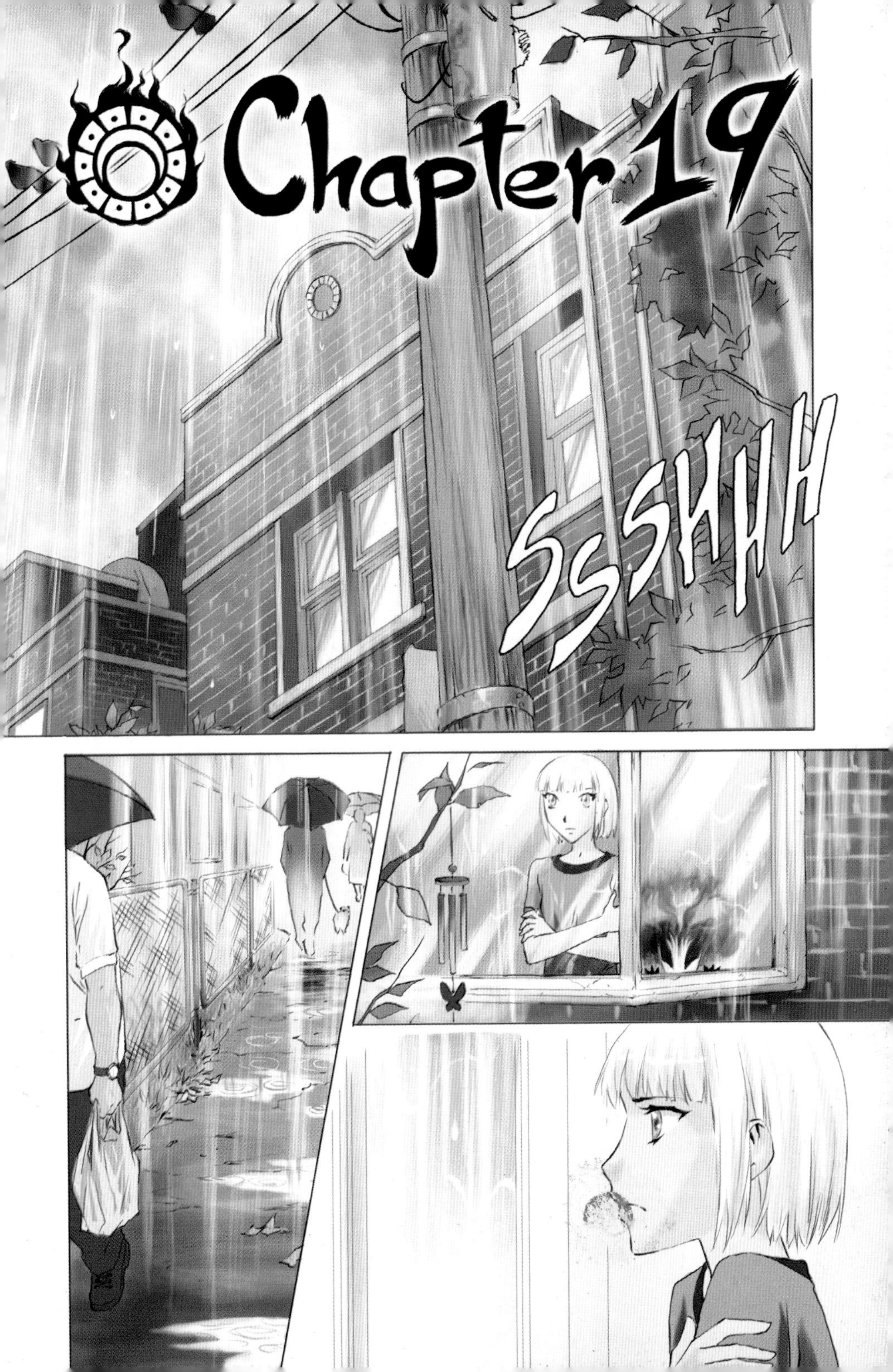
Chapter 19
SSSHHH

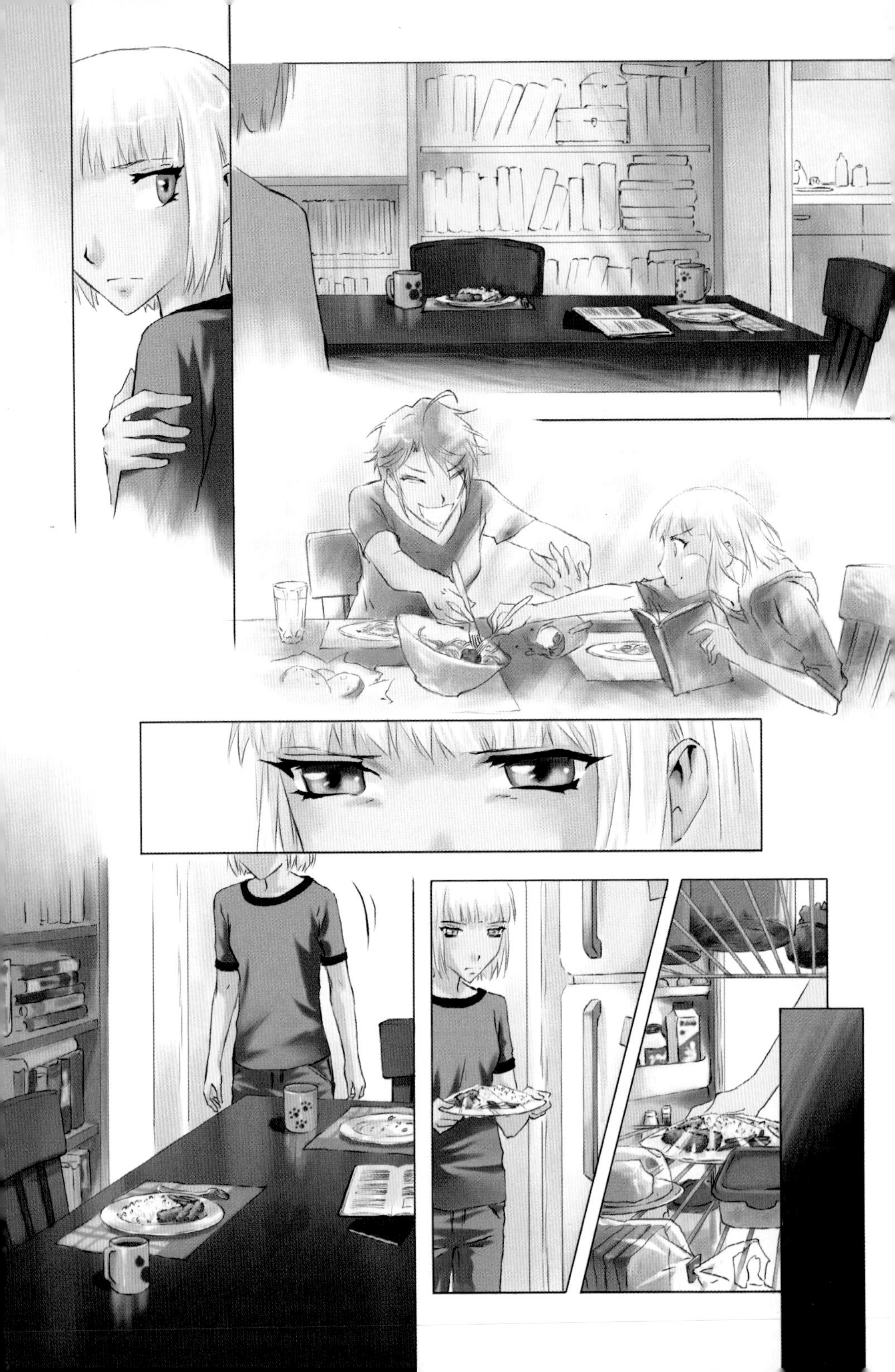

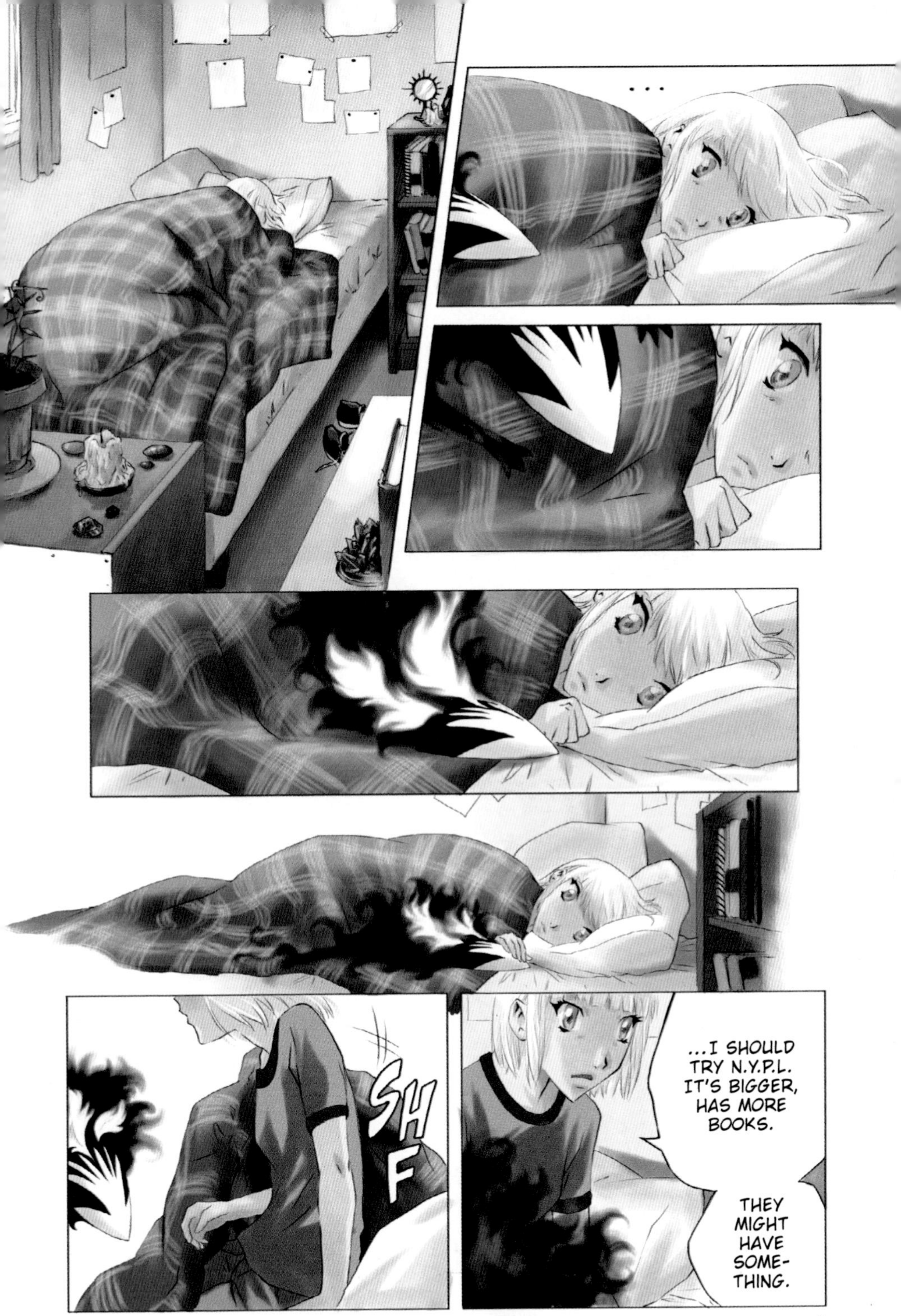
. . .
SH
F
...I SHOULD TRY N.Y.P.L. IT'S BIGGER, HAS MORE BOOKS.
THEY MIGHT HAVE SOME-THING.

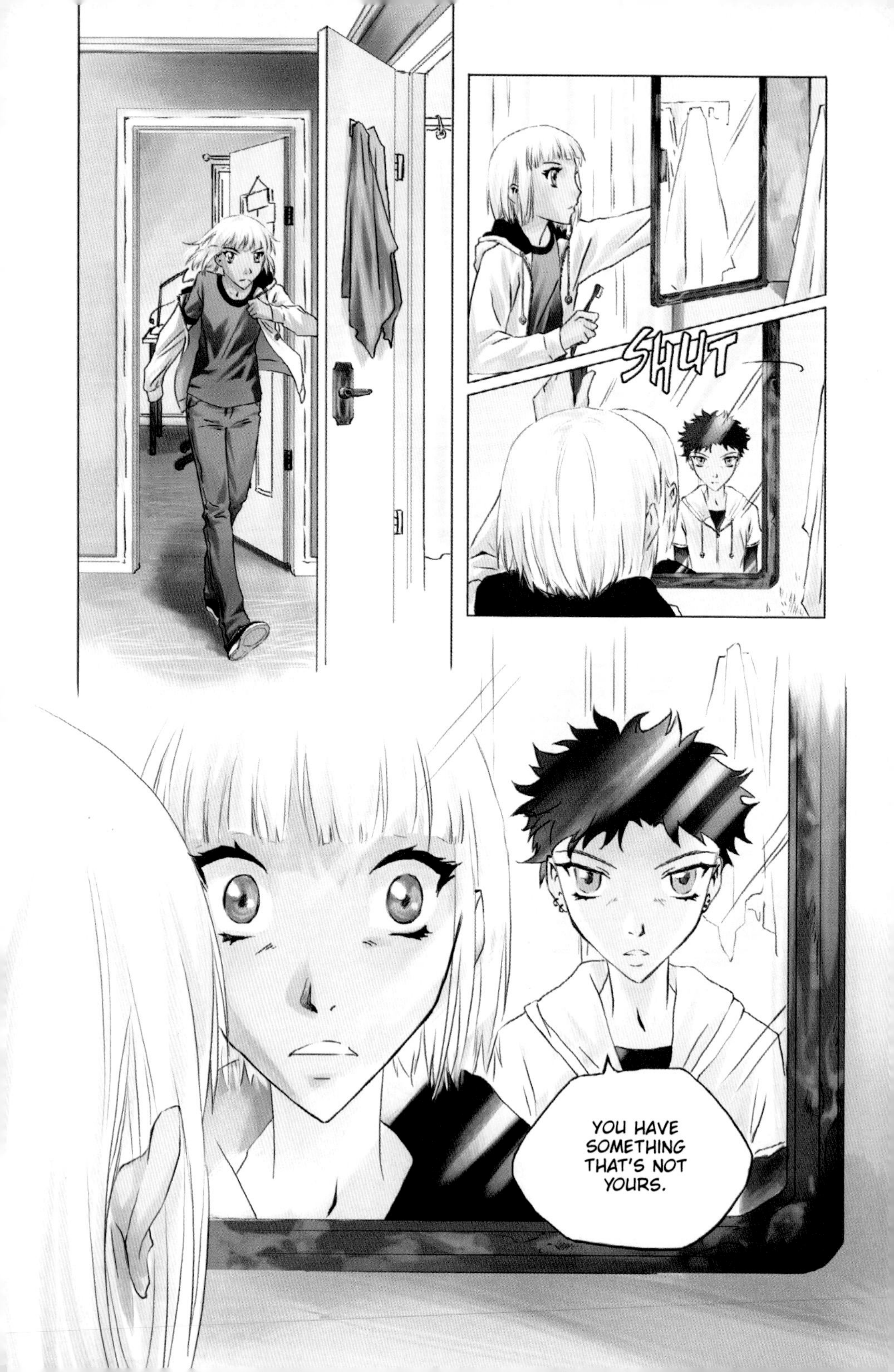
SHUT
YOU HAVE SOMETHING THAT'S NOT YOURS.

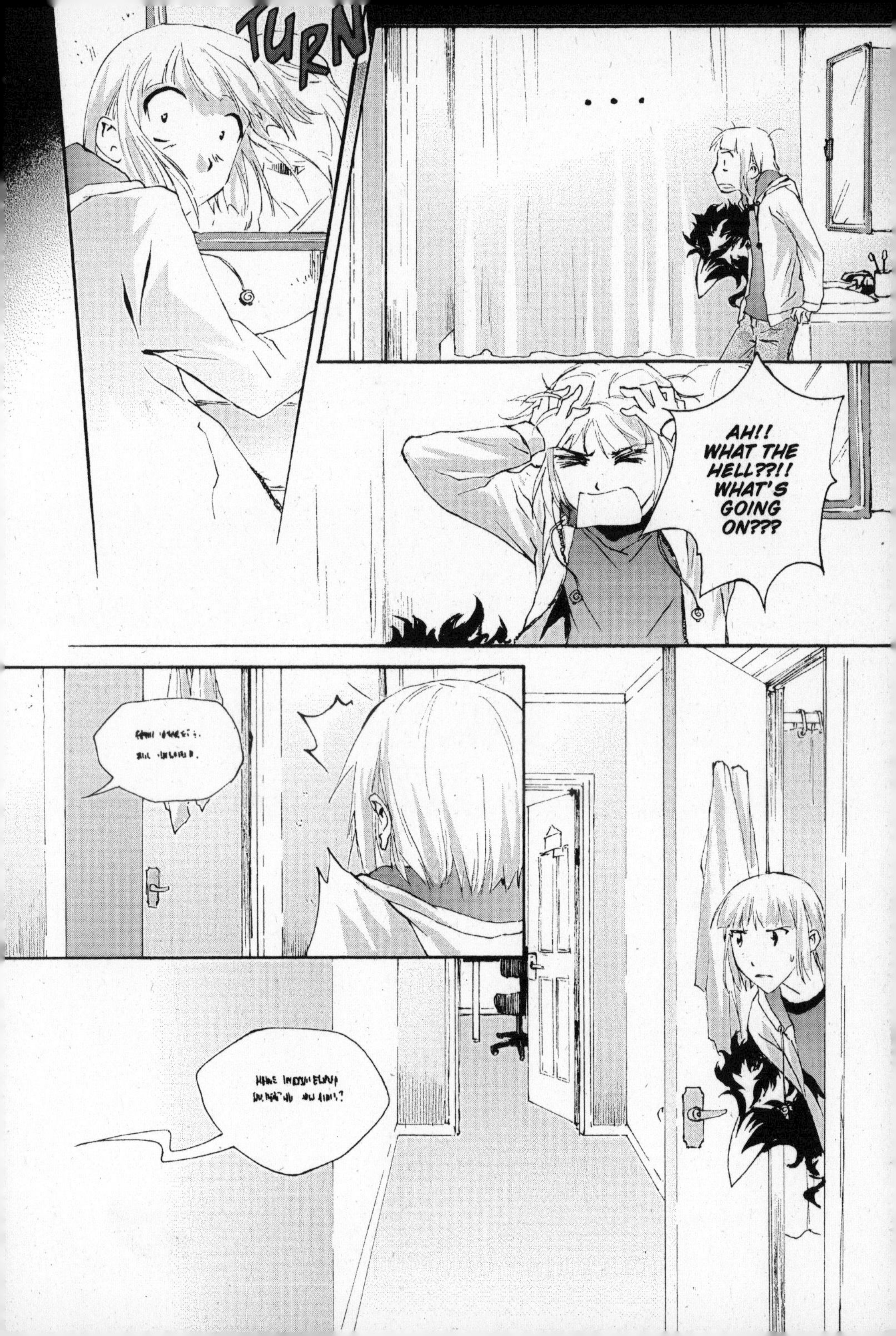
TURN
...
AH!! WHAT THE HELL??!! WHAT'S GOING ON???

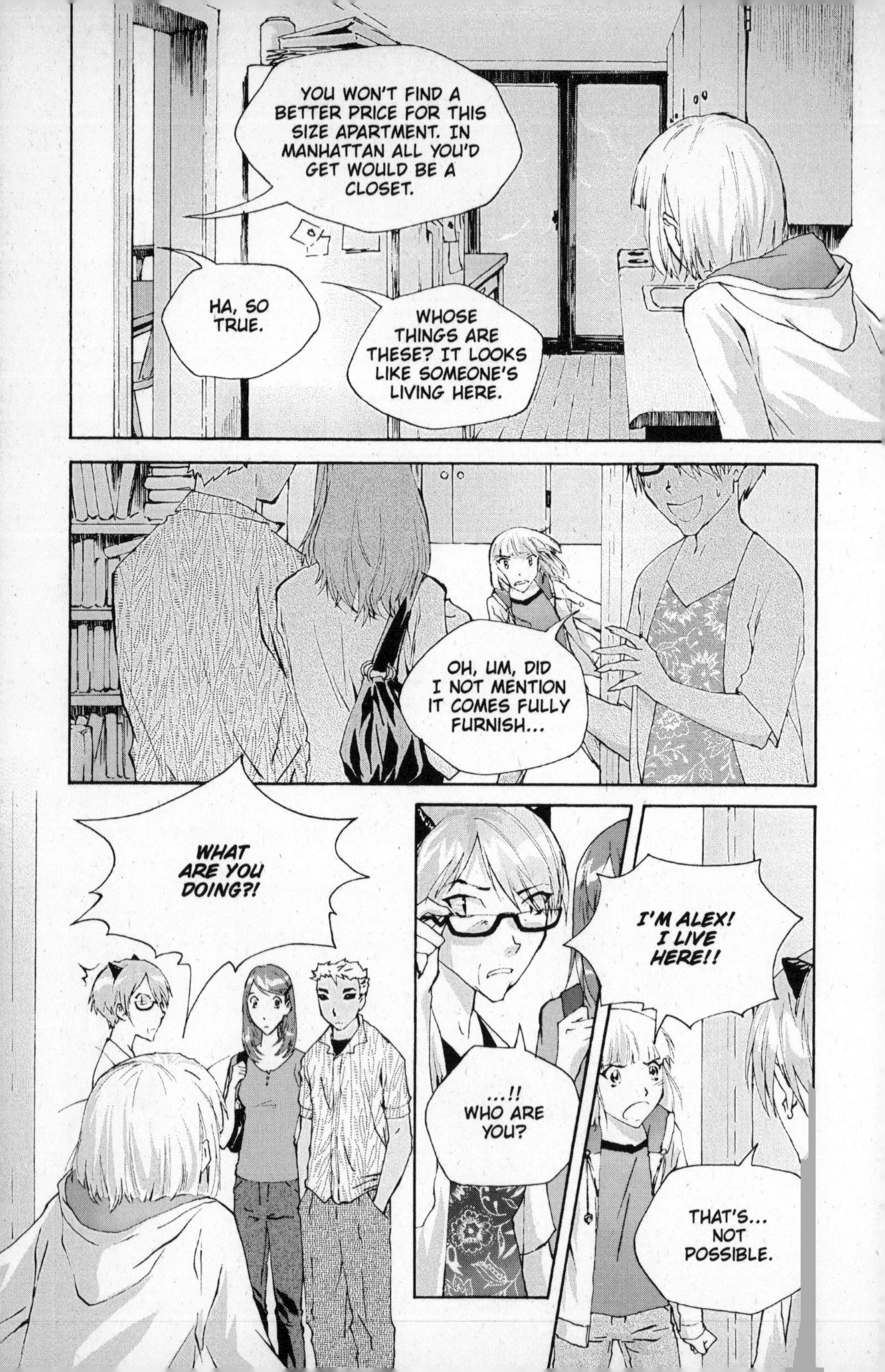
YOU WON'T FIND A BETTER PRICE FOR THIS SIZE APARTMENT. IN MANHATTAN ALL YOU'D GET WOULD BE A CLOSET.
HA, SO TRUE.
WHOSE THINGS ARE THESE? IT LOOKS LIKE SOMEONE'S LIVING HERE.
OH, UM, DID I NOT MENTION IT COMES FULLY FURNISH...
WHAT ARE YOU DOING?!
I'M ALEX! I LIVE HERE!!
...!! WHO ARE YOU?
THAT'S... NOT POSSIBLE.

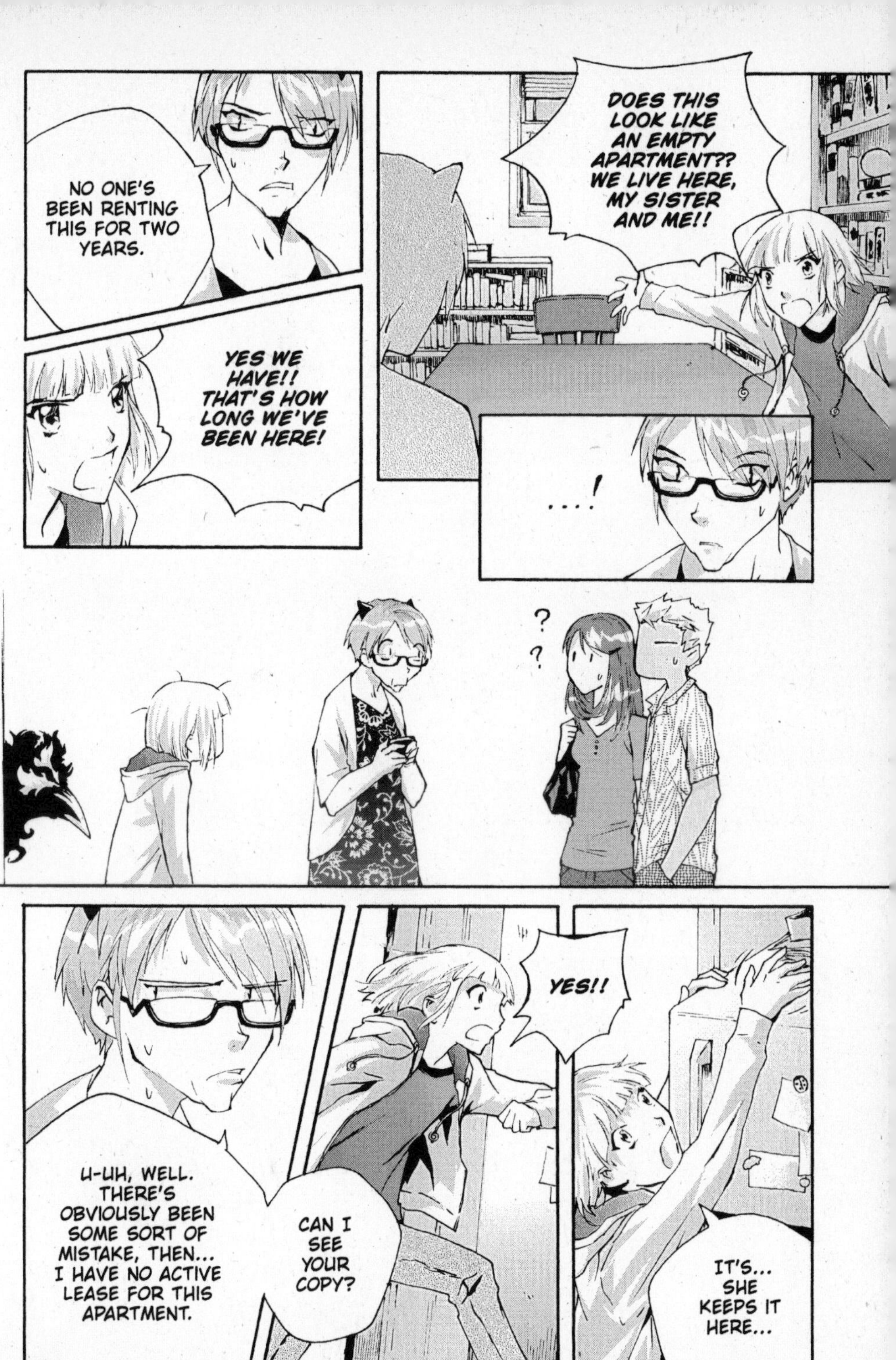
NO ONE'S BEEN RENTING THIS FOR TWO YEARS.
YES WE HAVE!! THAT'S HOW LONG WE'VE BEEN HERE!
DOES THIS LOOK LIKE AN EMPTY APARTMENT?? WE LIVE HERE, MY SISTER AND ME!!
...!
?
?
U-UH, WELL. THERE'S OBVIOUSLY BEEN SOME SORT OF MISTAKE, THEN... I HAVE NO ACTIVE LEASE FOR THIS APARTMENT.
YES!!
CAN I SEE YOUR COPY?
IT'S... SHE KEEPS IT HERE...

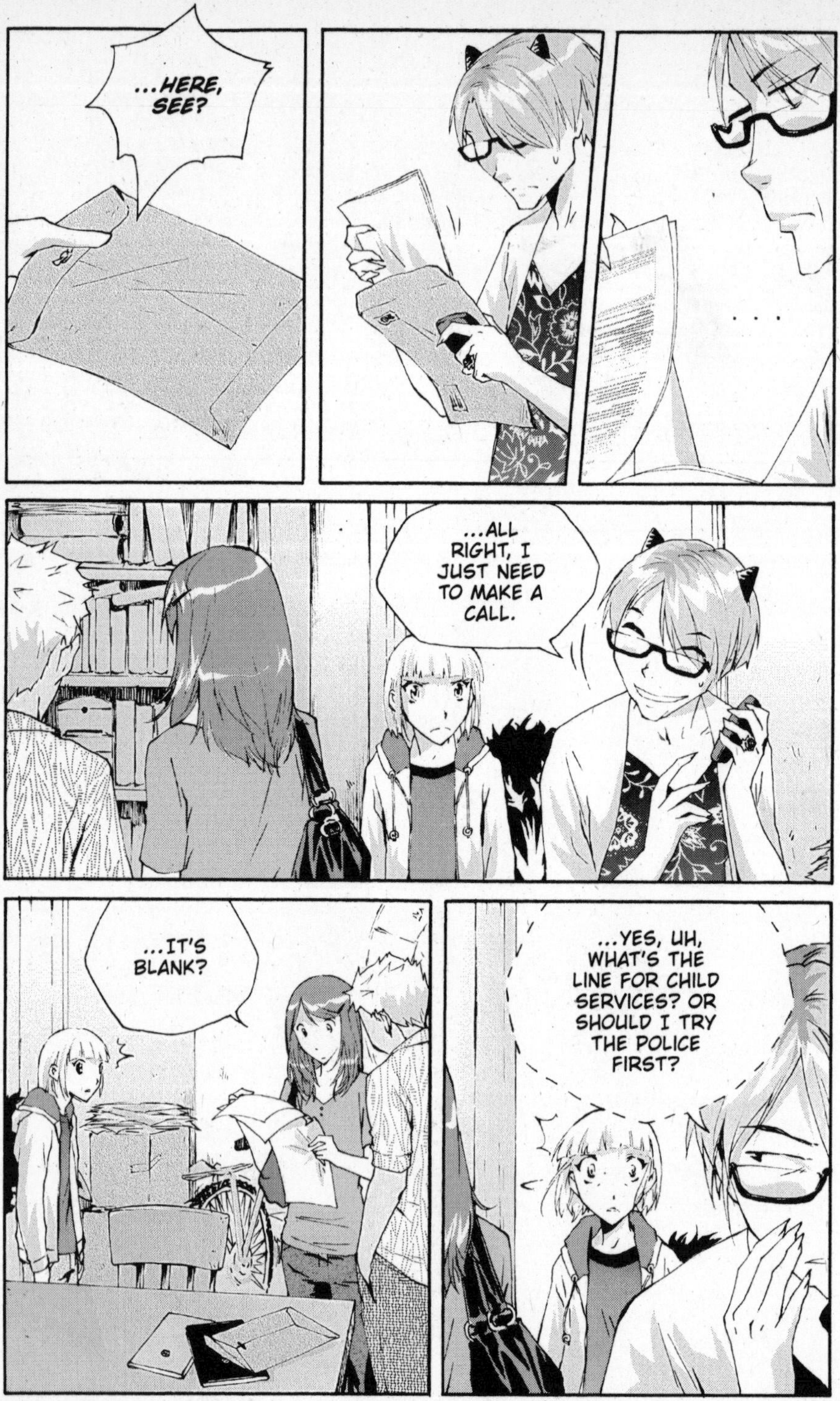
...HERE, SEE?
. . .
...ALL RIGHT, I JUST NEED TO MAKE A CALL.
...IT'S BLANK?
...YES, UH, WHAT'S THE LINE FOR CHILD SERVICES? OR SHOULD I TRY THE POLICE FIRST?

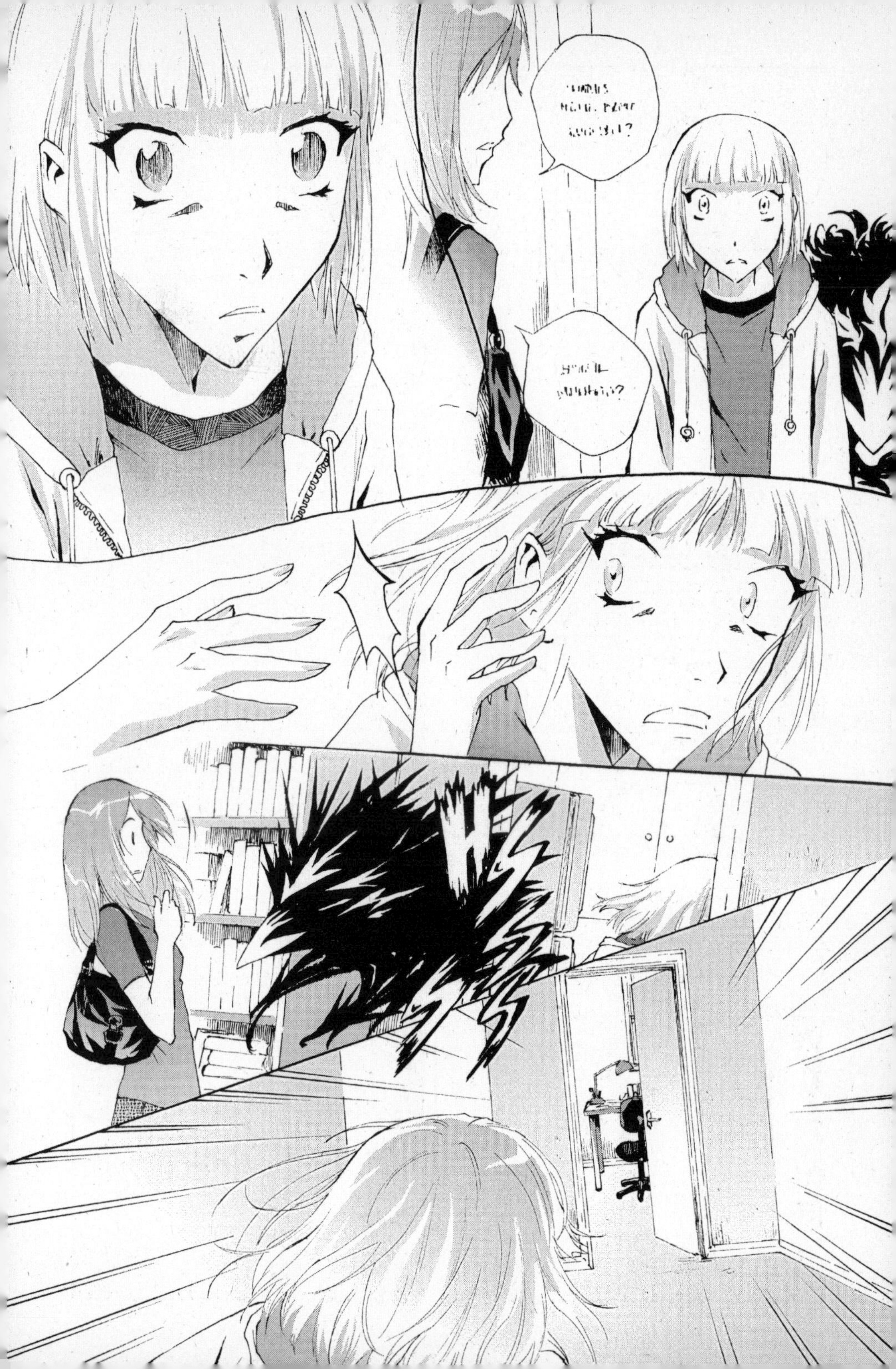

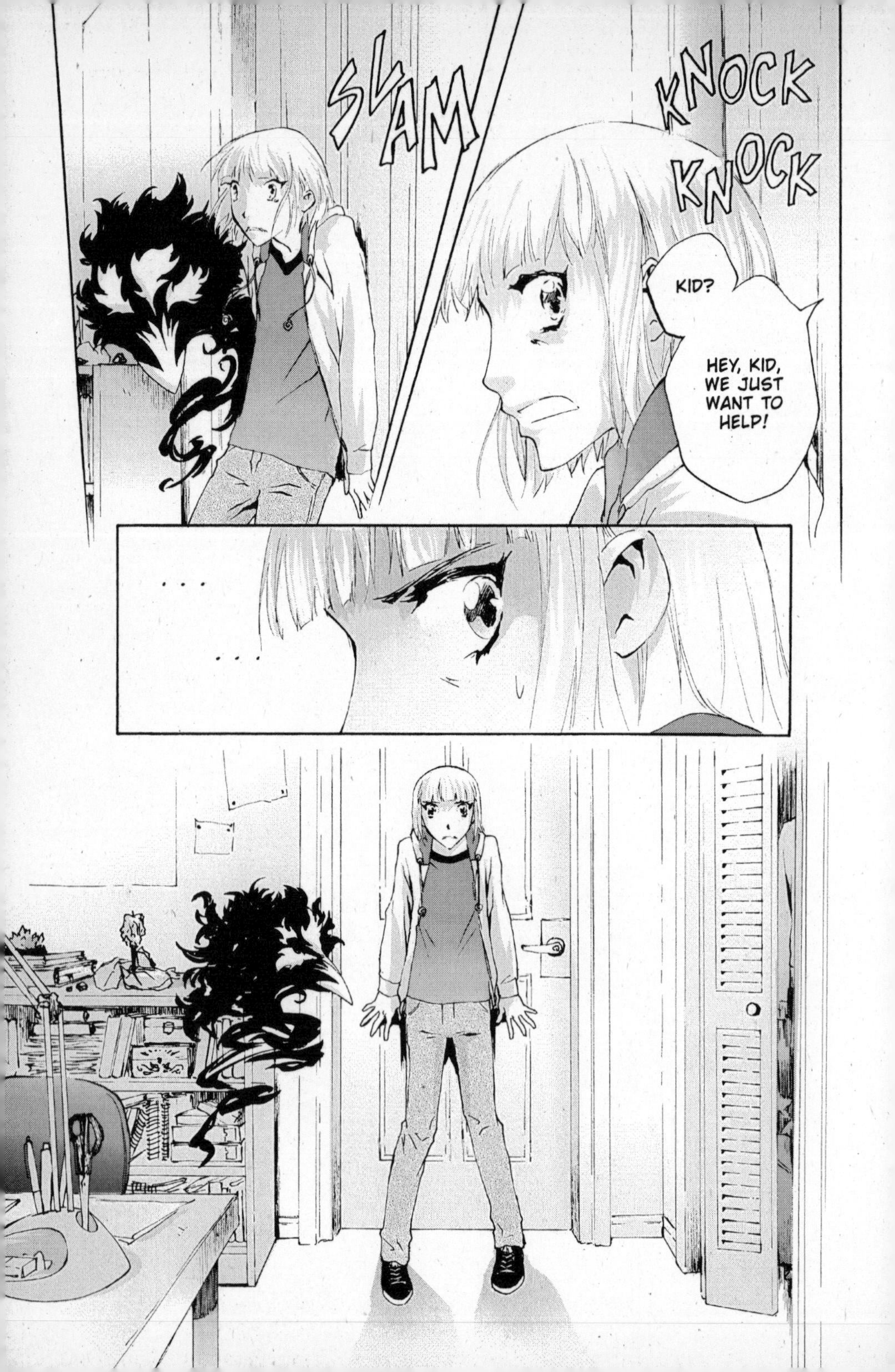
SLAM
KNOCK KNOCK
KID?
HEY, KID, WE JUST WANT TO HELP!
...
...

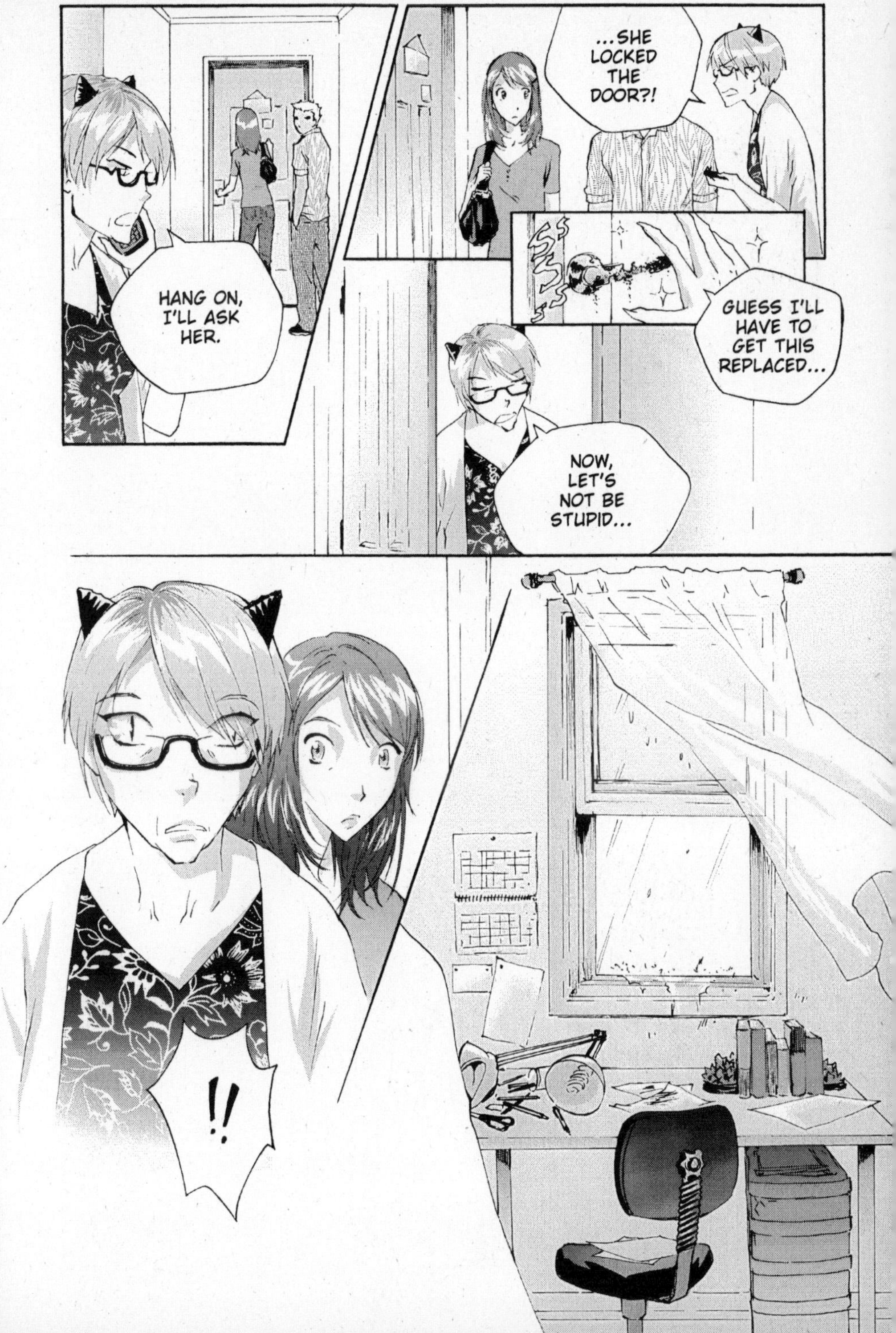
HANG ON, I'LL ASK HER.
...SHE LOCKED THE DOOR?!
GUESS I'LL HAVE TO GET THIS REPLACED...
NOW, LET'S NOT BE STUPID...
!!

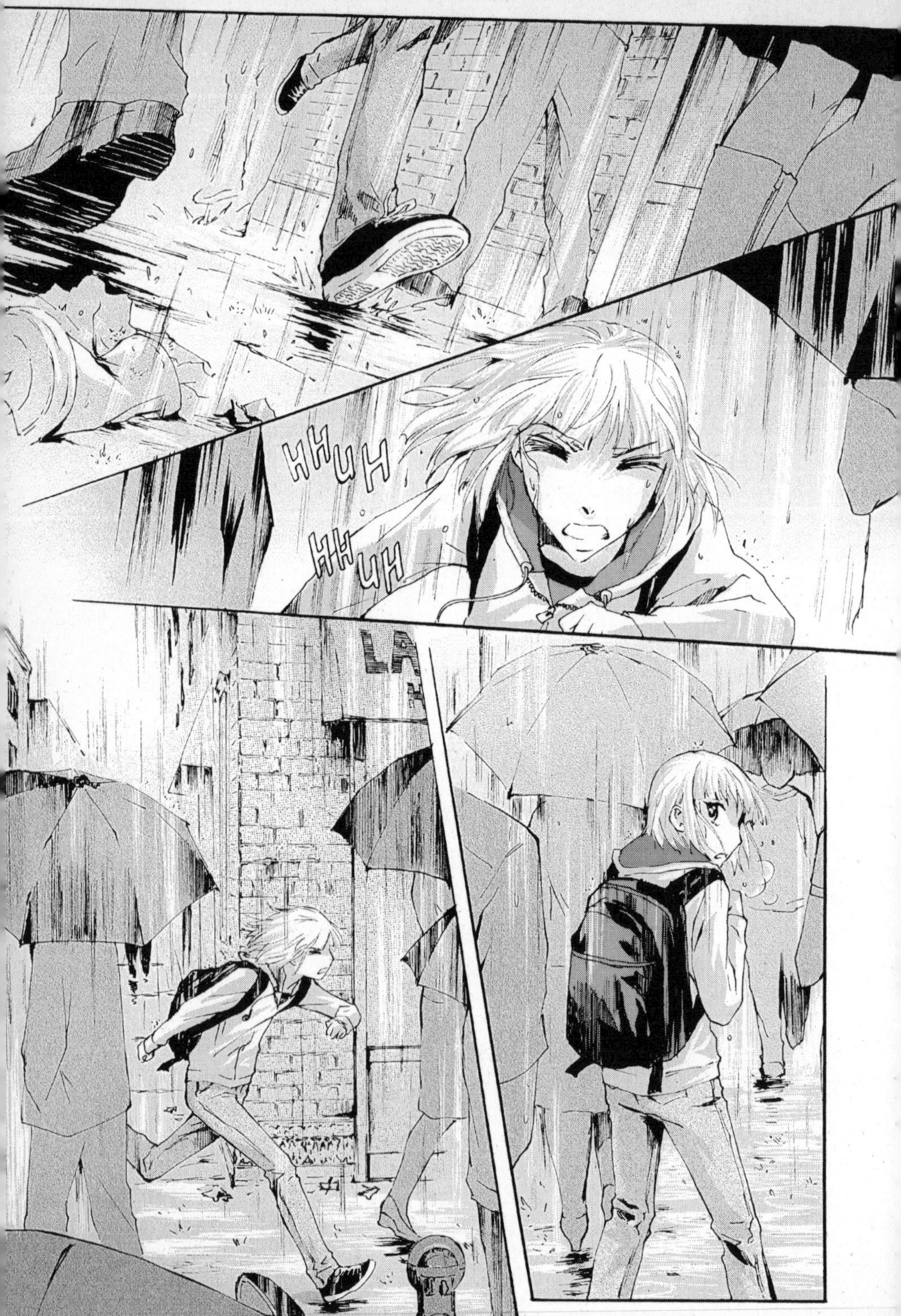
HHUH
HHUH

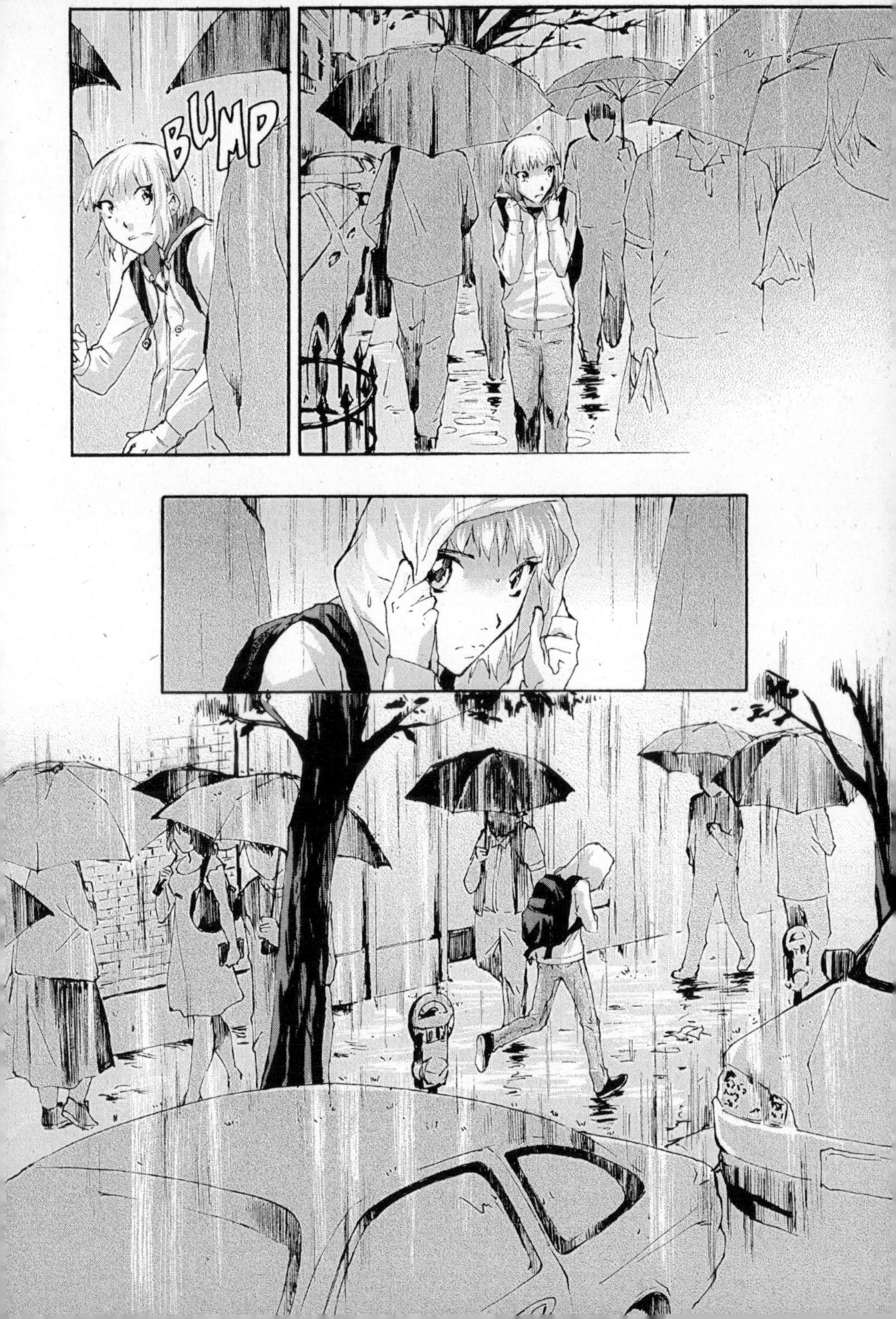
BUMP

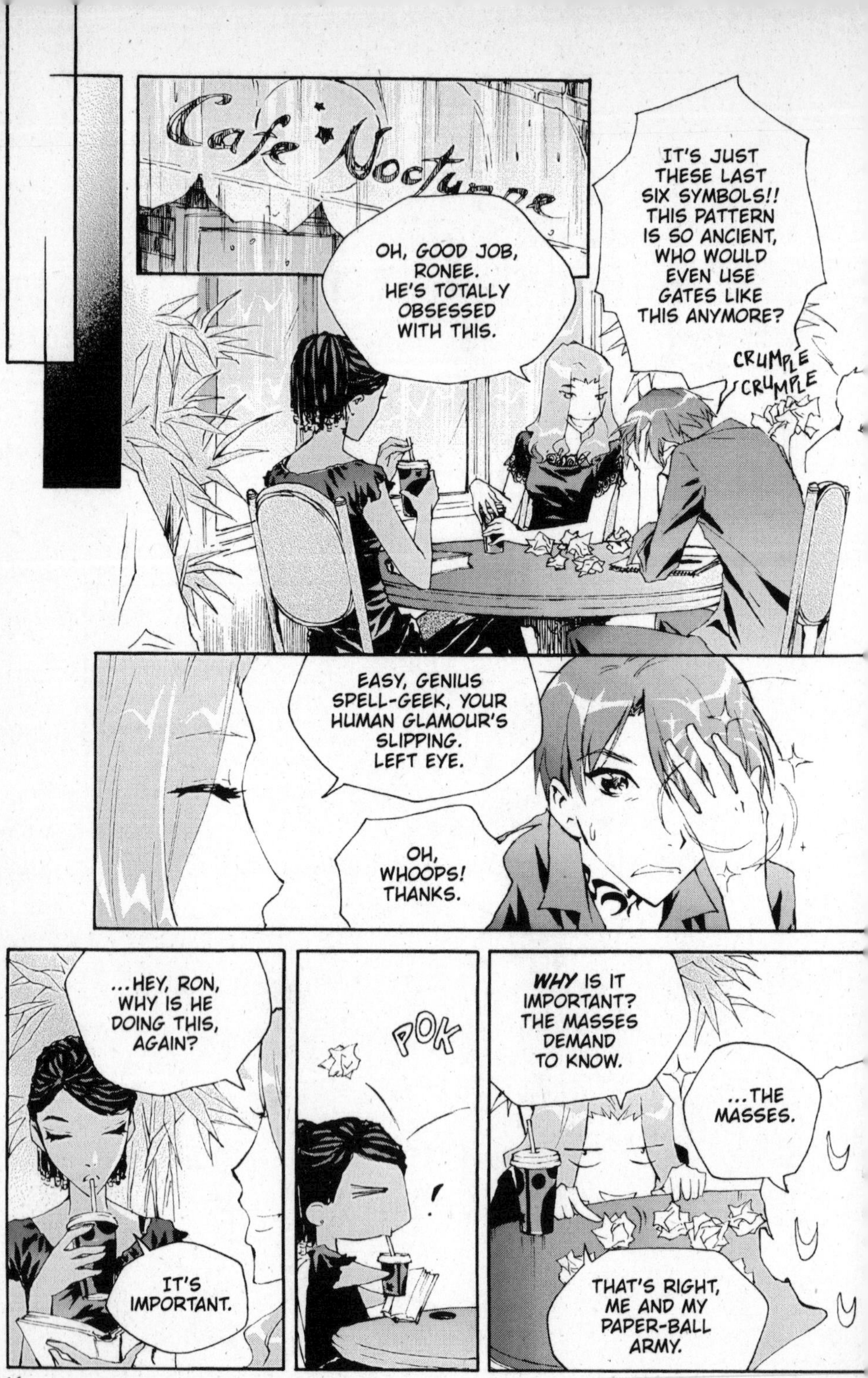
IT'S JUST THESE LAST SIX SYMBOLS!! THIS PATTERN IS SO ANCIENT, WHO WOULD EVEN USE GATES LIKE THIS ANYMORE?
OH, GOOD JOB, RONEE. HE'S TOTALLY OBSESSED WITH THIS.
CRUMPLE CRUMPLE
EASY, GENIUS SPELL-GEEK, YOUR HUMAN GLAMOUR'S SLIPPING. LEFT EYE.
OH, WHOOPS! THANKS.
...HEY, RON, WHY IS HE DOING THIS, AGAIN?
IT'S IMPORTANT.
POK
!
WHY IS IT IMPORTANT? THE MASSES DEMAND TO KNOW.
...THE MASSES.
THAT'S RIGHT, ME AND MY PAPER-BALL ARMY.

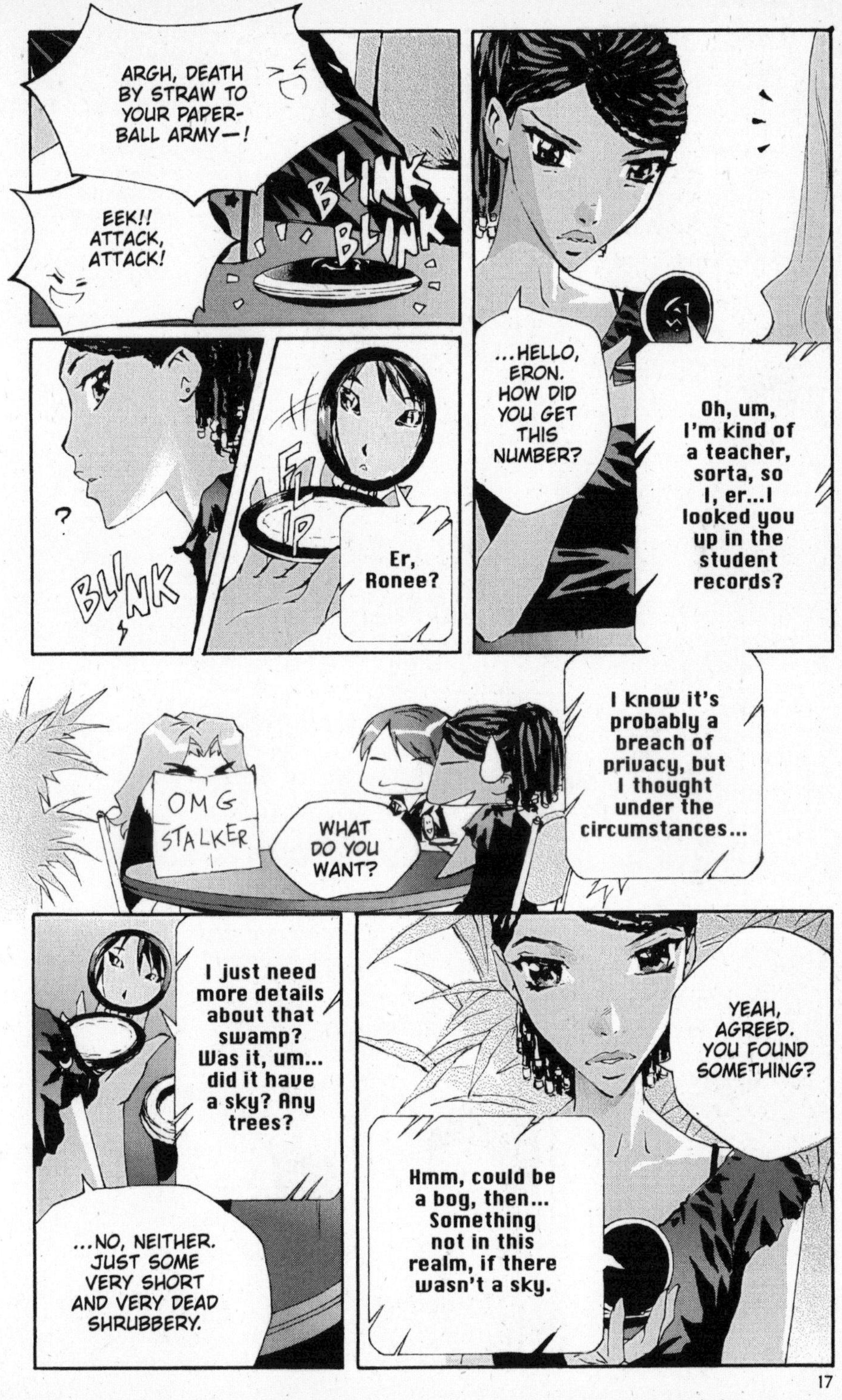
ARGH, DEATH BY STRAW TO YOUR PAPER-BALL ARMY—!
EEK!! ATTACK, ATTACK!
BLINK BLINK
?
BLINK
FLIP
Er, Ronee?
...HELLO, ERON. HOW DID YOU GET THIS NUMBER?
Oh, um, I'm kind of a teacher, sorta, so I, er...I looked you up in the student records?
OMG STALKER
WHAT DO YOU WANT?
I know it's probably a breach of privacy, but I thought under the circumstances...
I just need more details about that swamp? Was it, um... did it have a sky? Any trees?
...NO, NEITHER. JUST SOME VERY SHORT AND VERY DEAD SHRUBBERY.
YEAH, AGREED. YOU FOUND SOMETHING?
Hmm, could be a bog, then... Something not in this realm, if there wasn't a sky.

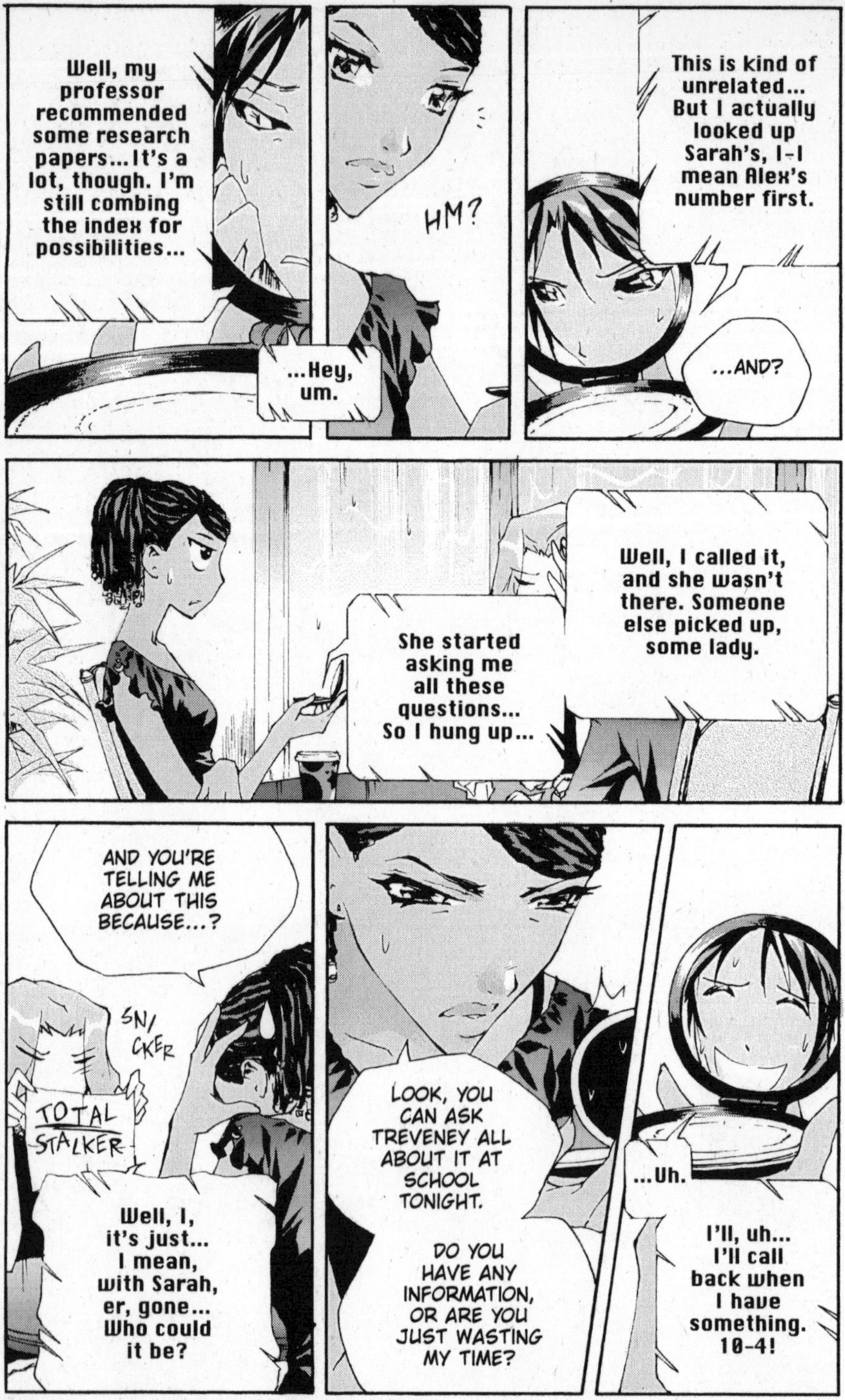
Well, my professor recommended some research papers... It's a lot, though. I'm still combing the index for possibilities...
...Hey, um.
HM?
This is kind of unrelated... But I actually looked up Sarah's, I-I mean Alex's number first.
...AND?
Well, I called it, and she wasn't there. Someone else picked up, some lady.
She started asking me all these questions... So I hung up...
AND YOU'RE TELLING ME ABOUT THIS BECAUSE...?
SNI CKER
TOTAL STALKER
Well, I, it's just... I mean, with Sarah, er, gone... Who could it be?
LOOK, YOU CAN ASK TREVENEY ALL ABOUT IT AT SCHOOL TONIGHT.
DO YOU HAVE ANY INFORMATION, OR ARE YOU JUST WASTING MY TIME?
...Uh.
I'll, uh... I'll call back when I have something. 10-4!

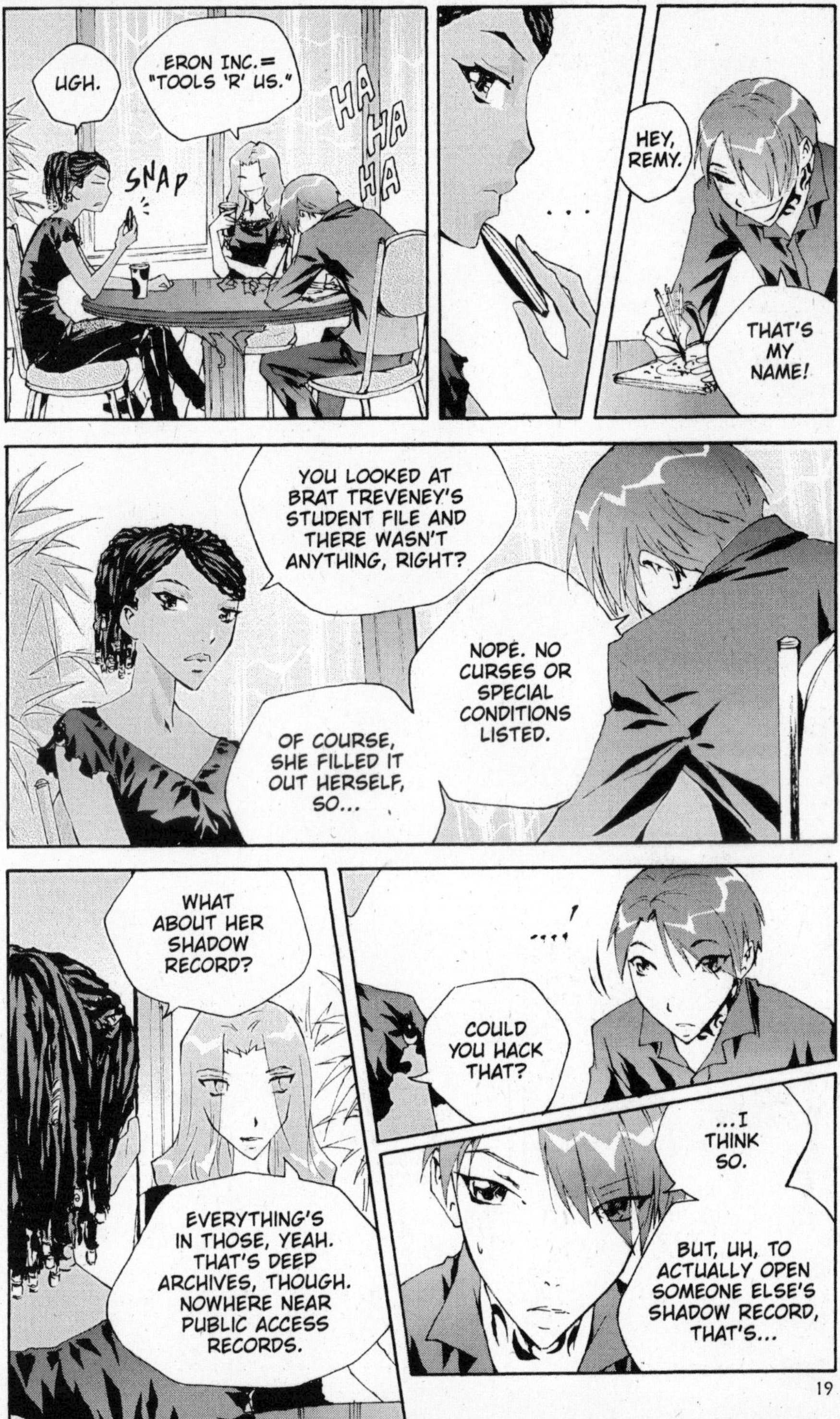
UGH.
ERON INC.= "TOOLS 'R' US."
SNAP
HA HA HA HA
. . .
HEY, REMY.
THAT'S MY NAME!
YOU LOOKED AT BRAT TREVENEY'S STUDENT FILE AND THERE WASN'T ANYTHING, RIGHT?
OF COURSE, SHE FILLED IT OUT HERSELF, SO...
NOPE. NO CURSES OR SPECIAL CONDITIONS LISTED.
WHAT ABOUT HER SHADOW RECORD?
EVERYTHING'S IN THOSE, YEAH. THAT'S DEEP ARCHIVES, THOUGH. NOWHERE NEAR PUBLIC ACCESS RECORDS.
...!
COULD YOU HACK THAT?
...I THINK SO.
BUT, UH, TO ACTUALLY OPEN SOMEONE ELSE'S SHADOW RECORD, THAT'S...

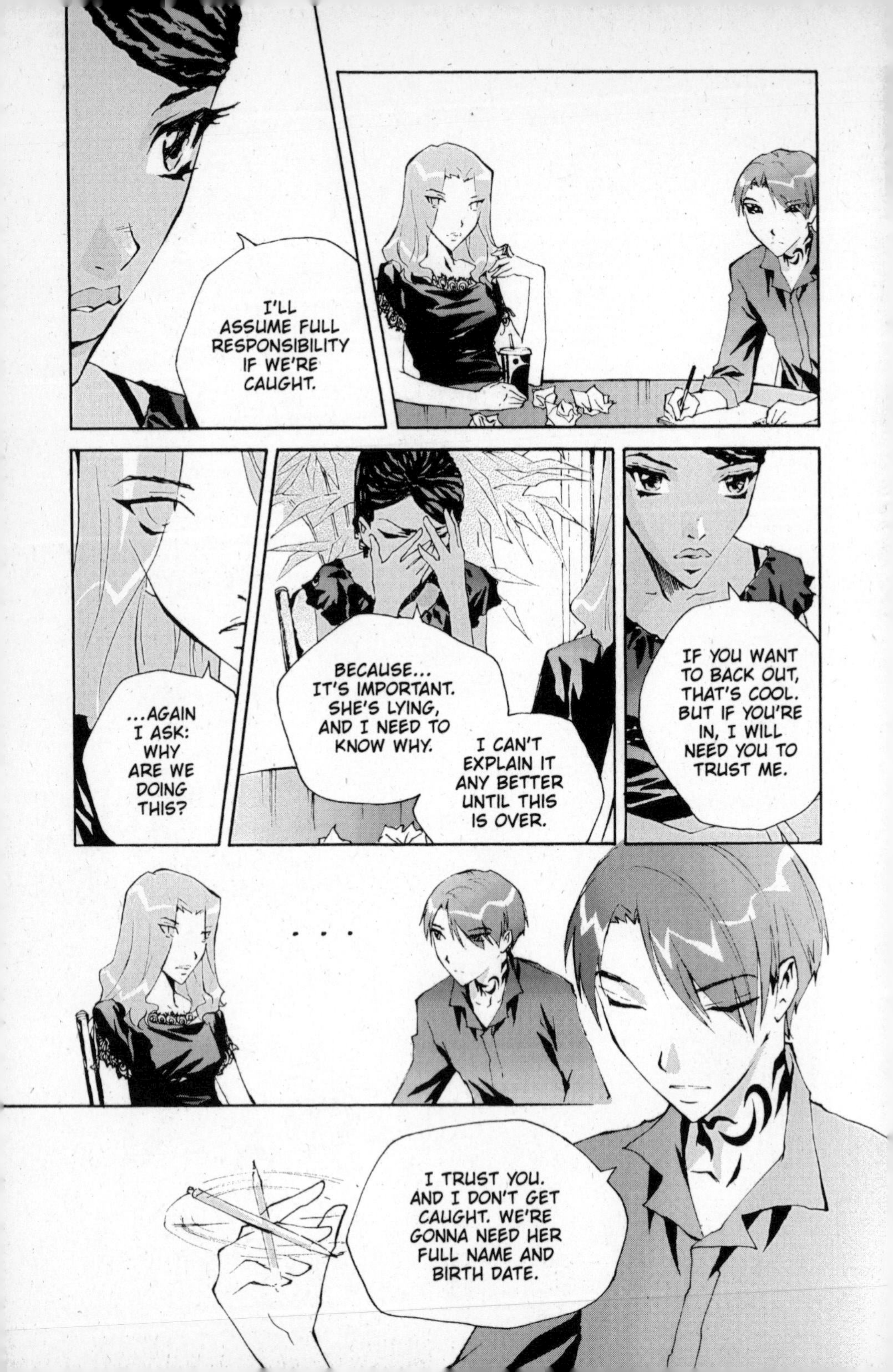
I'LL ASSUME FULL RESPONSIBILITY IF WE'RE CAUGHT.
...AGAIN I ASK: WHY ARE WE DOING THIS?
BECAUSE... IT'S IMPORTANT. SHE'S LYING, AND I NEED TO KNOW WHY.
I CAN'T EXPLAIN IT ANY BETTER UNTIL THIS IS OVER.
IF YOU WANT TO BACK OUT, THAT'S COOL. BUT IF YOU'RE IN, I WILL NEED YOU TO TRUST ME.
. . .
I TRUST YOU. AND I DON'T GET CAUGHT. WE'RE GONNA NEED HER FULL NAME AND BIRTH DATE.

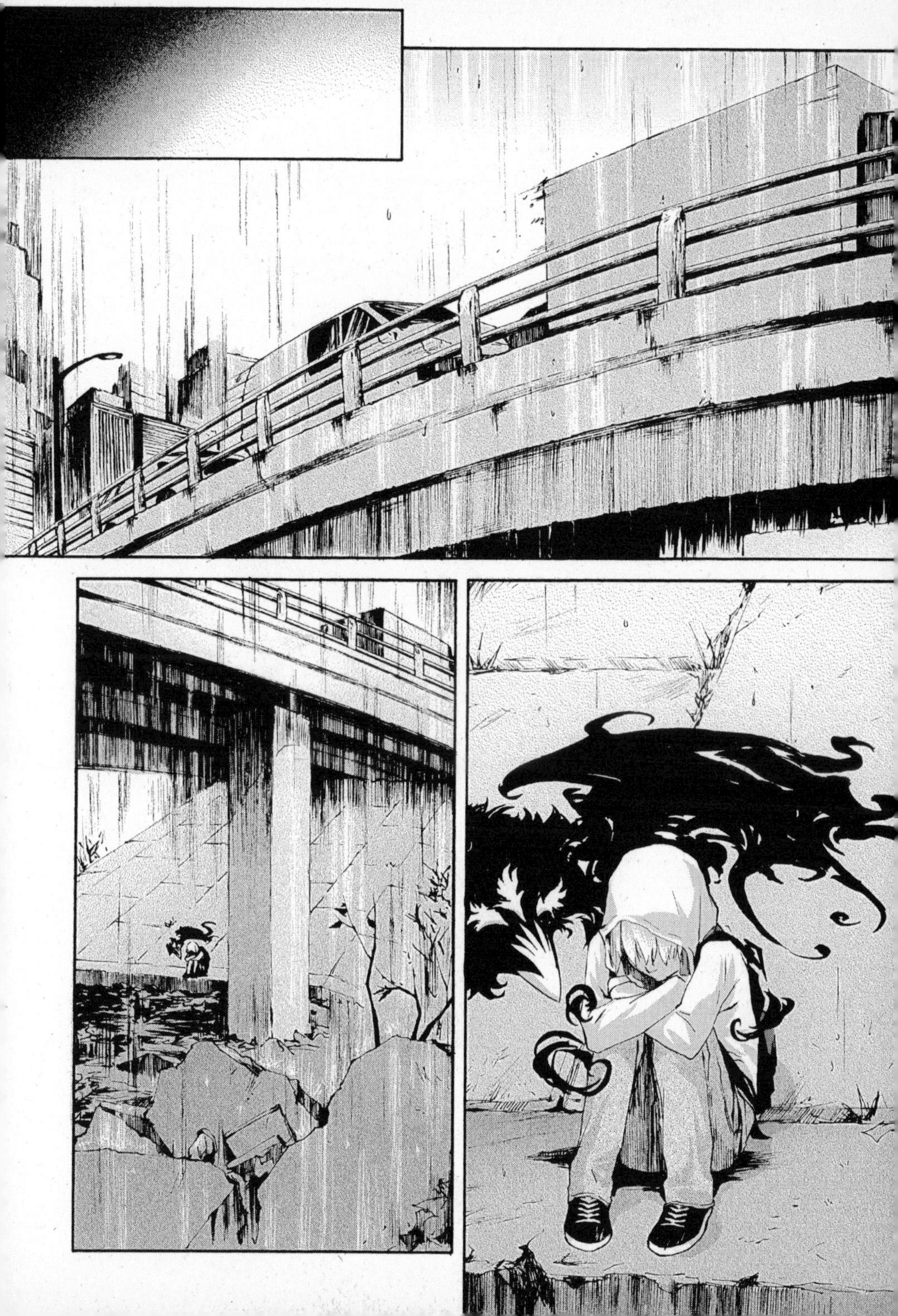

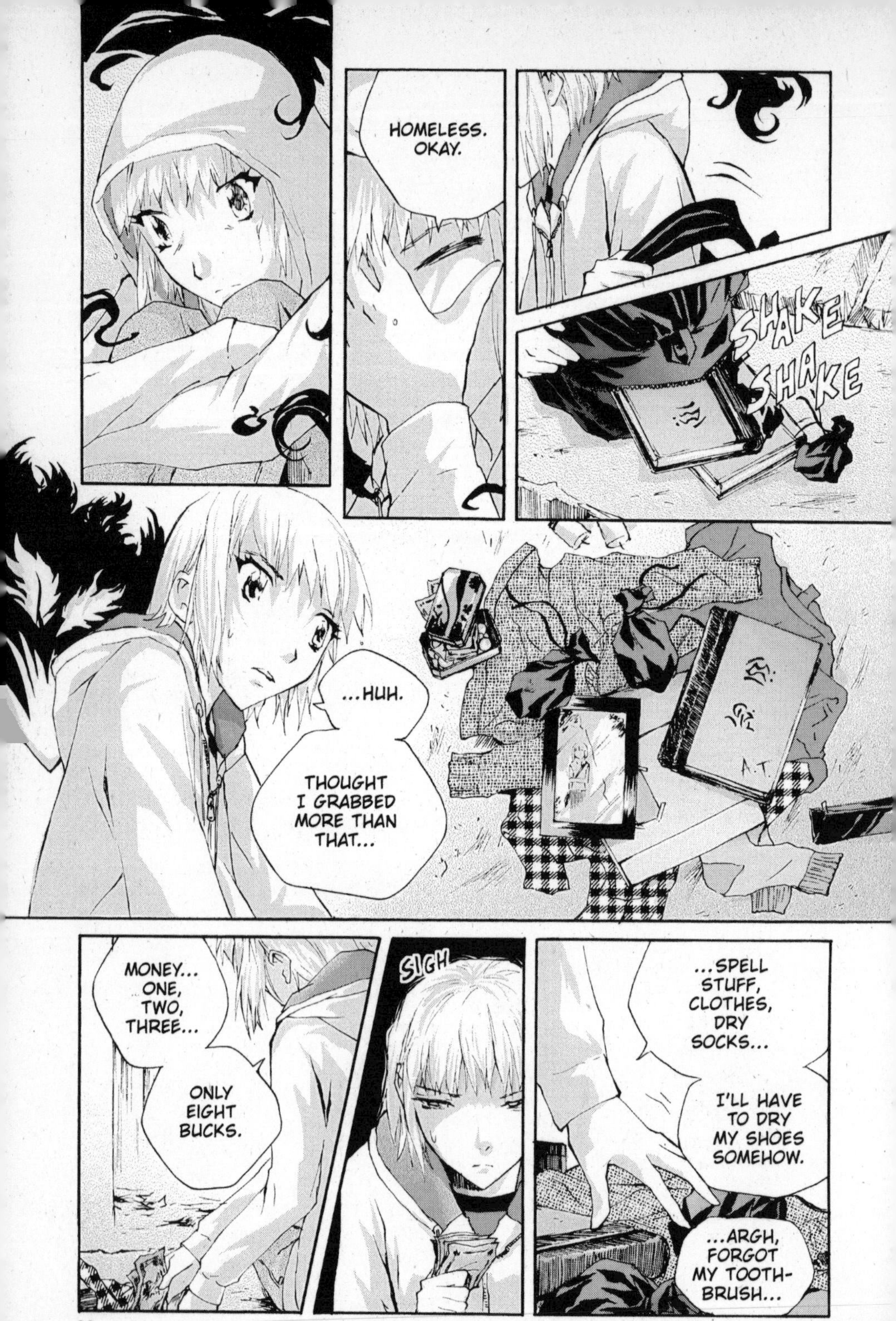
HOMELESS. OKAY.
SHAKE SHAKE
...HUH.
THOUGHT I GRABBED MORE THAN THAT...
MONEY... ONE, TWO, THREE...
ONLY EIGHT BUCKS.
SIGH
...SPELL STUFF, CLOTHES, DRY SOCKS...
I'LL HAVE TO DRY MY SHOES SOMEHOW.
...ARGH, FORGOT MY TOOTH-BRUSH...

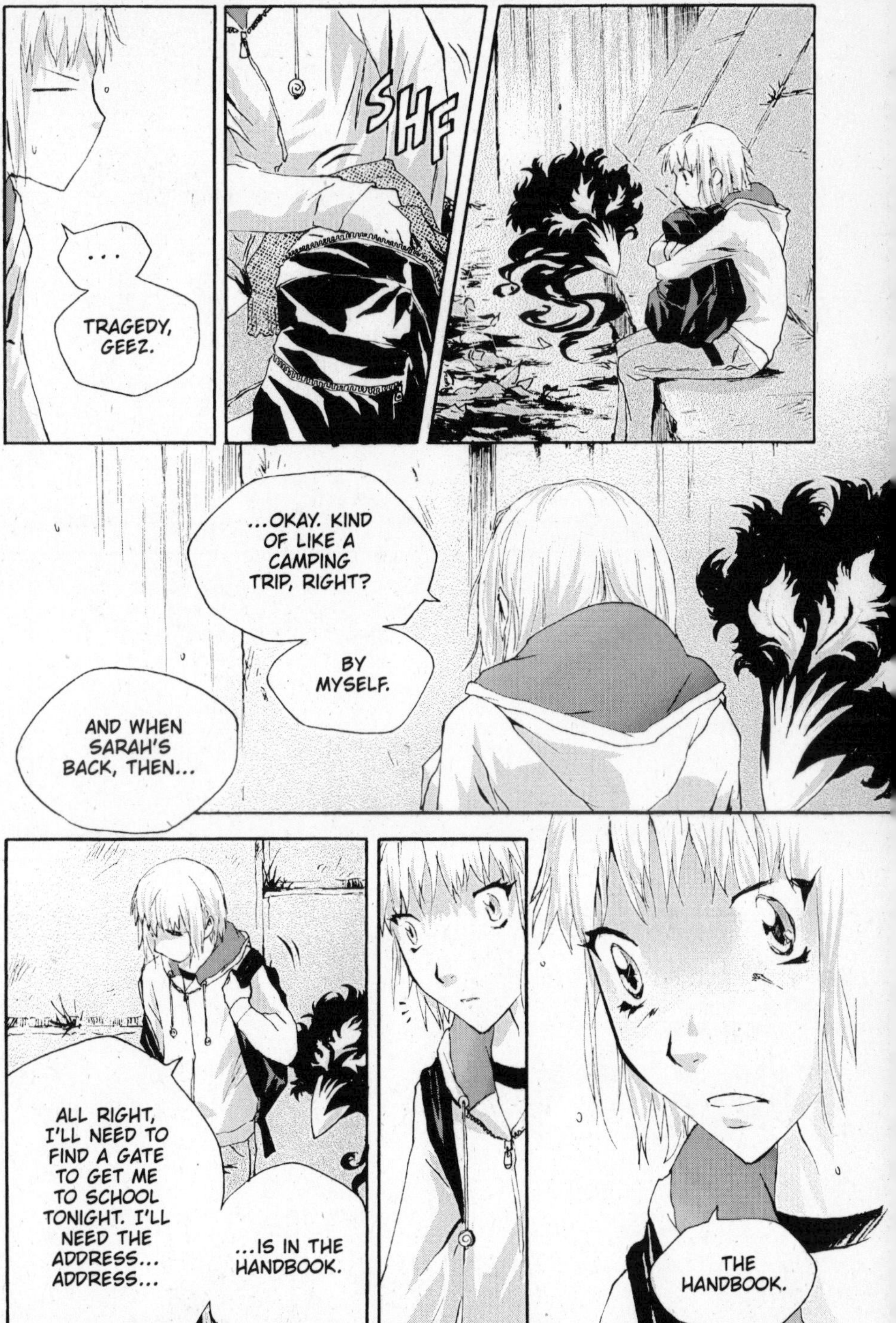
...
TRAGEDY, GEEZ.
SHF
...OKAY. KIND OF LIKE A CAMPING TRIP, RIGHT?
BY MYSELF.
AND WHEN SARAH'S BACK, THEN...
ALL RIGHT, I'LL NEED TO FIND A GATE TO GET ME TO SCHOOL TONIGHT. I'LL NEED THE ADDRESS... ADDRESS...
...IS IN THE HANDBOOK.
THE HANDBOOK.

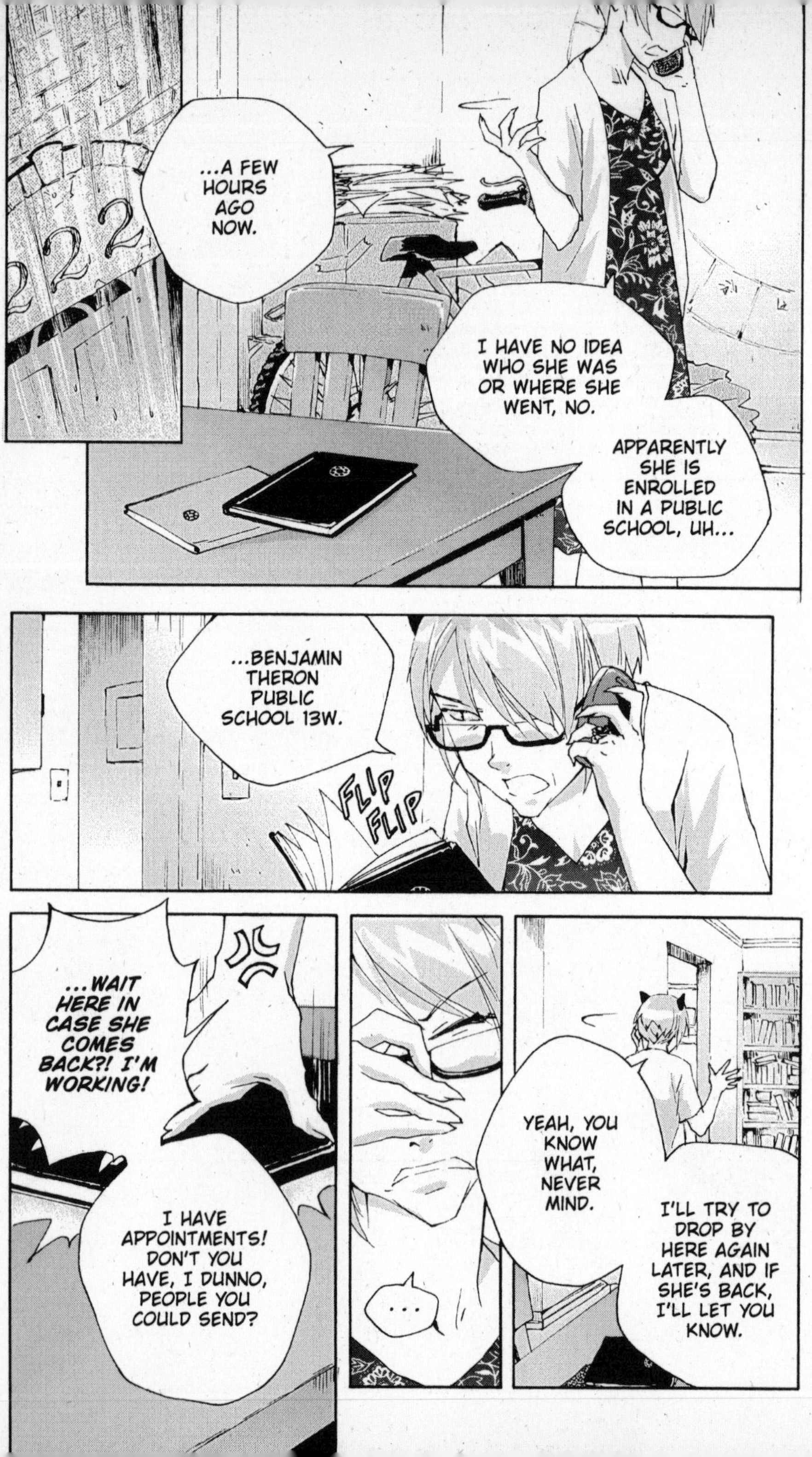
...A FEW HOURS AGO NOW.
I HAVE NO IDEA WHO SHE WAS OR WHERE SHE WENT, NO.
APPARENTLY SHE IS ENROLLED IN A PUBLIC SCHOOL, UH...
...BENJAMIN THERON PUBLIC SCHOOL 13W.
FLIP FLIP
...WAIT HERE IN CASE SHE COMES BACK?! I'M WORKING!
I HAVE APPOINTMENTS! DON'T YOU HAVE, I DUNNO, PEOPLE YOU COULD SEND?
...
YEAH, YOU KNOW WHAT, NEVER MIND.
I'LL TRY TO DROP BY HERE AGAIN LATER, AND IF SHE'S BACK, I'LL LET YOU KNOW.

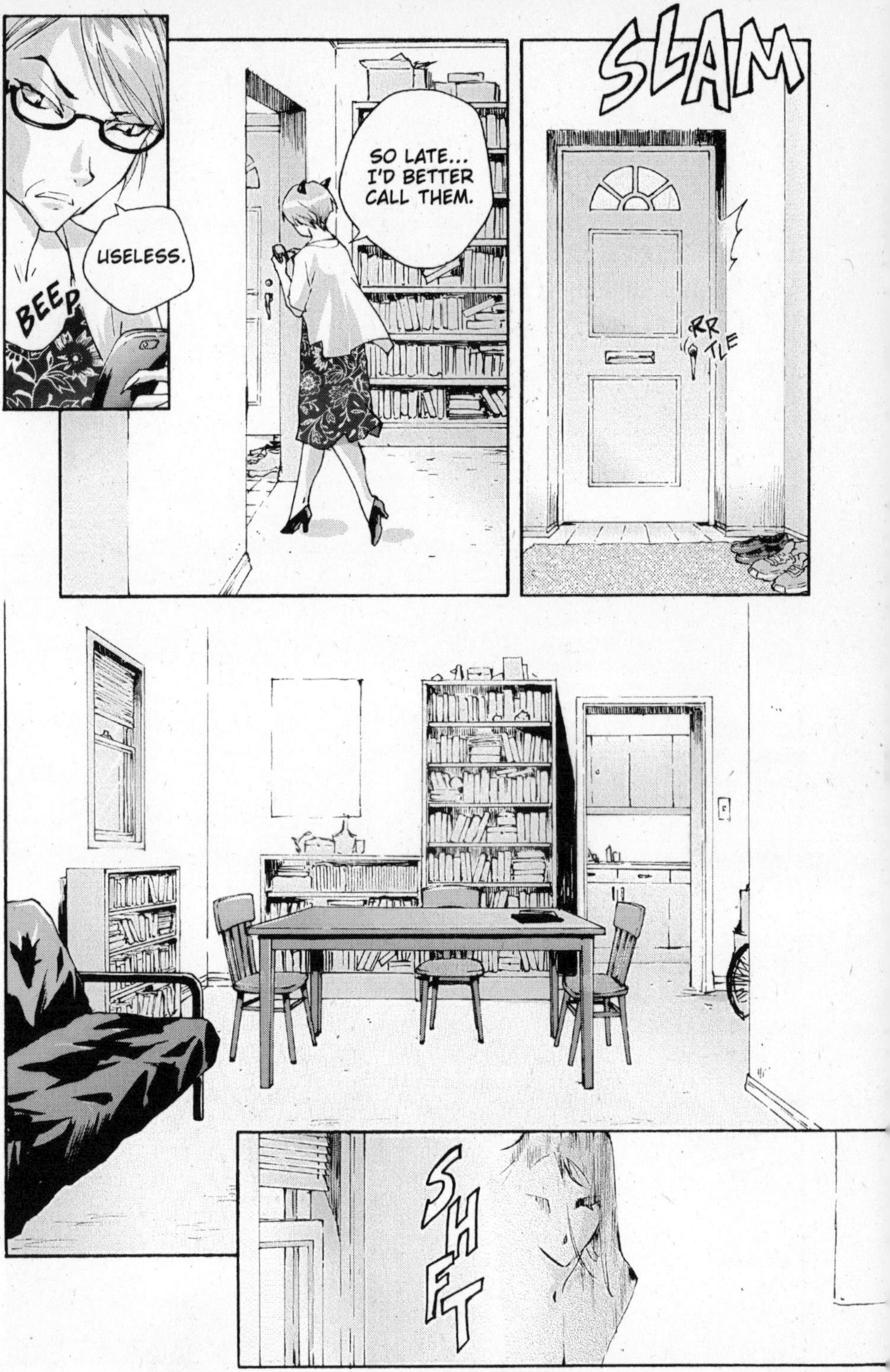
BEEP
USELESS.
SO LATE... I'D BETTER CALL THEM.
SLAM
RR TLE
SHFT

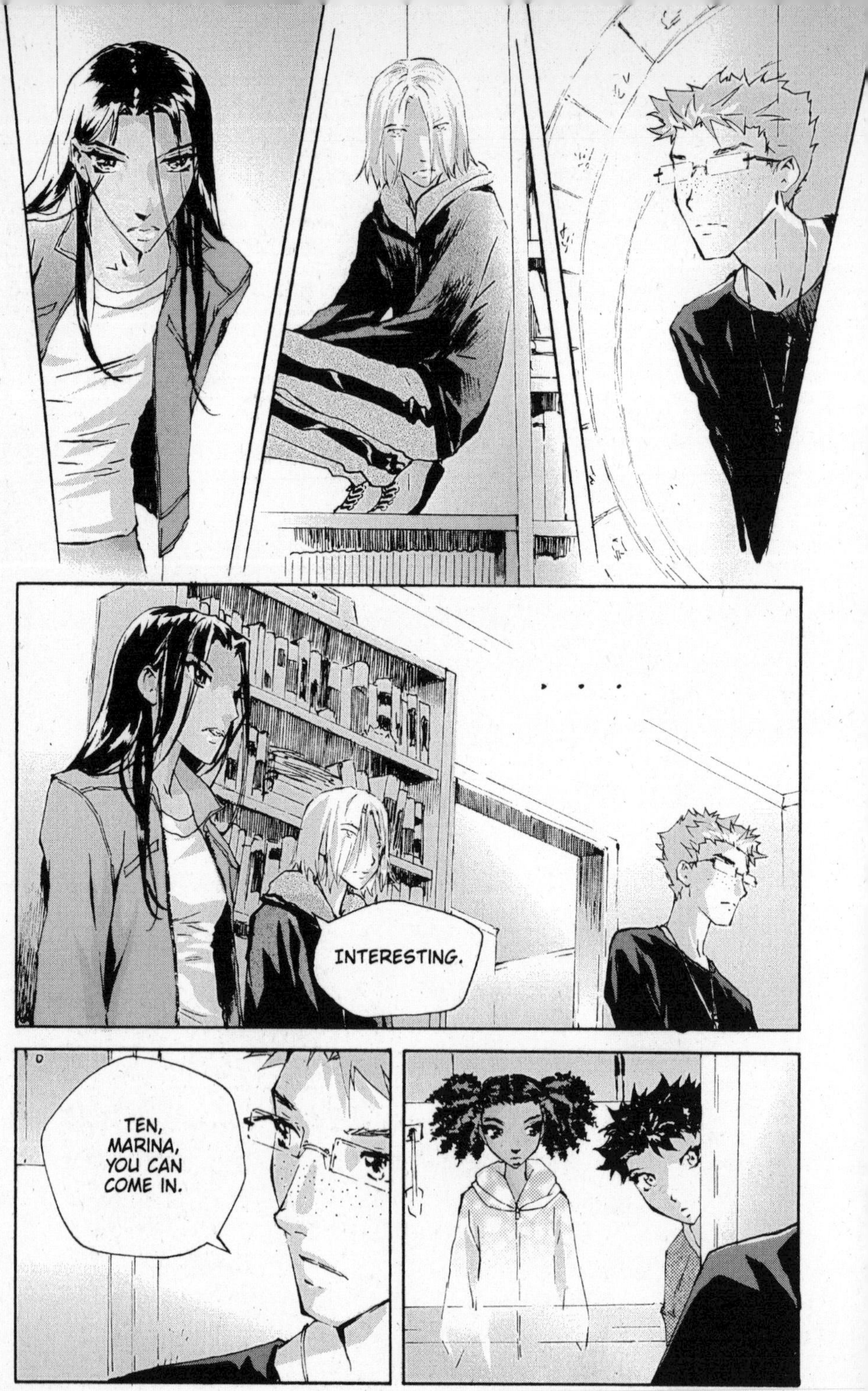
. . .
INTERESTING.
TEN, MARINA, YOU CAN COME IN.

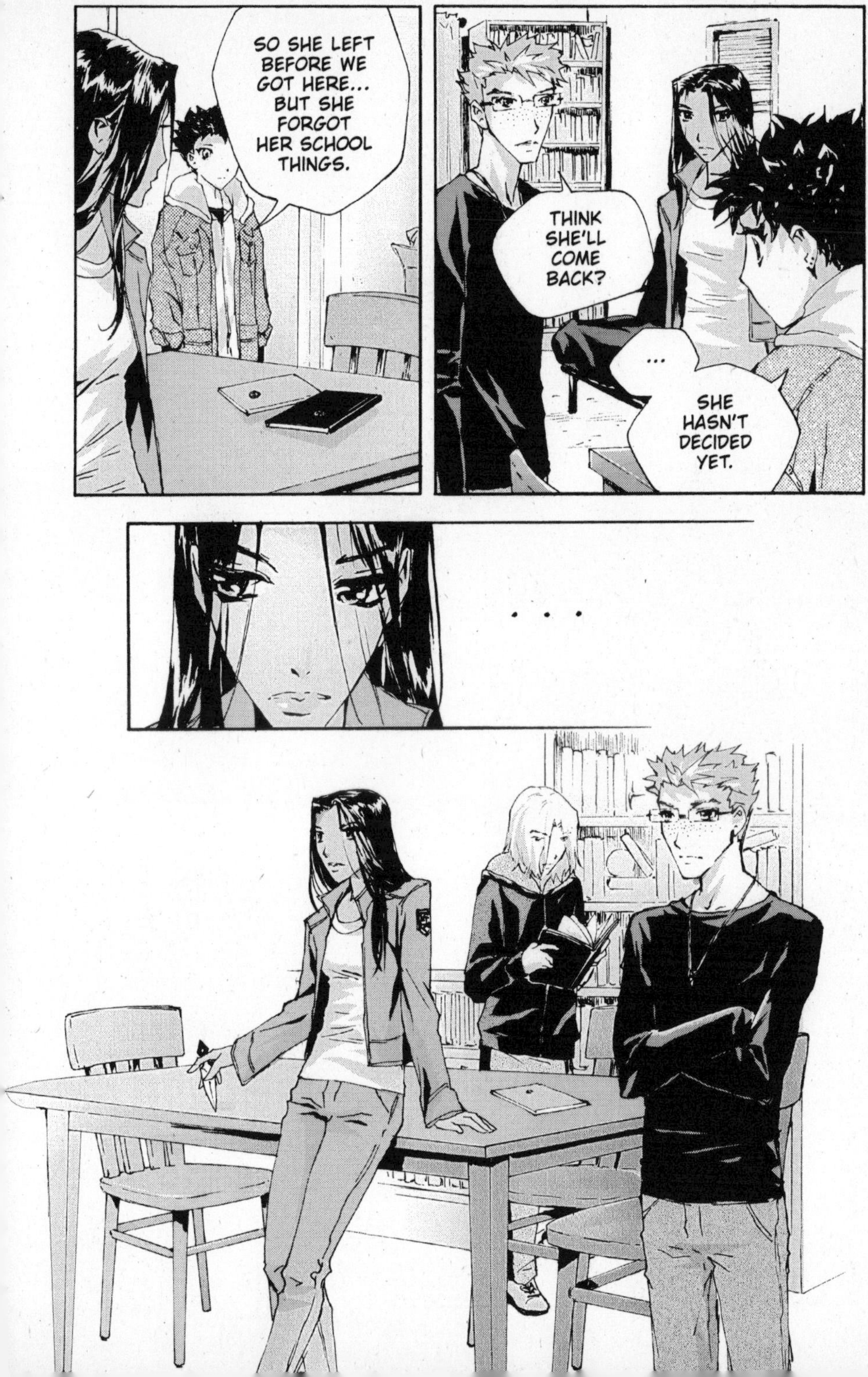
SO SHE LEFT BEFORE WE GOT HERE... BUT SHE FORGOT HER SCHOOL THINGS.
THINK SHE'LL COME BACK?
...
SHE HASN'T DECIDED YET.
. . .

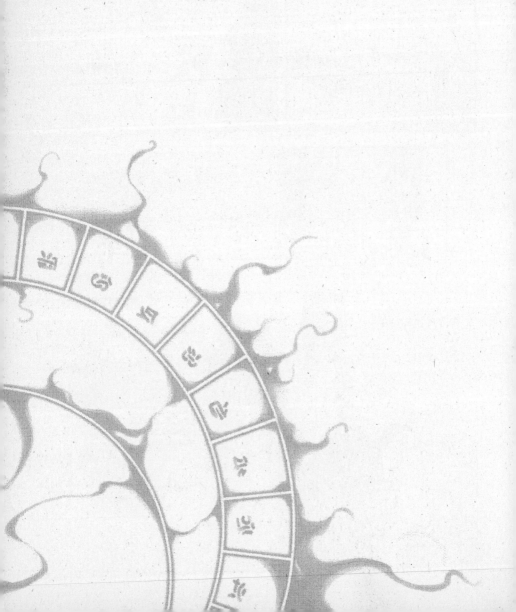

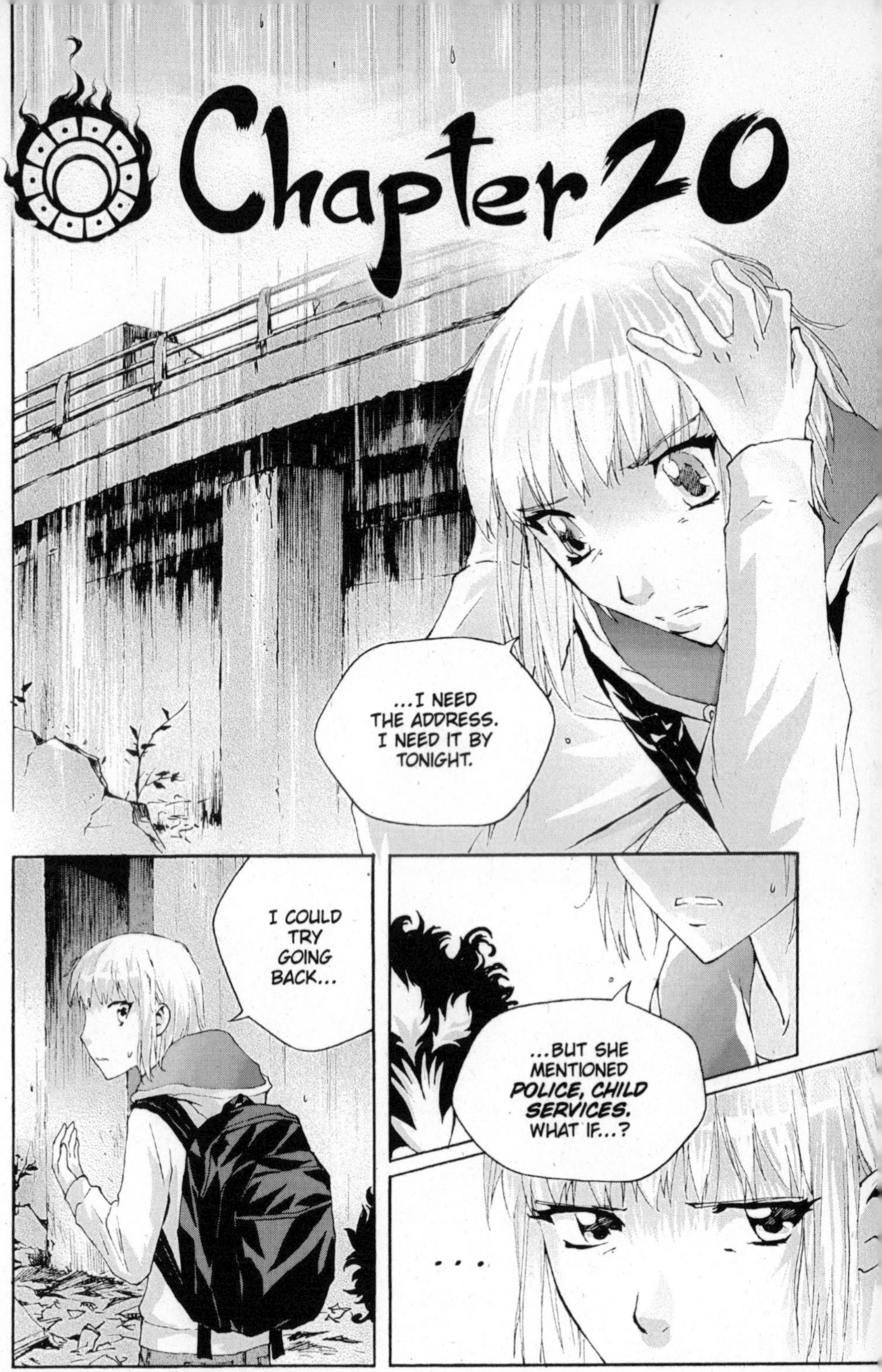
Chapter 20
...I NEED THE ADDRESS. I NEED IT BY TONIGHT.
I COULD TRY GOING BACK...
...BUT SHE MENTIONED POLICE, CHILD SERVICES. WHAT IF...?
...

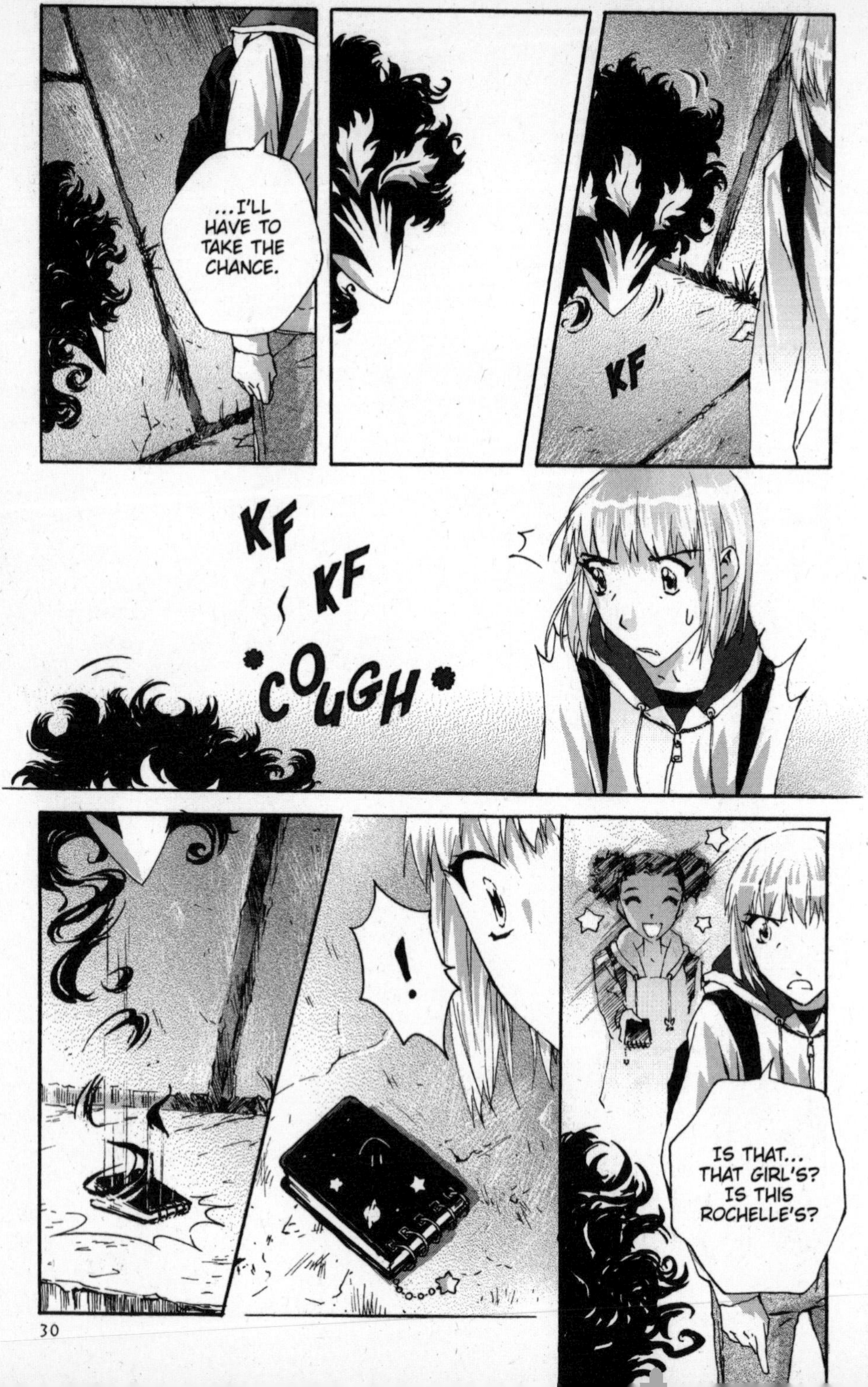
...I'LL HAVE TO TAKE THE CHANCE.
KF
KF
KF
COUGH
!
IS THAT... THAT GIRL'S? IS THIS ROCHELLE'S?

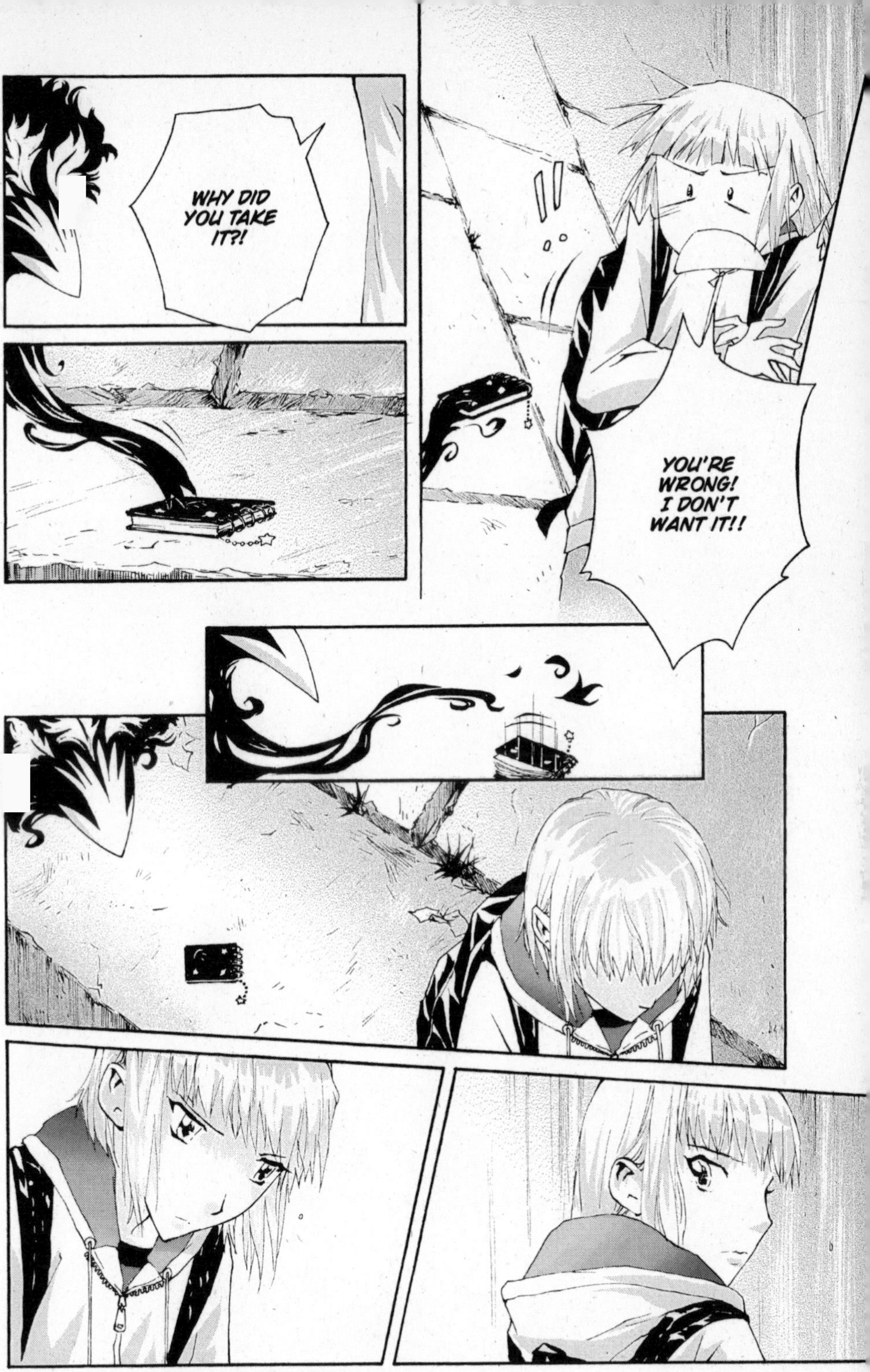
WHY DID YOU TAKE IT?!
YOU'RE WRONG! I DON'T WANT IT!!

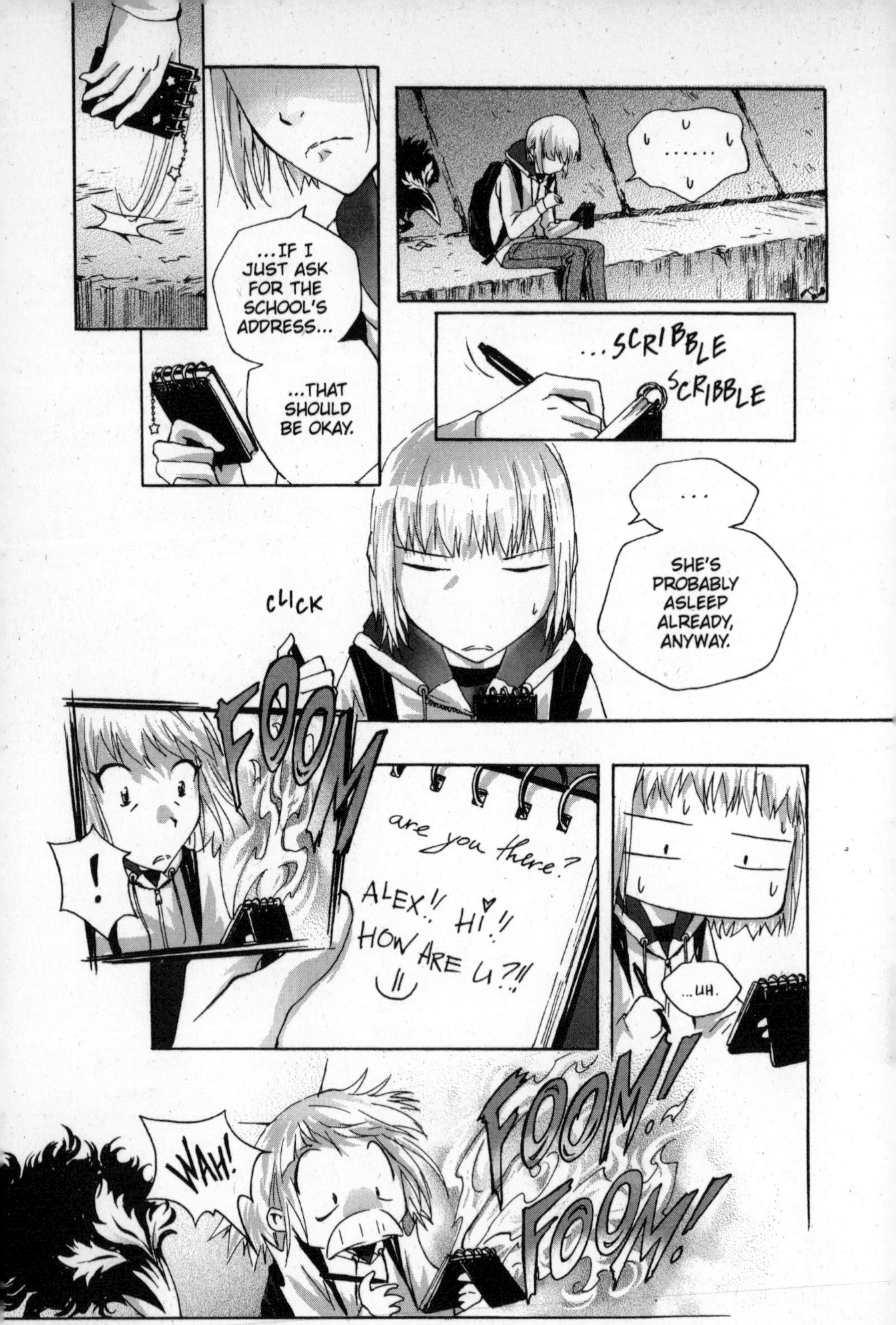
...IF I JUST ASK FOR THE SCHOOL'S ADDRESS...
...THAT SHOULD BE OKAY.
....
...SCRIBBLE
SCRIBBLE
CLICK
...
SHE'S PROBABLY ASLEEP ALREADY, ANYWAY.
FOOM
!
are you there?
ALEX!! HI!! HOW ARE U?!!
...UH.
WAH!
FOOM!
FOOM!

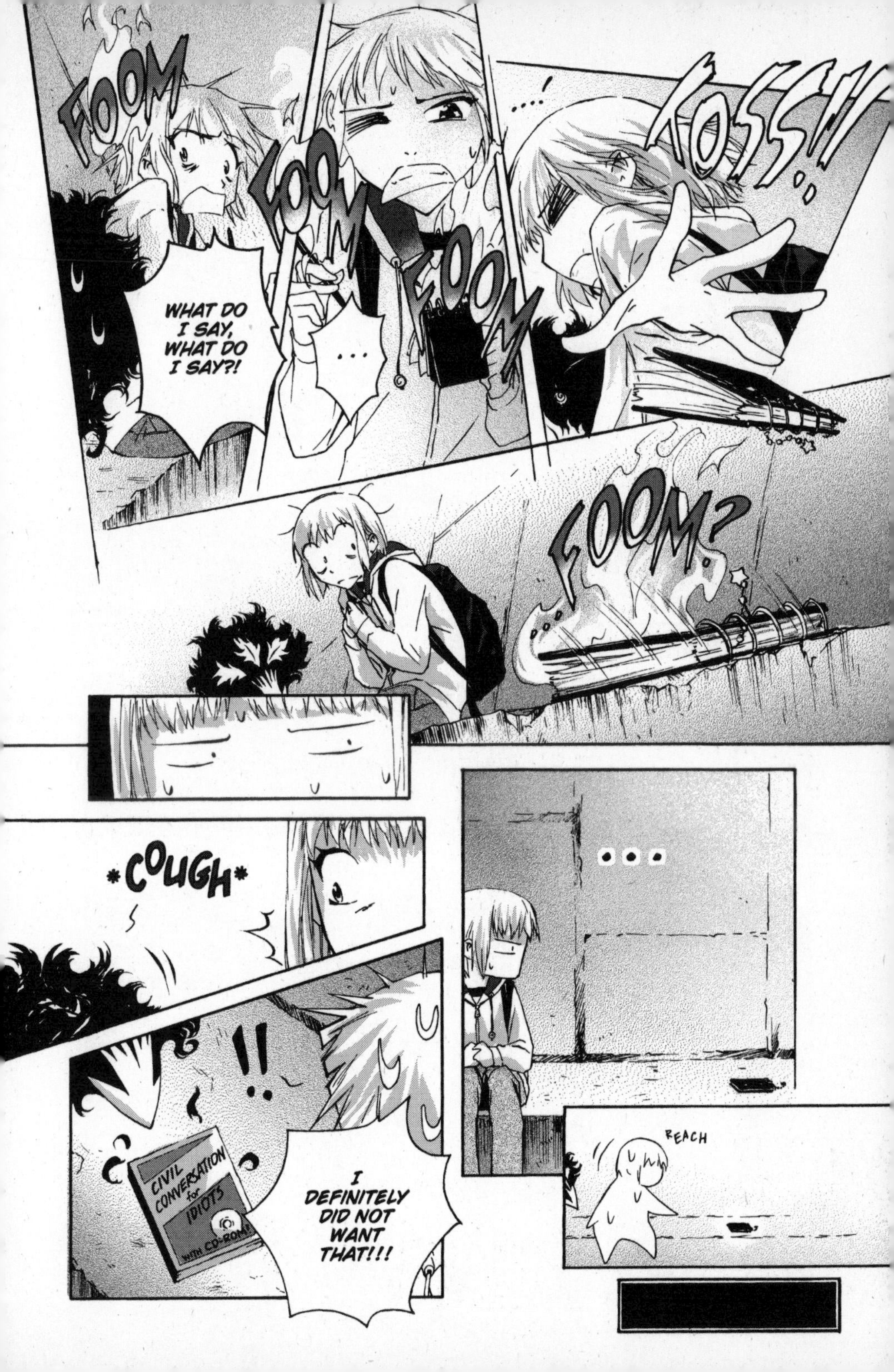
FOOM
WHAT DO I SAY, WHAT DO I SAY?!
FOOM
FOOM
. . .
....!
KOSSH!!
FOOM?
COUGH
!!
CIVIL CONVERSATION for IDIOTS
WITH CD-ROM!
I DEFINITELY DID NOT WANT THAT!!!
• • •
REACH

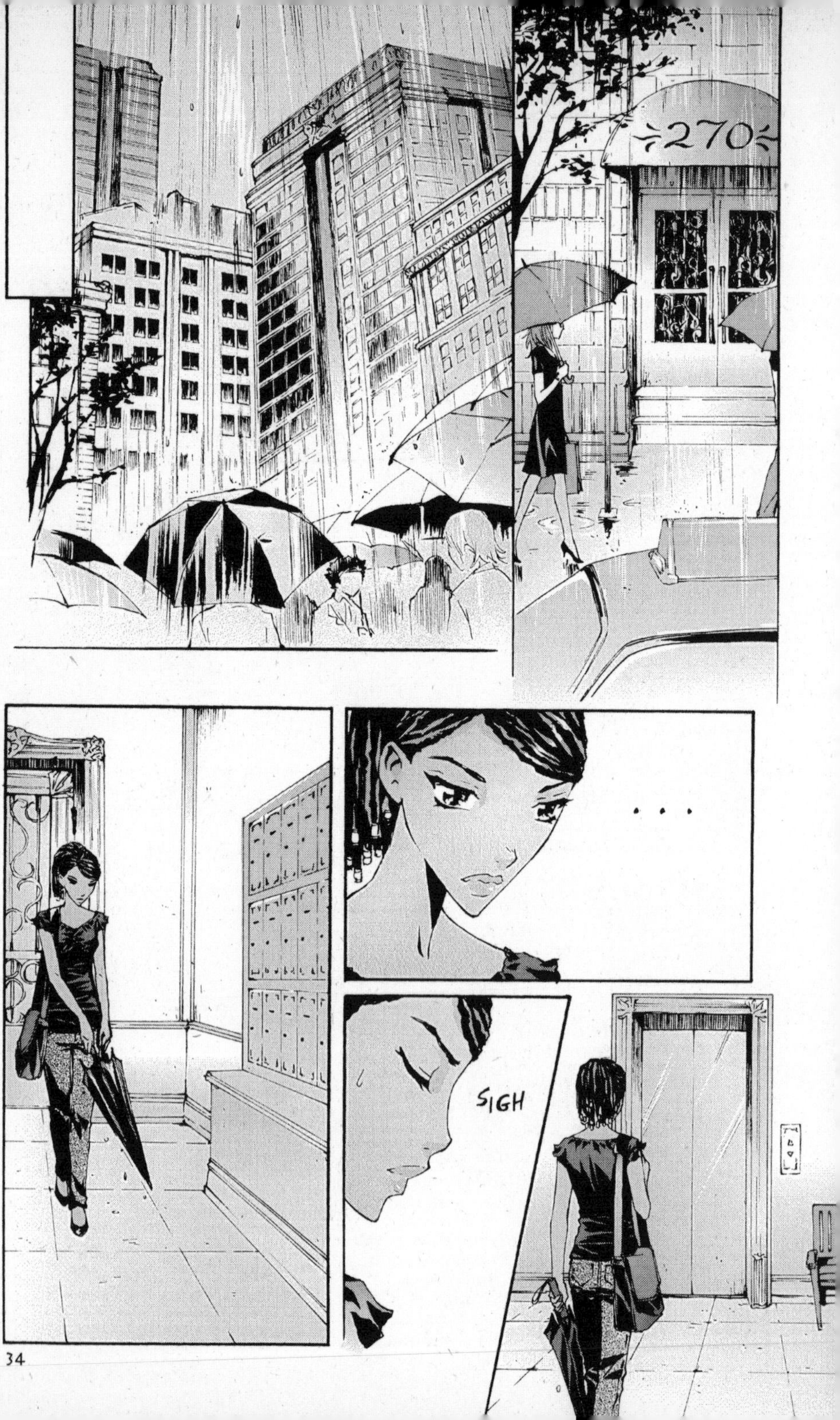
270
. . .
SIGH

I'M HOME.

YOU'RE BACK!!

JUST IN TIME! I'M MAKING PASTA! SEAFOOD— SHRIMP AND SCALLOPS!

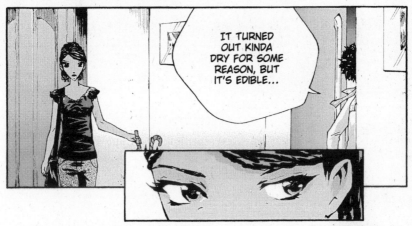

IT TURNED OUT KINDA DRY FOR SOME REASON, BUT IT'S EDIBLE...

HEY, HOW WELL DO YOU KNOW THAT ALEX GIRL?

...UM, NOT VERY, I GUESS. WHY?

• • •

YOU SHOULD STAY AWAY FROM HER.

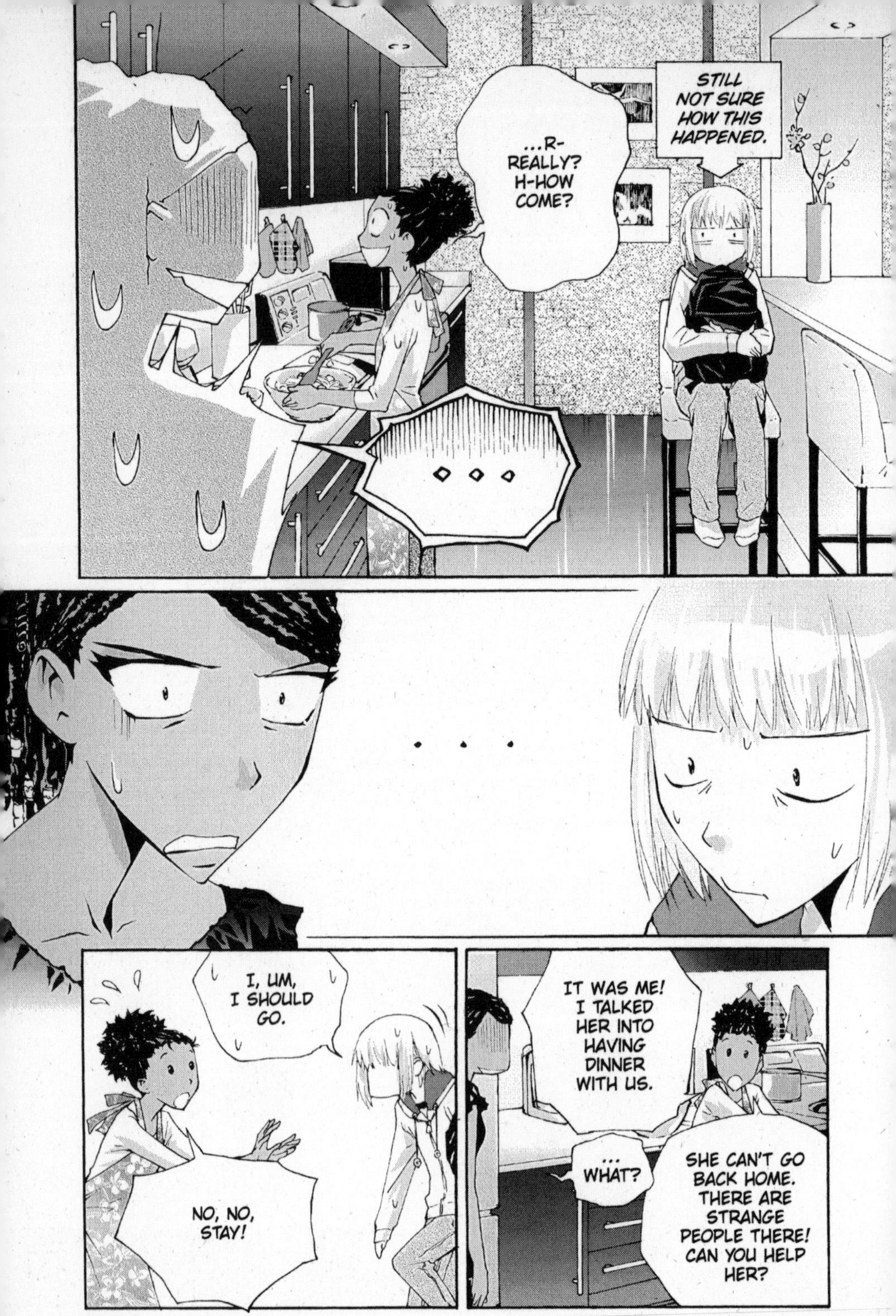
...R-
REALLY?
H-HOW
COME?
STILL
NOT SURE
HOW THIS
HAPPENED.
...
I, UM,
I SHOULD
GO.
NO, NO,
STAY!
IT WAS ME!
I TALKED
HER INTO
HAVING
DINNER
WITH US.
...
WHAT?
SHE CAN'T GO
BACK HOME.
THERE ARE
STRANGE
PEOPLE THERE!
CAN YOU HELP
HER?

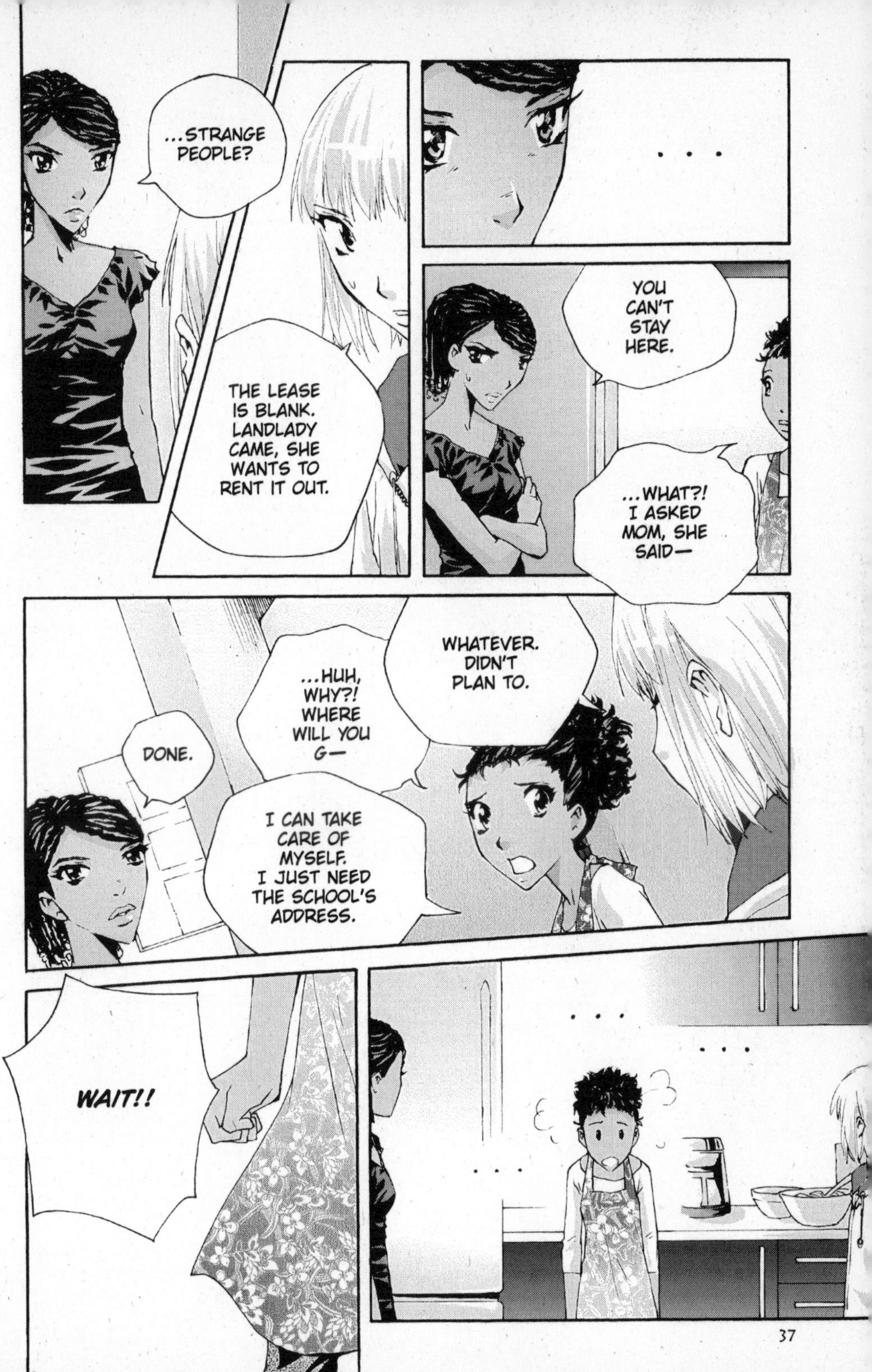
...STRANGE PEOPLE?
THE LEASE IS BLANK. LANDLADY CAME, SHE WANTS TO RENT IT OUT.
. . .
YOU CAN'T STAY HERE.
...WHAT?! I ASKED MOM, SHE SAID—
DONE.
...HUH, WHY?! WHERE WILL YOU G—
WHATEVER. DIDN'T PLAN TO.
I CAN TAKE CARE OF MYSELF. I JUST NEED THE SCHOOL'S ADDRESS.
WAIT!!
. . .
. . .
. . .

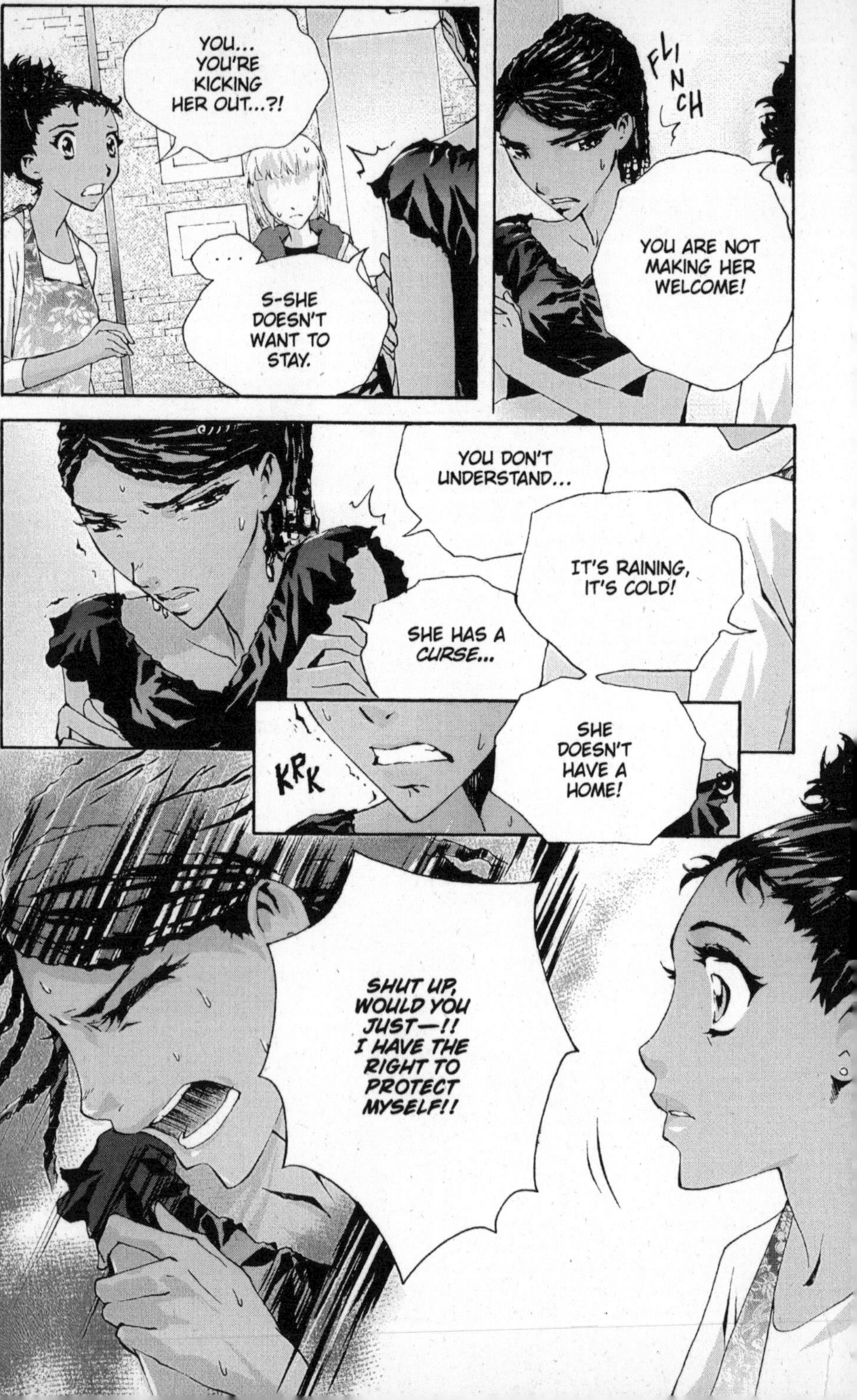
YOU... YOU'RE KICKING HER OUT...?!
...
S-SHE DOESN'T WANT TO STAY.
FLINCH
YOU ARE NOT MAKING HER WELCOME!
YOU DON'T UNDERSTAND...
IT'S RAINING, IT'S COLD!
SHE HAS A CURSE...
KRK
SHE DOESN'T HAVE A HOME!
SHUT UP, WOULD YOU JUST—!! I HAVE THE RIGHT TO PROTECT MYSELF!!

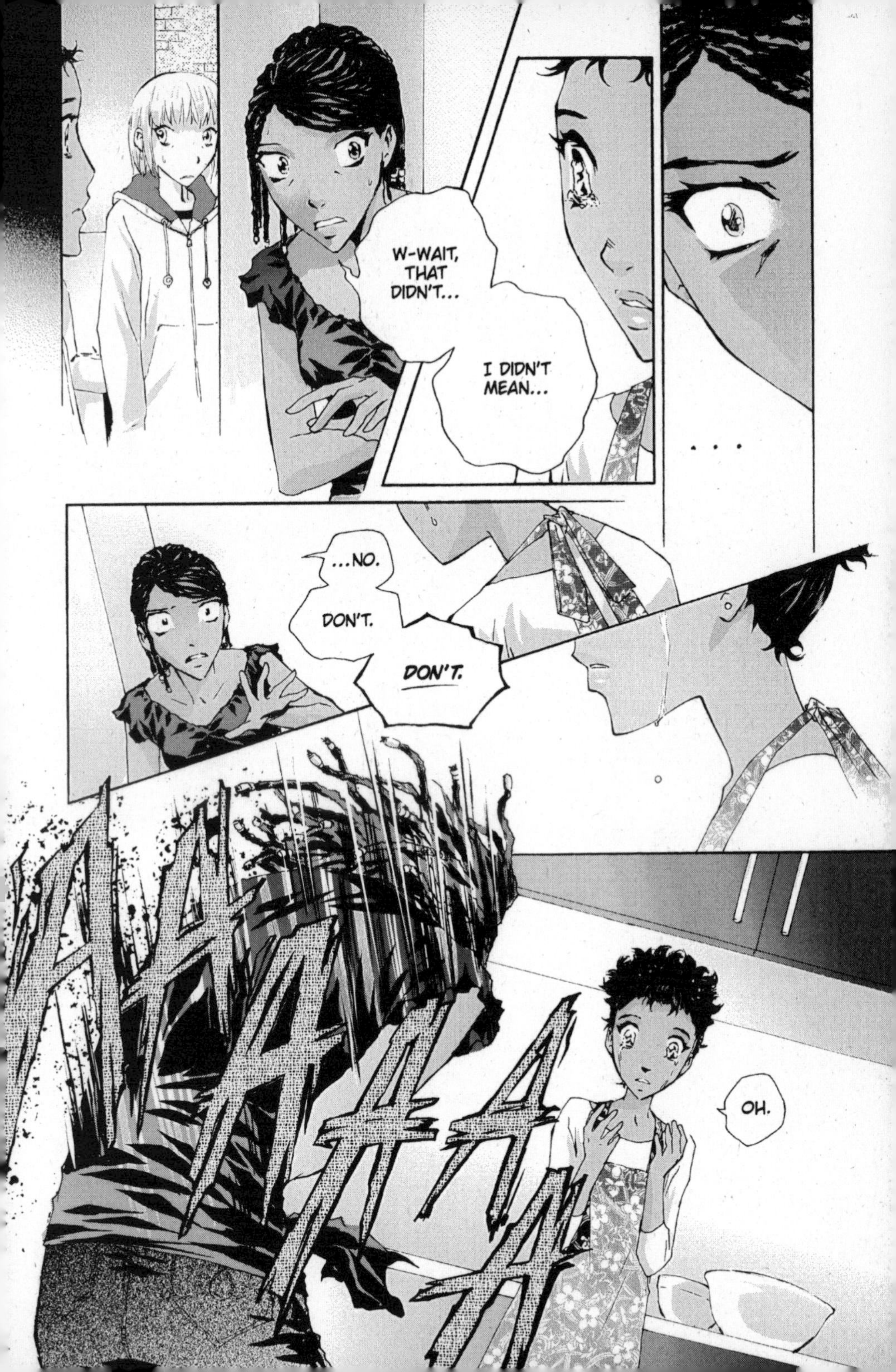
W-WAIT, THAT DIDN'T...
I DIDN'T MEAN...
...
...NO.
DON'T.
DON'T.
OH.

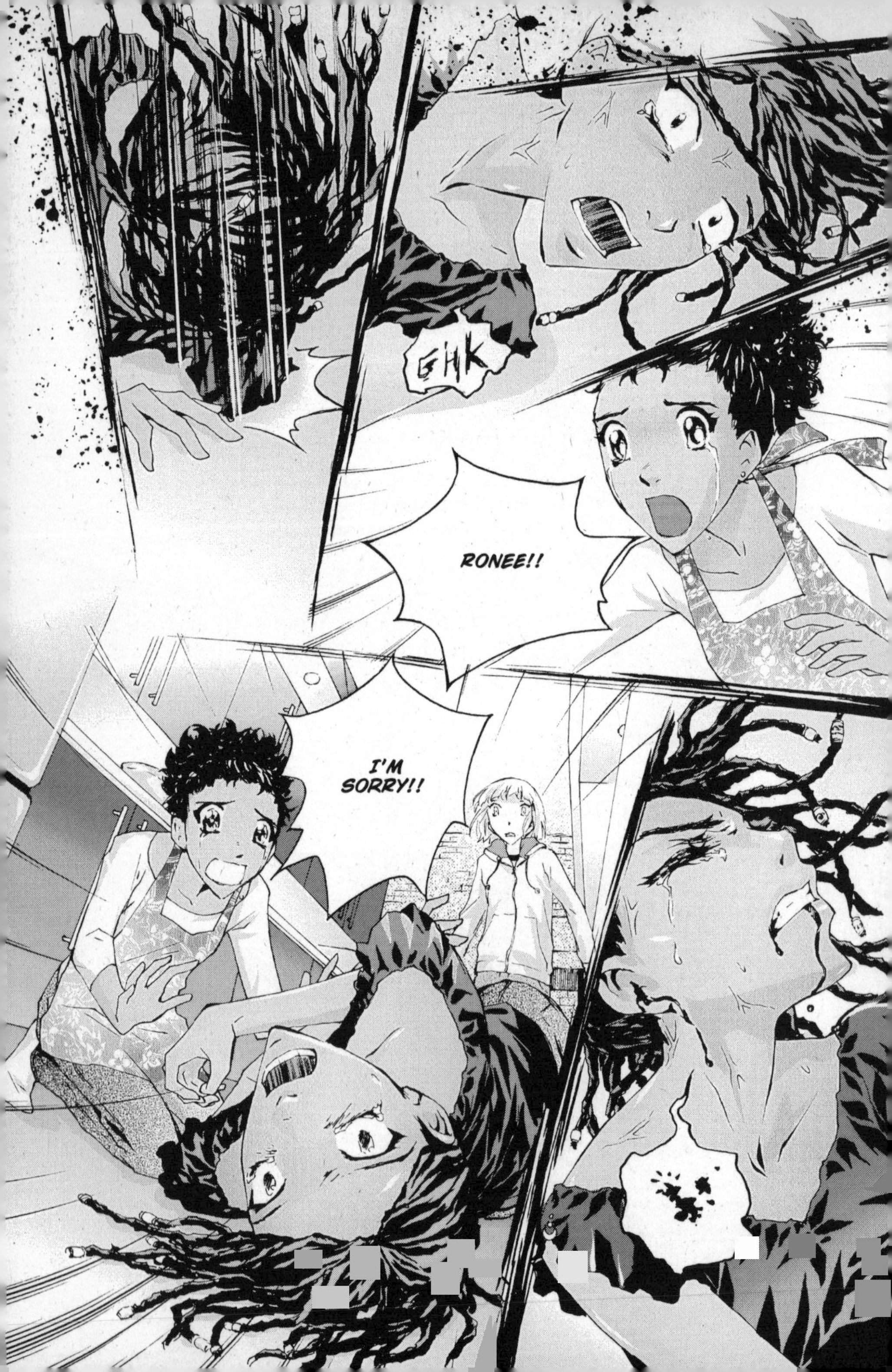
GHK
RONEE!!
I'M SORRY!!

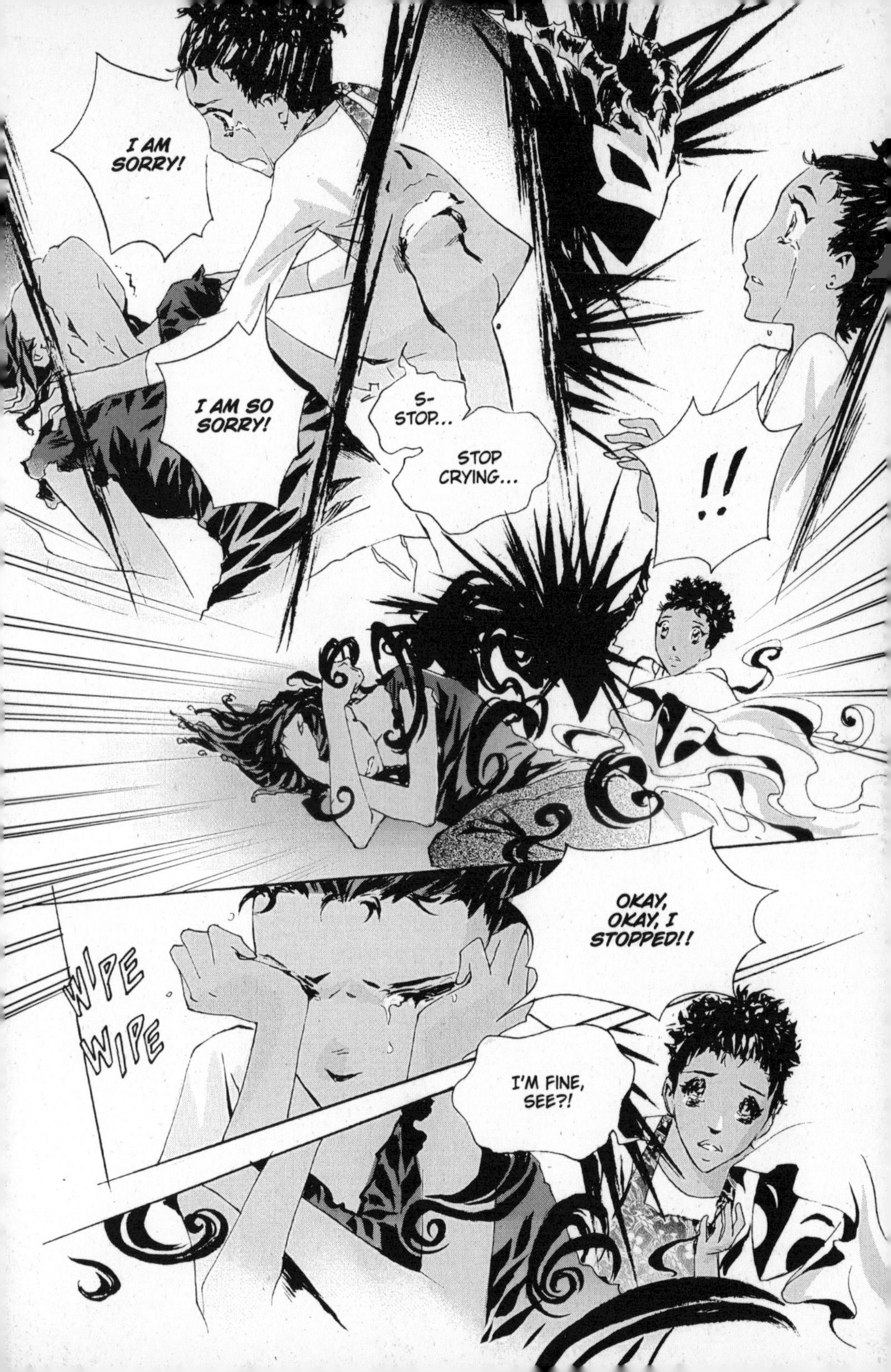
I AM SORRY!
I AM SO SORRY!
S-STOP...
STOP CRYING...
!!
OKAY, OKAY, I STOPPED!!
WIPE WIPE
I'M FINE, SEE?!

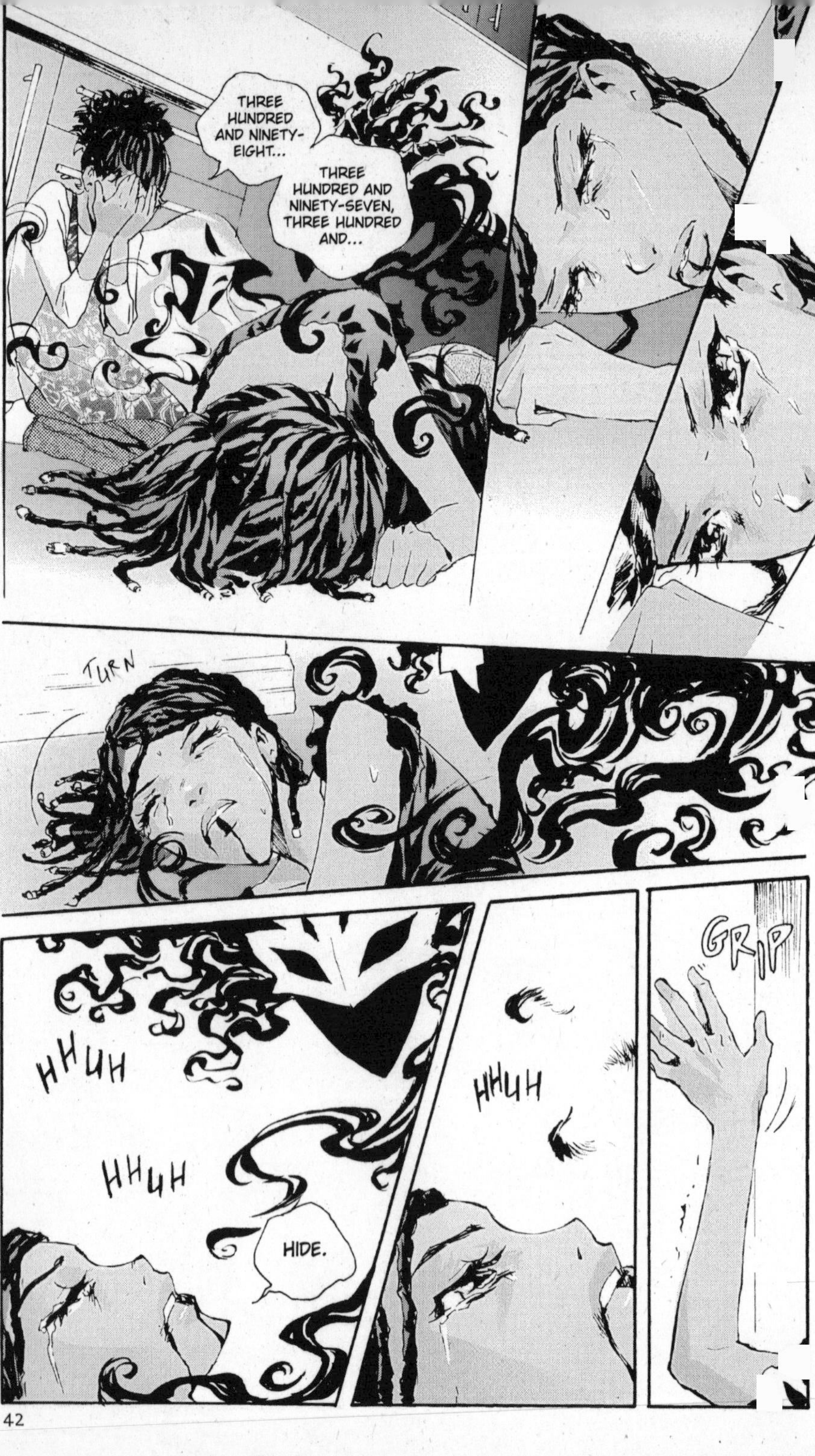
THREE HUNDRED AND NINETY-EIGHT...
THREE HUNDRED AND NINETY-SEVEN, THREE HUNDRED AND...
TURN
HHUH
HHUH
HIDE.
HHUH
GRIP

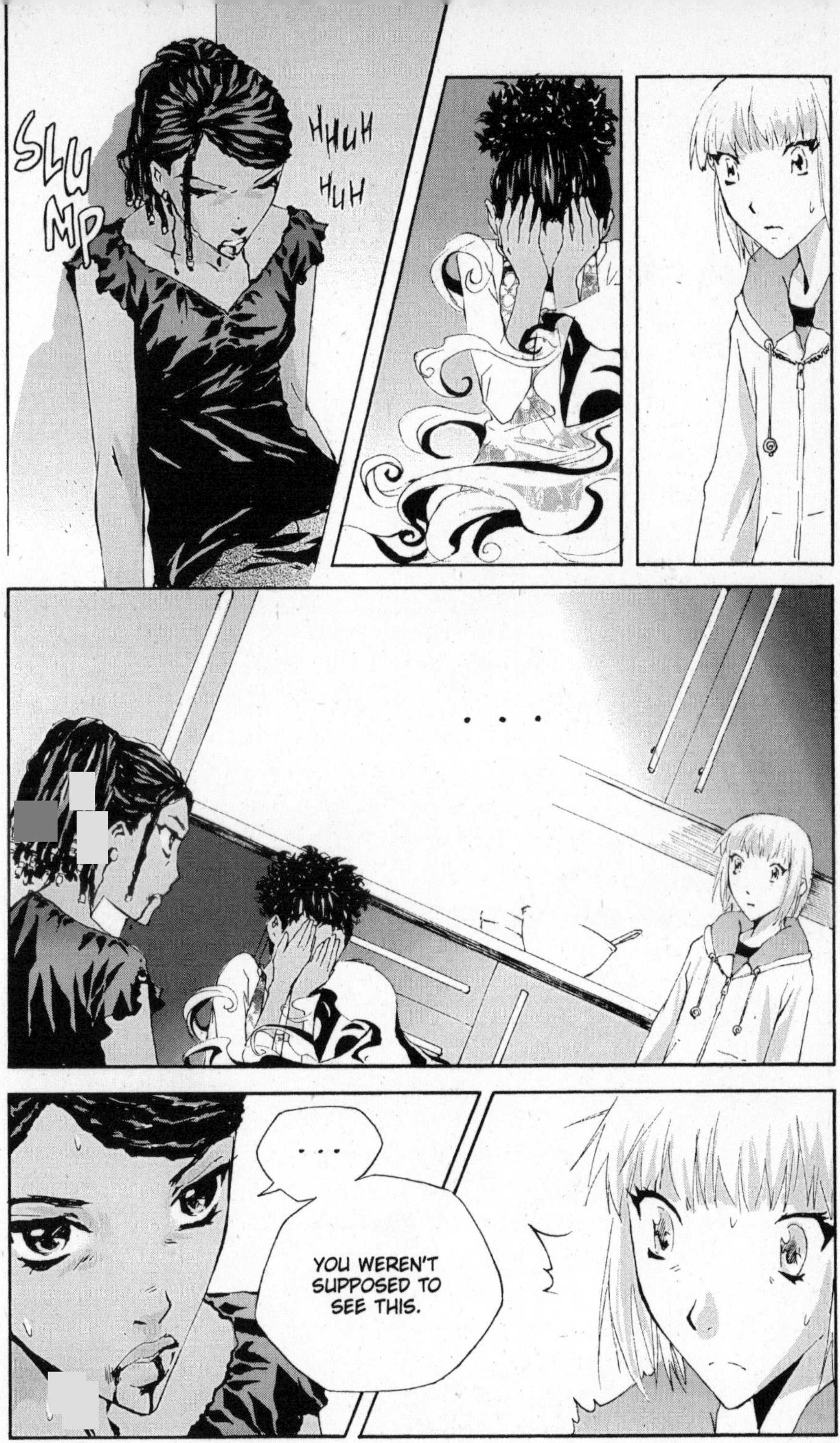
SLUMP
HHUH HUH
. . .
. . .
YOU WEREN'T SUPPOSED TO SEE THIS.

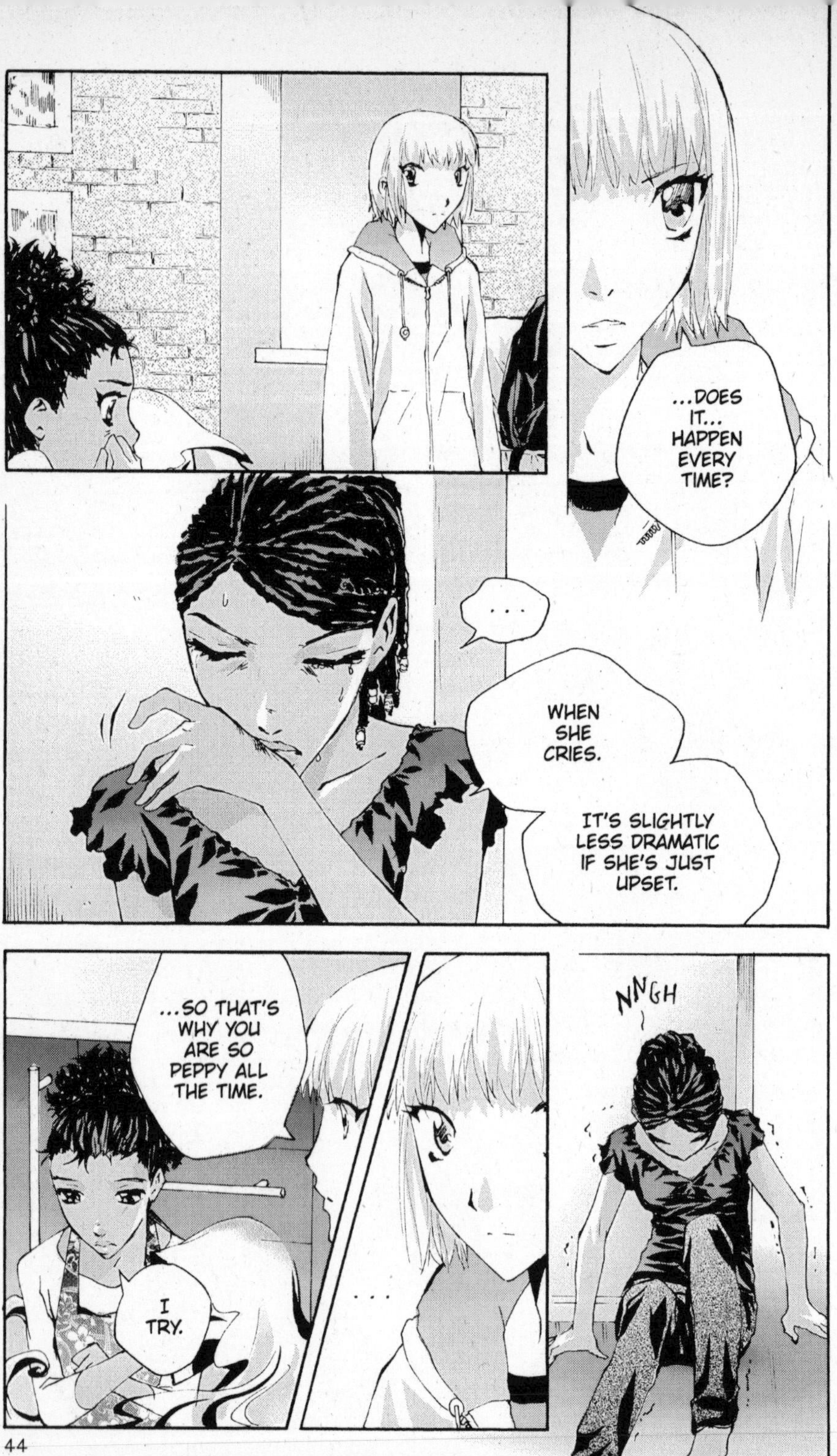
...DOES IT... HAPPEN EVERY TIME?
...
WHEN SHE CRIES.
IT'S SLIGHTLY LESS DRAMATIC IF SHE'S JUST UPSET.
...SO THAT'S WHY YOU ARE SO PEPPY ALL THE TIME.
I TRY.
...
NNGH

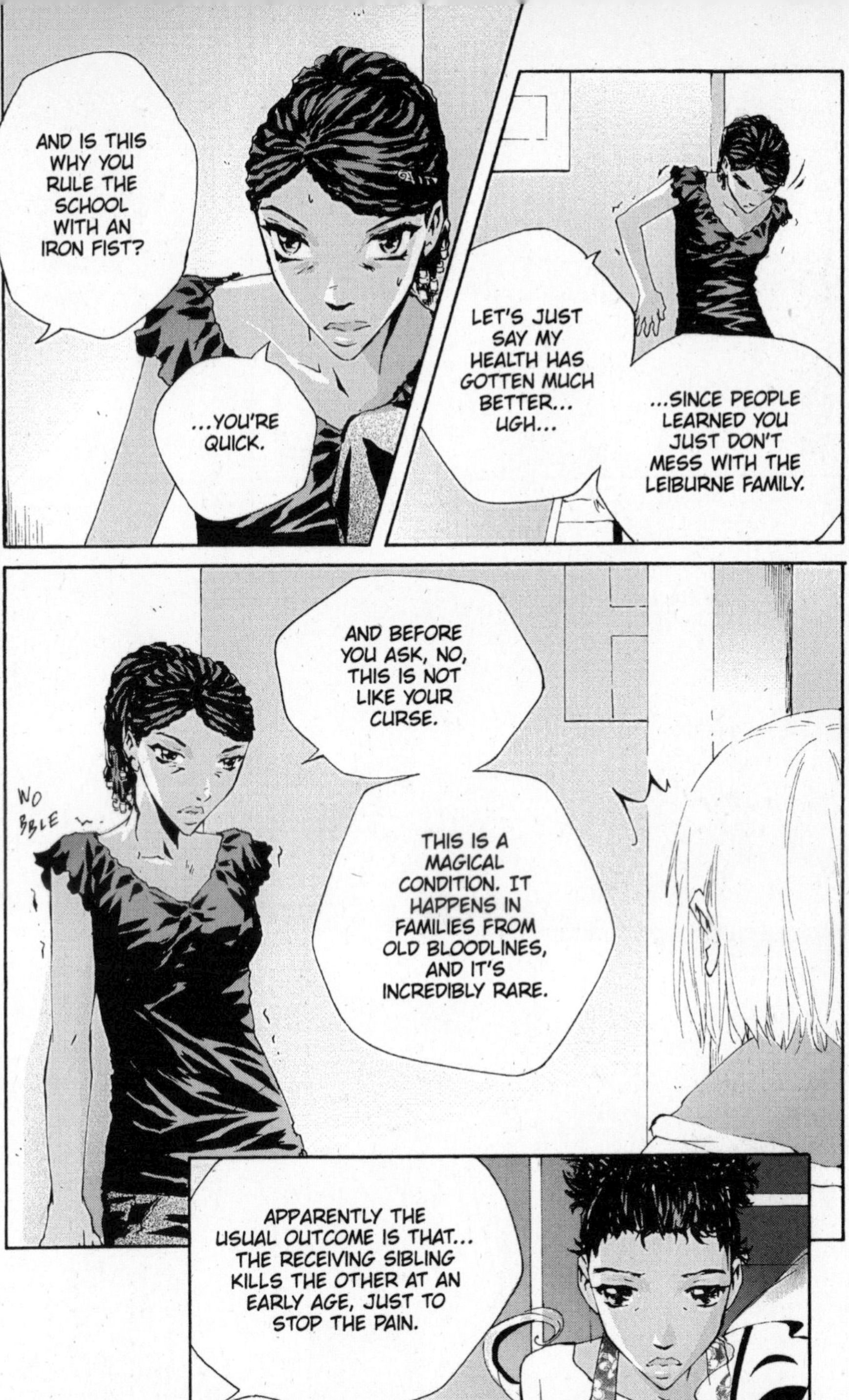
AND IS THIS WHY YOU RULE THE SCHOOL WITH AN IRON FIST?
...YOU'RE QUICK.
LET'S JUST SAY MY HEALTH HAS GOTTEN MUCH BETTER... UGH...
...SINCE PEOPLE LEARNED YOU JUST DON'T MESS WITH THE LEIBURNE FAMILY.
AND BEFORE YOU ASK, NO, THIS IS NOT LIKE YOUR CURSE.
WOBBLE
THIS IS A MAGICAL CONDITION. IT HAPPENS IN FAMILIES FROM OLD BLOODLINES, AND IT'S INCREDIBLY RARE.
APPARENTLY THE USUAL OUTCOME IS THAT... THE RECEIVING SIBLING KILLS THE OTHER AT AN EARLY AGE, JUST TO STOP THE PAIN.

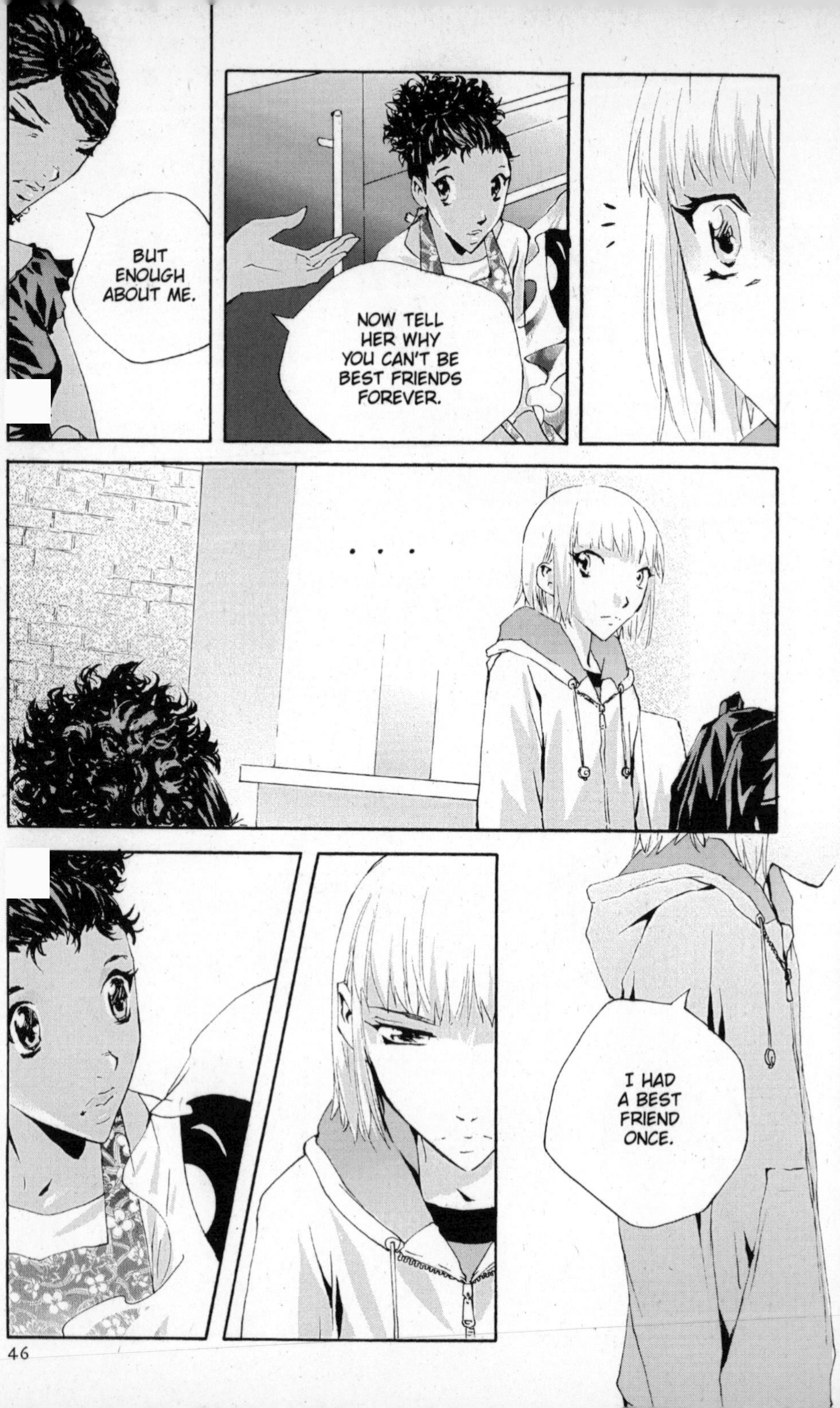
BUT ENOUGH ABOUT ME.
NOW TELL HER WHY YOU CAN'T BE BEST FRIENDS FOREVER.
...
I HAD A BEST FRIEND ONCE.

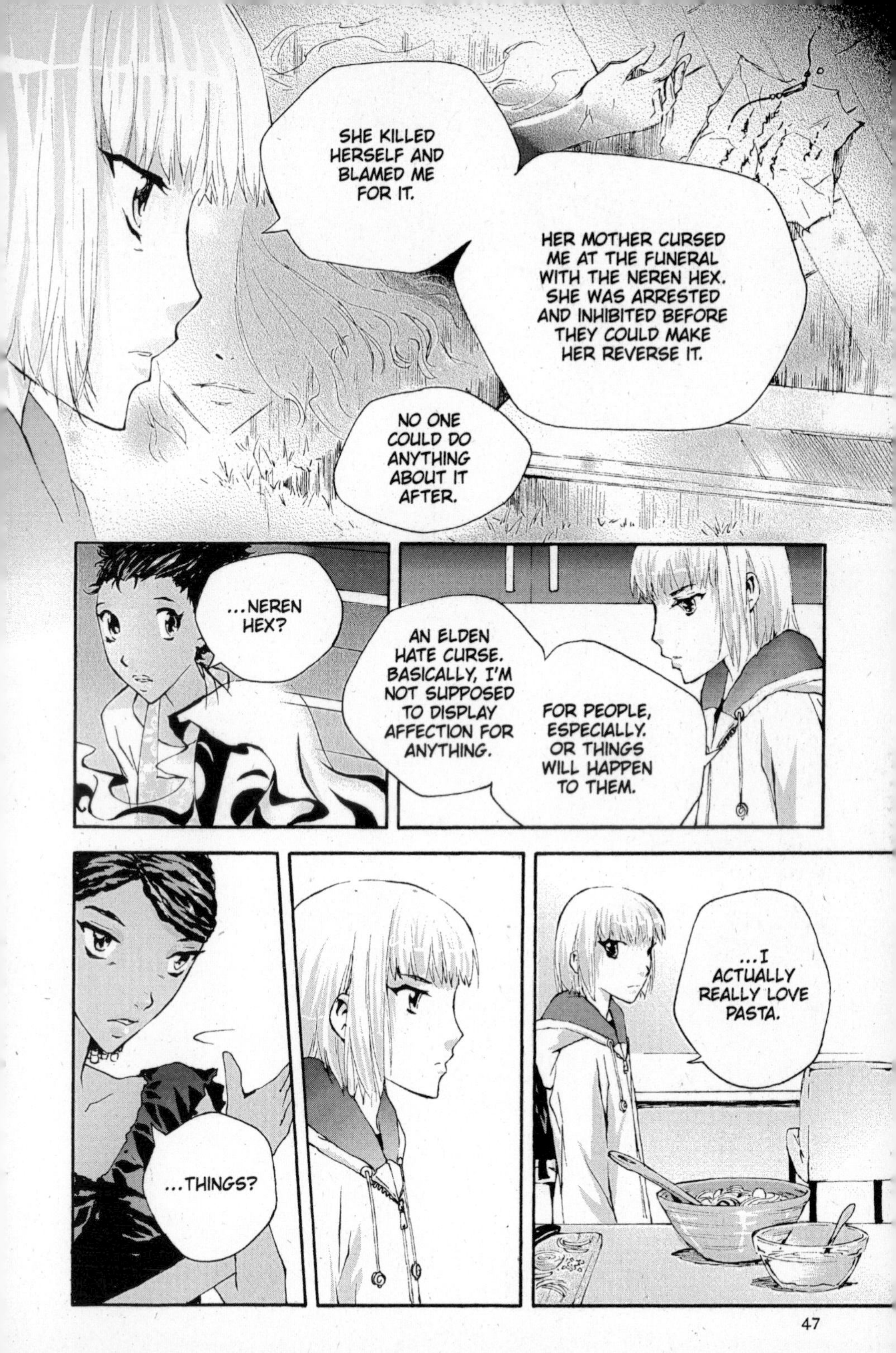
SHE KILLED HERSELF AND BLAMED ME FOR IT.
HER MOTHER CURSED ME AT THE FUNERAL WITH THE NEREN HEX. SHE WAS ARRESTED AND INHIBITED BEFORE THEY COULD MAKE HER REVERSE IT.
NO ONE COULD DO ANYTHING ABOUT IT AFTER.
...NEREN HEX?
AN ELDEN HATE CURSE. BASICALLY, I'M NOT SUPPOSED TO DISPLAY AFFECTION FOR ANYTHING.
FOR PEOPLE, ESPECIALLY. OR THINGS WILL HAPPEN TO THEM.
...THINGS?
...I ACTUALLY REALLY LOVE PASTA.

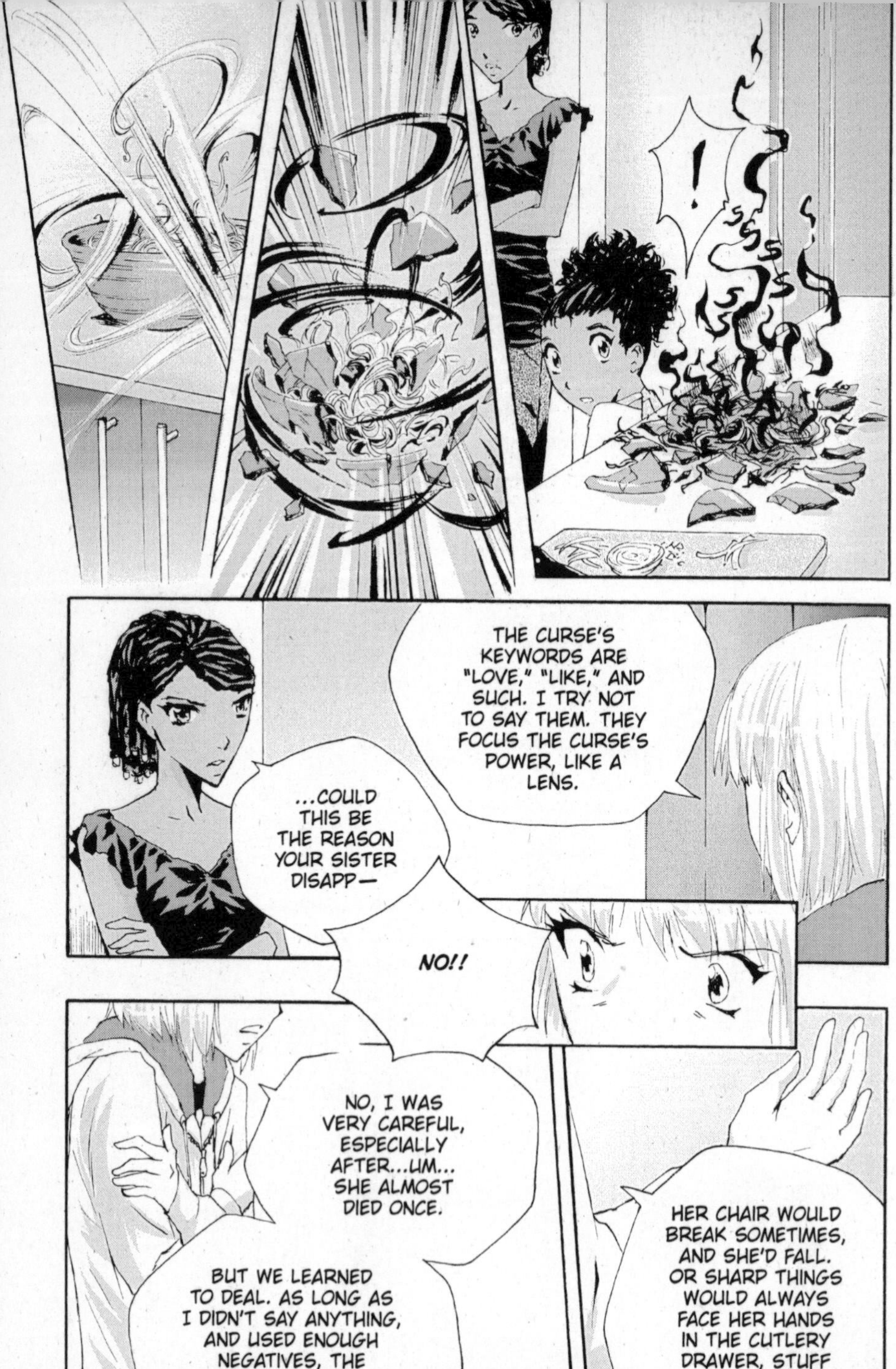
!
THE CURSE'S KEYWORDS ARE "LOVE," "LIKE," AND SUCH. I TRY NOT TO SAY THEM. THEY FOCUS THE CURSE'S POWER, LIKE A LENS.
...COULD THIS BE THE REASON YOUR SISTER DISAPP—
NO!!
NO, I WAS VERY CAREFUL, ESPECIALLY AFTER...UM... SHE ALMOST DIED ONCE.
BUT WE LEARNED TO DEAL. AS LONG AS I DIDN'T SAY ANYTHING, AND USED ENOUGH NEGATIVES, THE EFFECTS WERE... MILDER.
HER CHAIR WOULD BREAK SOMETIMES, AND SHE'D FALL. OR SHARP THINGS WOULD ALWAYS FACE HER HANDS IN THE CUTLERY DRAWER, STUFF LIKE THAT. NOTHING, UM...

NOTHING FINAL.

SO YOU CAN HAVE FRIENDS, THEN? IF YOU'RE CAREFUL?

DO YOU KNOW WHAT FRIENDS REALLY ARE?

PEOPLE WHO KNOW EXACTLY WHERE TO HIT SO IT HURTS FOR THE REST OF YOUR LIFE.

DON'T NEED ANY MORE, THANKS.

SHF

LOOK, I'M ALL FOR MAKING THIS EASY FOR EVERYONE.

I NEED THE SCHOOL'S ADDRESS, AND I NEED MY SISTER BACK.

YOU NEED TO FIND OUT WHO'S MESSING WITH YOUR TURF AND TO KEEP THE DANGEROUS ELEMENT AWAY FROM YOUR SISTER.

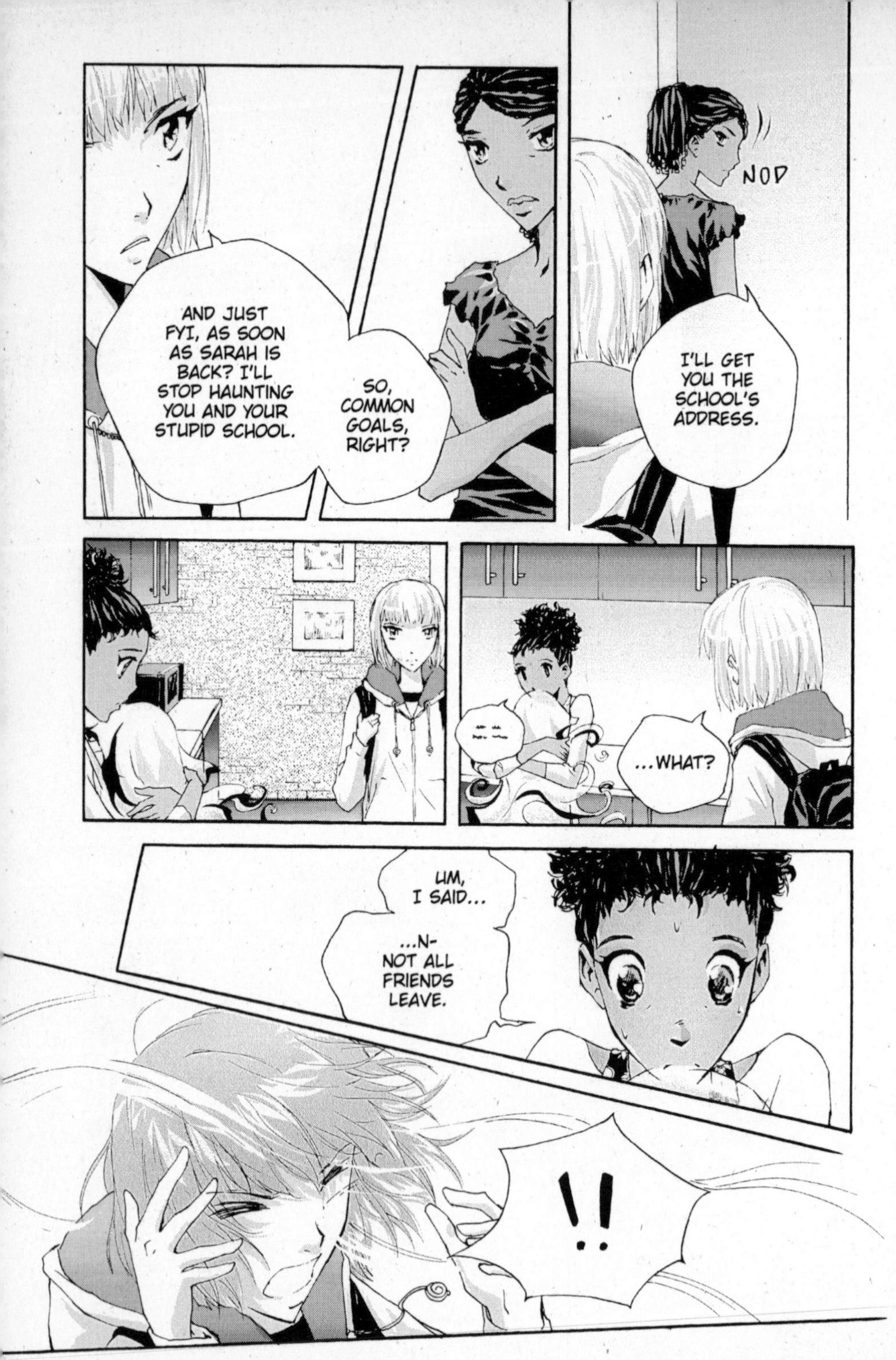
AND JUST FYI, AS SOON AS SARAH IS BACK? I'LL STOP HAUNTING YOU AND YOUR STUPID SCHOOL.
SO, COMMON GOALS, RIGHT?
NOD
I'LL GET YOU THE SCHOOL'S ADDRESS.
...WHAT?
UM, I SAID...
...N-NOT ALL FRIENDS LEAVE.
!!

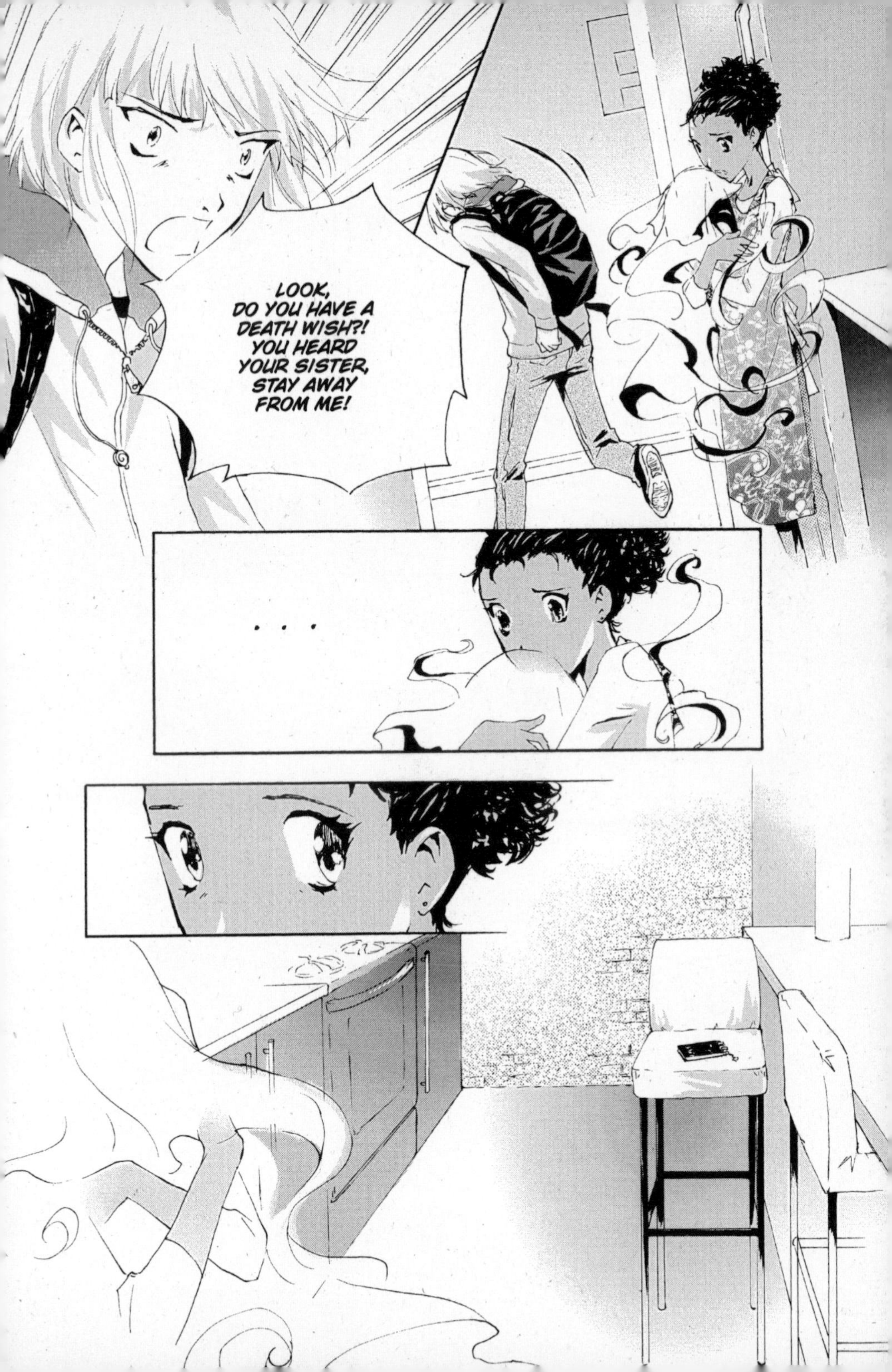
LOOK, DO YOU HAVE A DEATH WISH?! YOU HEARD YOUR SISTER, STAY AWAY FROM ME!
. . .

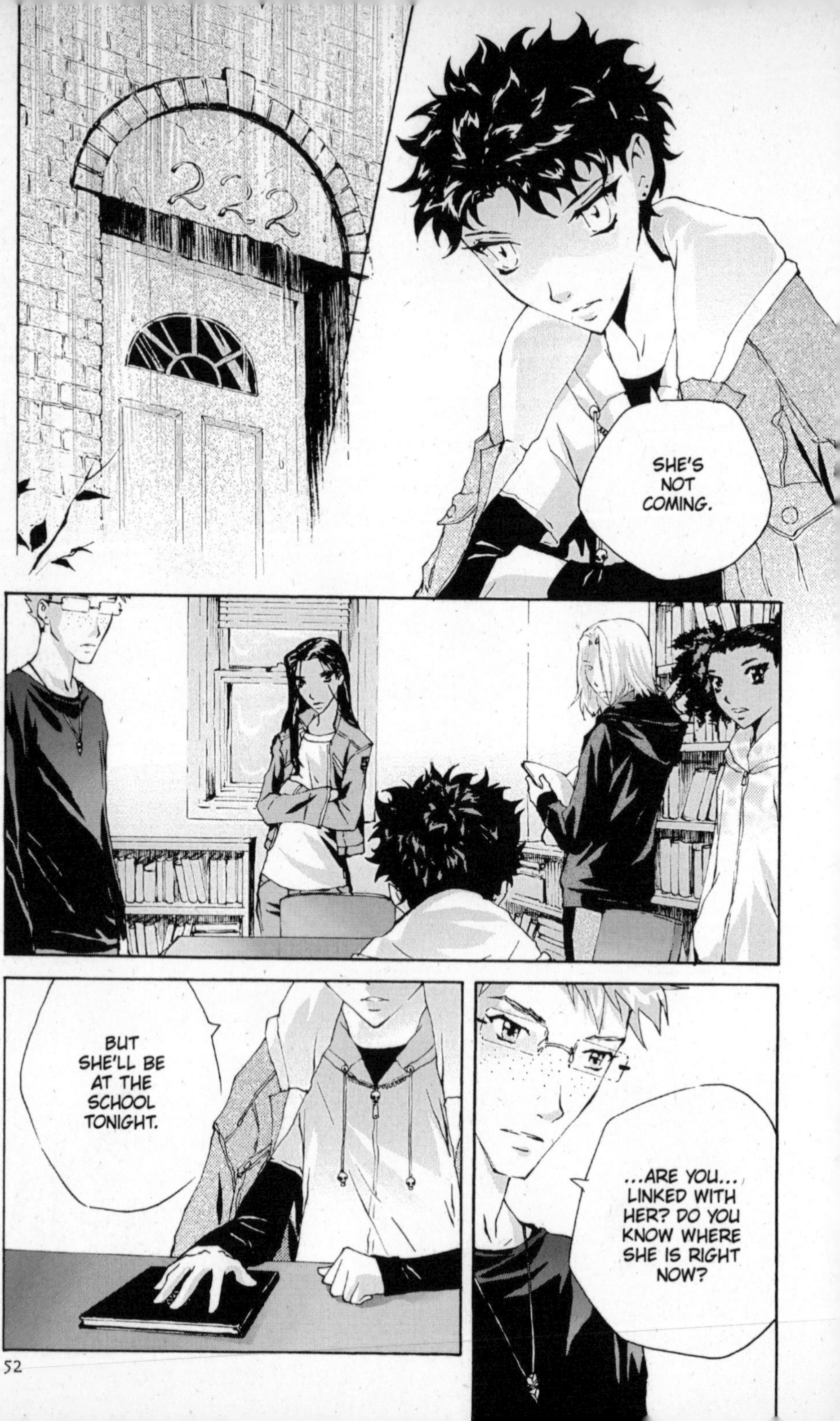
222
SHE'S NOT COMING.
BUT SHE'LL BE AT THE SCHOOL TONIGHT.
...ARE YOU... LINKED WITH HER? DO YOU KNOW WHERE SHE IS RIGHT NOW?

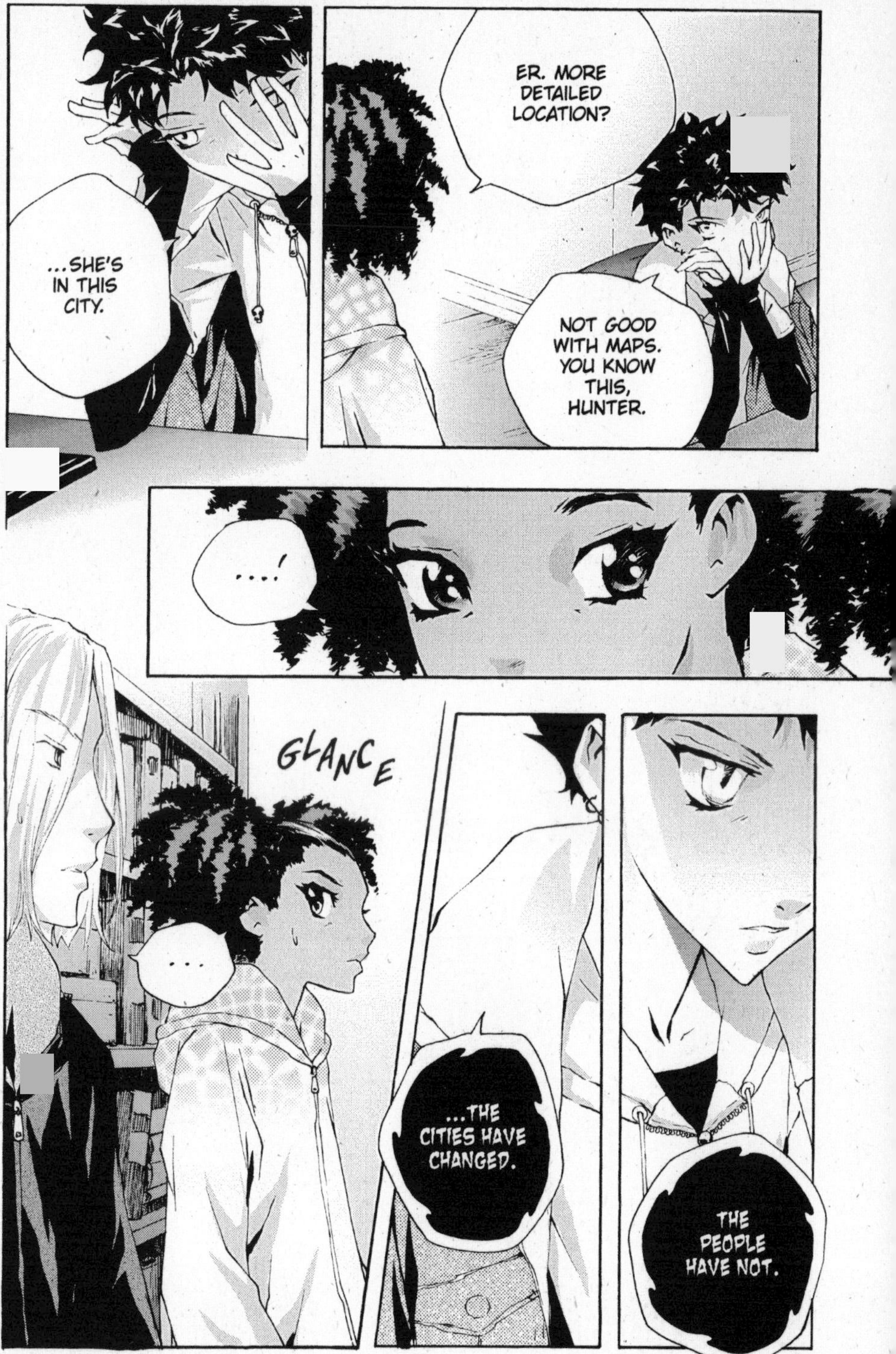
...SHE'S IN THIS CITY.
ER. MORE DETAILED LOCATION?
NOT GOOD WITH MAPS. YOU KNOW THIS, HUNTER.
...!
GLANCE
...
...THE CITIES HAVE CHANGED.
THE PEOPLE HAVE NOT.

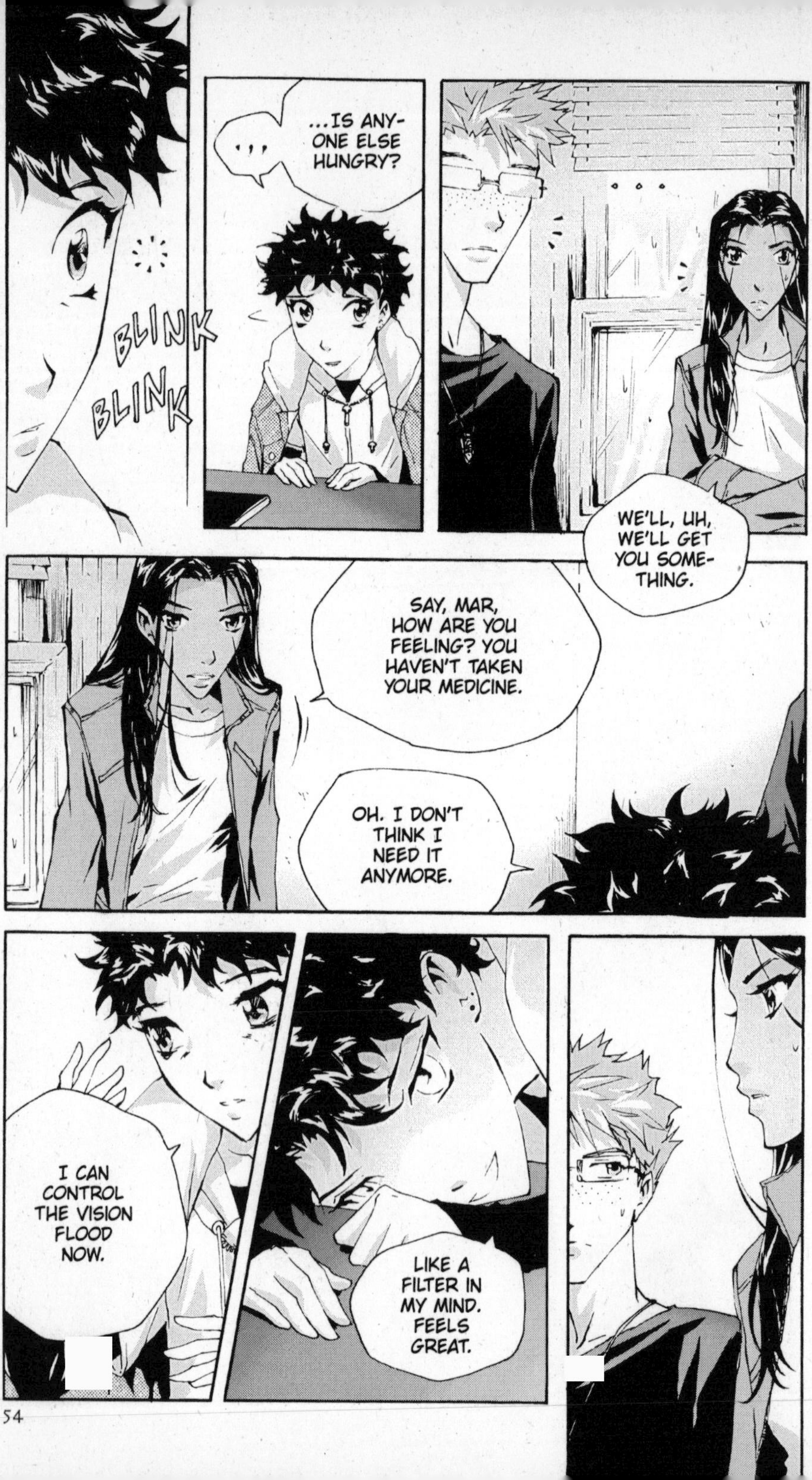
BLINK
BLINK
...
...IS ANY-ONE ELSE HUNGRY?
...
WE'LL, UH, WE'LL GET YOU SOME-THING.
SAY, MAR, HOW ARE YOU FEELING? YOU HAVEN'T TAKEN YOUR MEDICINE.
OH. I DON'T THINK I NEED IT ANYMORE.
I CAN CONTROL THE VISION FLOOD NOW.
LIKE A FILTER IN MY MIND. FEELS GREAT.

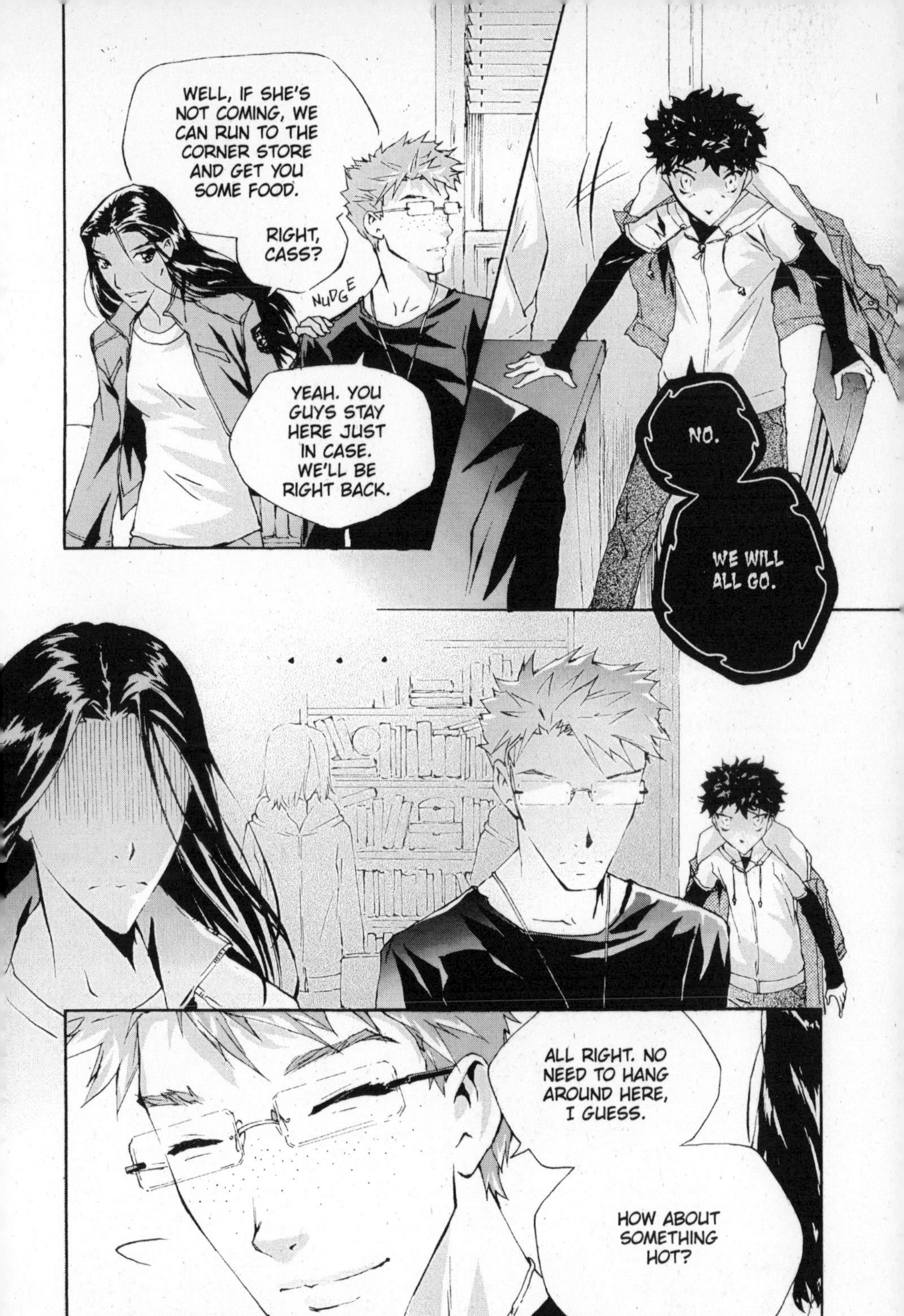

WELL, IF SHE'S NOT COMING, WE CAN RUN TO THE CORNER STORE AND GET YOU SOME FOOD.
RIGHT, CASS?
NUDGE
YEAH. YOU GUYS STAY HERE JUST IN CASE. WE'LL BE RIGHT BACK.
NO.
WE WILL ALL GO.
...
ALL RIGHT. NO NEED TO HANG AROUND HERE, I GUESS.
HOW ABOUT SOMETHING HOT?

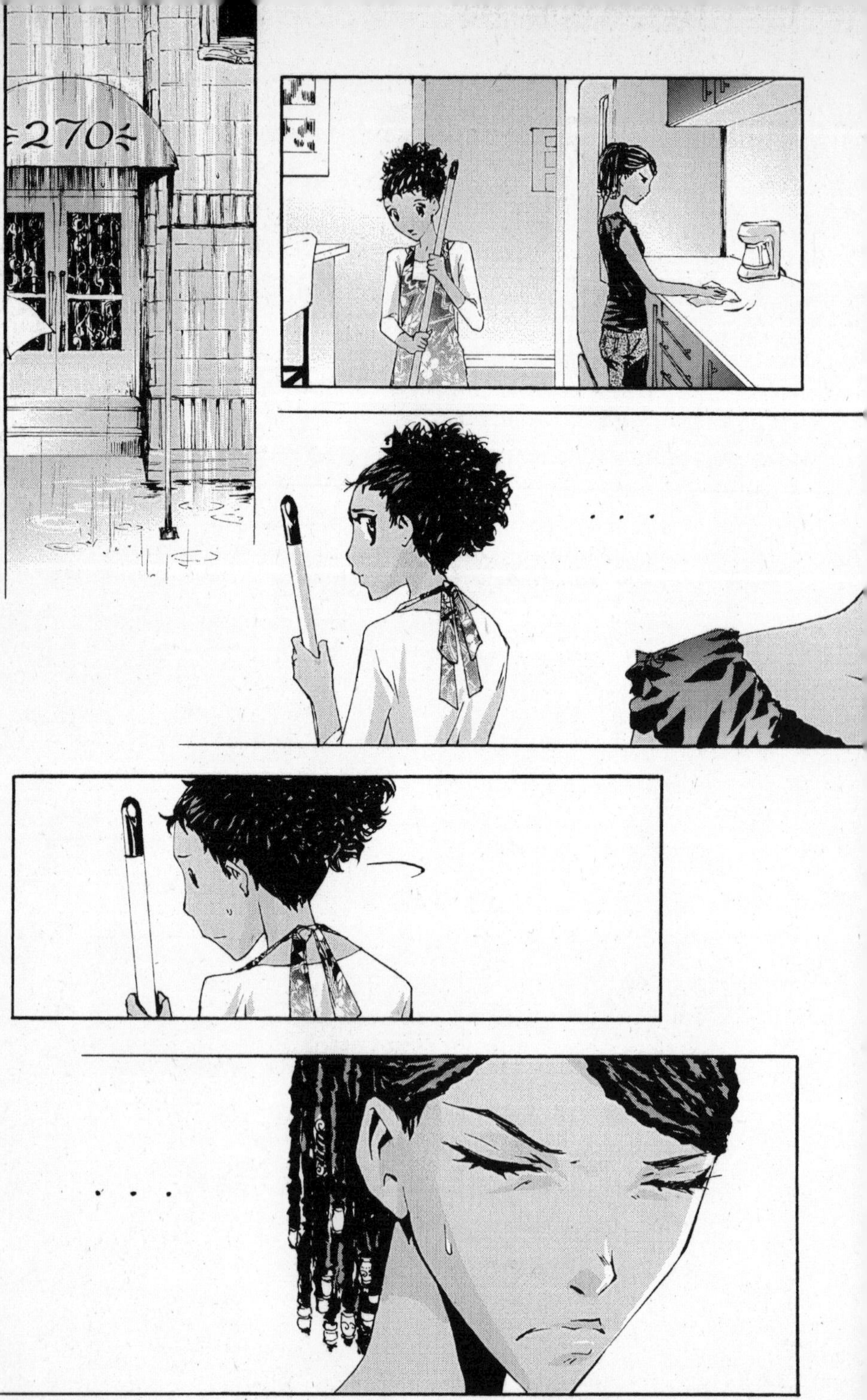
270
. . .
. . .

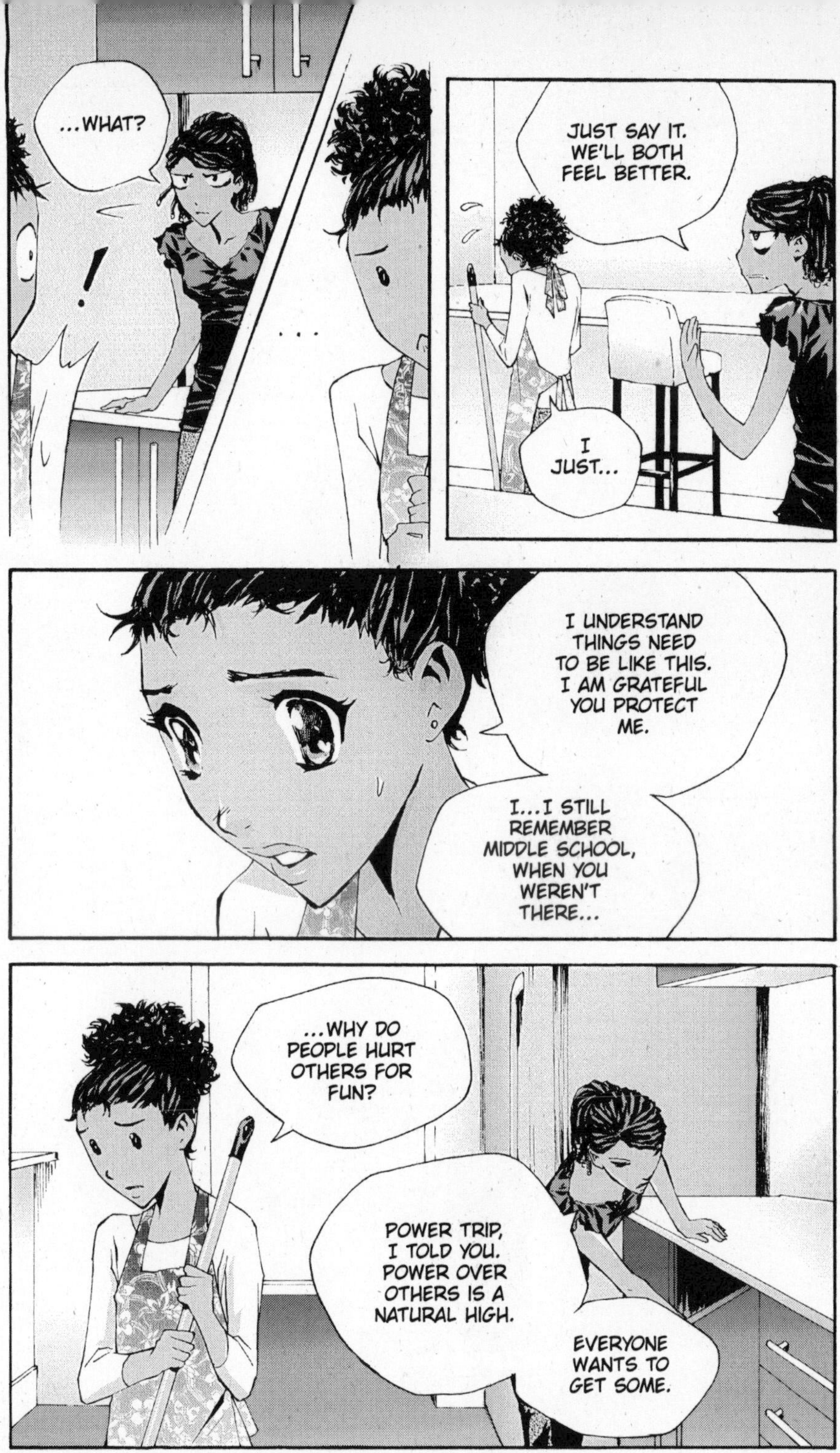
...WHAT?
!
...
JUST SAY IT. WE'LL BOTH FEEL BETTER.
I JUST...
I UNDERSTAND THINGS NEED TO BE LIKE THIS. I AM GRATEFUL YOU PROTECT ME.
I...I STILL REMEMBER MIDDLE SCHOOL, WHEN YOU WEREN'T THERE...
...WHY DO PEOPLE HURT OTHERS FOR FUN?
POWER TRIP, I TOLD YOU. POWER OVER OTHERS IS A NATURAL HIGH.
EVERYONE WANTS TO GET SOME.

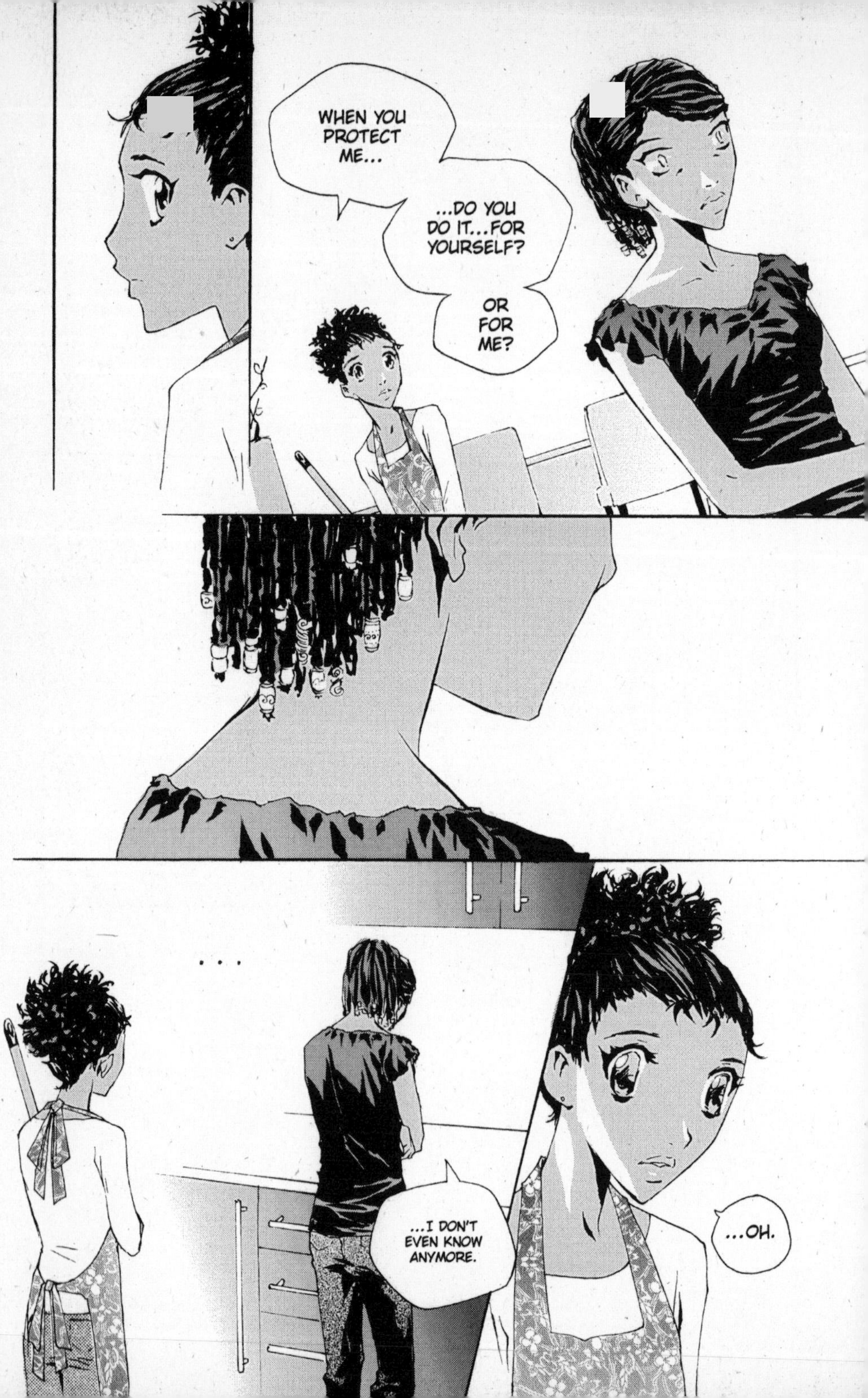
WHEN YOU PROTECT ME...
...DO YOU DO IT...FOR YOURSELF?
OR FOR ME?
...
...I DON'T EVEN KNOW ANYMORE.
...OH.

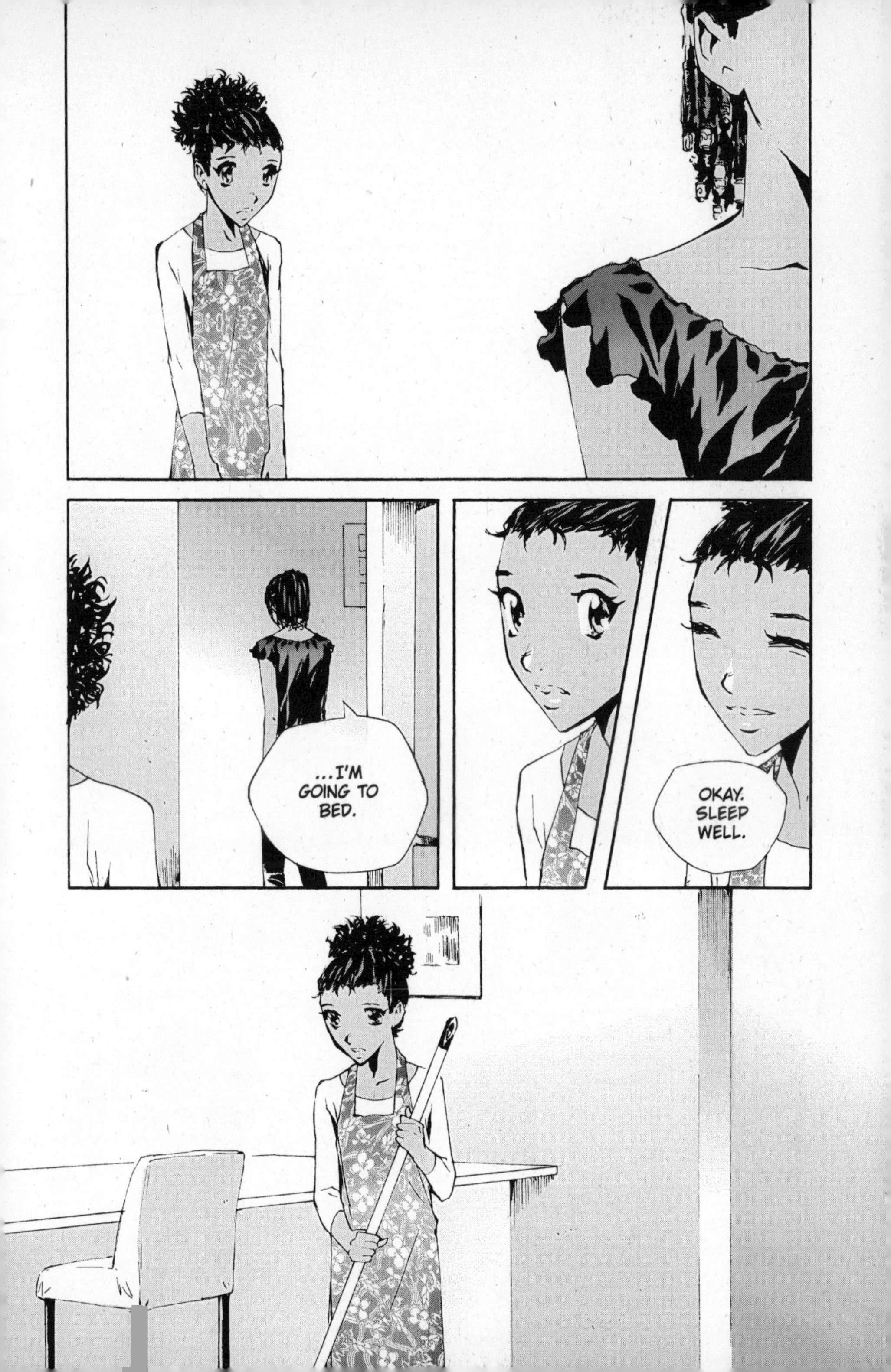
...I'M GOING TO BED.
OKAY. SLEEP WELL.

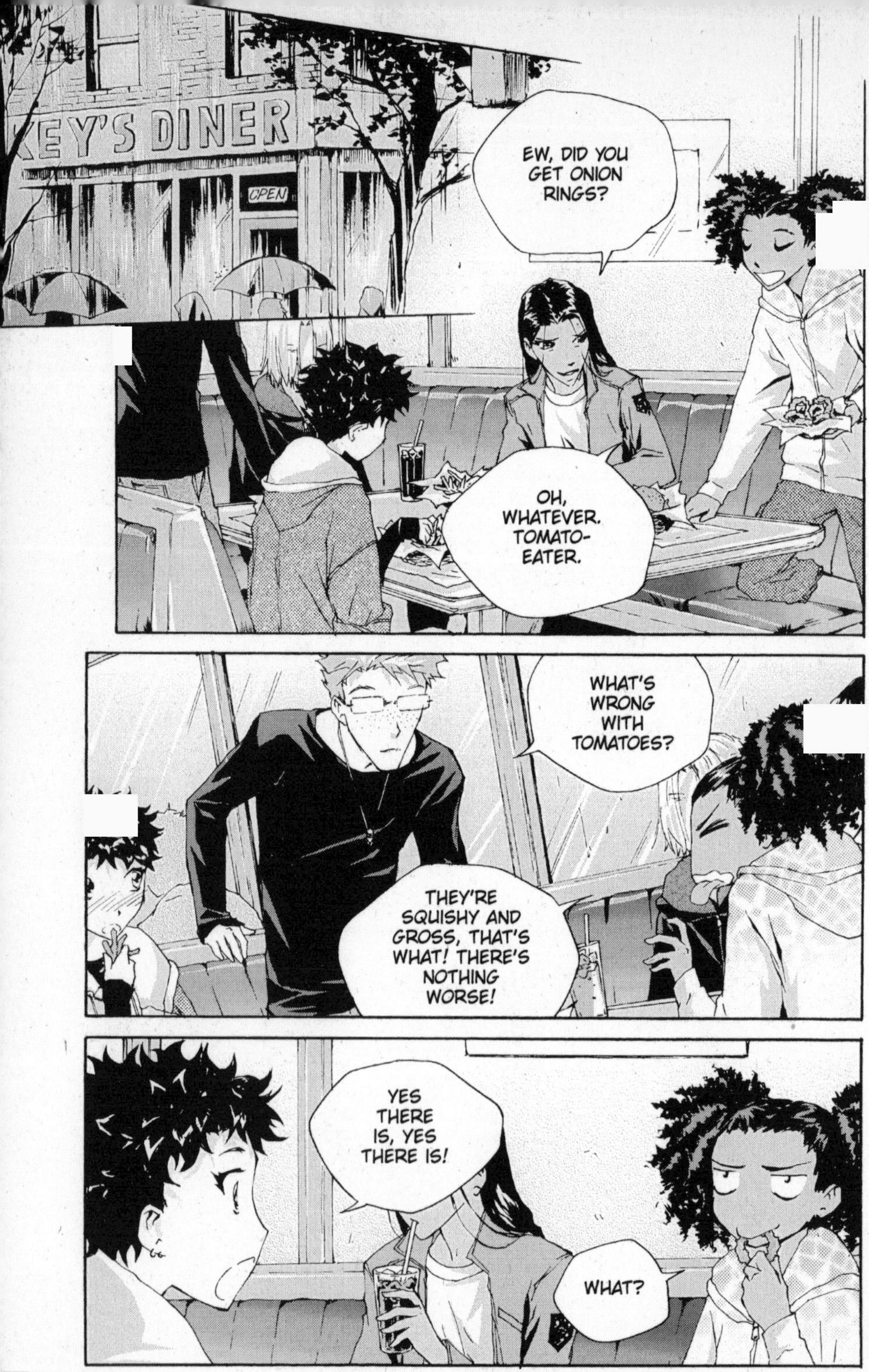

KEY'S DINER
OPEN
EW, DID YOU GET ONION RINGS?
OH, WHATEVER. TOMATO-EATER.
WHAT'S WRONG WITH TOMATOES?
THEY'RE SQUISHY AND GROSS, THAT'S WHAT! THERE'S NOTHING WORSE!
YES THERE IS, YES THERE IS!
WHAT?

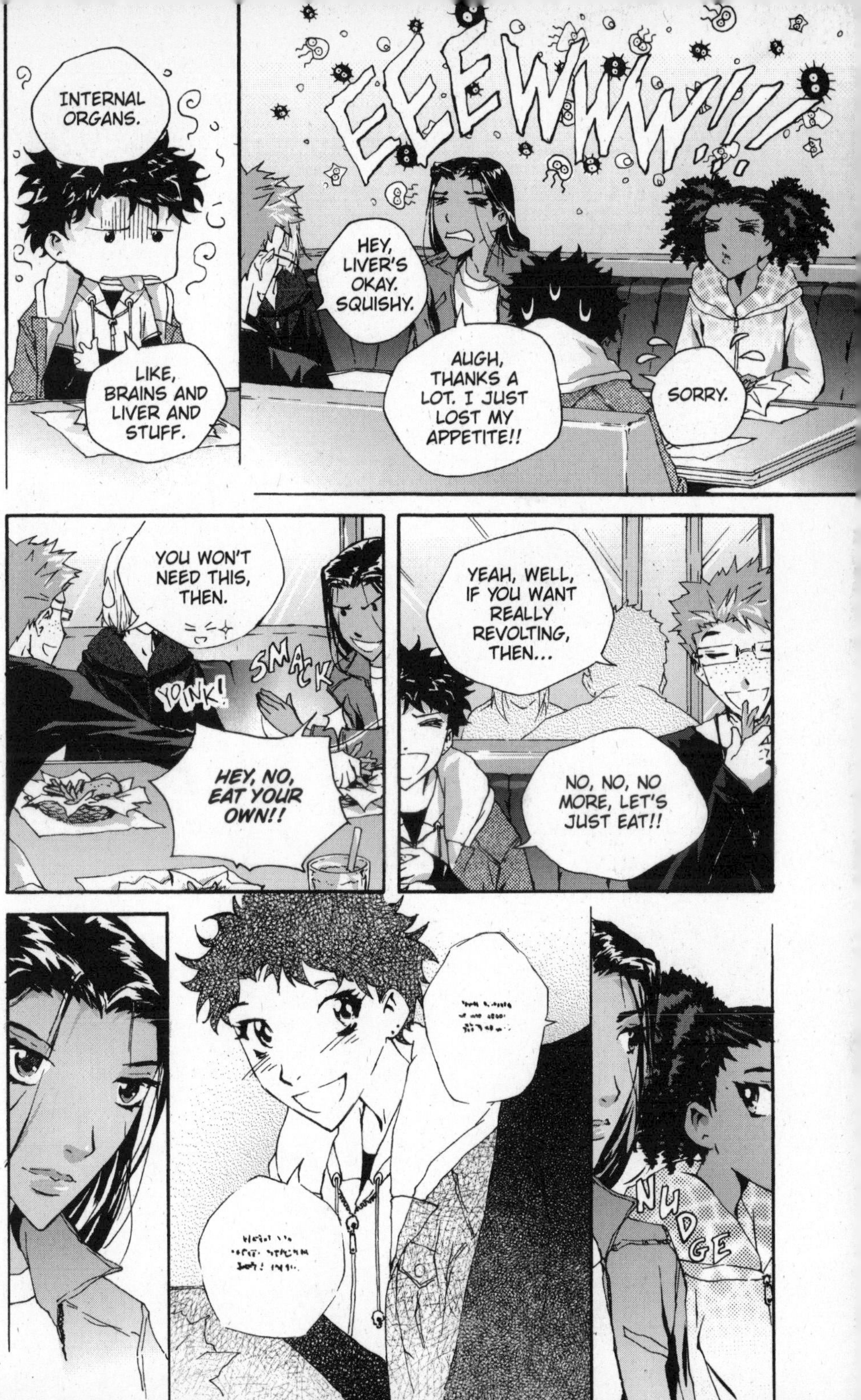
INTERNAL ORGANS.
LIKE, BRAINS AND LIVER AND STUFF.
EEEWWWW!!!
HEY, LIVER'S OKAY. SQUISHY.
AUGH, THANKS A LOT. I JUST LOST MY APPETITE!!
SORRY.
YOU WON'T NEED THIS, THEN.
YOINK!
SMACK
HEY, NO, EAT YOUR OWN!!
YEAH, WELL, IF YOU WANT REALLY REVOLTING, THEN...
NO, NO, NO MORE, LET'S JUST EAT!!
NUDGE

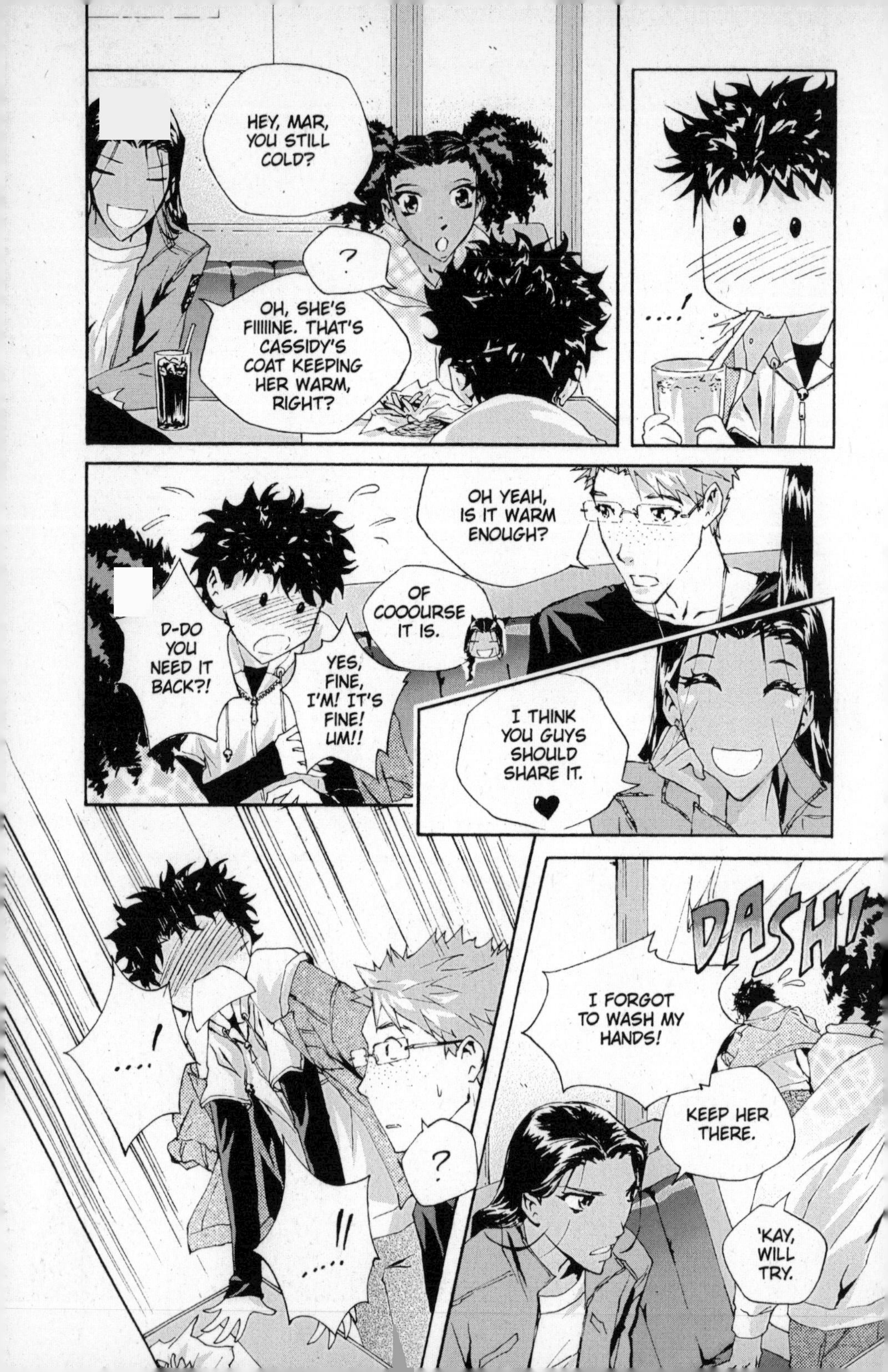
HEY, MAR, YOU STILL COLD?
?
OH, SHE'S FIIIIINE. THAT'S CASSIDY'S COAT KEEPING HER WARM, RIGHT?
....!
OH YEAH, IS IT WARM ENOUGH?
D-DO YOU NEED IT BACK?!
YES, FINE, I'M! IT'S FINE! UM!!
OF COOOURSE IT IS.
I THINK YOU GUYS SHOULD SHARE IT. ♥
....!
?
....!!
DASH!
I FORGOT TO WASH MY HANDS!
KEEP HER THERE.
'KAY, WILL TRY.

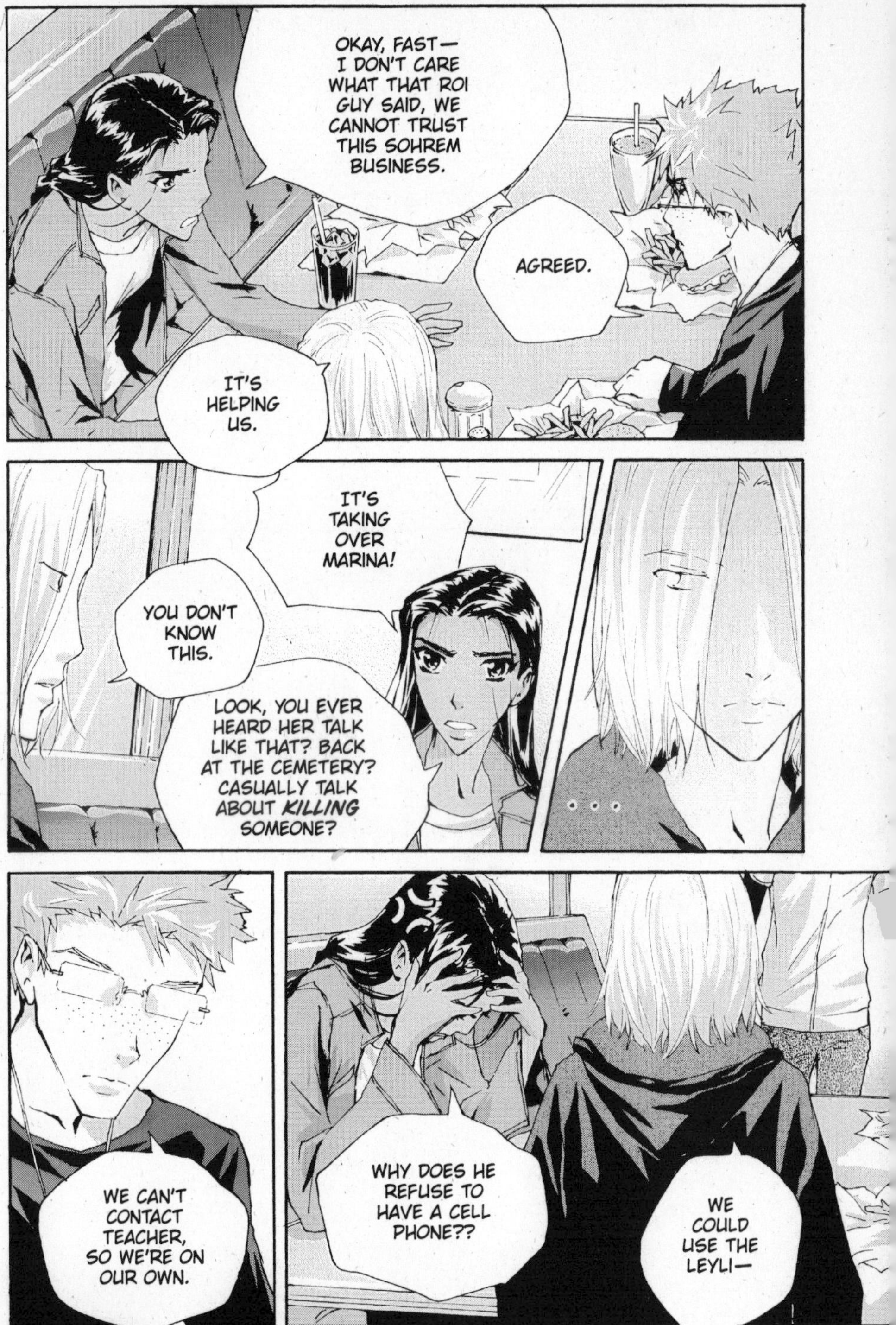
OKAY, FAST— I DON'T CARE WHAT THAT ROI GUY SAID, WE CANNOT TRUST THIS SOHREM BUSINESS.
AGREED.
IT'S HELPING US.
IT'S TAKING OVER MARINA!
YOU DON'T KNOW THIS.
LOOK, YOU EVER HEARD HER TALK LIKE THAT? BACK AT THE CEMETERY? CASUALLY TALK ABOUT *KILLING* SOMEONE?
WE CAN'T CONTACT TEACHER, SO WE'RE ON OUR OWN.
WHY DOES HE REFUSE TO HAVE A CELL PHONE??
WE COULD USE THE LEYLI—

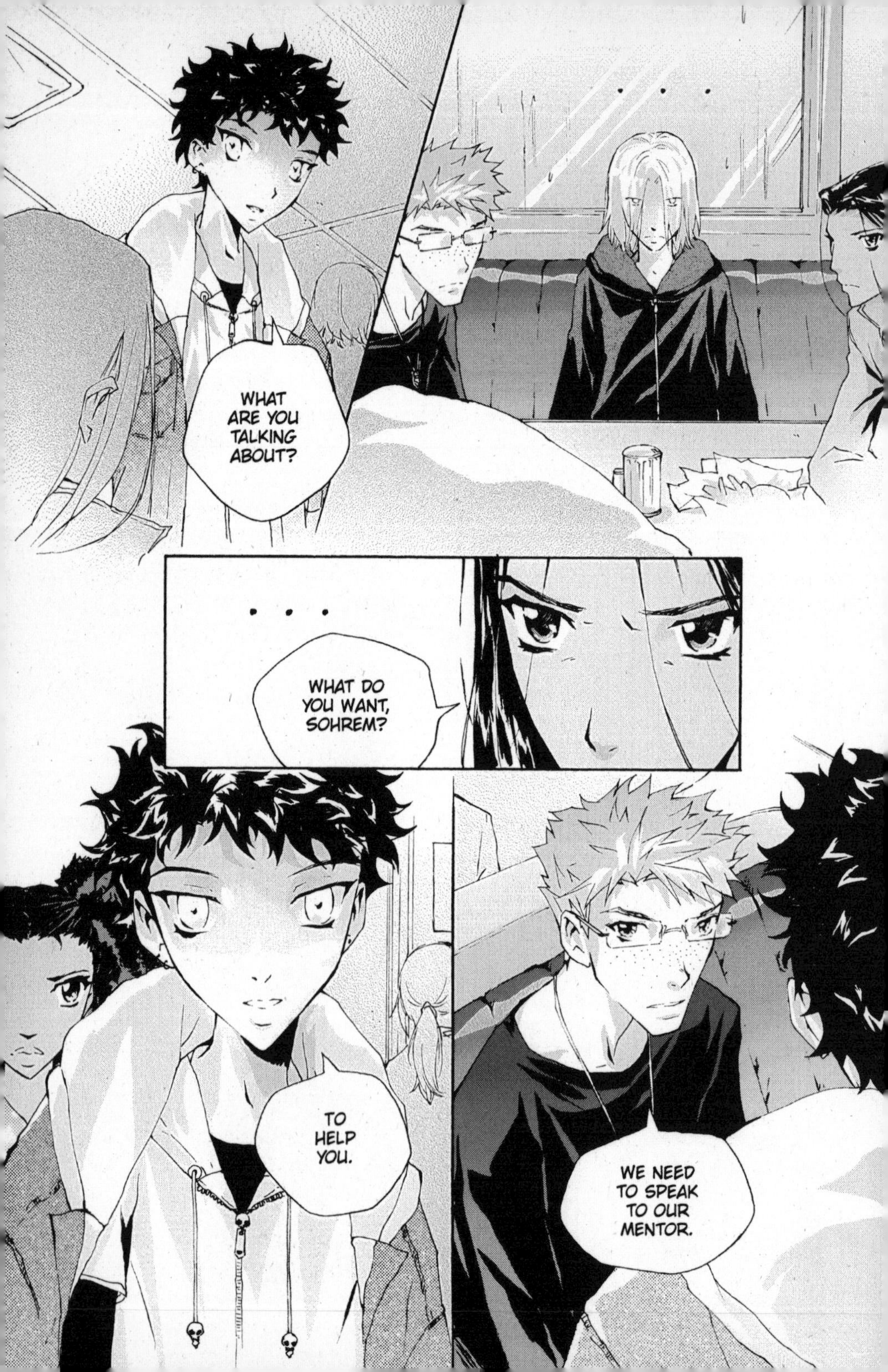
WHAT ARE YOU TALKING ABOUT?
...
...
WHAT DO YOU WANT, SOHREM?
TO HELP YOU.
WE NEED TO SPEAK TO OUR MENTOR.

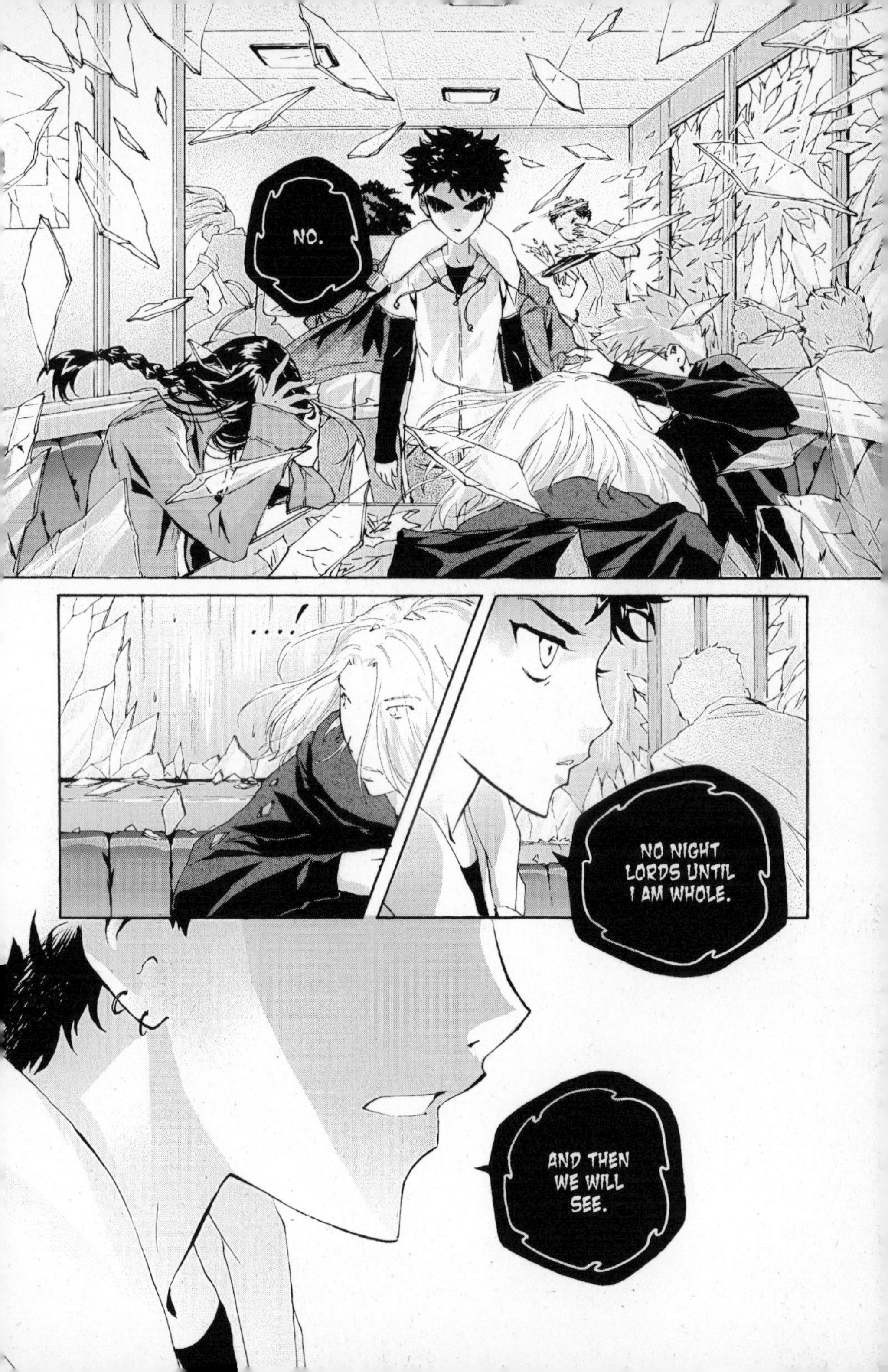
NO.
....!
NO NIGHT LORDS UNTIL I AM WHOLE.
AND THEN WE WILL SEE.

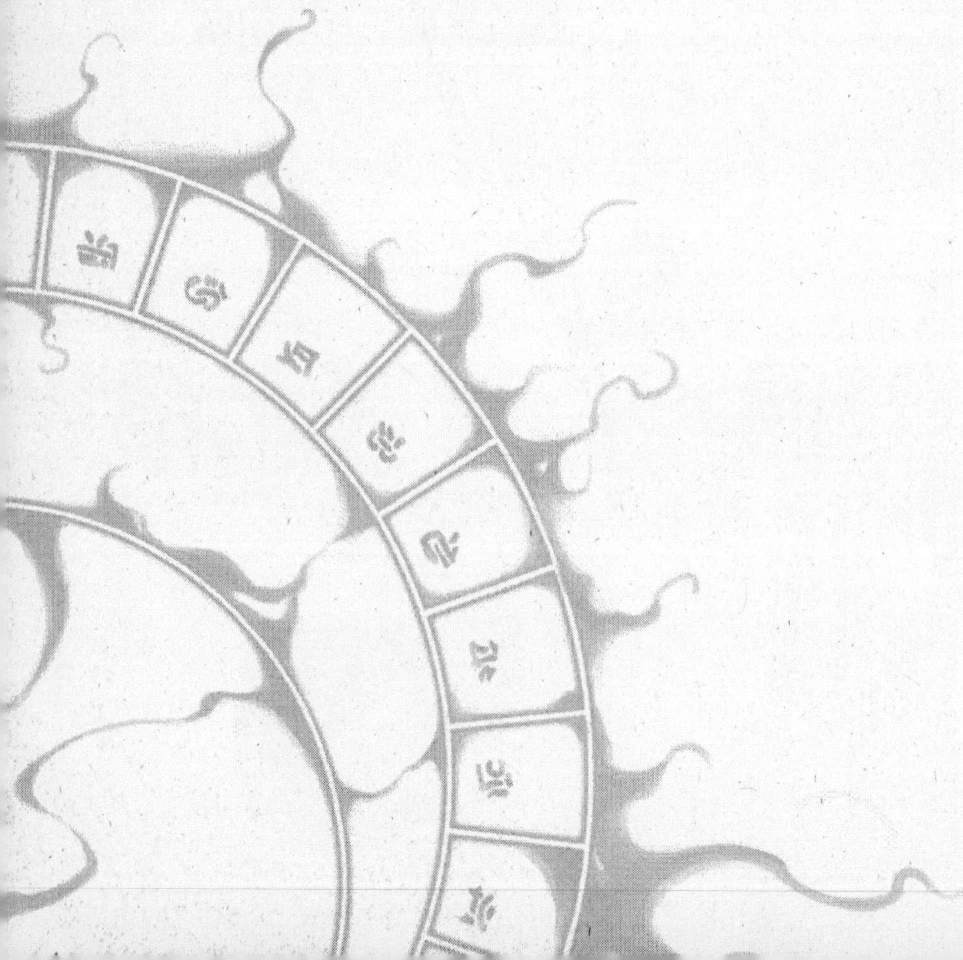

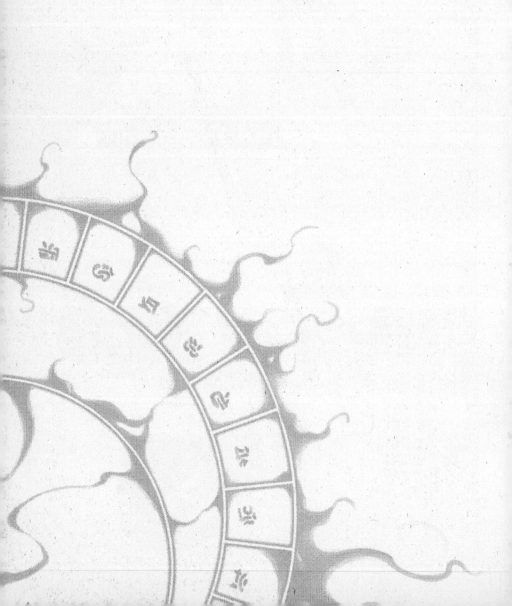

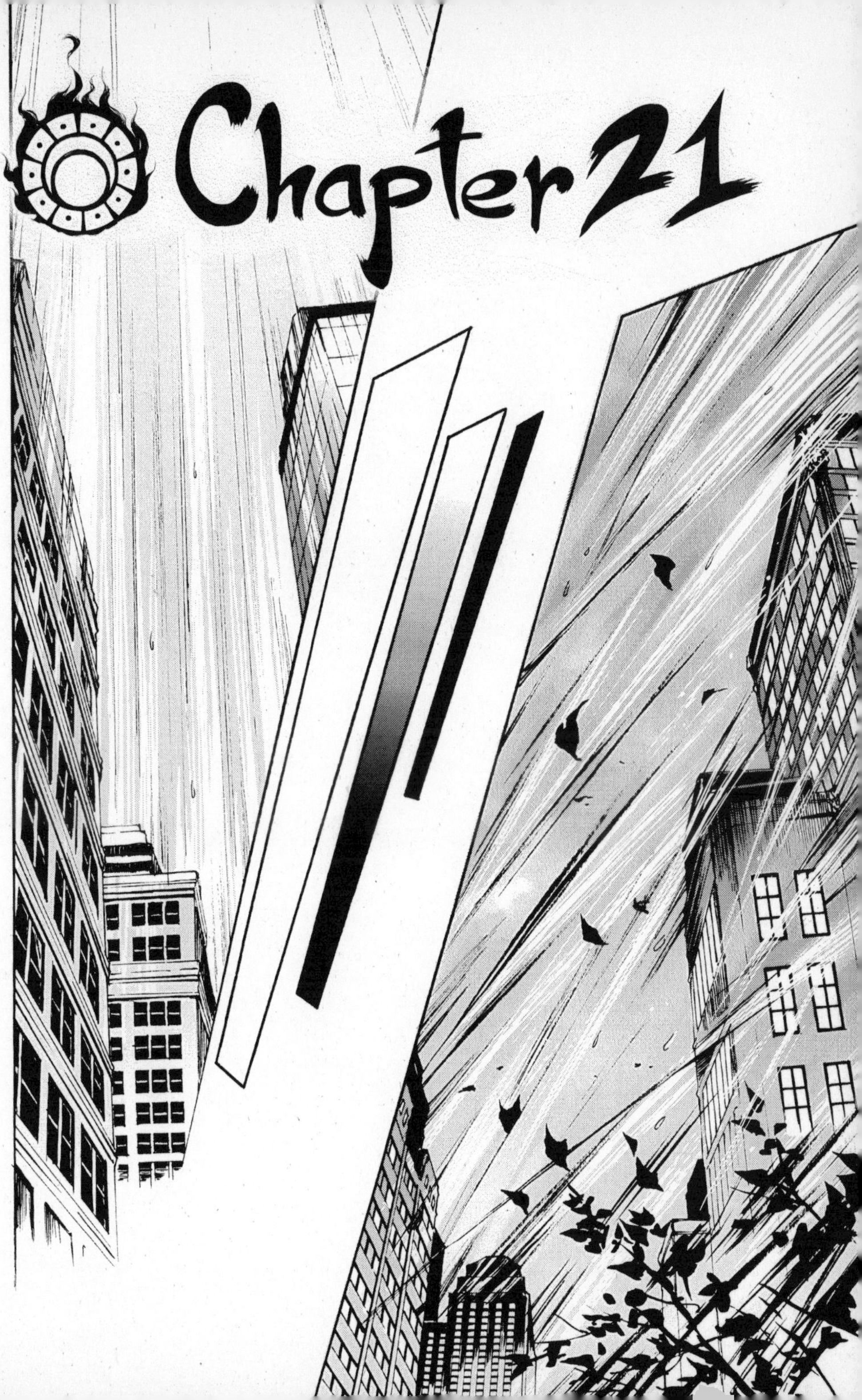
Chapter 21

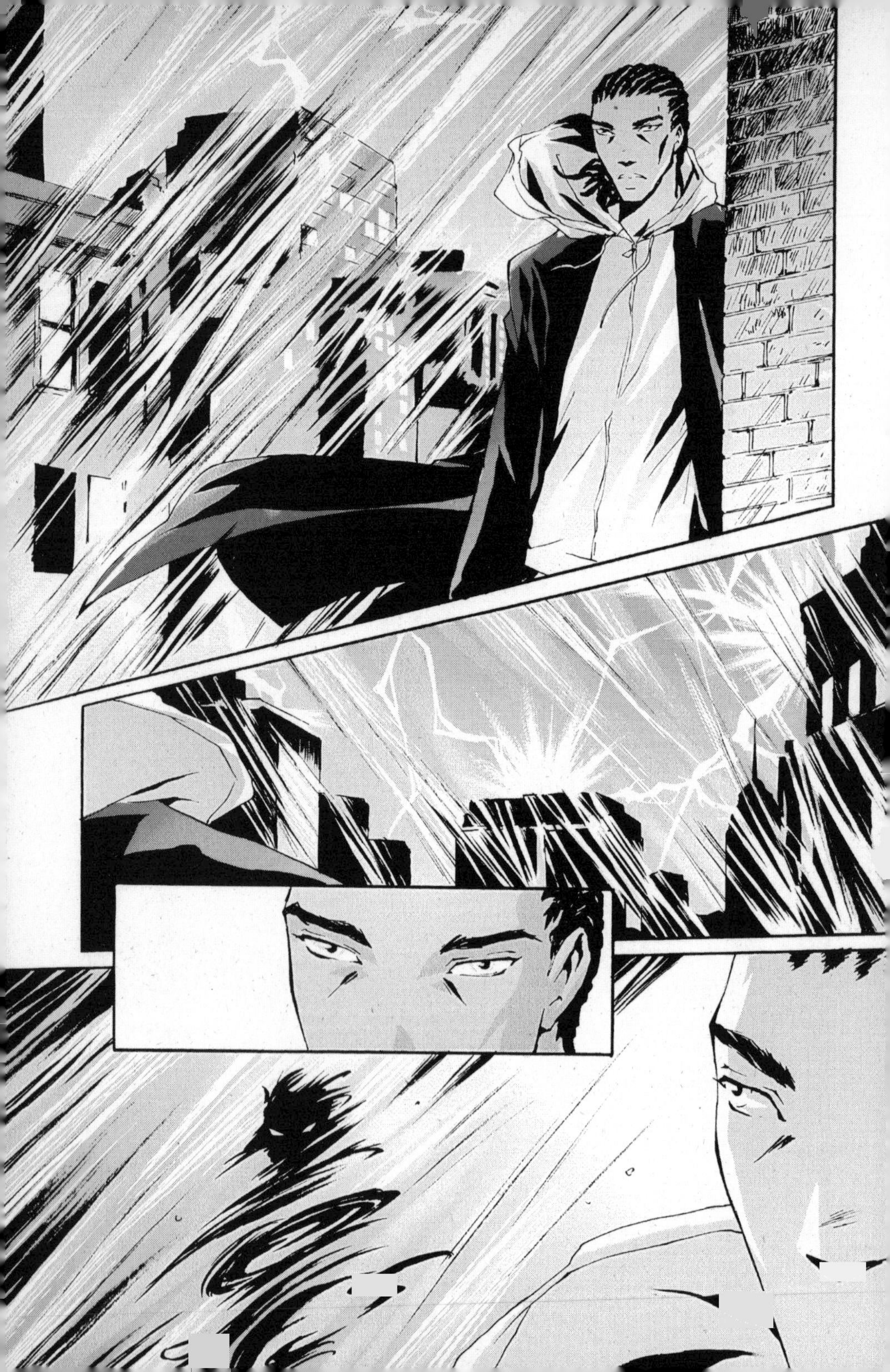

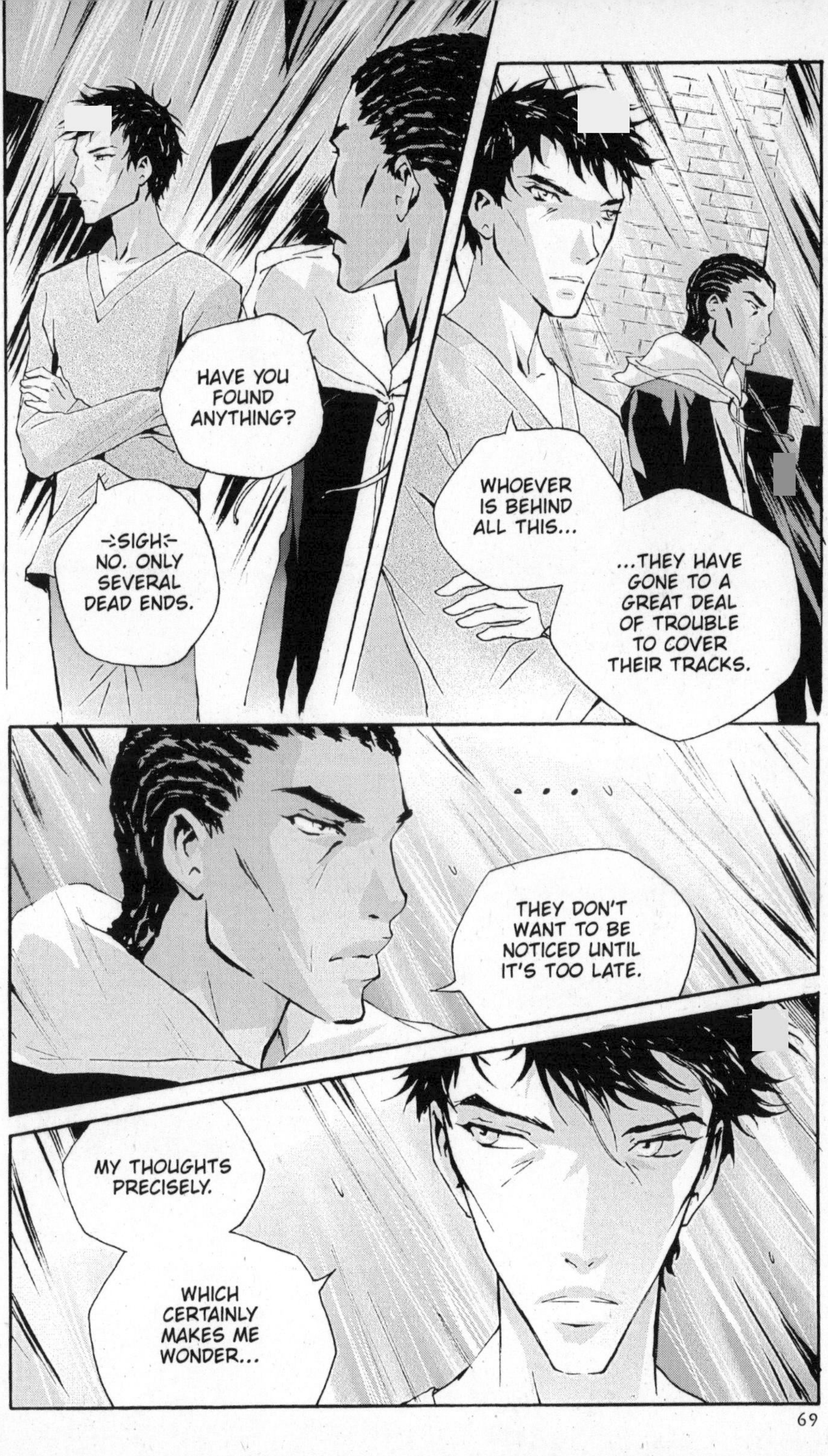
HAVE YOU FOUND ANYTHING?
-SIGH- NO. ONLY SEVERAL DEAD ENDS.
WHOEVER IS BEHIND ALL THIS...
...THEY HAVE GONE TO A GREAT DEAL OF TROUBLE TO COVER THEIR TRACKS.
...
THEY DON'T WANT TO BE NOTICED UNTIL IT'S TOO LATE.
MY THOUGHTS PRECISELY.
WHICH CERTAINLY MAKES ME WONDER...

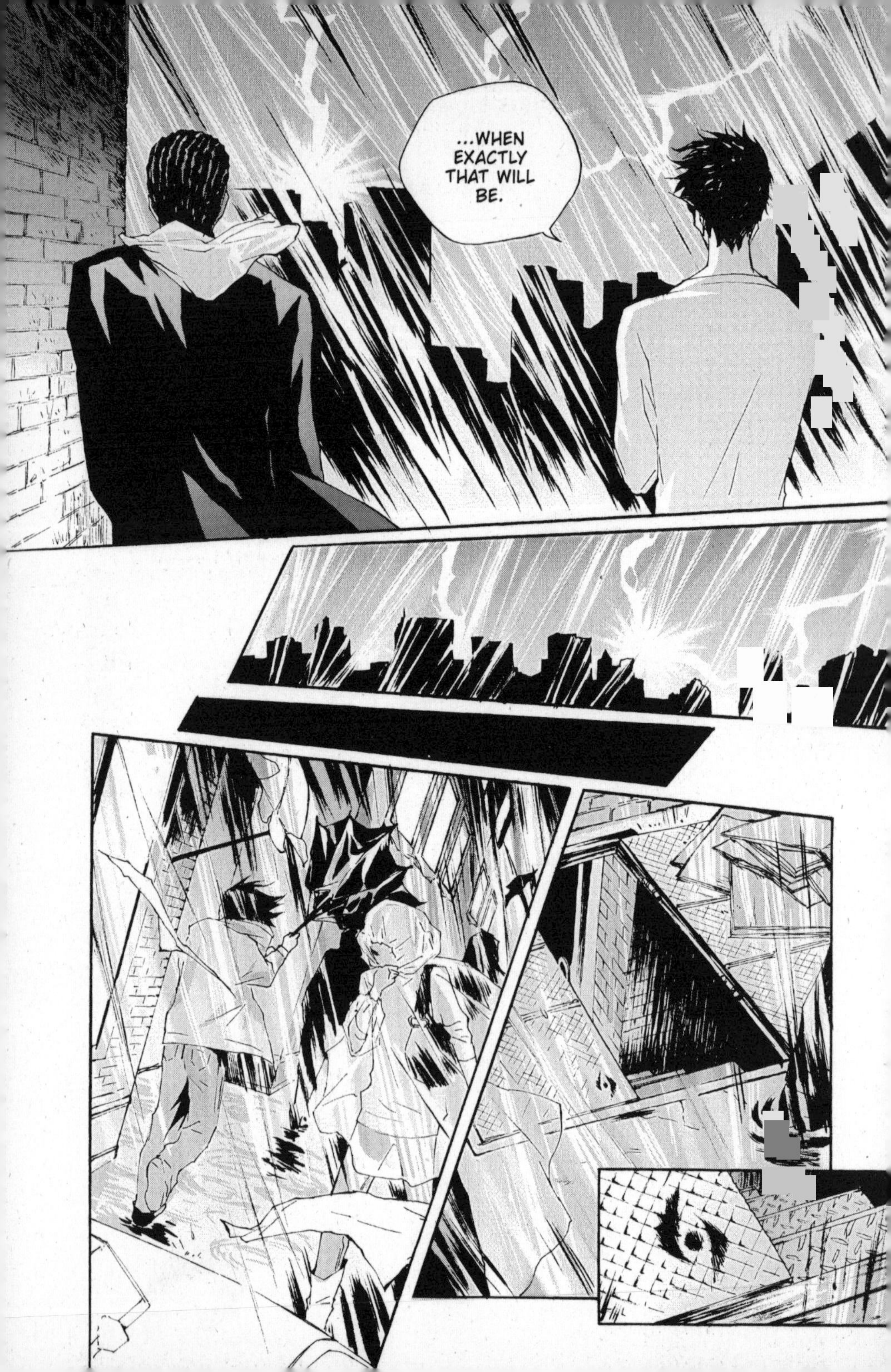
...WHEN EXACTLY THAT WILL BE.

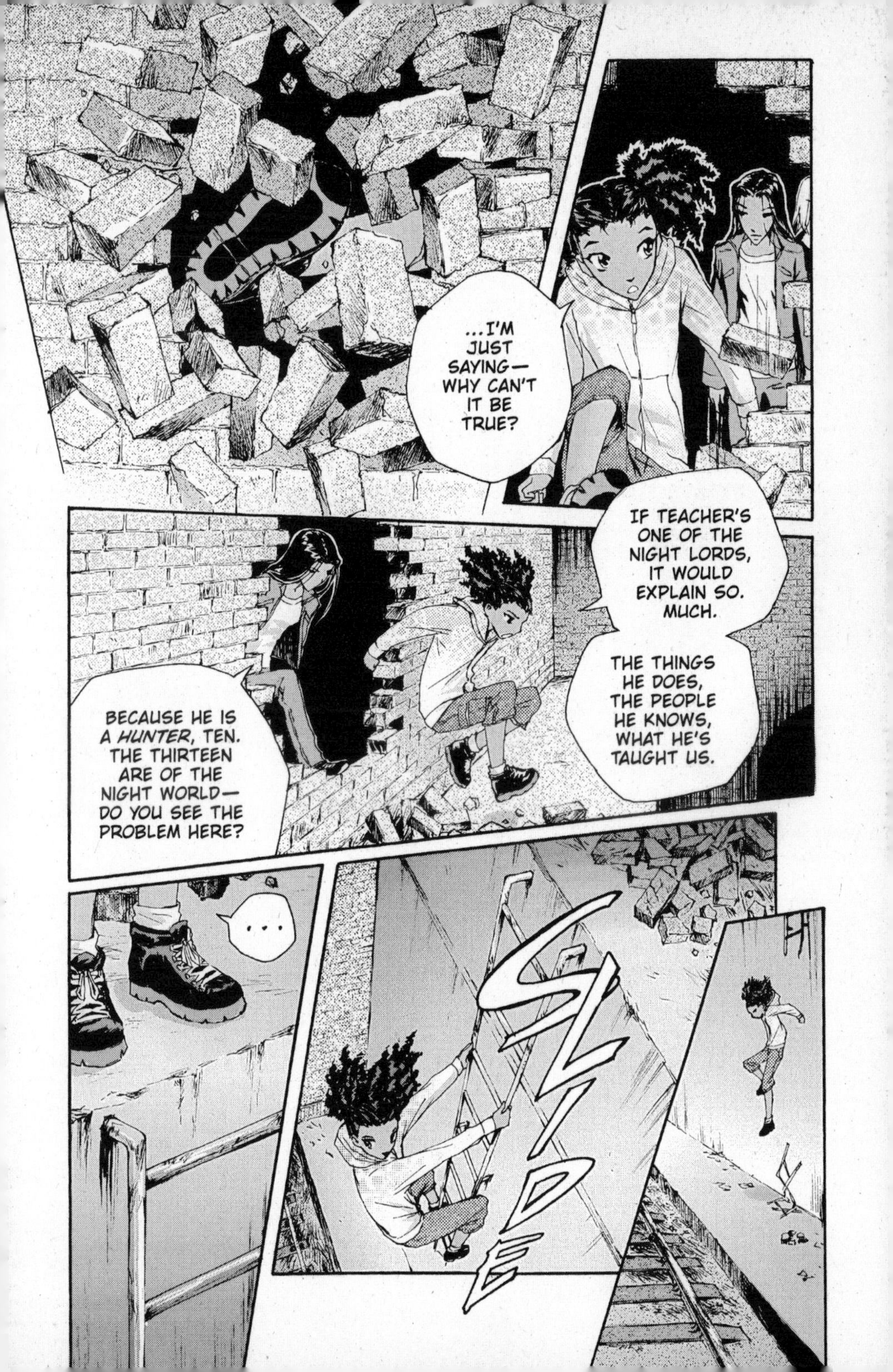
...I'M JUST SAYING—WHY CAN'T IT BE TRUE?
IF TEACHER'S ONE OF THE NIGHT LORDS, IT WOULD EXPLAIN SO. MUCH.
THE THINGS HE DOES, THE PEOPLE HE KNOWS, WHAT HE'S TAUGHT US.
BECAUSE HE IS A *HUNTER*, TEN. THE THIRTEEN ARE OF THE NIGHT WORLD—DO YOU SEE THE PROBLEM HERE?
...
SLIDE

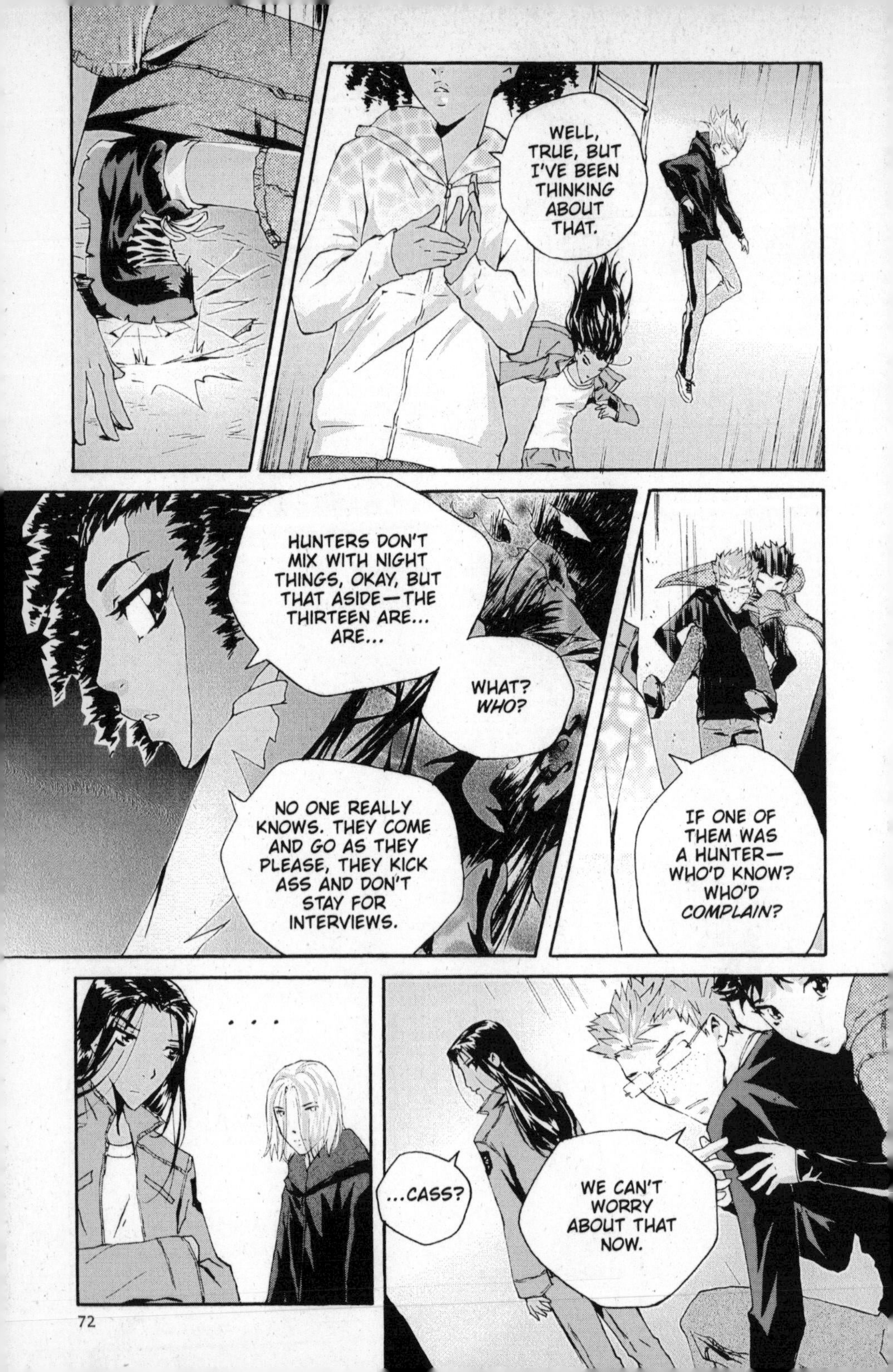
WELL, TRUE, BUT I'VE BEEN THINKING ABOUT THAT.
HUNTERS DON'T MIX WITH NIGHT THINGS, OKAY, BUT THAT ASIDE—THE THIRTEEN ARE... ARE...
WHAT? *WHO?*
NO ONE REALLY KNOWS. THEY COME AND GO AS THEY PLEASE, THEY KICK ASS AND DON'T STAY FOR INTERVIEWS.
IF ONE OF THEM WAS A HUNTER—WHO'D KNOW? WHO'D *COMPLAIN?*
. . .
...CASS?
WE CAN'T WORRY ABOUT THAT NOW.

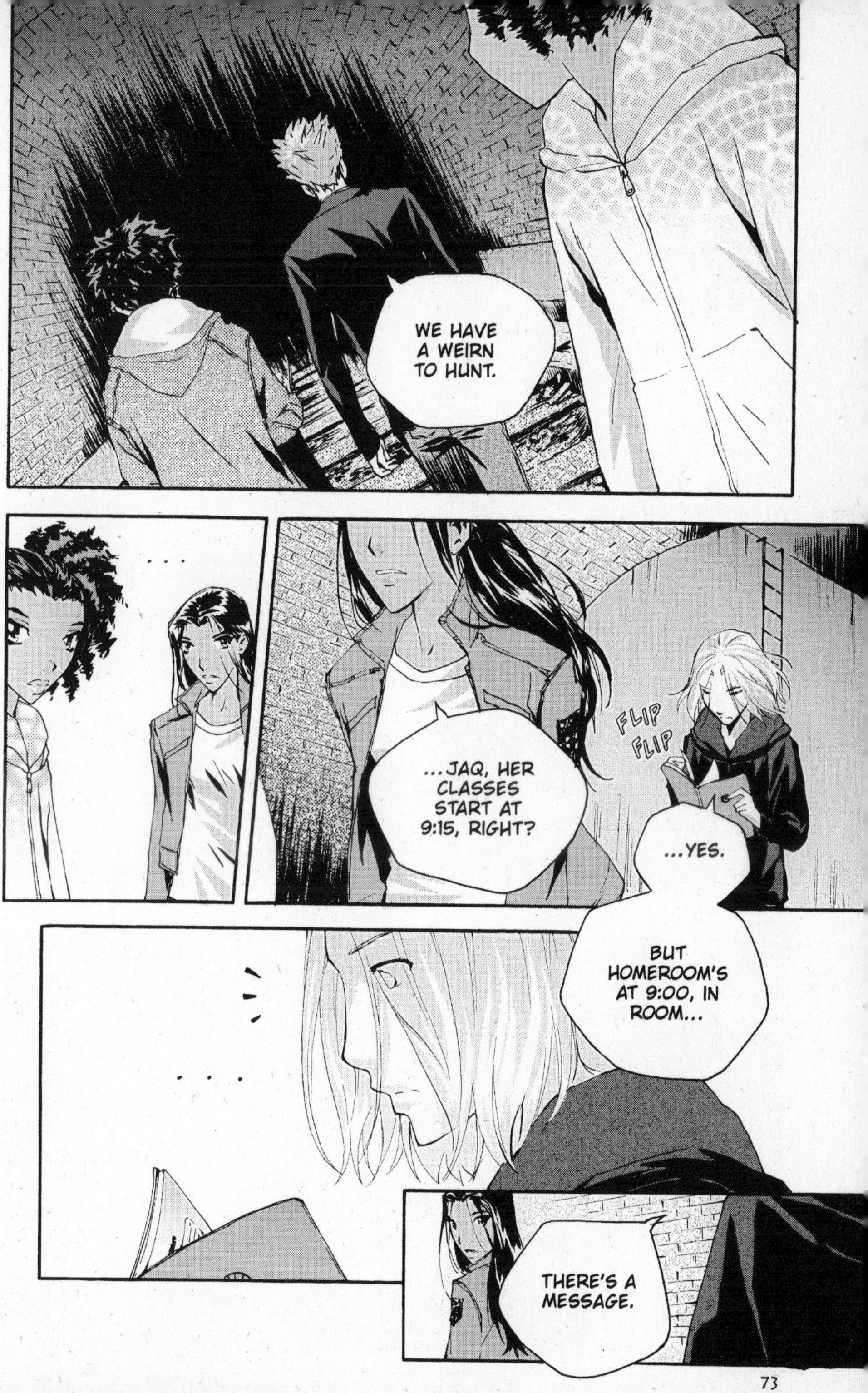
WE HAVE A WEIRN TO HUNT.
...
...JAQ, HER CLASSES START AT 9:15, RIGHT?
FLIP FLIP
...YES.
BUT HOMEROOM'S AT 9:00, IN ROOM...
...
THERE'S A MESSAGE.

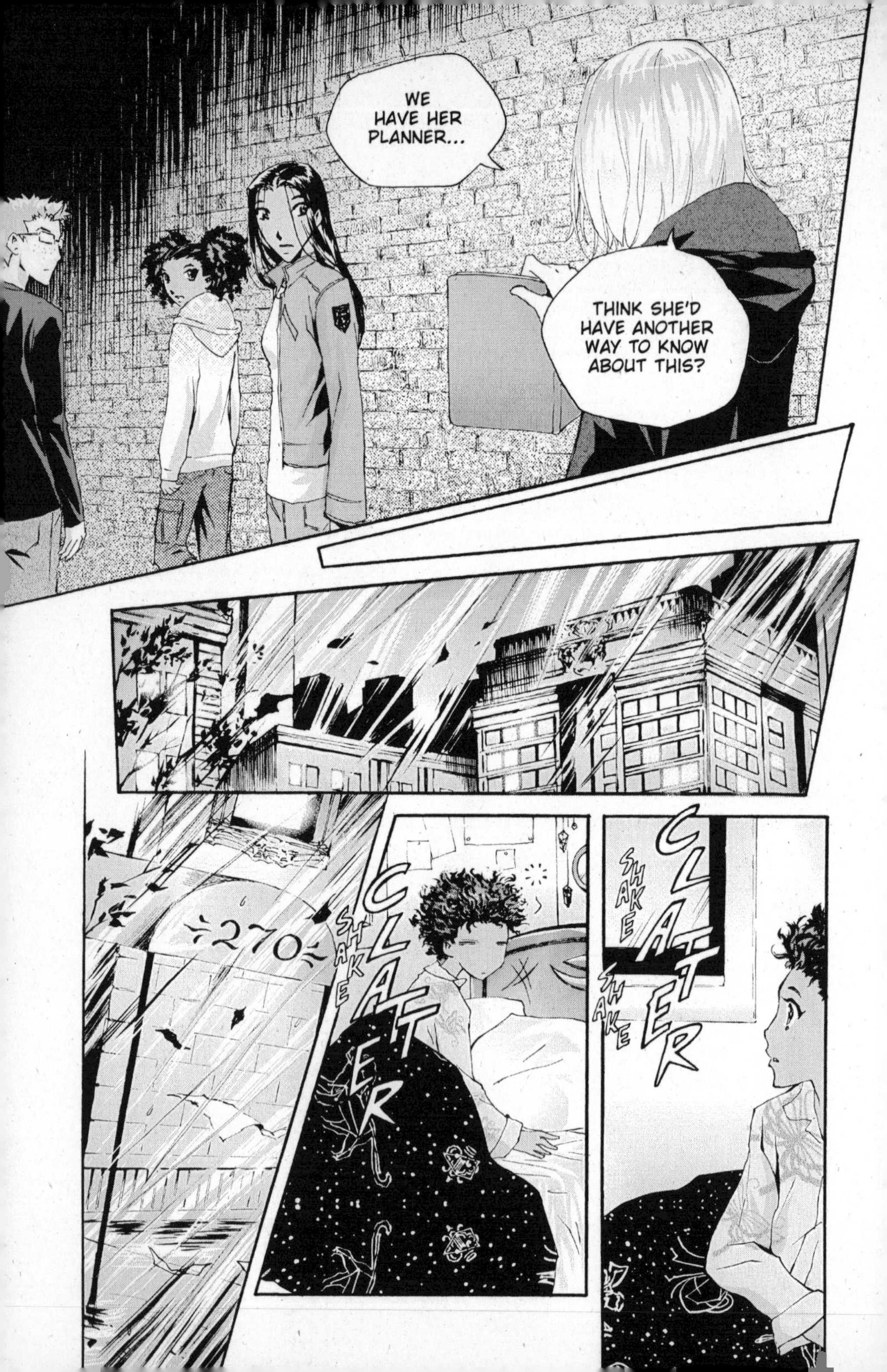
WE HAVE HER PLANNER...
THINK SHE'D HAVE ANOTHER WAY TO KNOW ABOUT THIS?
270
SHAKE
CLATTER
SHAKE
SHAKE
CLATTER

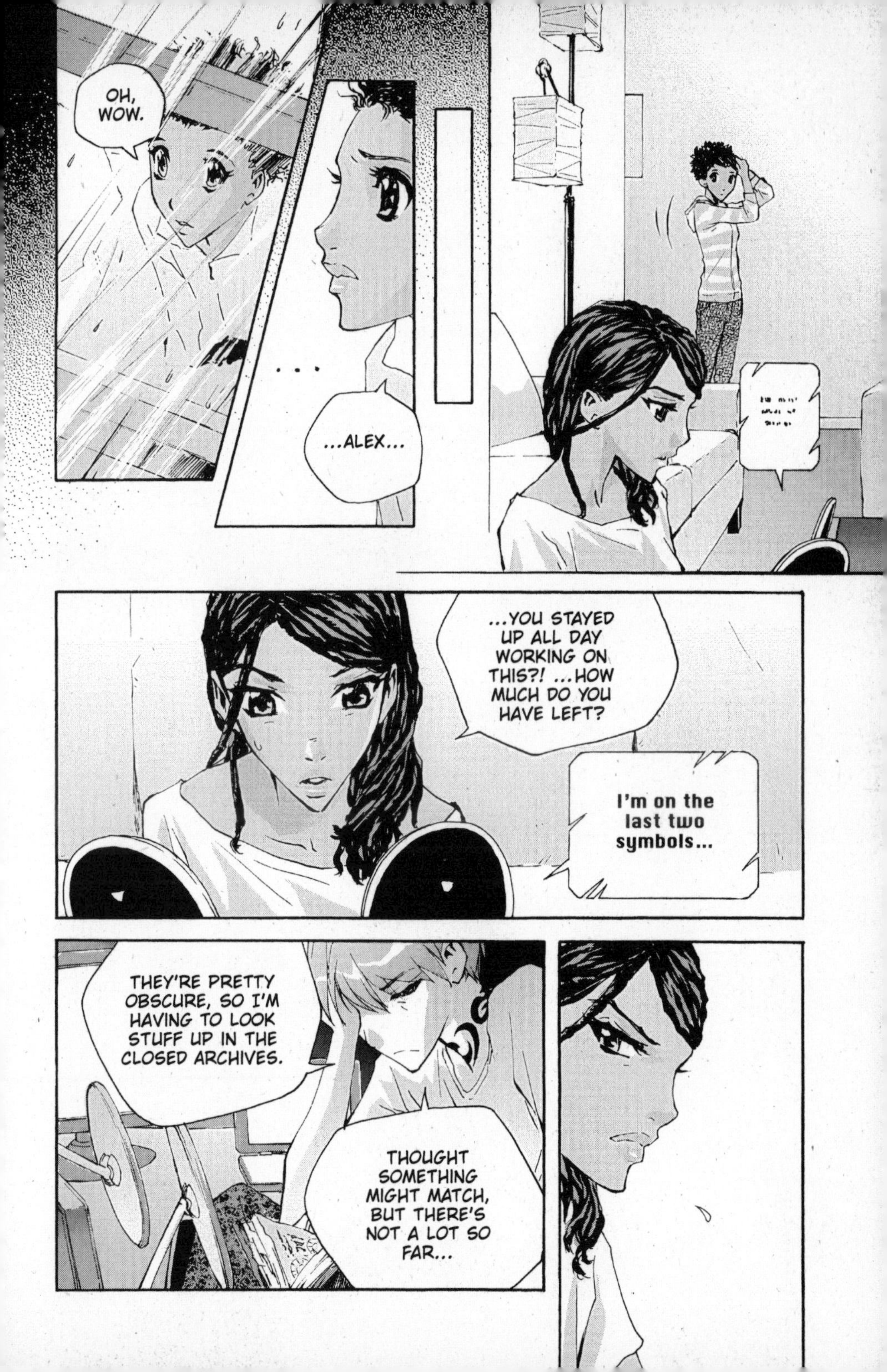
OH, WOW.
...
...ALEX...
...YOU STAYED UP ALL DAY WORKING ON THIS?! ...HOW MUCH DO YOU HAVE LEFT?
I'm on the last two symbols...
THEY'RE PRETTY OBSCURE, SO I'M HAVING TO LOOK STUFF UP IN THE CLOSED ARCHIVES.
THOUGHT SOMETHING MIGHT MATCH, BUT THERE'S NOT A LOT SO FAR...

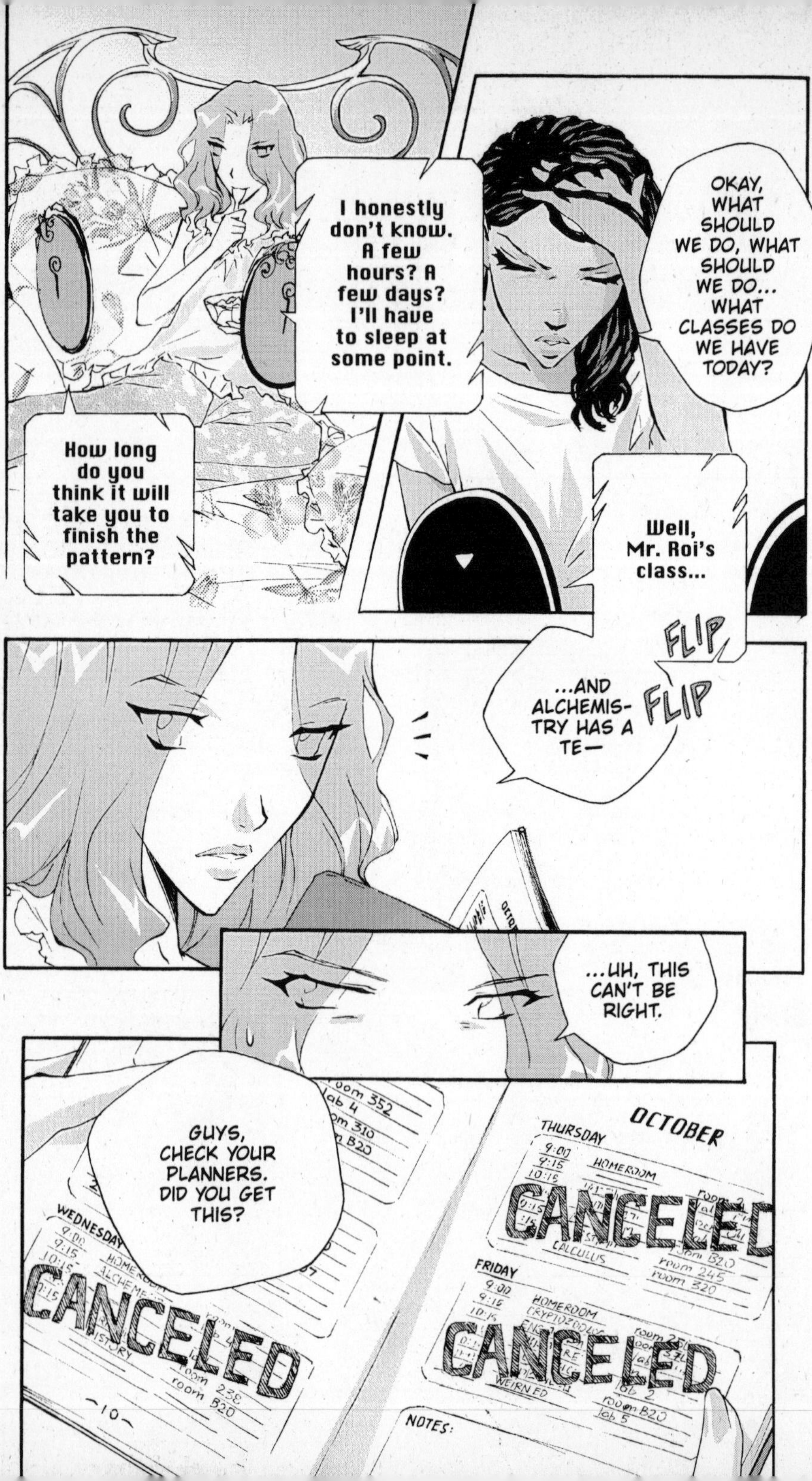
How long do you think it will take you to finish the pattern?
I honestly don't know. A few hours? A few days? I'll have to sleep at some point.
OKAY, WHAT SHOULD WE DO, WHAT SHOULD WE DO... WHAT CLASSES DO WE HAVE TODAY?
Well, Mr. Roi's class...
FLIP
...AND ALCHEMIS-TRY HAS A TE—
FLIP
...UH, THIS CAN'T BE RIGHT.
GUYS, CHECK YOUR PLANNERS. DID YOU GET THIS?
OCTOBER
WEDNESDAY
CANCELED
THURSDAY
CANCELED
FRIDAY
CANCELED
NOTES:

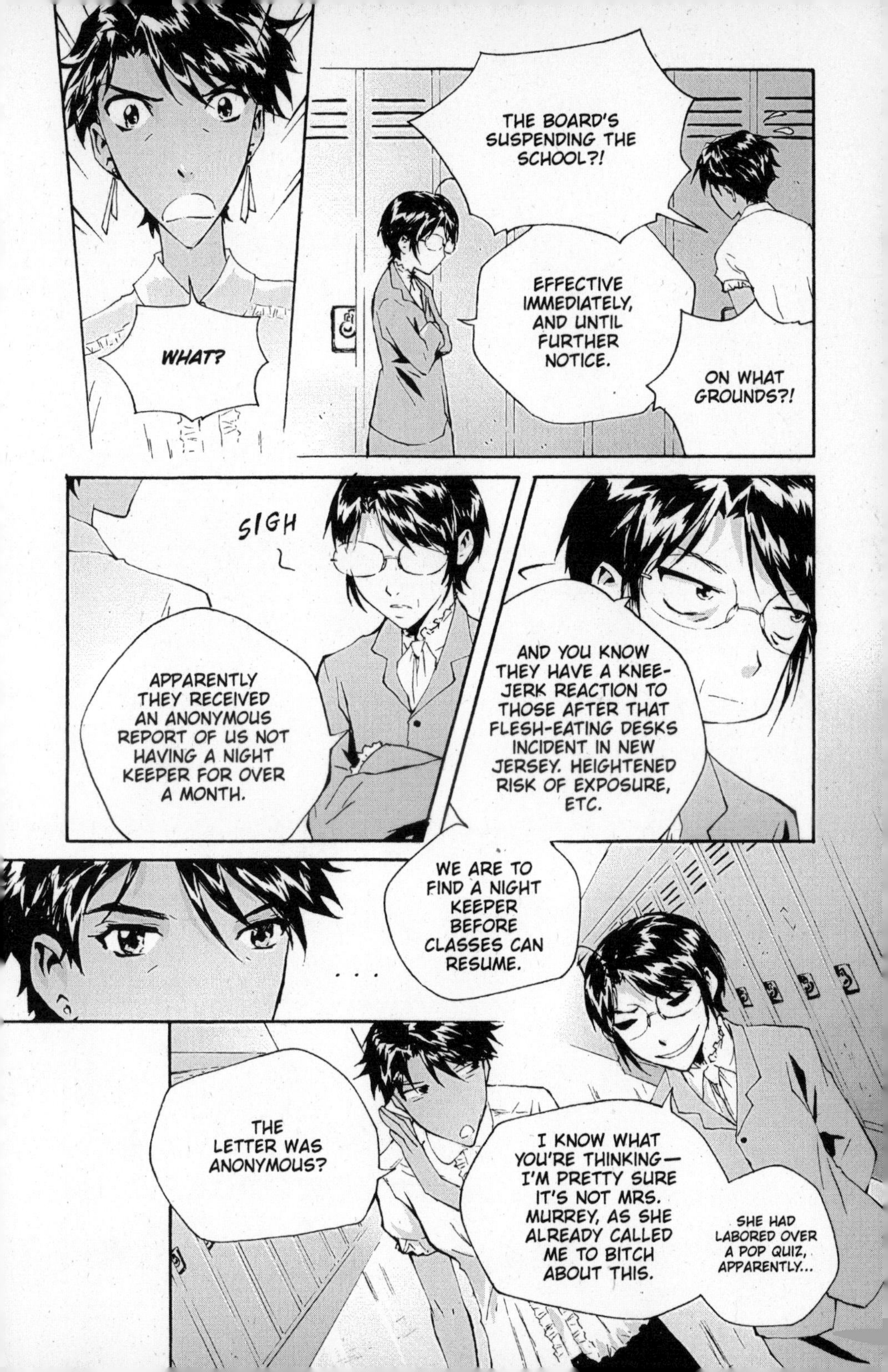
WHAT?
THE BOARD'S SUSPENDING THE SCHOOL?!
EFFECTIVE IMMEDIATELY, AND UNTIL FURTHER NOTICE.
ON WHAT GROUNDS?!
SIGH
APPARENTLY THEY RECEIVED AN ANONYMOUS REPORT OF US NOT HAVING A NIGHT KEEPER FOR OVER A MONTH.
AND YOU KNOW THEY HAVE A KNEE-JERK REACTION TO THOSE AFTER THAT FLESH-EATING DESKS INCIDENT IN NEW JERSEY. HEIGHTENED RISK OF EXPOSURE, ETC.
. . .
WE ARE TO FIND A NIGHT KEEPER BEFORE CLASSES CAN RESUME.
THE LETTER WAS ANONYMOUS?
I KNOW WHAT YOU'RE THINKING— I'M PRETTY SURE IT'S NOT MRS. MURREY, AS SHE ALREADY CALLED ME TO BITCH ABOUT THIS.
SHE HAD LABORED OVER A POP QUIZ, APPARENTLY...

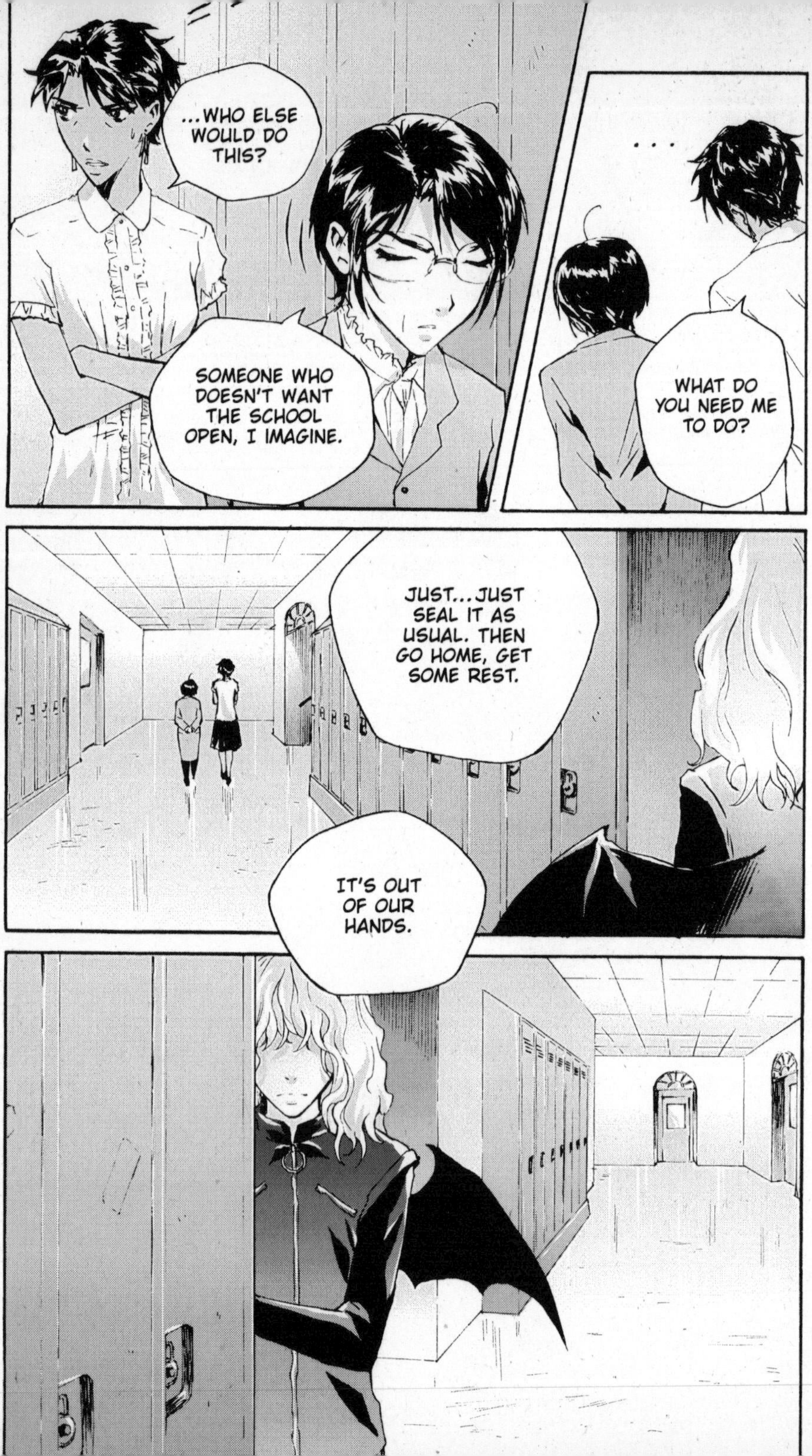
...WHO ELSE WOULD DO THIS?
SOMEONE WHO DOESN'T WANT THE SCHOOL OPEN, I IMAGINE.
. . .
WHAT DO YOU NEED ME TO DO?
JUST...JUST SEAL IT AS USUAL. THEN GO HOME, GET SOME REST.
IT'S OUT OF OUR HANDS.

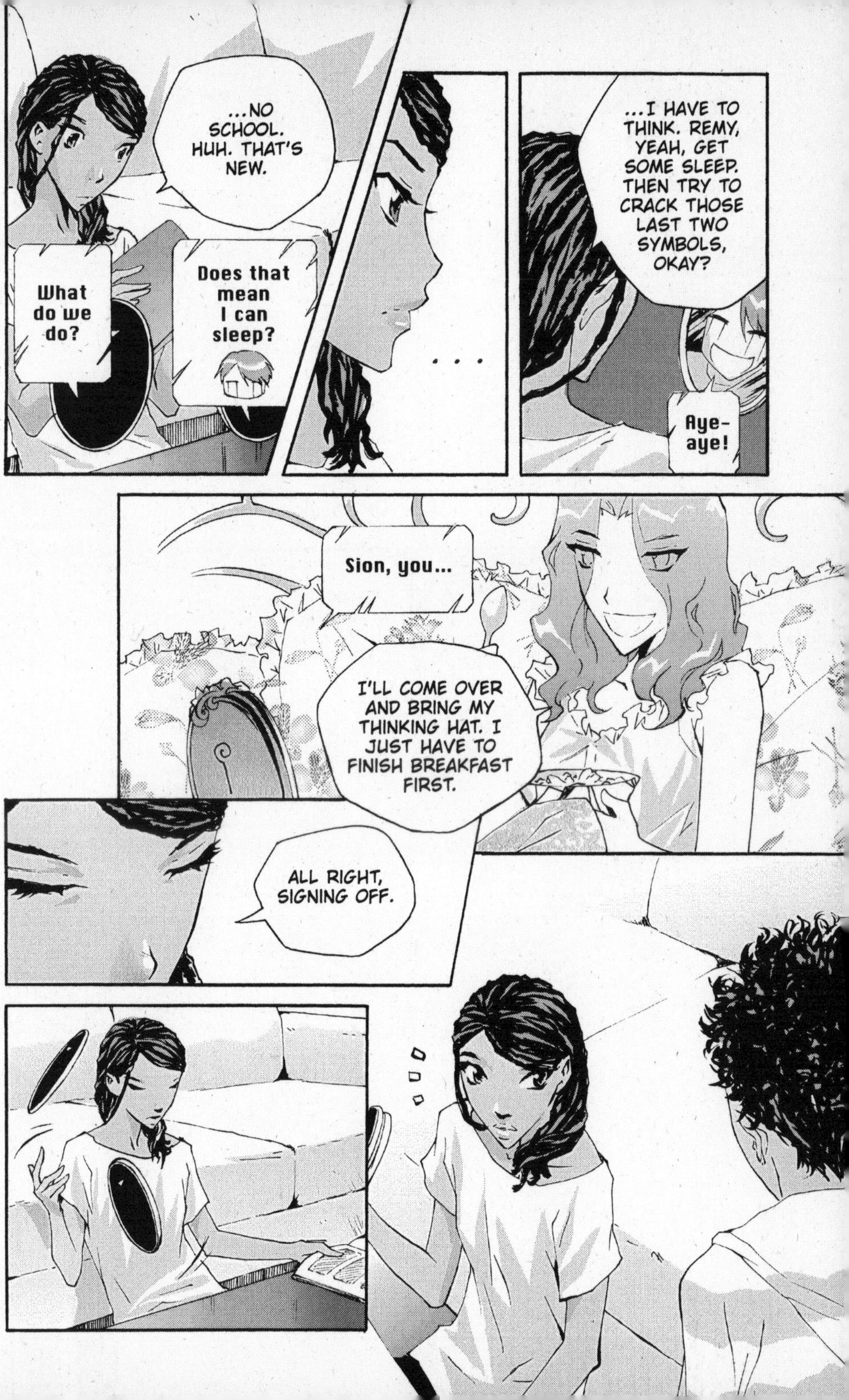
...NO SCHOOL. HUH. THAT'S NEW.
What do we do?
Does that mean I can sleep?
. . .
...I HAVE TO THINK. REMY, YEAH, GET SOME SLEEP. THEN TRY TO CRACK THOSE LAST TWO SYMBOLS, OKAY?
Aye-aye!
Sion, you...
I'LL COME OVER AND BRING MY THINKING HAT. I JUST HAVE TO FINISH BREAKFAST FIRST.
ALL RIGHT, SIGNING OFF.

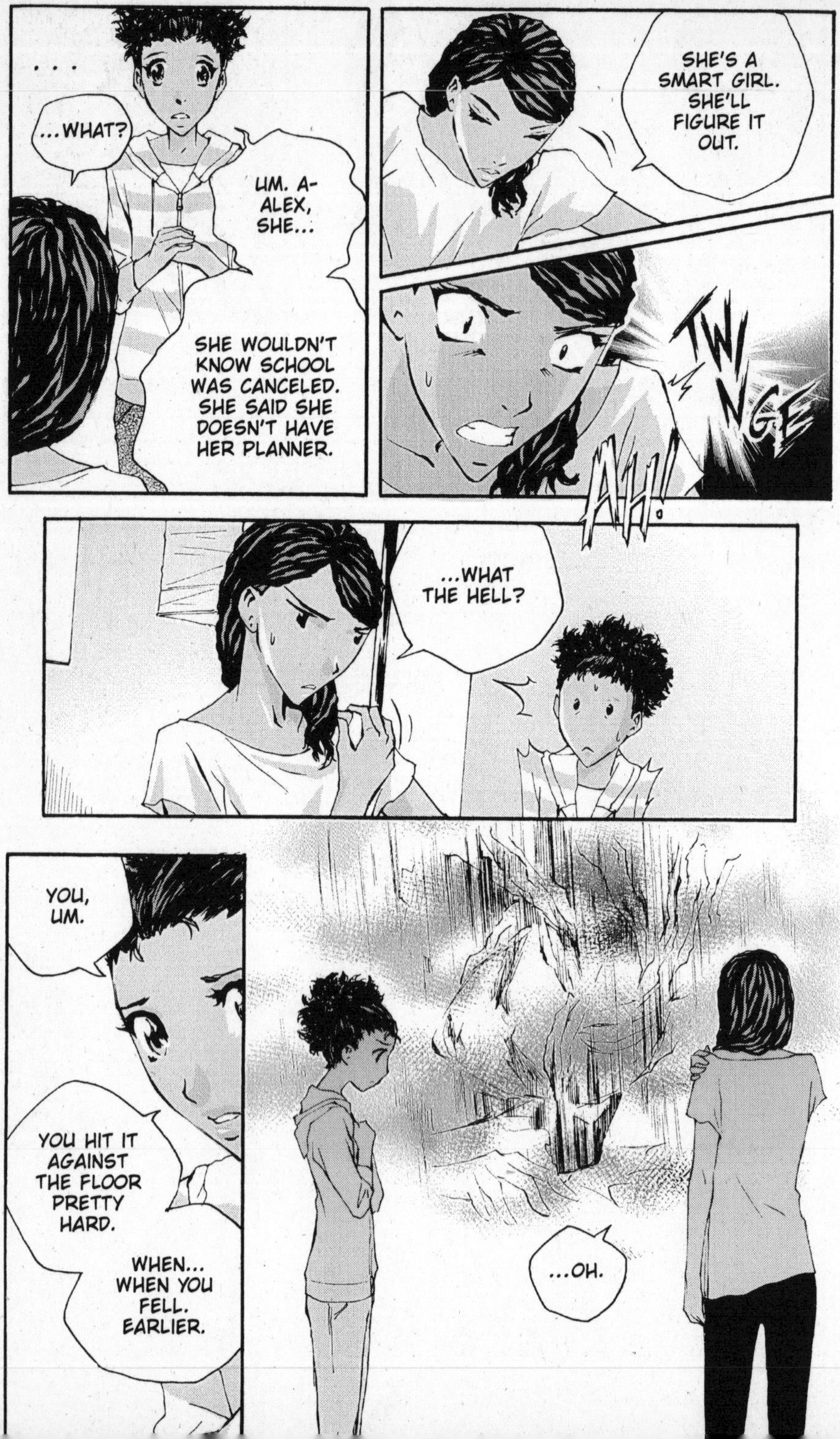
. . .
...WHAT?
UM. A-ALEX, SHE...
SHE WOULDN'T KNOW SCHOOL WAS CANCELED. SHE SAID SHE DOESN'T HAVE HER PLANNER.
SHE'S A SMART GIRL. SHE'LL FIGURE IT OUT.
TWINGE
AH!
...WHAT THE HELL?
YOU, UM.
YOU HIT IT AGAINST THE FLOOR PRETTY HARD.
WHEN... WHEN YOU FELL. EARLIER.
...OH.

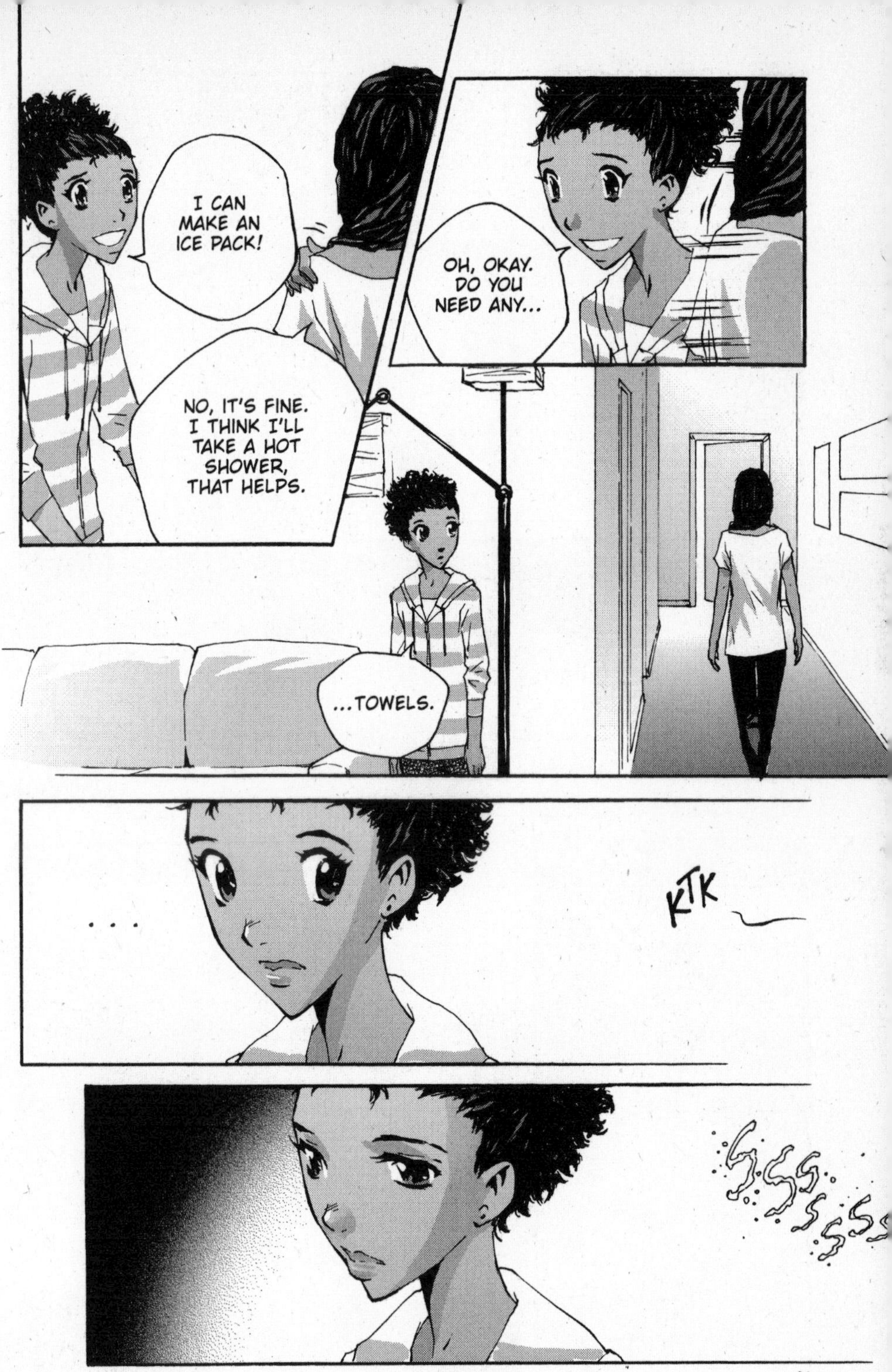
I CAN MAKE AN ICE PACK!
NO, IT'S FINE. I THINK I'LL TAKE A HOT SHOWER, THAT HELPS.
OH, OKAY. DO YOU NEED ANY...
...TOWELS.
. . .
KTK

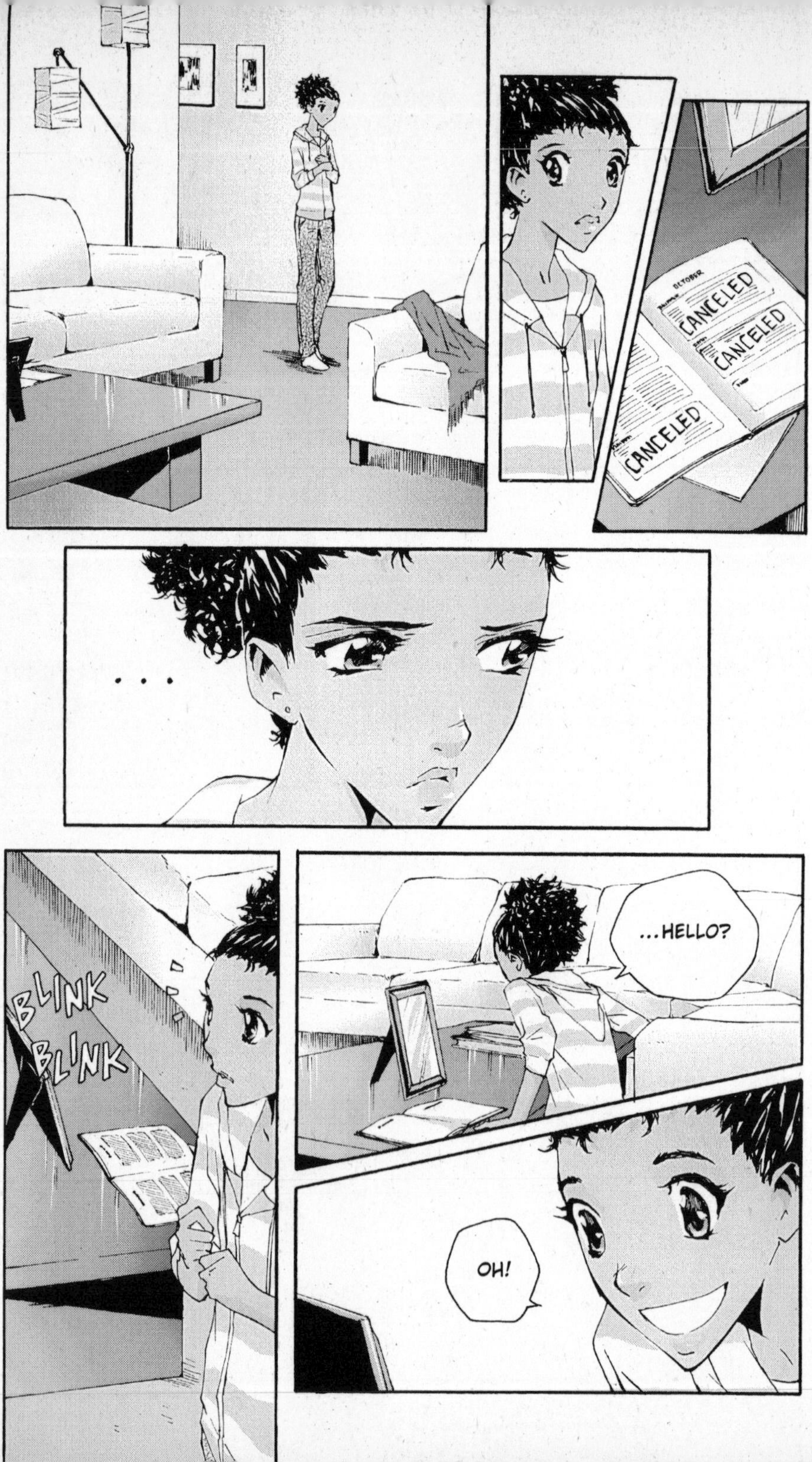
OCTOBER
CANCELED
CANCELED
CANCELED
. . .
BLINK
BLINK
...HELLO?
OH!

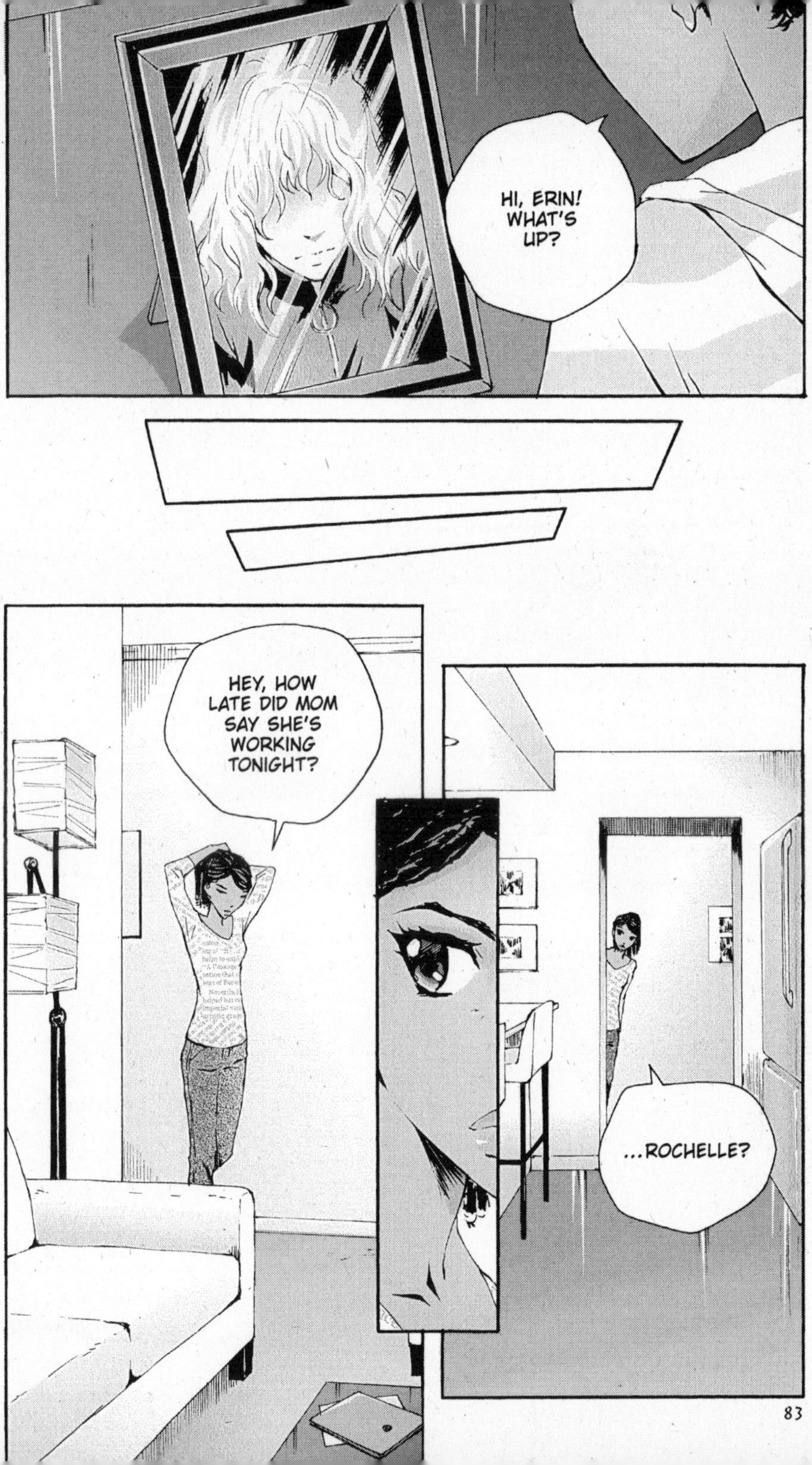
HI, ERIN! WHAT'S UP?
HEY, HOW LATE DID MOM SAY SHE'S WORKING TONIGHT?
...ROCHELLE?

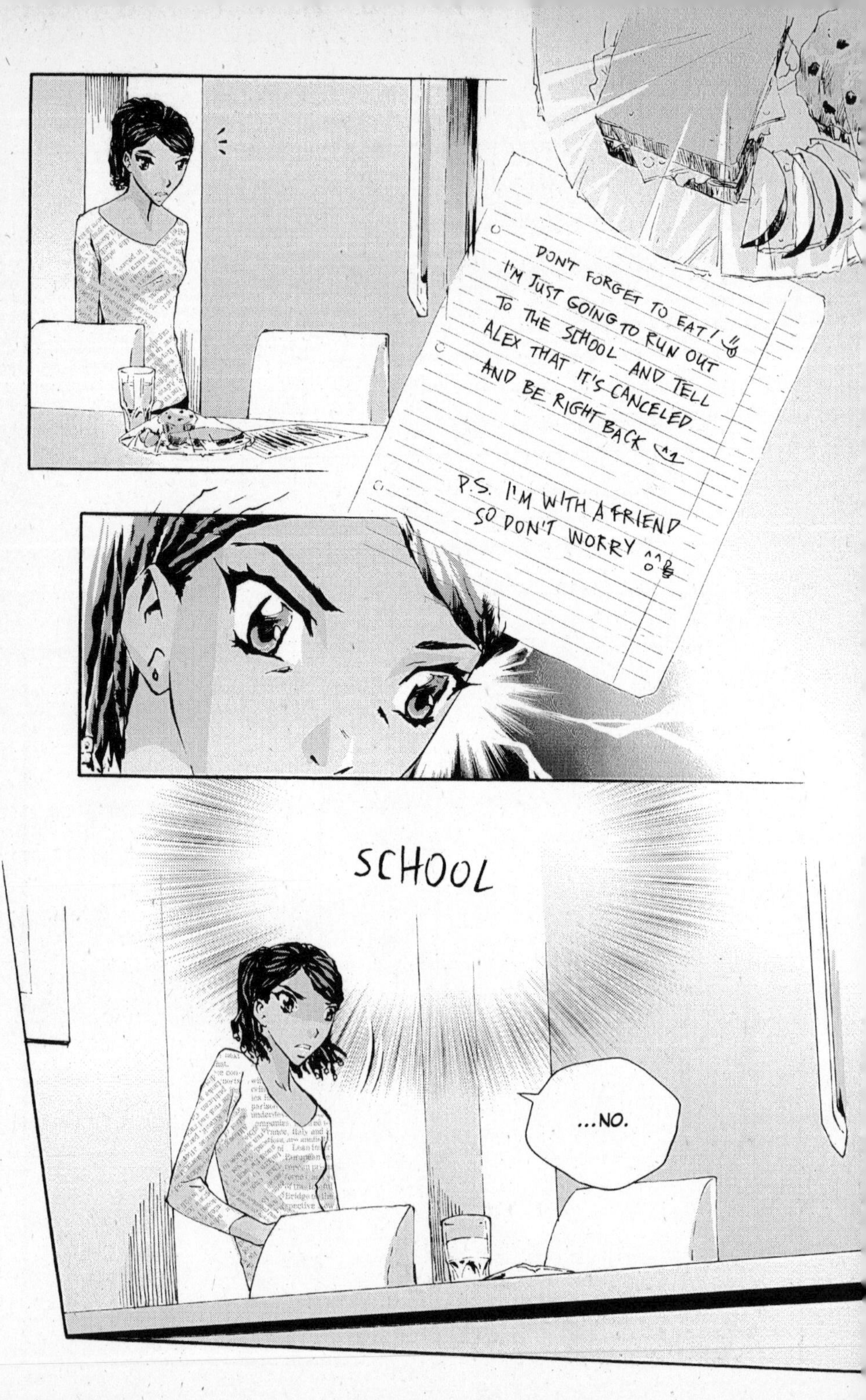
DON'T FORGET TO EAT!
I'M JUST GOING TO RUN OUT
TO THE SCHOOL AND TELL
ALEX THAT IT'S CANCELED
AND BE RIGHT BACK
P.S. I'M WITH A FRIEND
SO DON'T WORRY
SCHOOL
...NO.

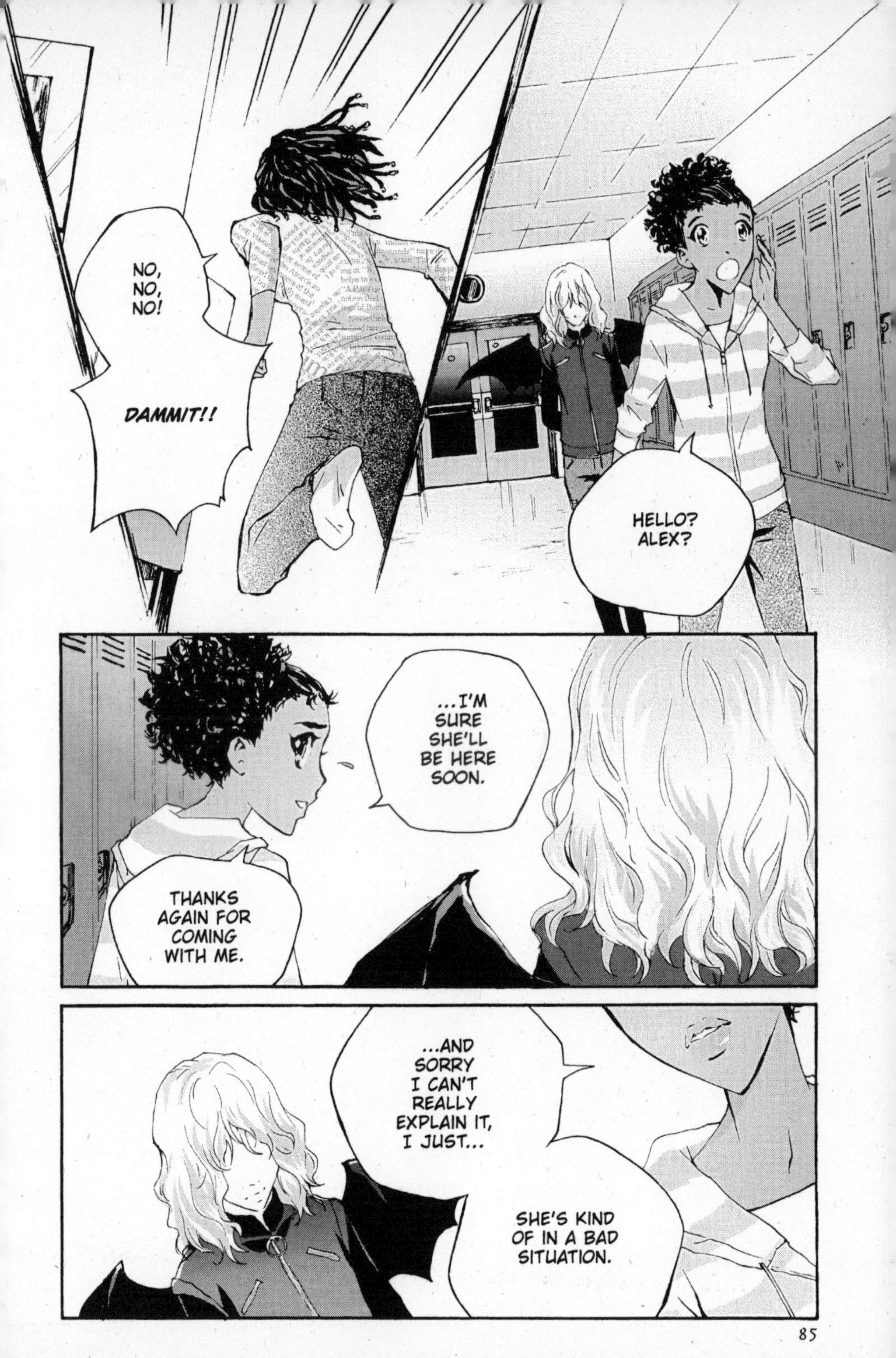
NO, NO, NO!
DAMMIT!!
HELLO? ALEX?
...I'M SURE SHE'LL BE HERE SOON.
THANKS AGAIN FOR COMING WITH ME.
...AND SORRY I CAN'T REALLY EXPLAIN IT, I JUST...
SHE'S KIND OF IN A BAD SITUATION.

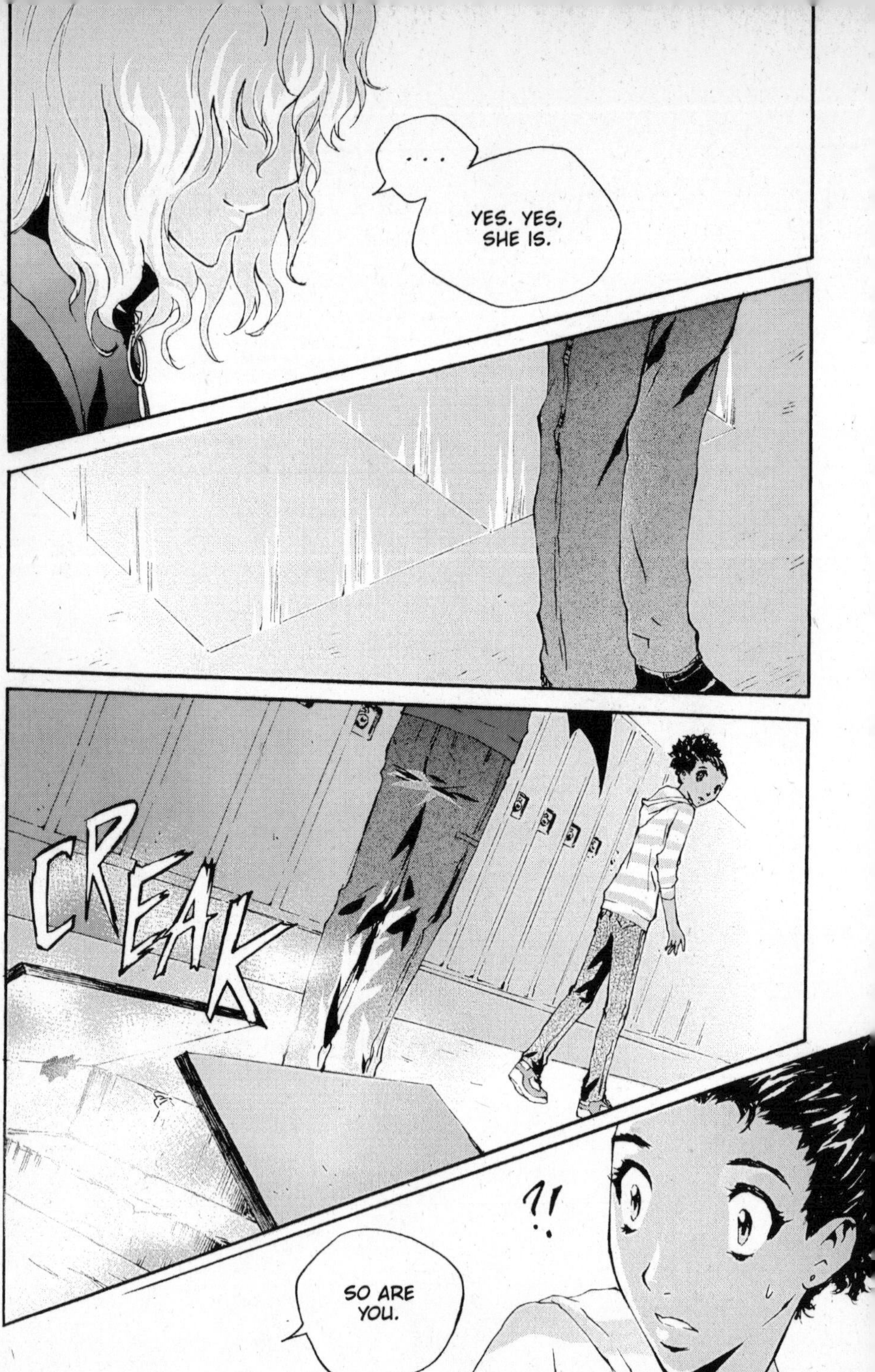
...
YES. YES, SHE IS.
CREAK
?!
SO ARE YOU.

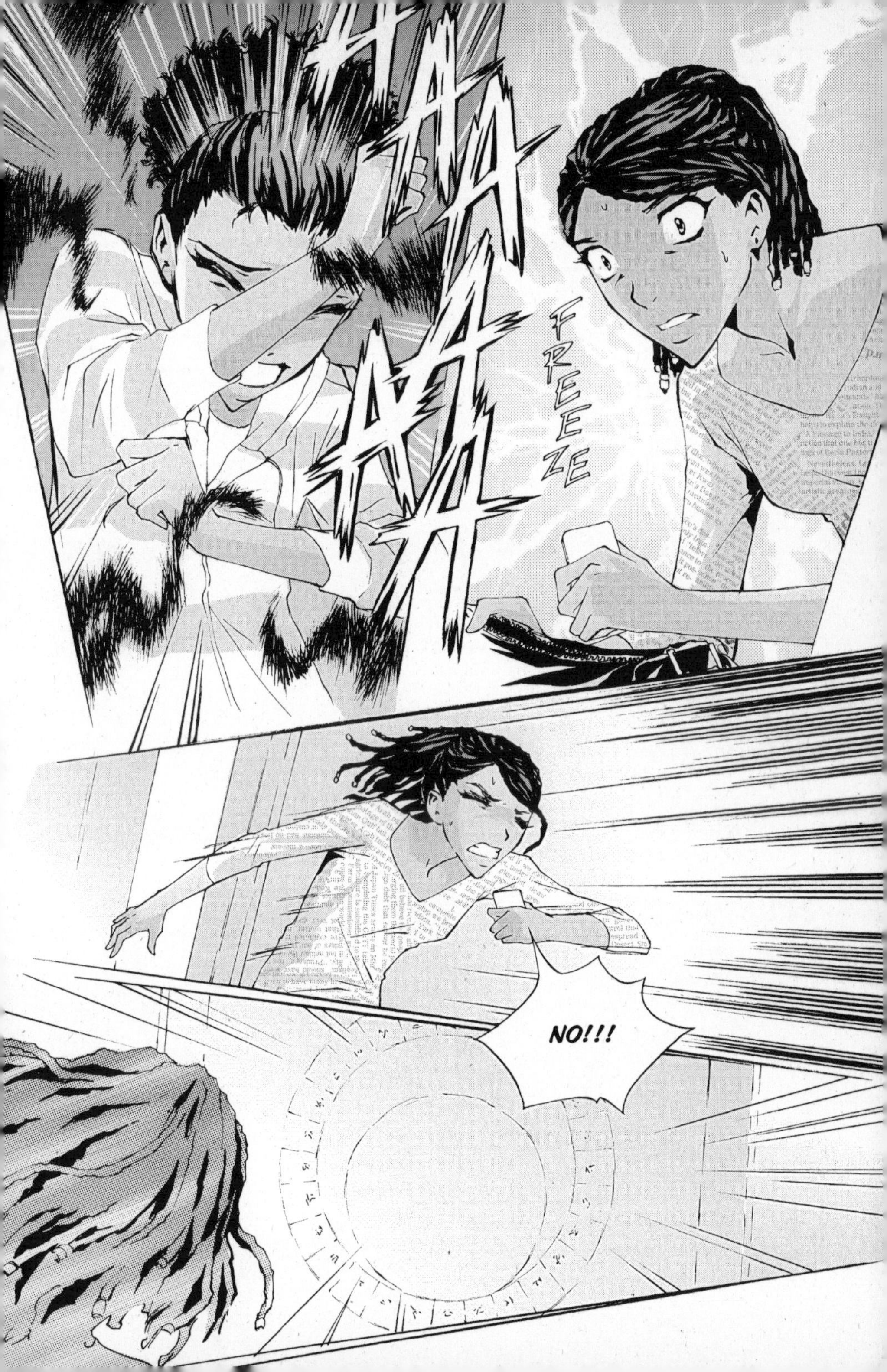
HAAAAA
FREEZE
NO!!!

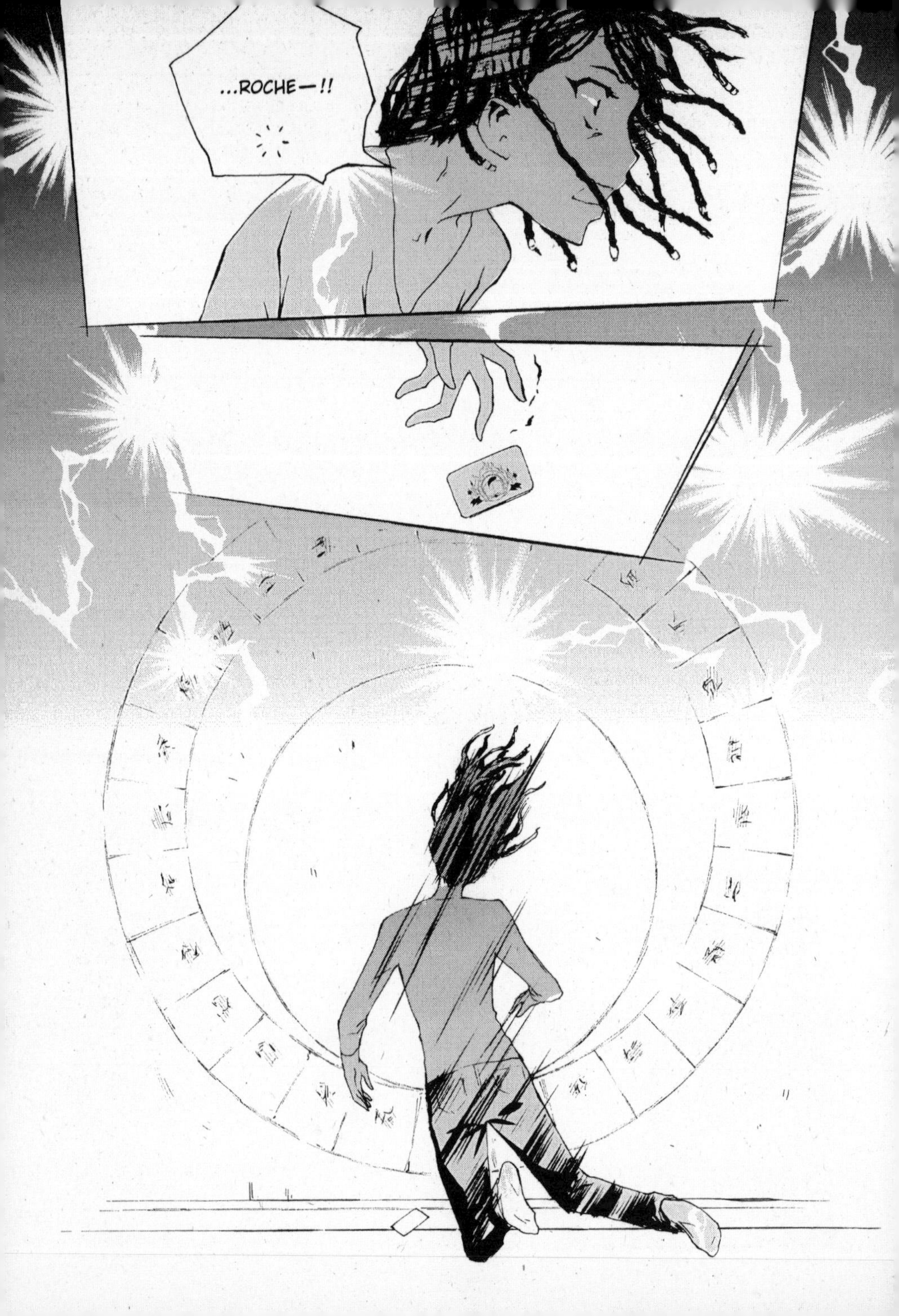
...ROCHE—!!

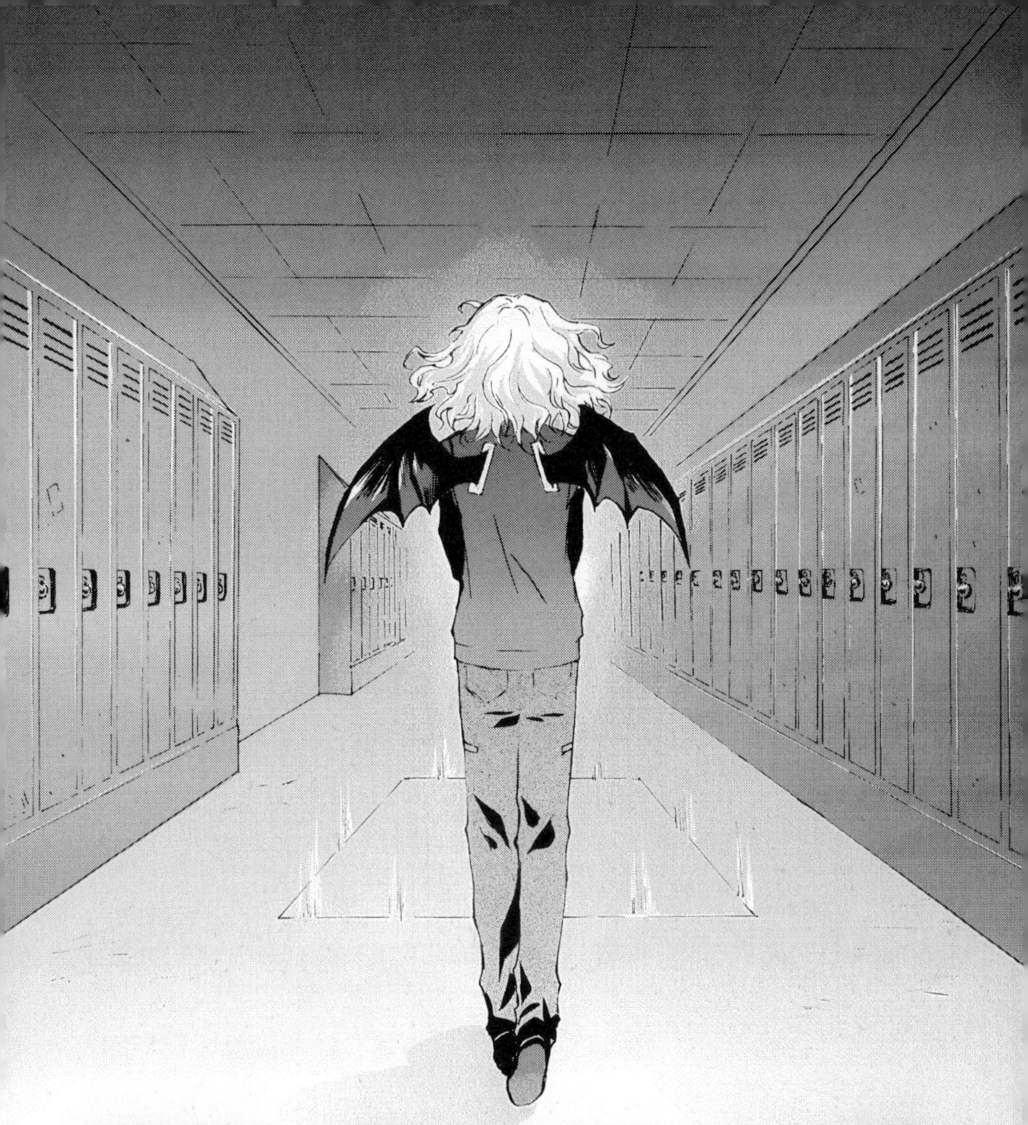

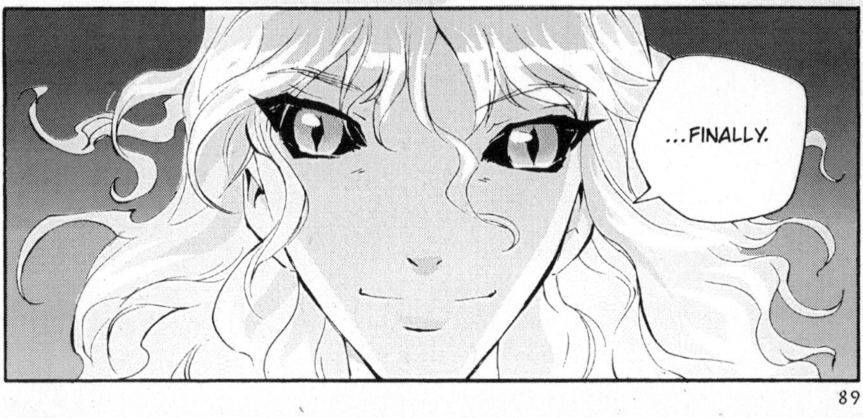
...FINALLY.

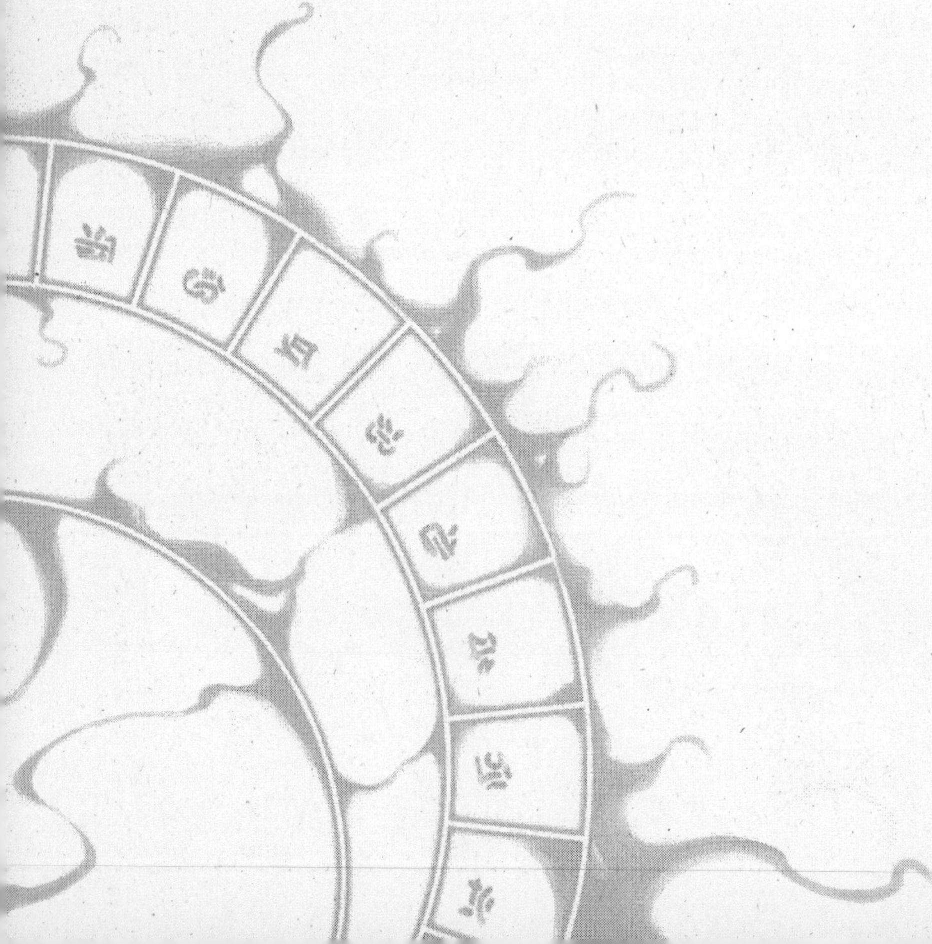

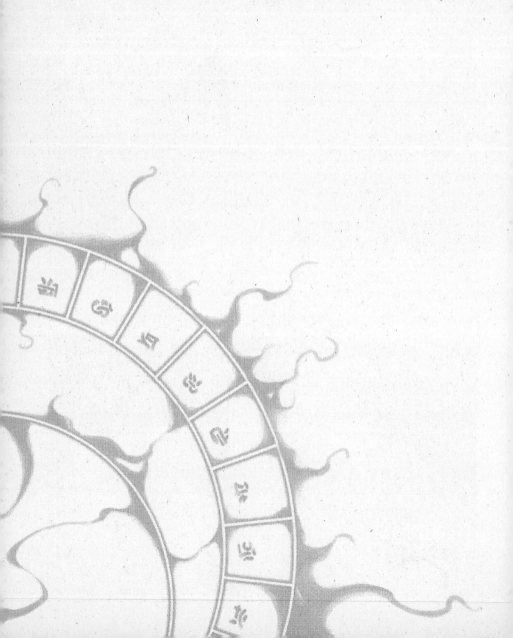

Chapter 22

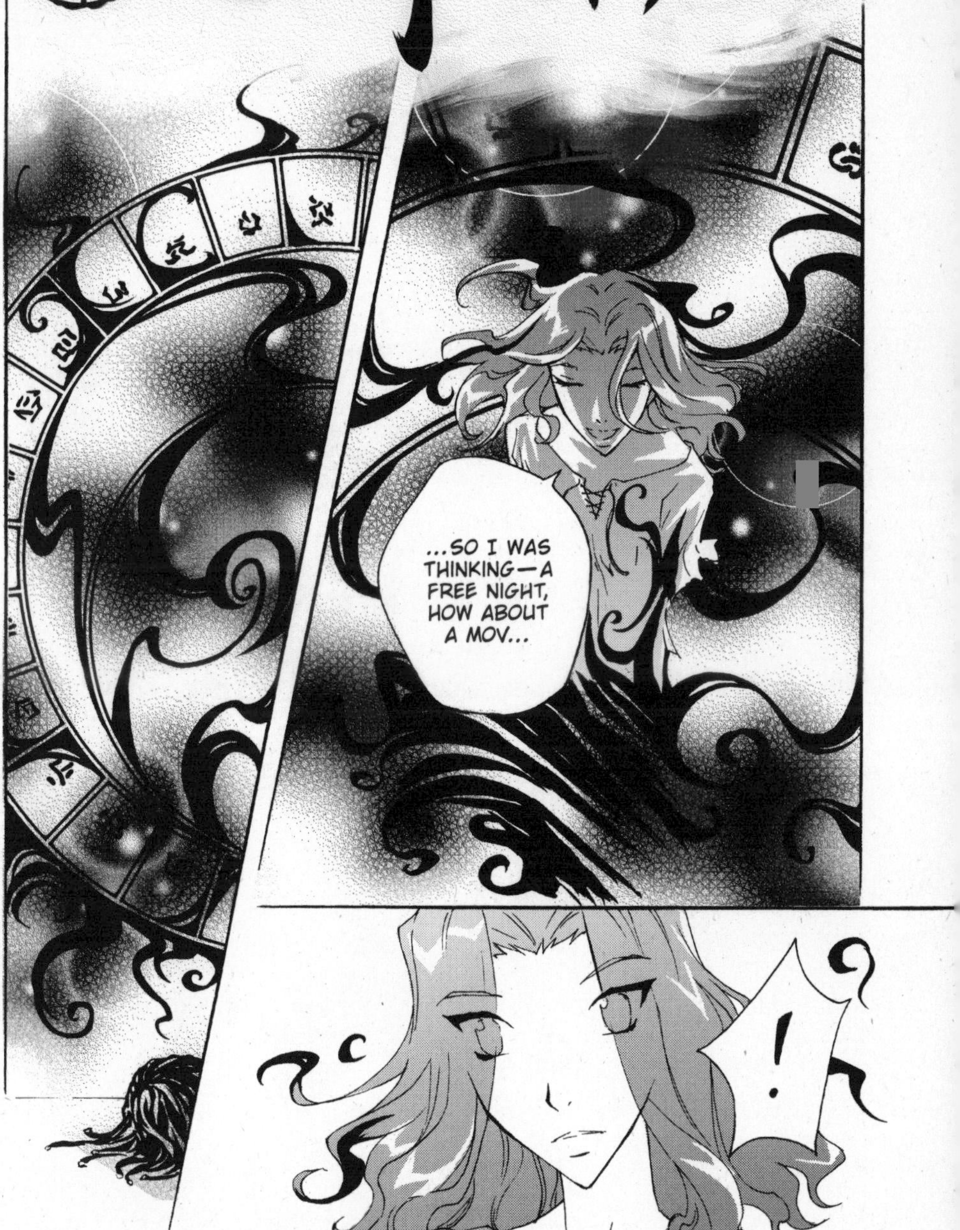

...SO I WAS THINKING—A FREE NIGHT, HOW ABOUT A MOV...
!

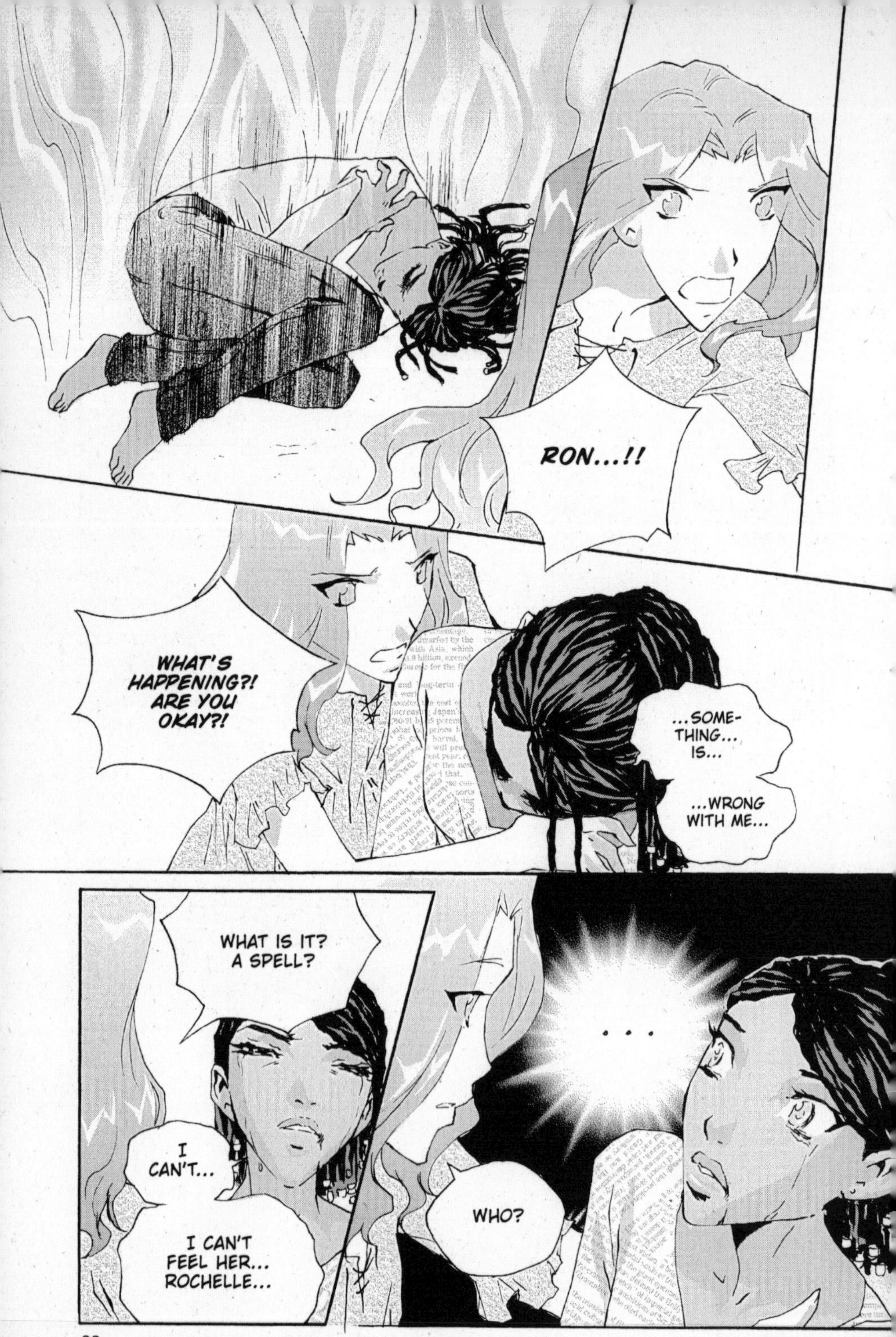
RON...!!
WHAT'S HAPPENING?! ARE YOU OKAY?!
...SOME-THING... IS...
...WRONG WITH ME...
WHAT IS IT? A SPELL?
I CAN'T...
I CAN'T FEEL HER... ROCHELLE...
WHO?
...

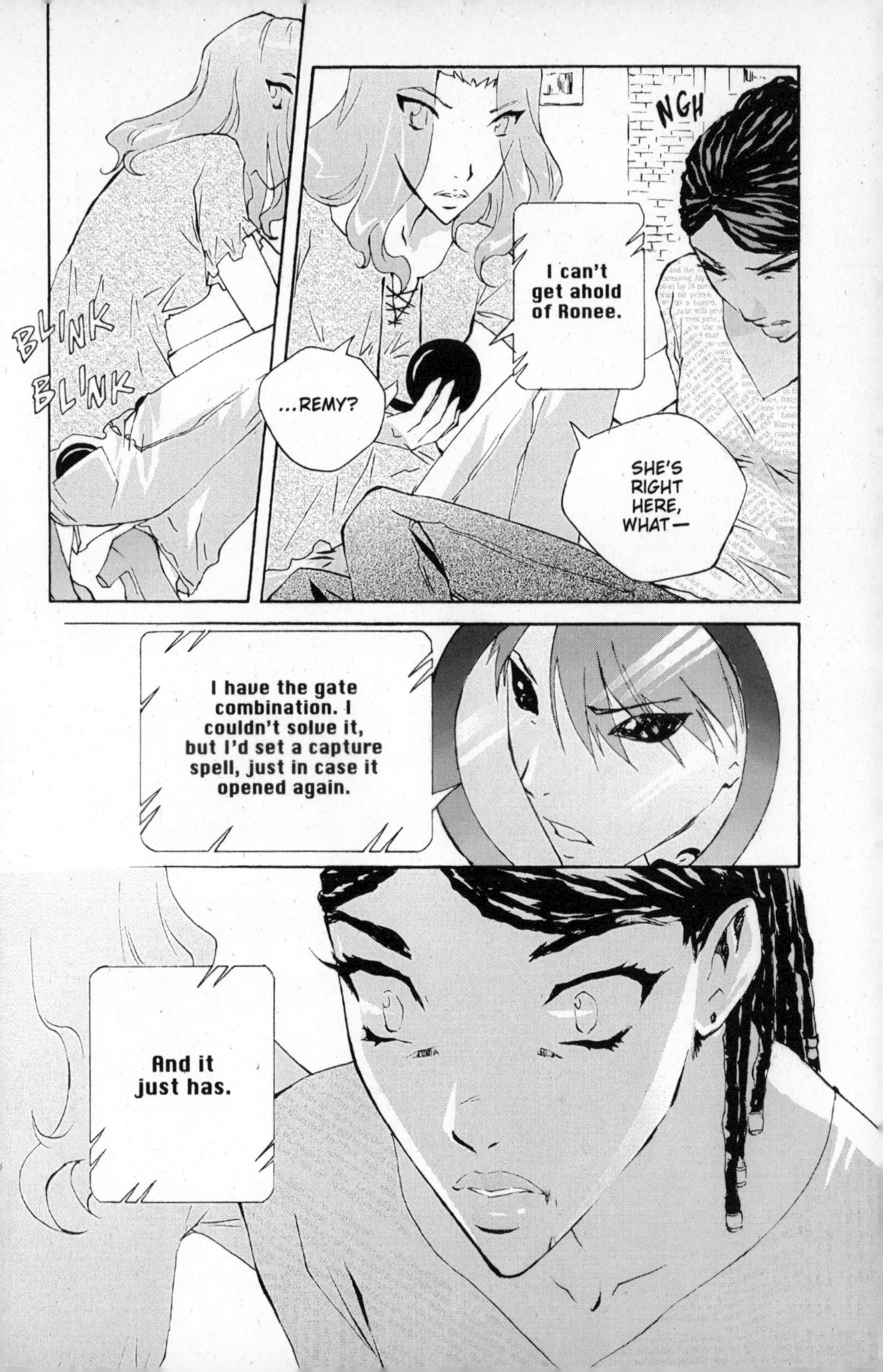
BLINK
BLINK
NGH
I can't get ahold of Ronee.
...REMY?
SHE'S RIGHT HERE, WHAT—
I have the gate combination. I couldn't solve it, but I'd set a capture spell, just in case it opened again.
And it just has.

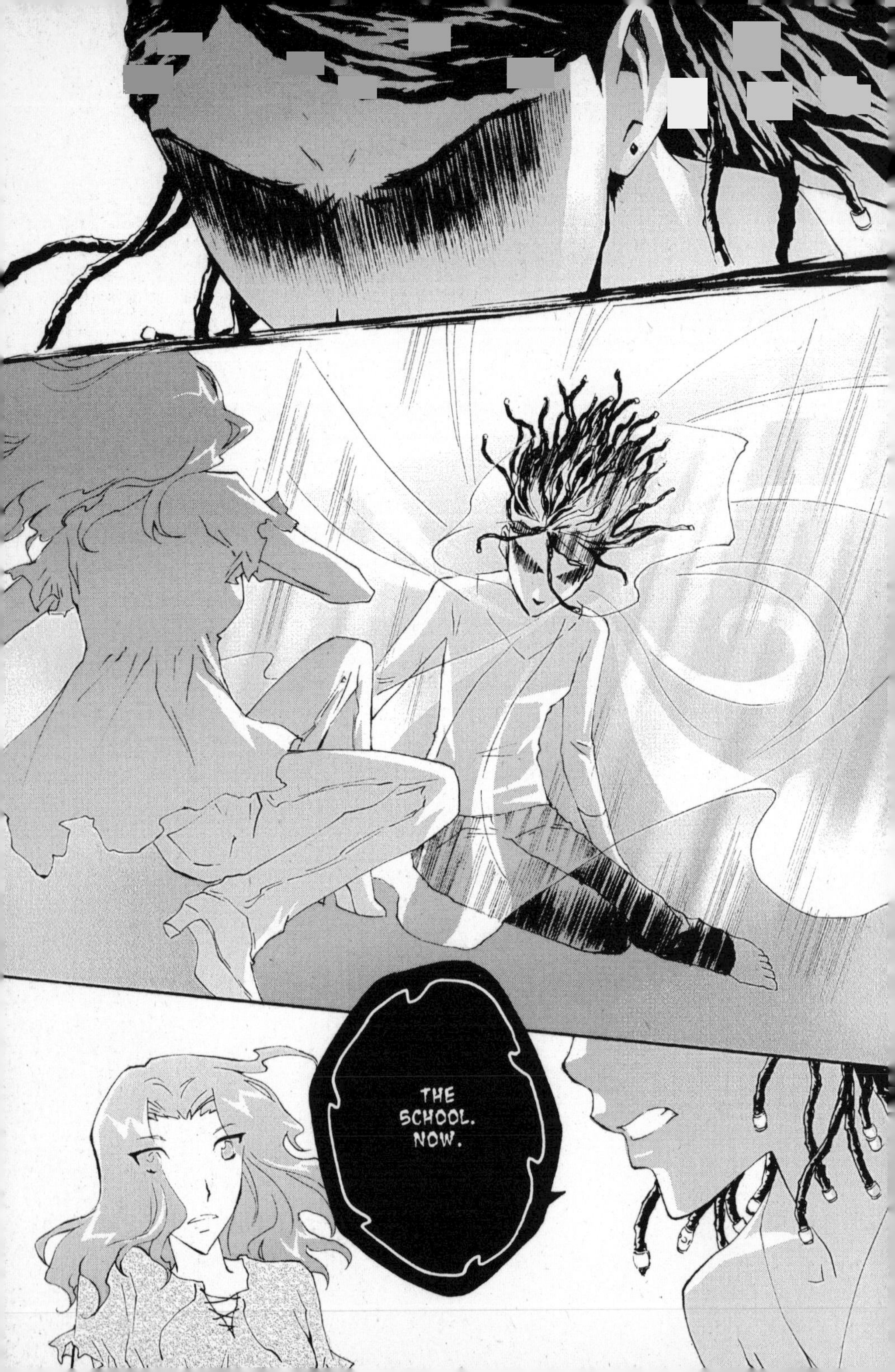
THE SCHOOL. NOW.

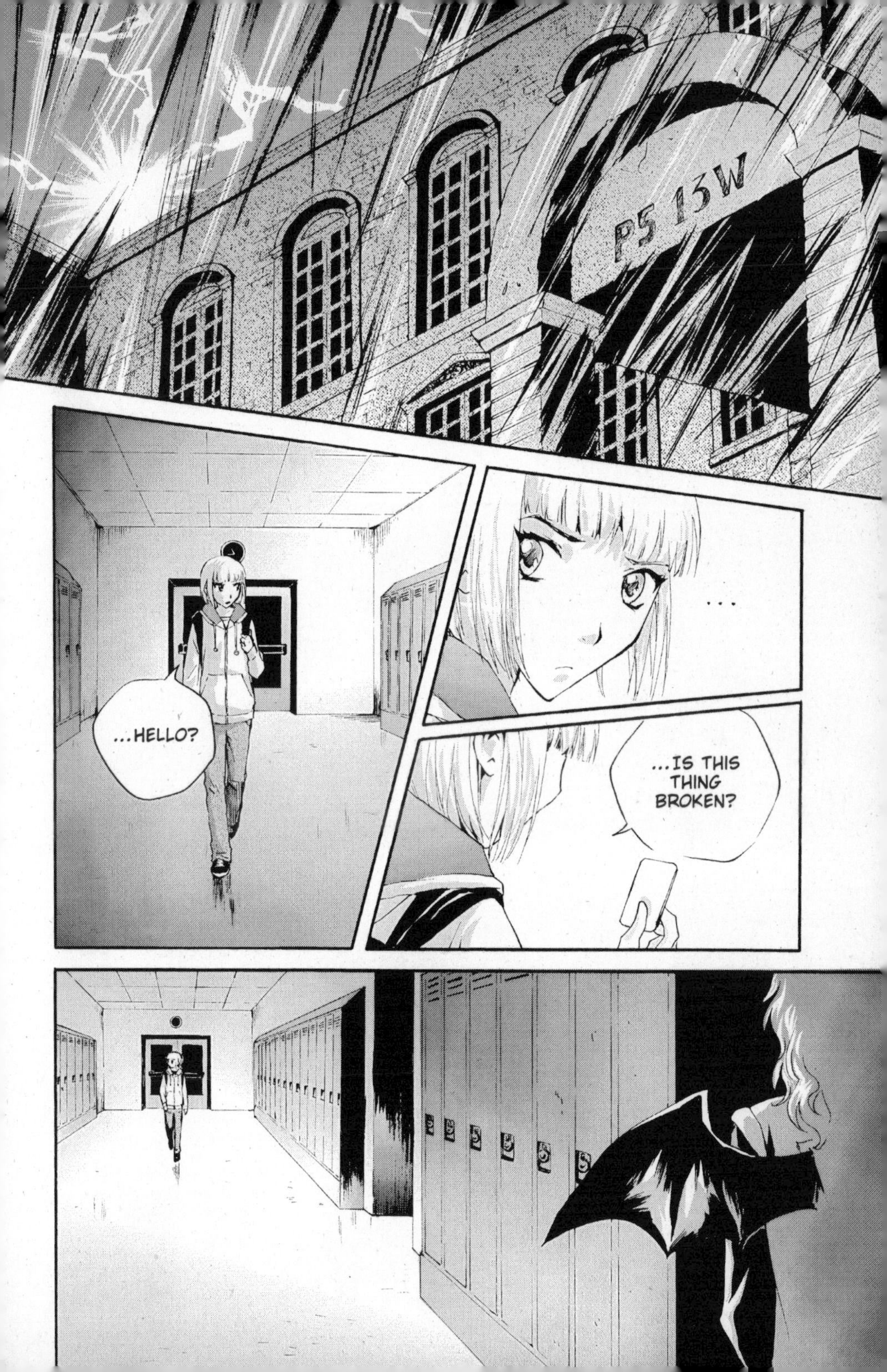
PS 13W
...HELLO?
...
...IS THIS THING BROKEN?

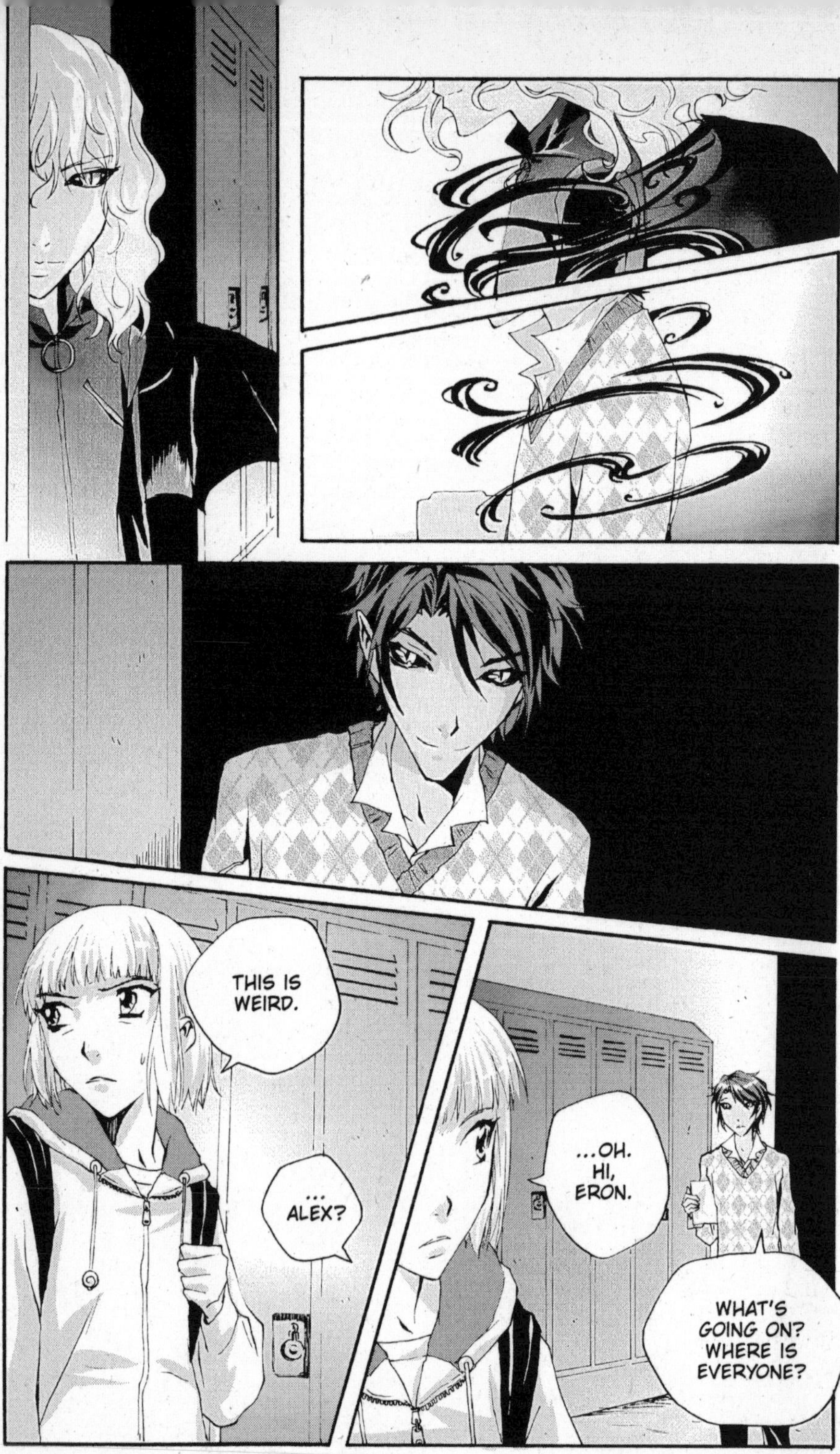
THIS IS WEIRD.
... ALEX?
...OH. HI, ERON.
WHAT'S GOING ON? WHERE IS EVERYONE?

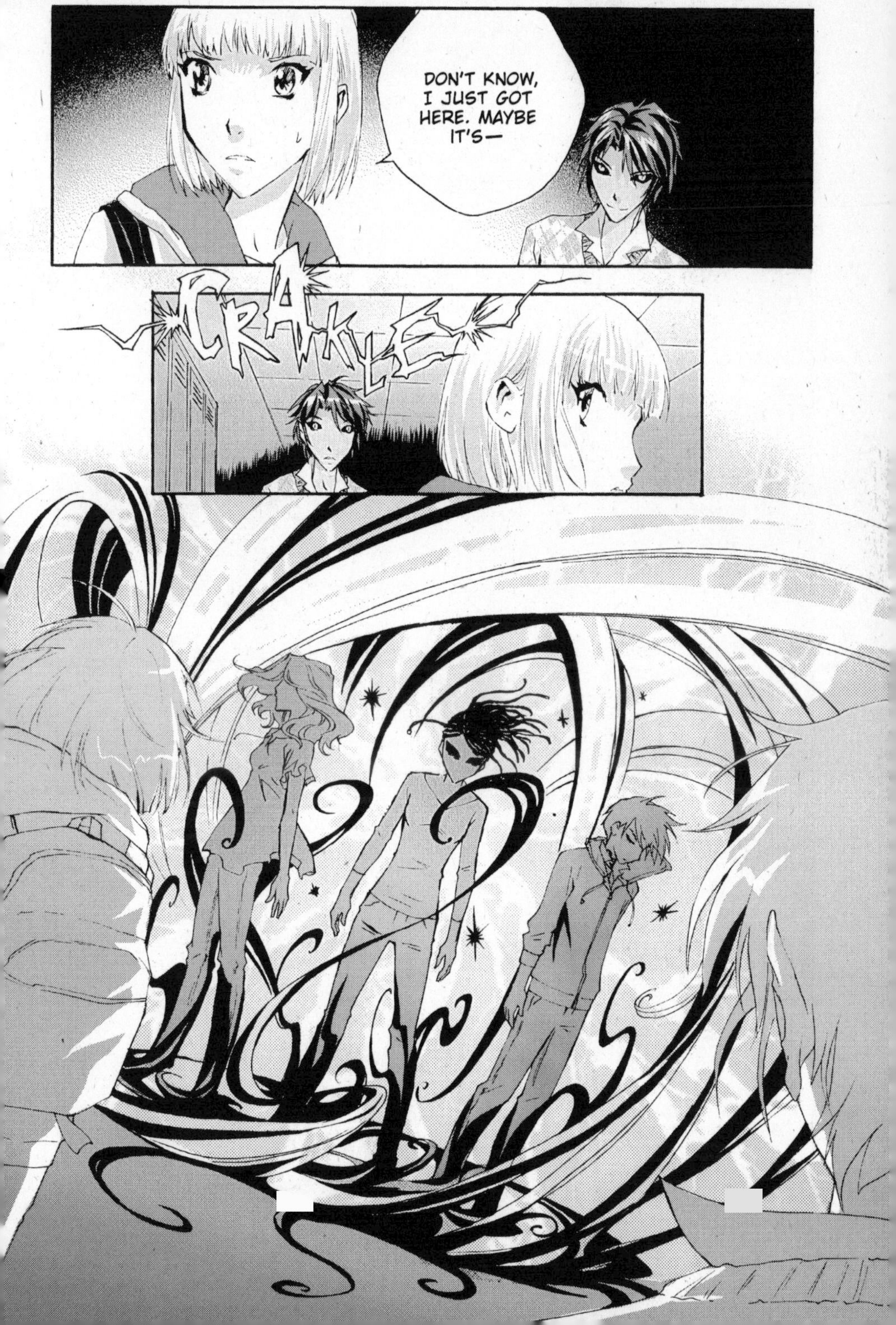
DON'T KNOW, I JUST GOT HERE. MAYBE IT'S—
CRAKKLE

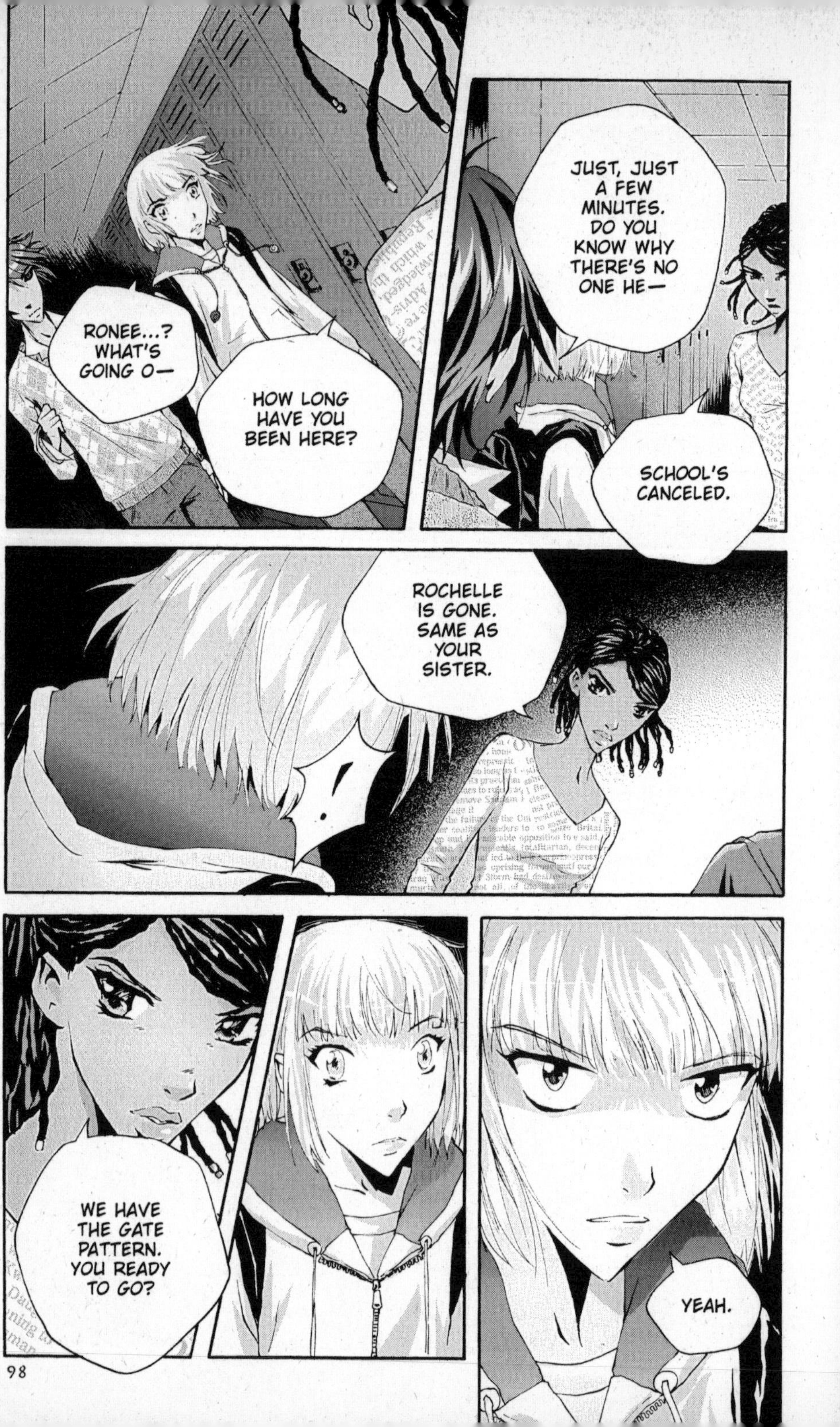
RONEE...? WHAT'S GOING O—
HOW LONG HAVE YOU BEEN HERE?
JUST, JUST A FEW MINUTES. DO YOU KNOW WHY THERE'S NO ONE HE—
SCHOOL'S CANCELED.
ROCHELLE IS GONE. SAME AS YOUR SISTER.
WE HAVE THE GATE PATTERN. YOU READY TO GO?
YEAH.

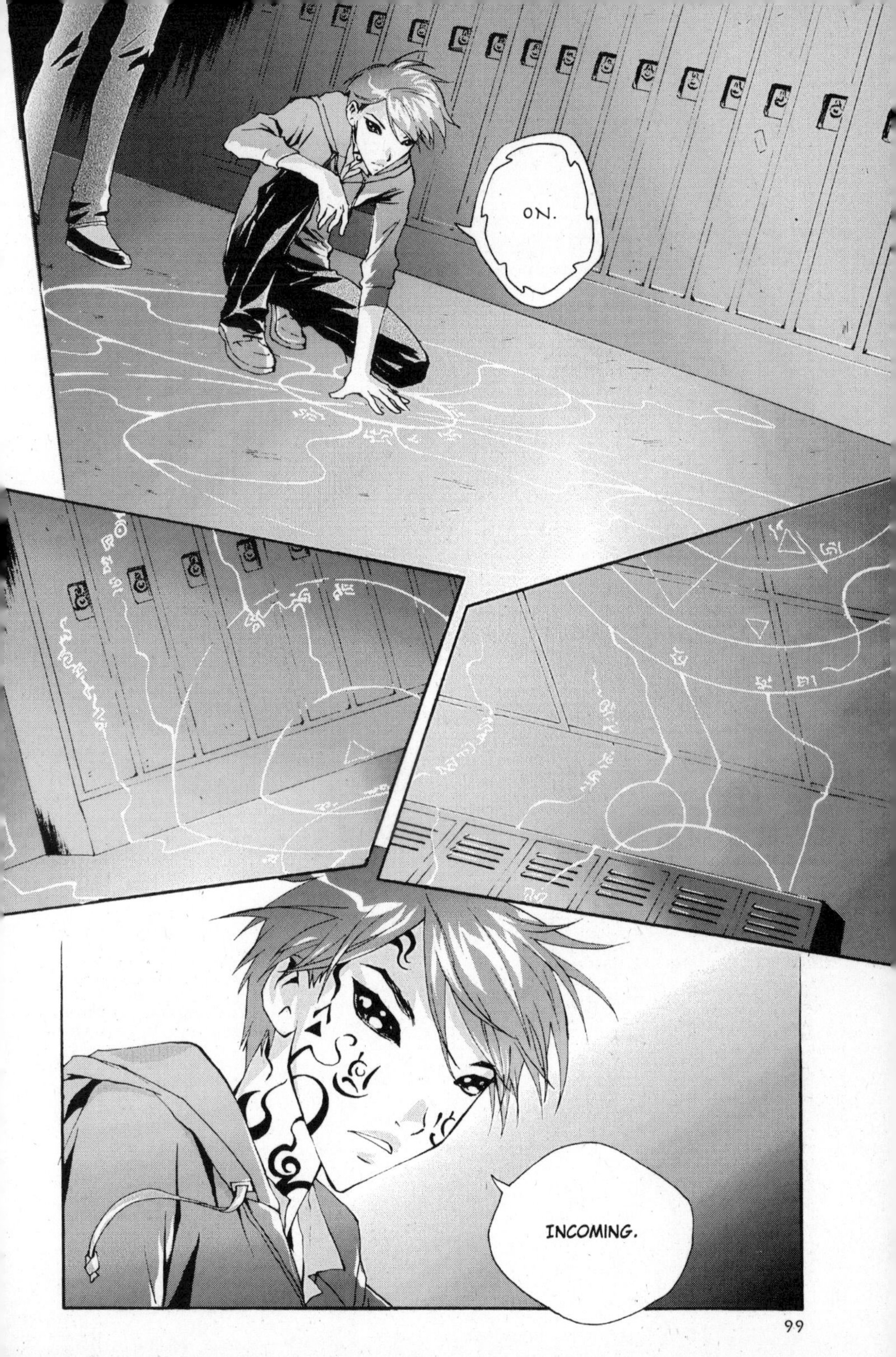
ON.
INCOMING.

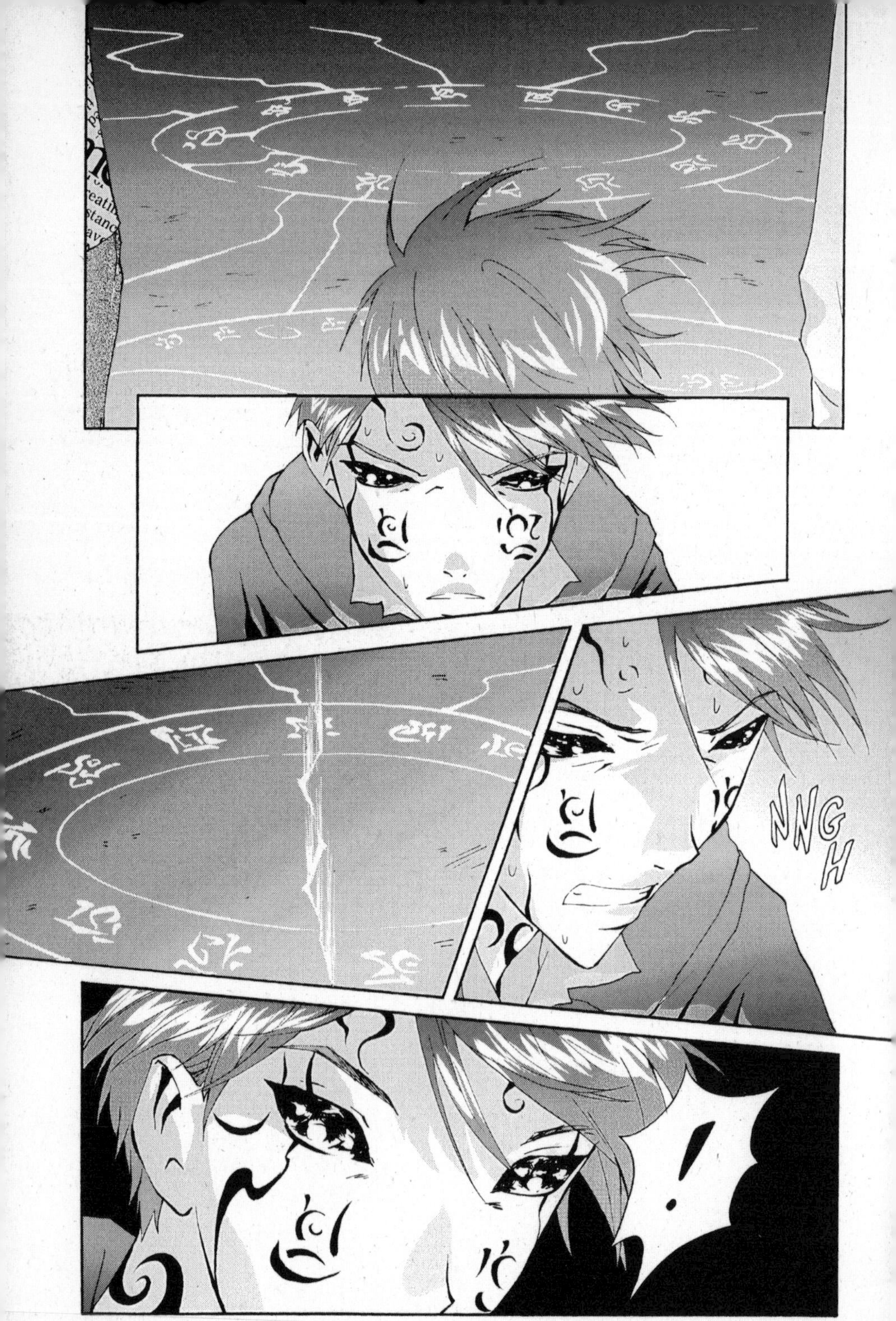
NNGH
!

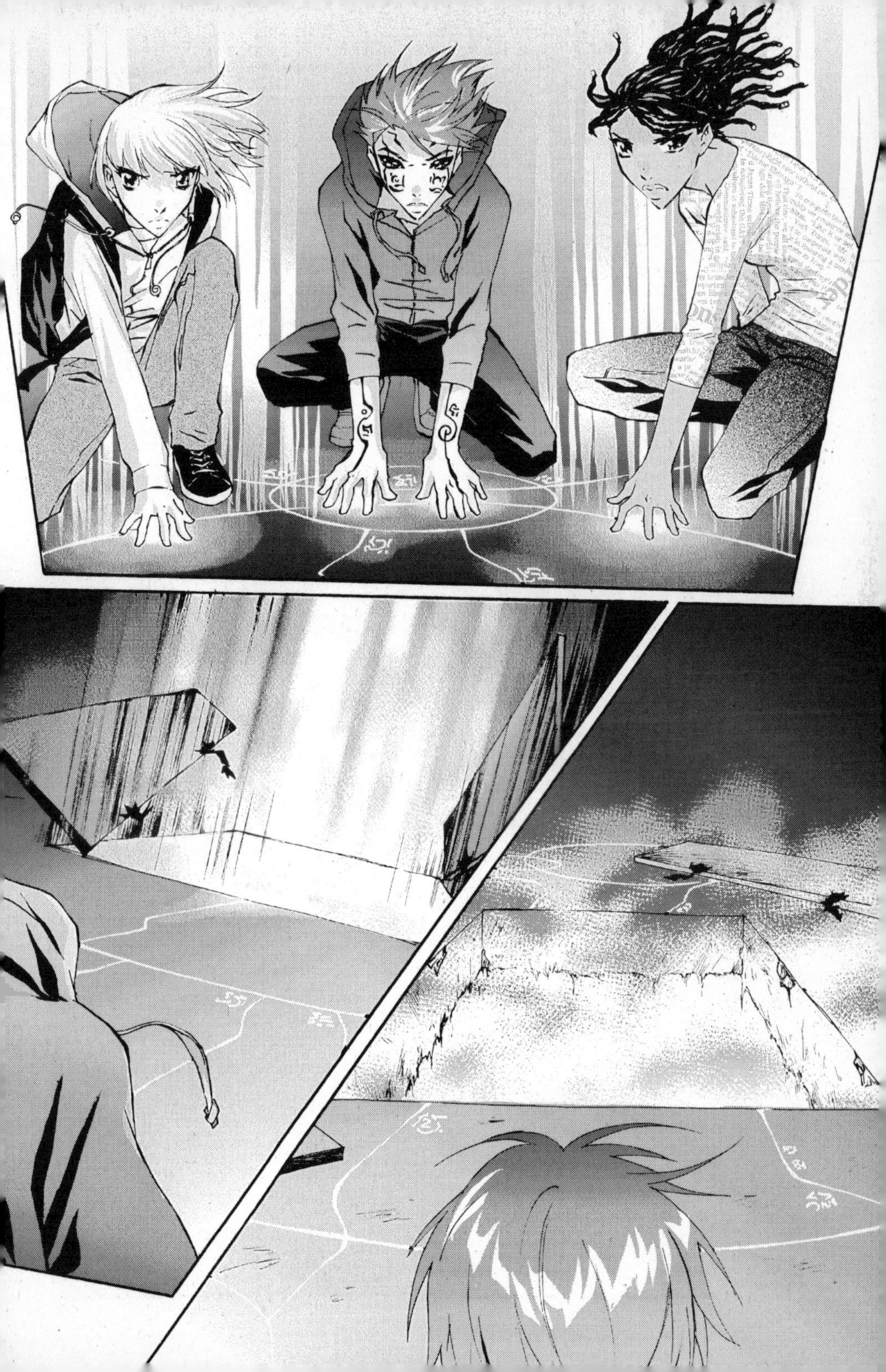

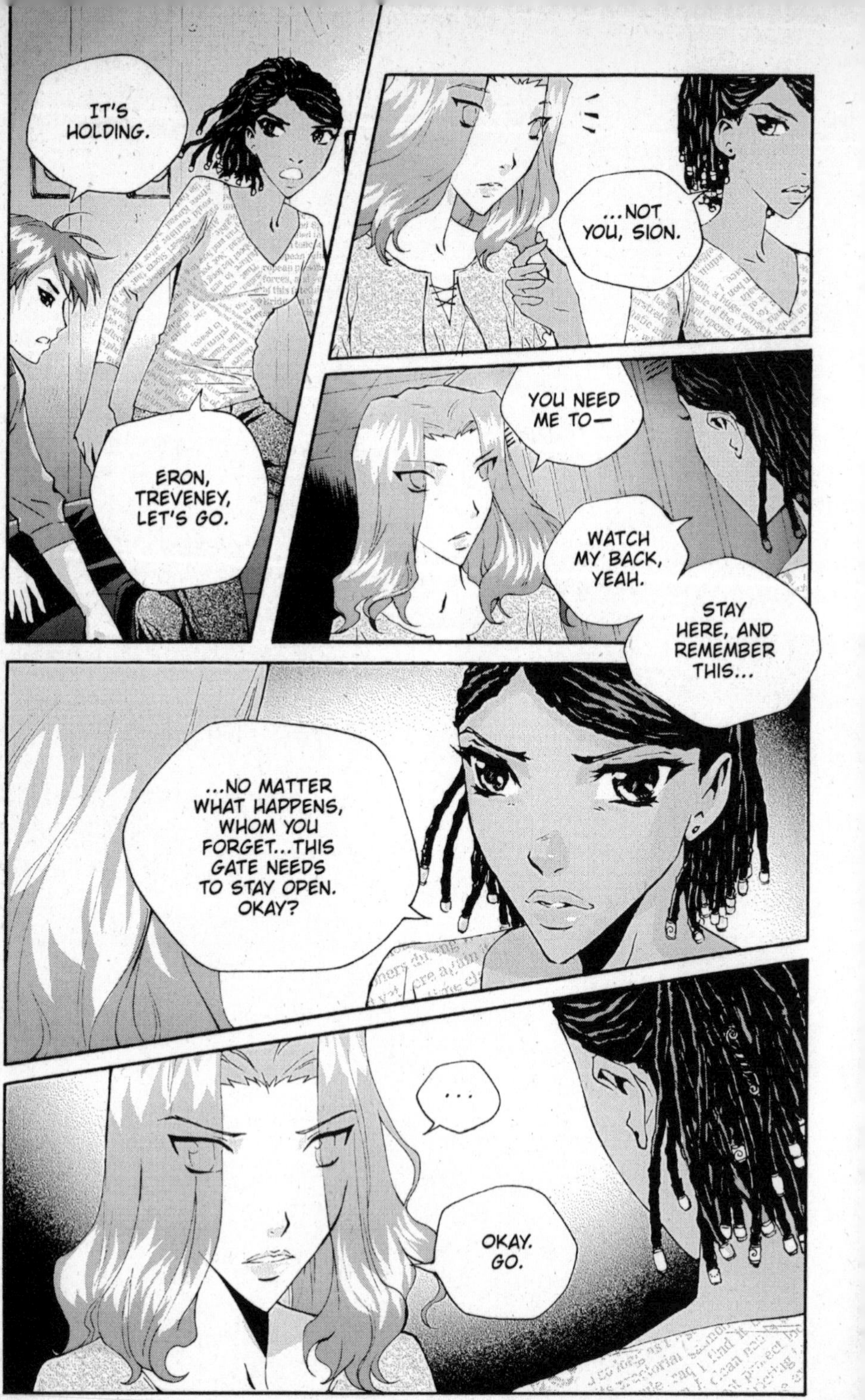
IT'S HOLDING.
ERON, TREVENEY, LET'S GO.
...NOT YOU, SION.
YOU NEED ME TO—
WATCH MY BACK, YEAH.
STAY HERE, AND REMEMBER THIS...
...NO MATTER WHAT HAPPENS, WHOM YOU FORGET...THIS GATE NEEDS TO STAY OPEN. OKAY?
...
OKAY. GO.

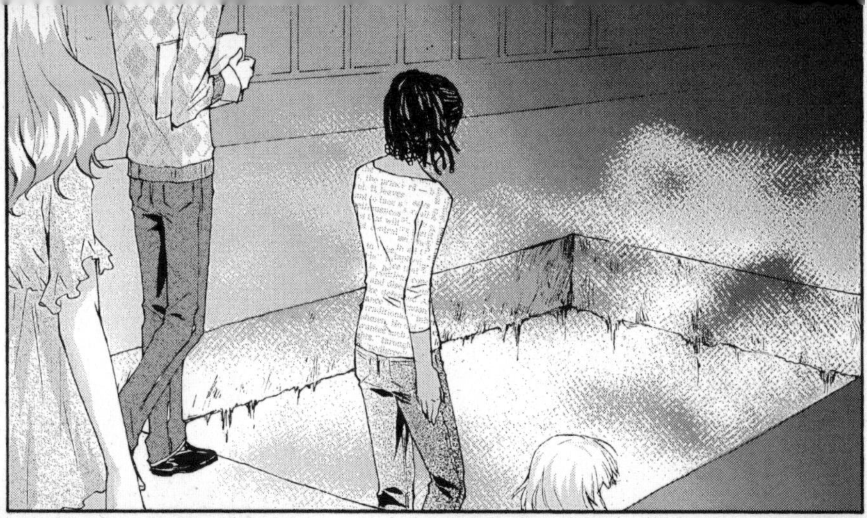

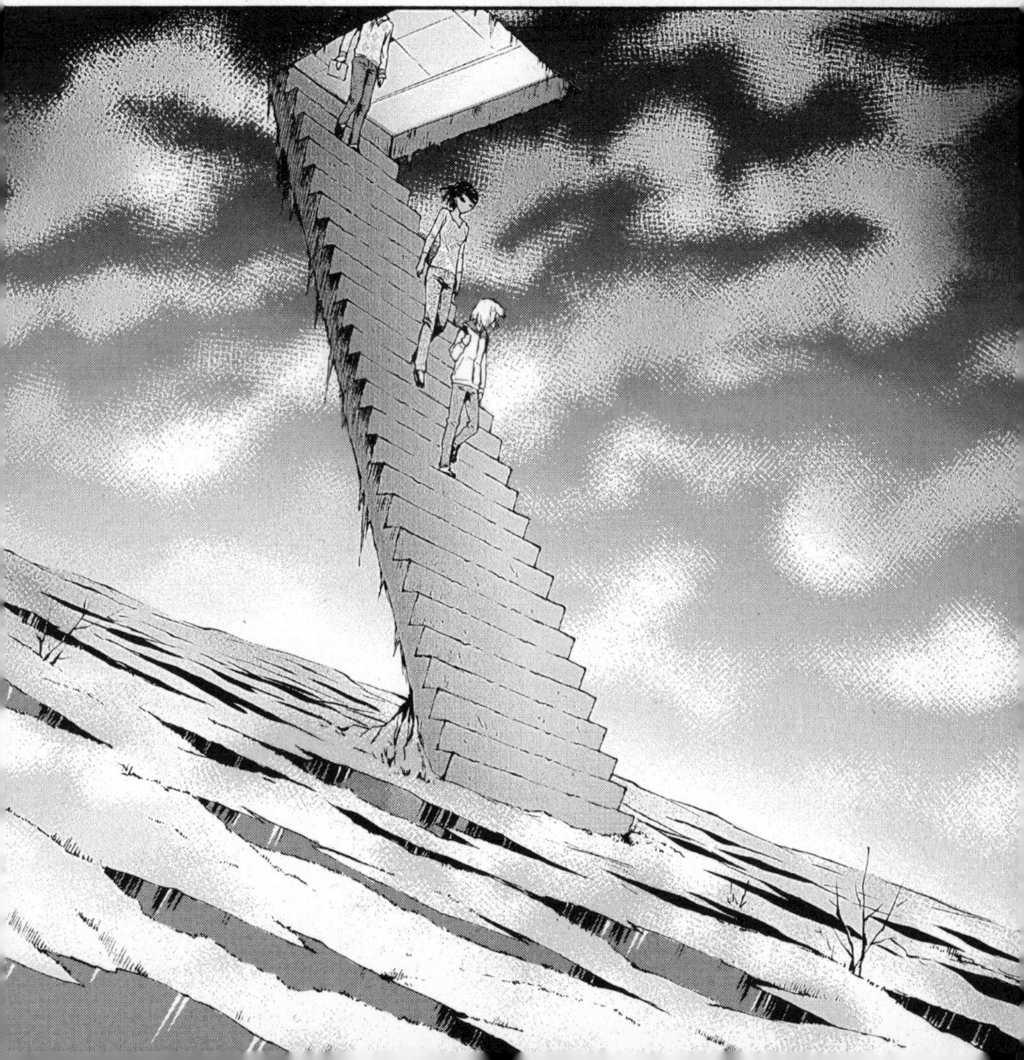

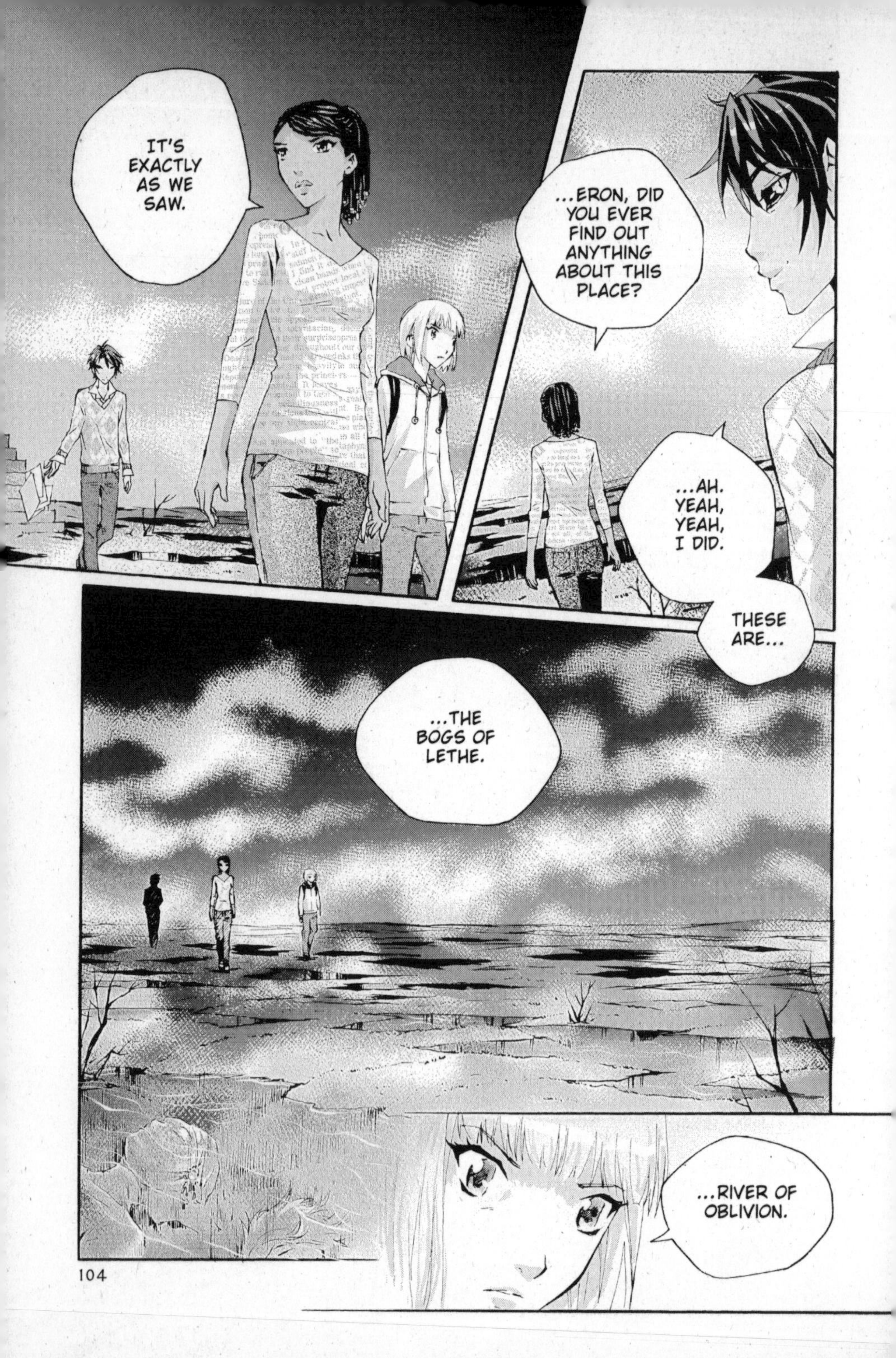
IT'S EXACTLY AS WE SAW.
...ERON, DID YOU EVER FIND OUT ANYTHING ABOUT THIS PLACE?
...AH. YEAH, YEAH, I DID.
THESE ARE...
...THE BOGS OF LETHE.
...RIVER OF OBLIVION.

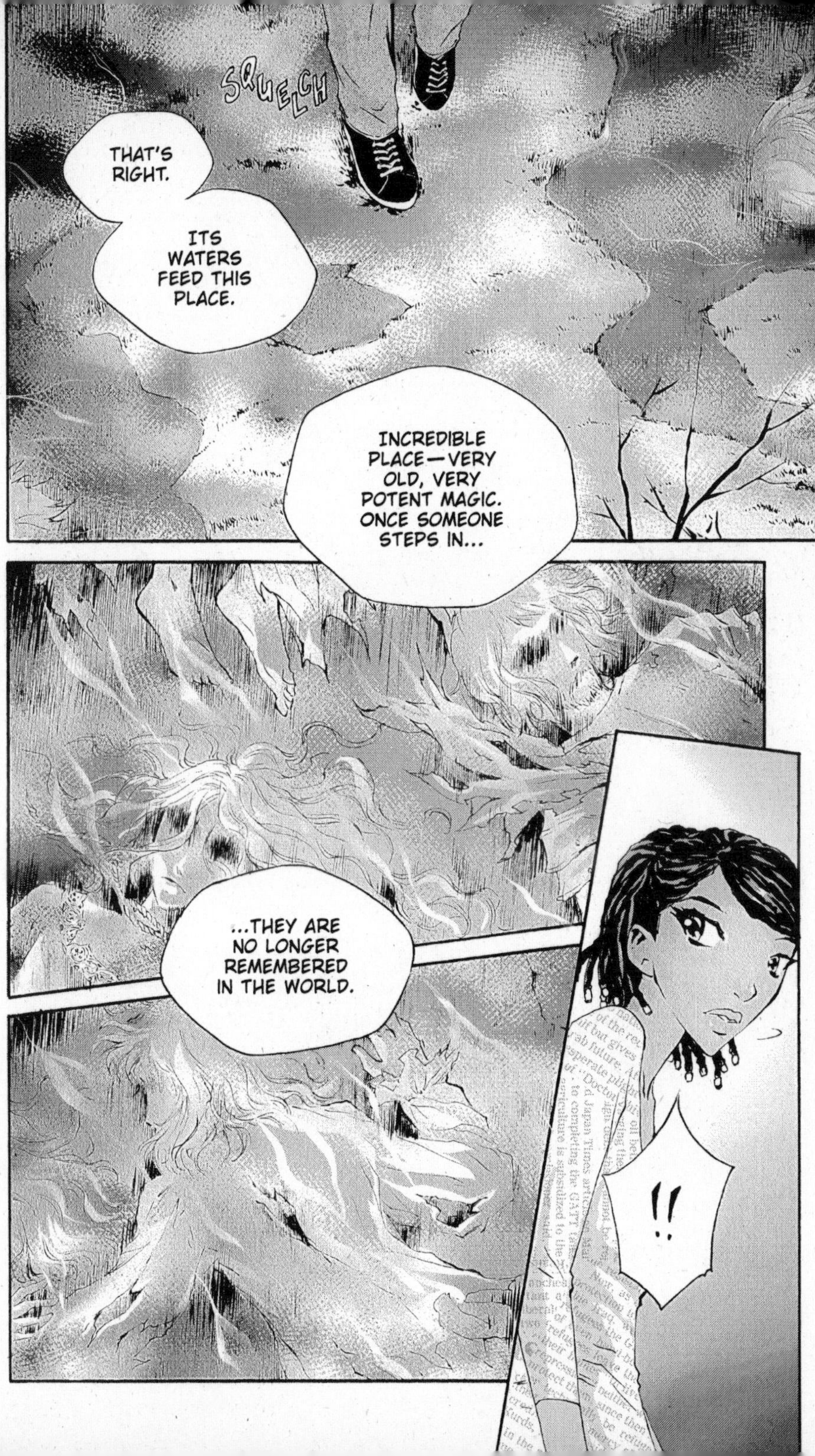
SQUELCH
THAT'S RIGHT.
ITS WATERS FEED THIS PLACE.
INCREDIBLE PLACE—VERY OLD, VERY POTENT MAGIC. ONCE SOMEONE STEPS IN...
...THEY ARE NO LONGER REMEMBERED IN THE WORLD.
!!

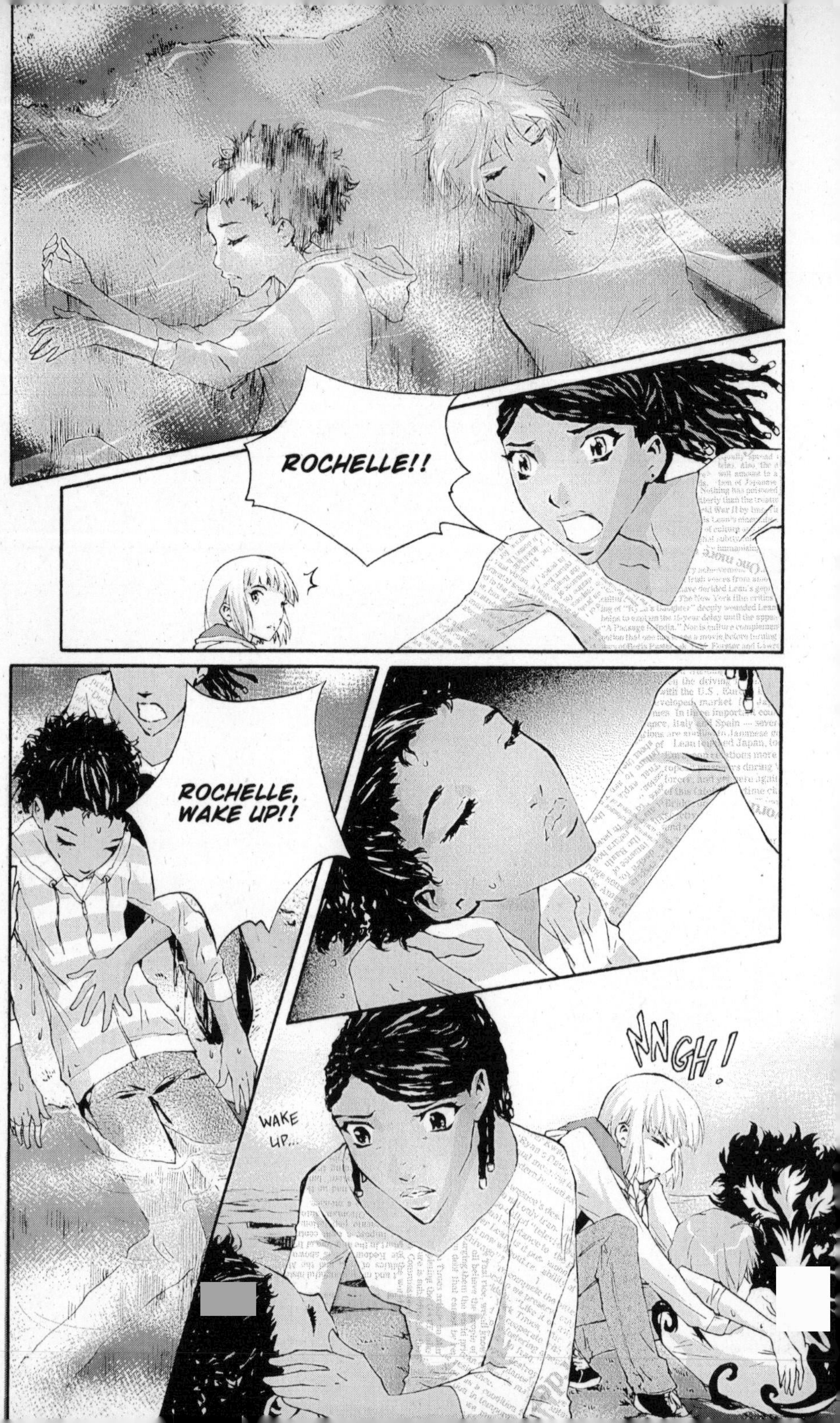
ROCHELLE!!
ROCHELLE, WAKE UP!!
WAKE UP...
NNGH!

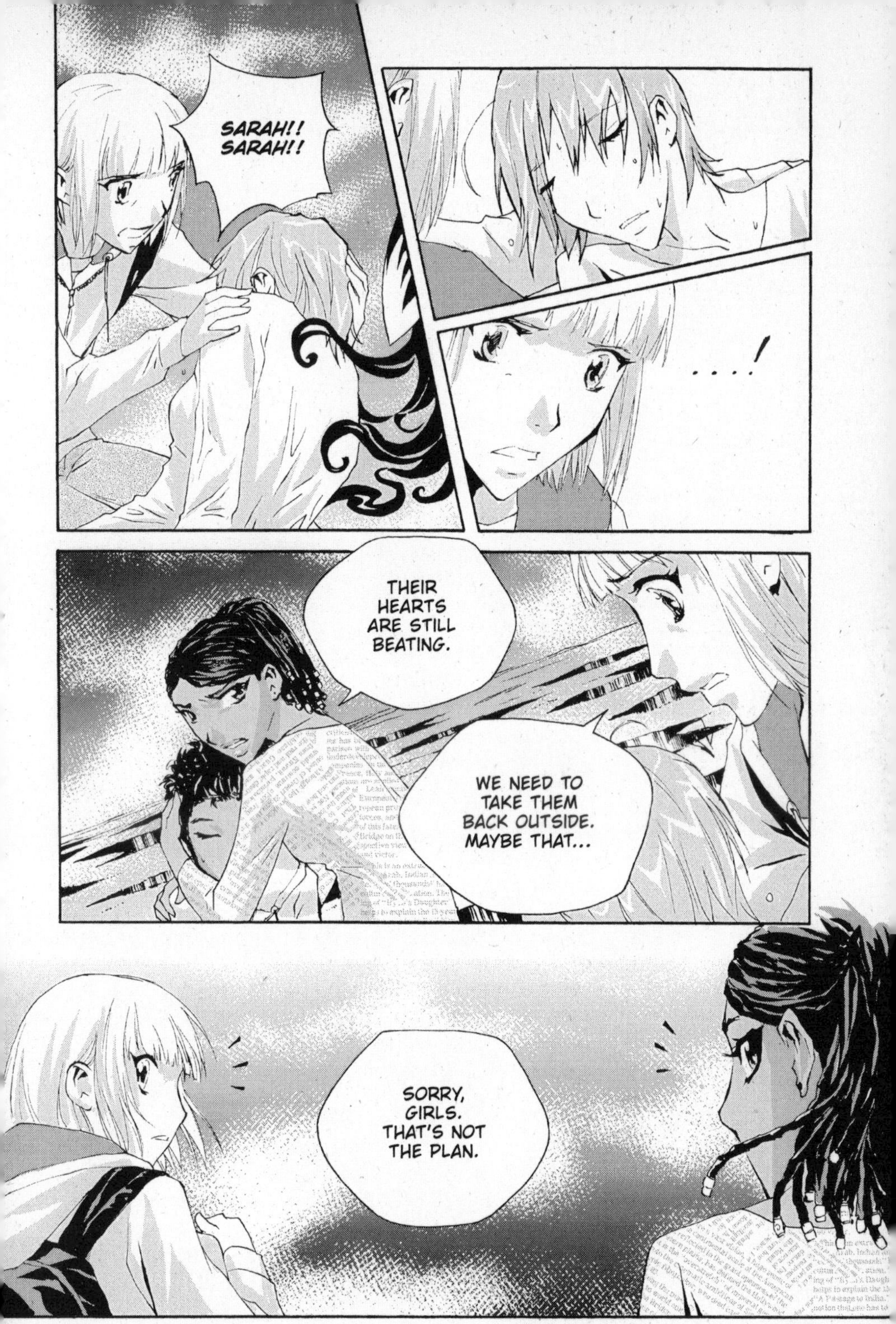
SARAH!! SARAH!!
...!
THEIR HEARTS ARE STILL BEATING.
WE NEED TO TAKE THEM BACK OUTSIDE. MAYBE THAT...
SORRY, GIRLS. THAT'S NOT THE PLAN.

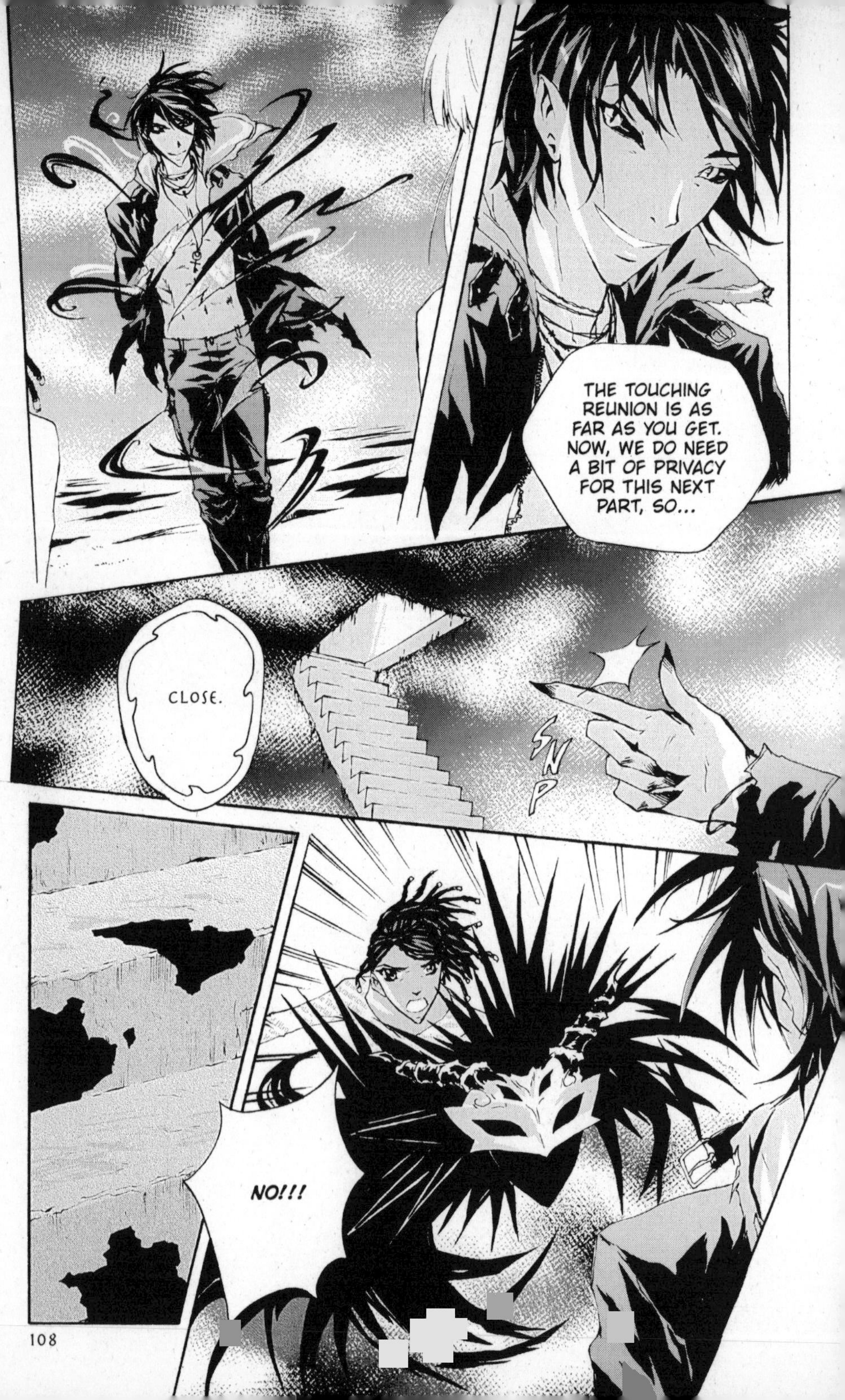
THE TOUCHING REUNION IS AS FAR AS YOU GET. NOW, WE DO NEED A BIT OF PRIVACY FOR THIS NEXT PART, SO...
CLOSE.
SNP
NO!!!

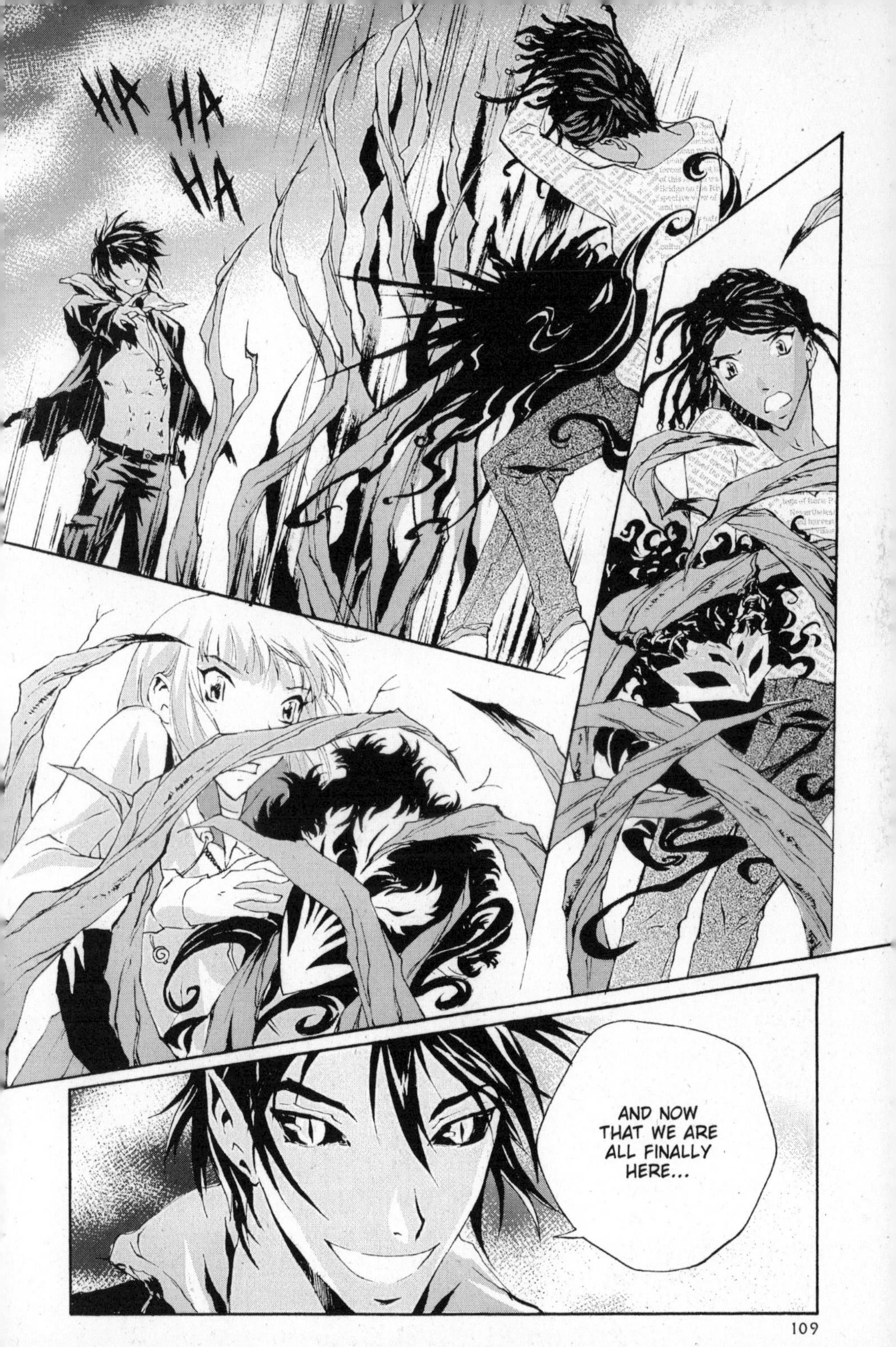
HA HA HA
AND NOW THAT WE ARE ALL FINALLY HERE...

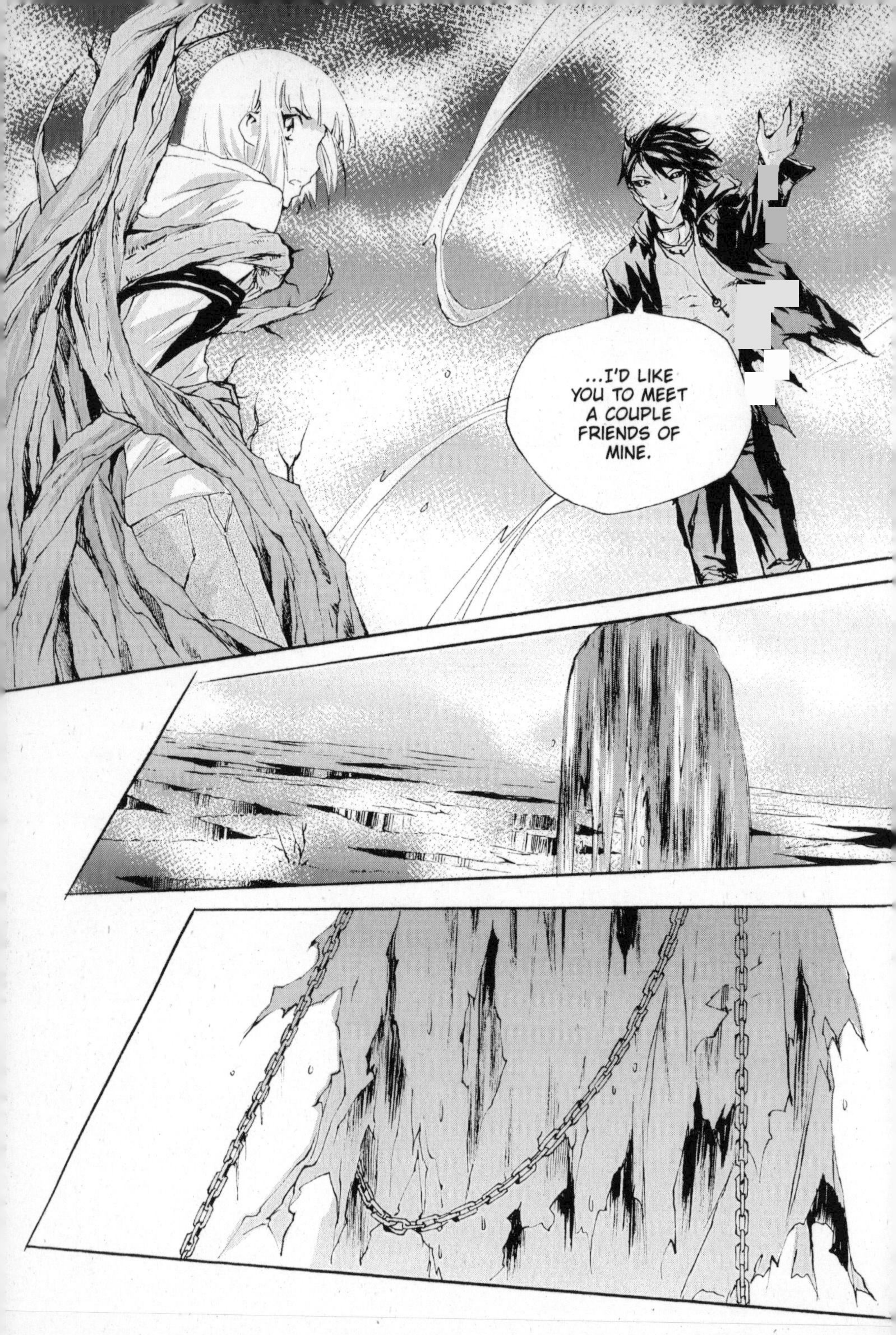
...I'D LIKE YOU TO MEET A COUPLE FRIENDS OF MINE.

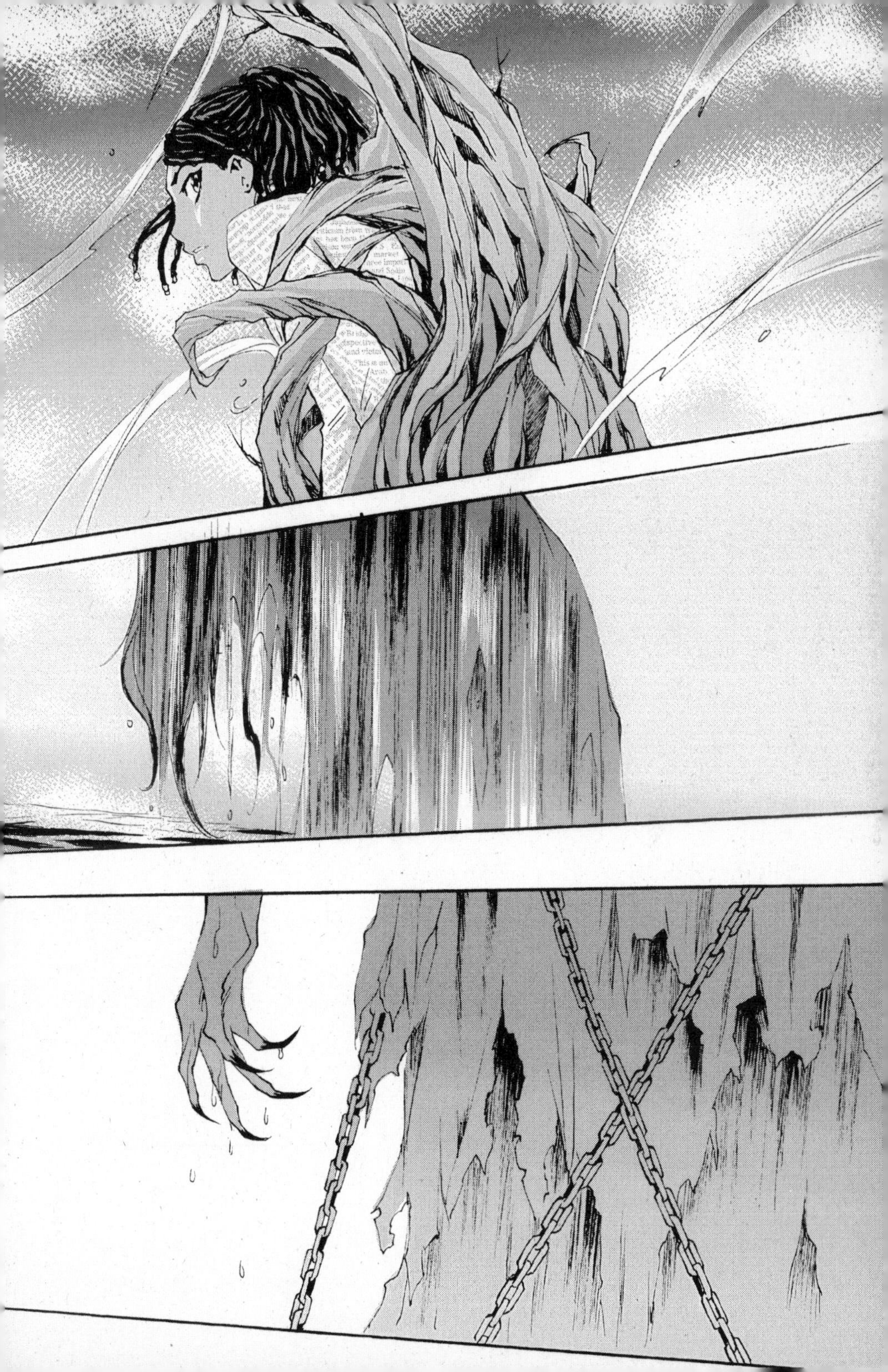

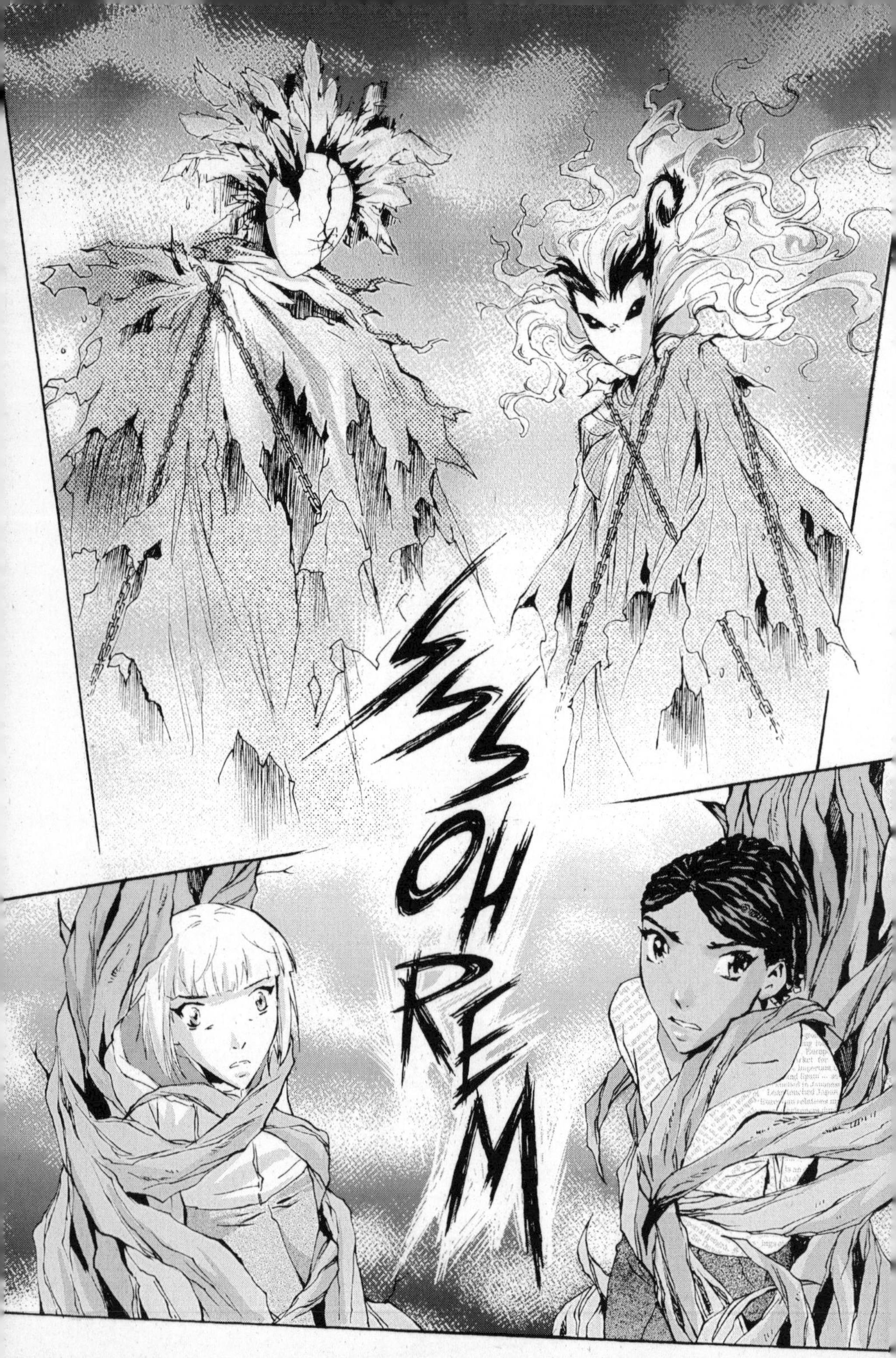
SWOHREM

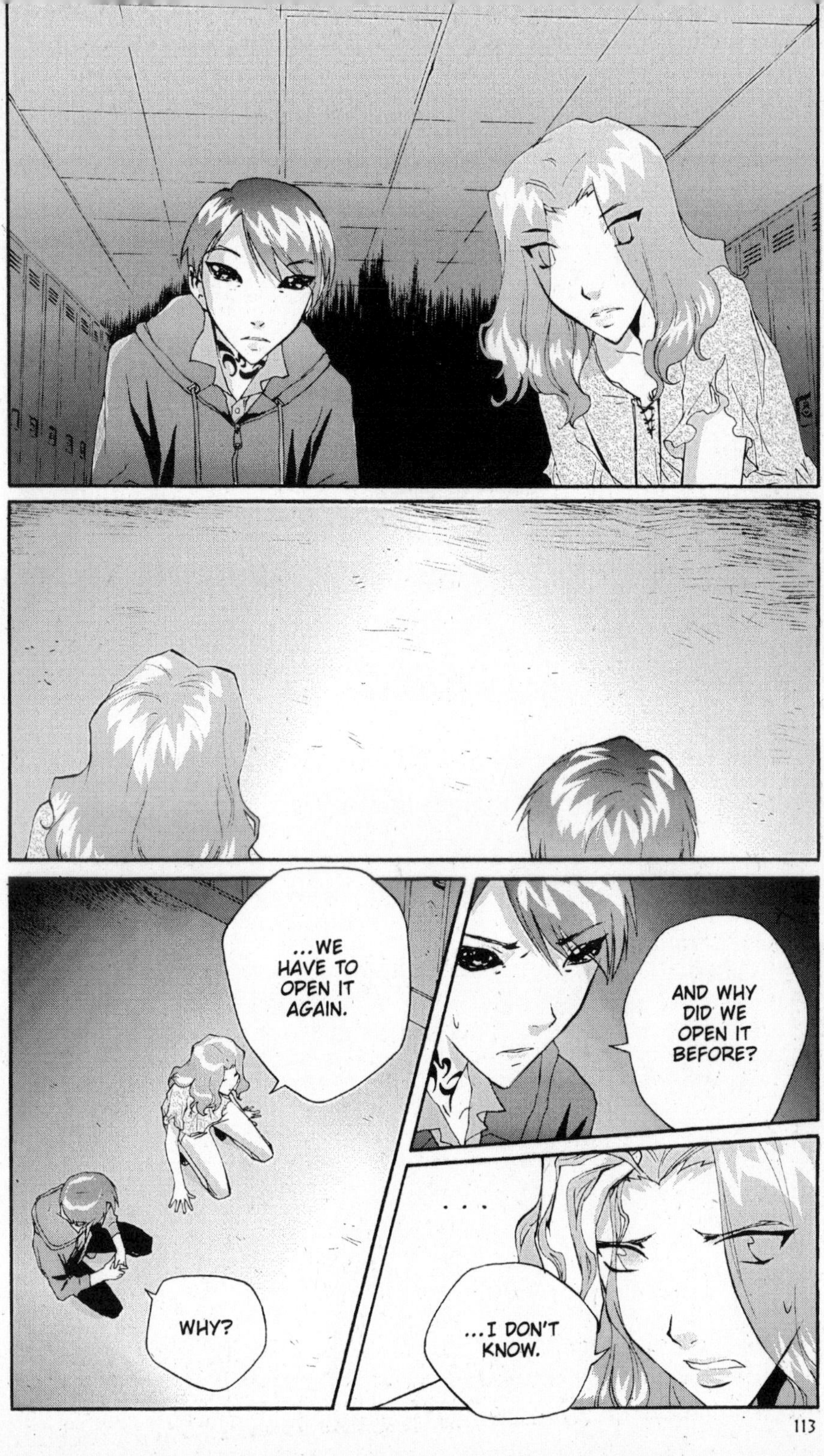
...WE HAVE TO OPEN IT AGAIN.
WHY?
AND WHY DID WE OPEN IT BEFORE?
...
...I DON'T KNOW.

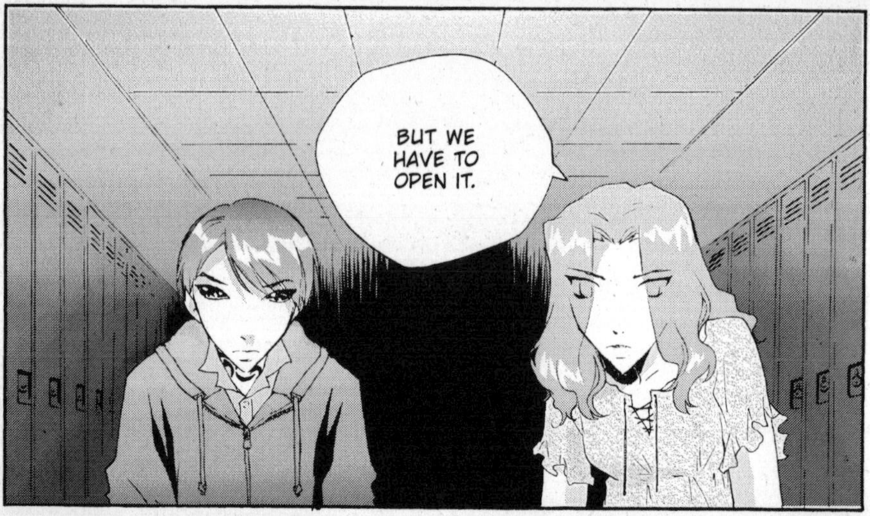
BUT WE HAVE TO OPEN IT.
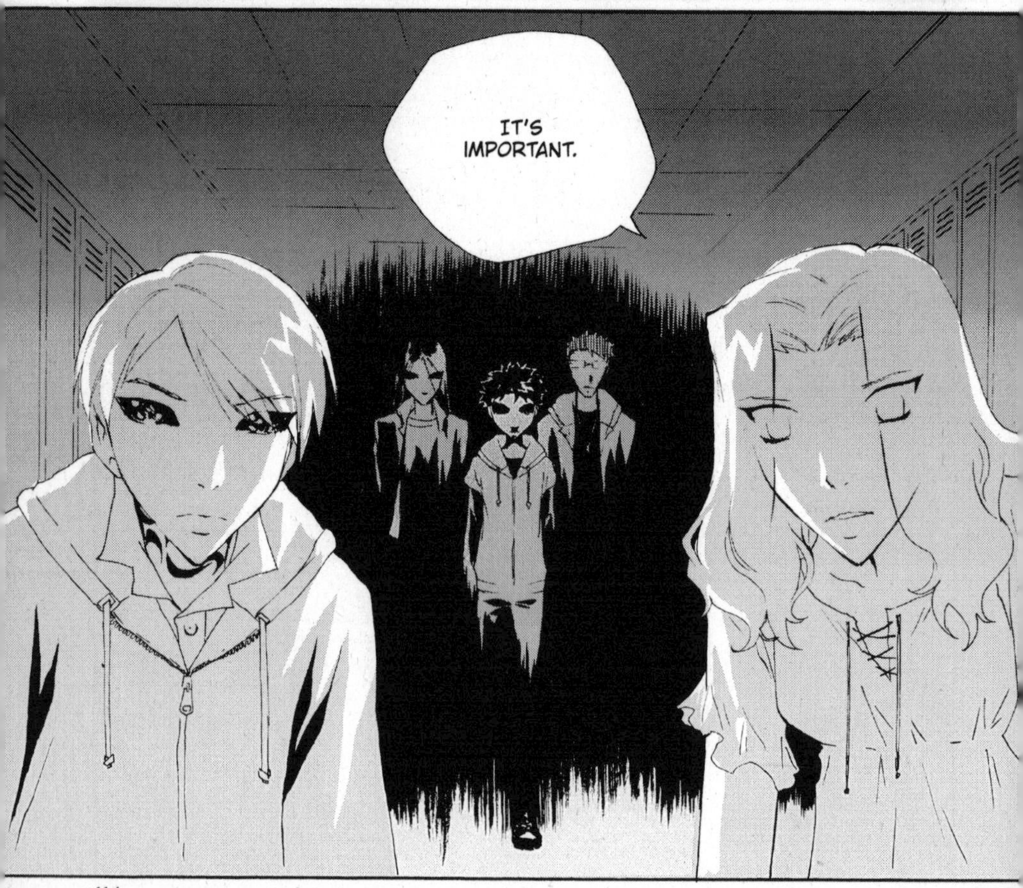
IT'S IMPORTANT.

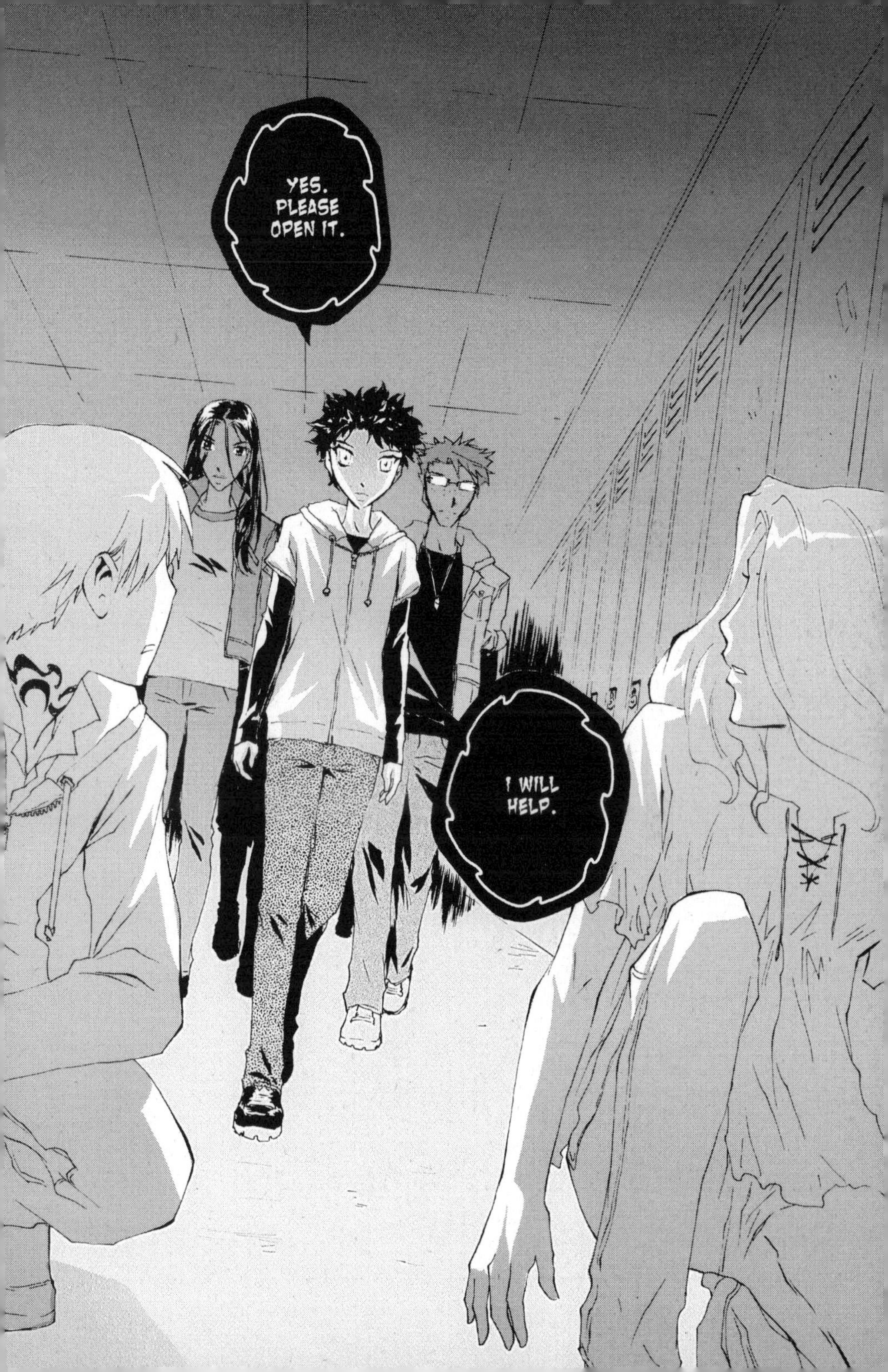
YES. PLEASE OPEN IT.
I WILL HELP.

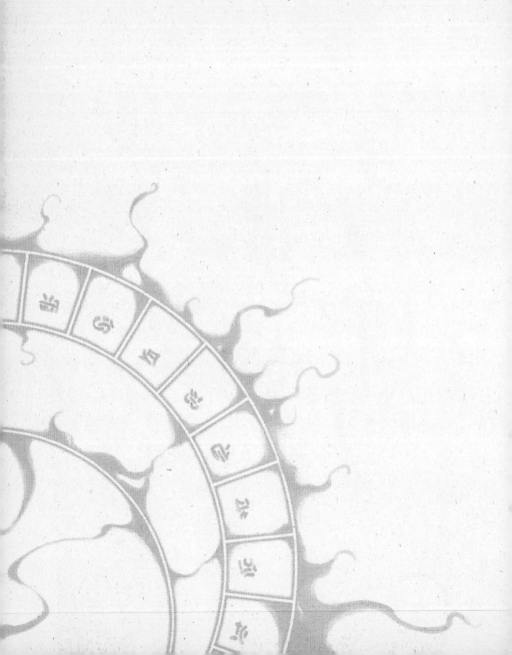

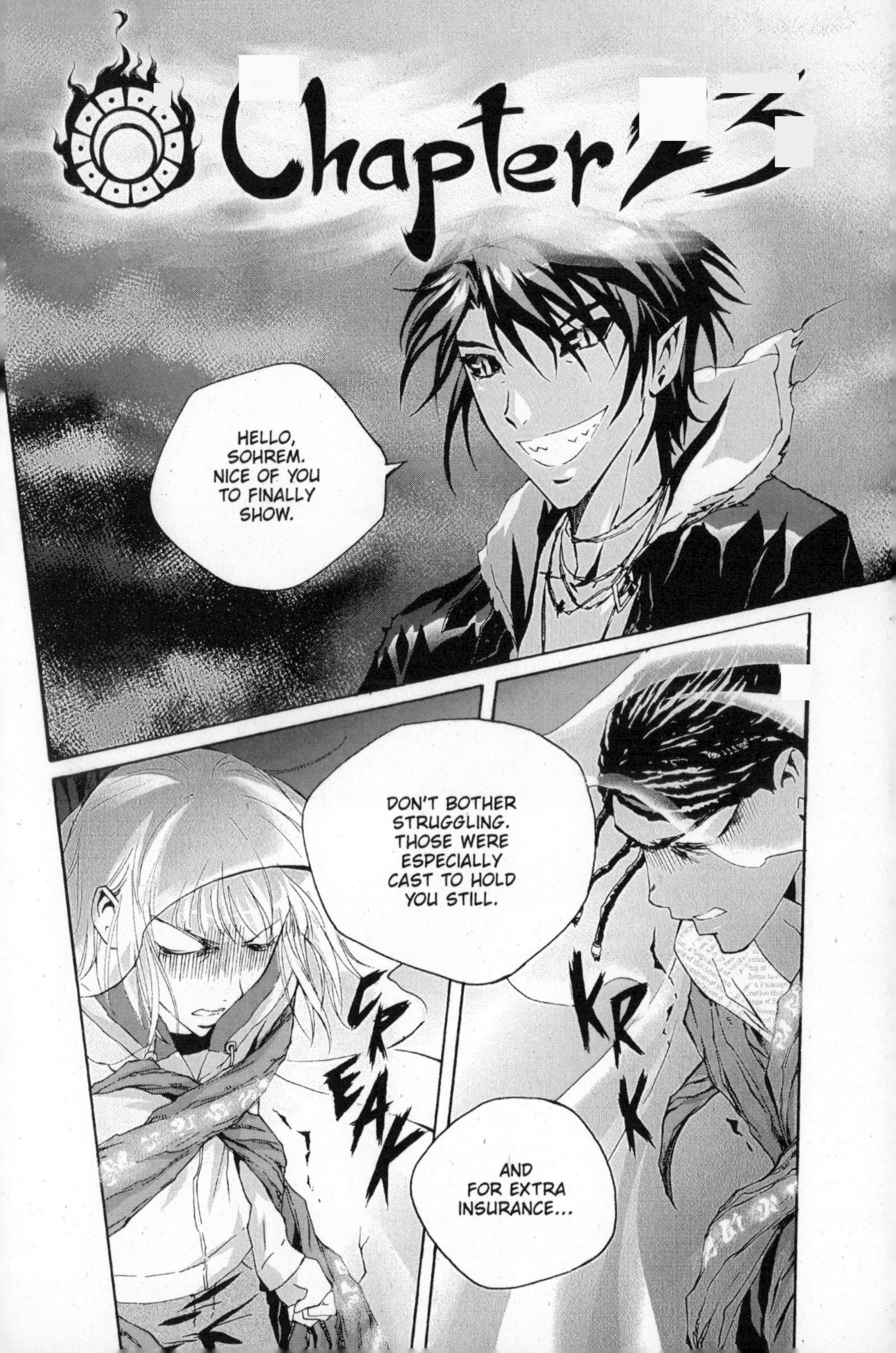
Chapter
HELLO, SOHREM. NICE OF YOU TO FINALLY SHOW.
DON'T BOTHER STRUGGLING. THOSE WERE ESPECIALLY CAST TO HOLD YOU STILL.
CREAK
KRKK
AND FOR EXTRA INSURANCE...

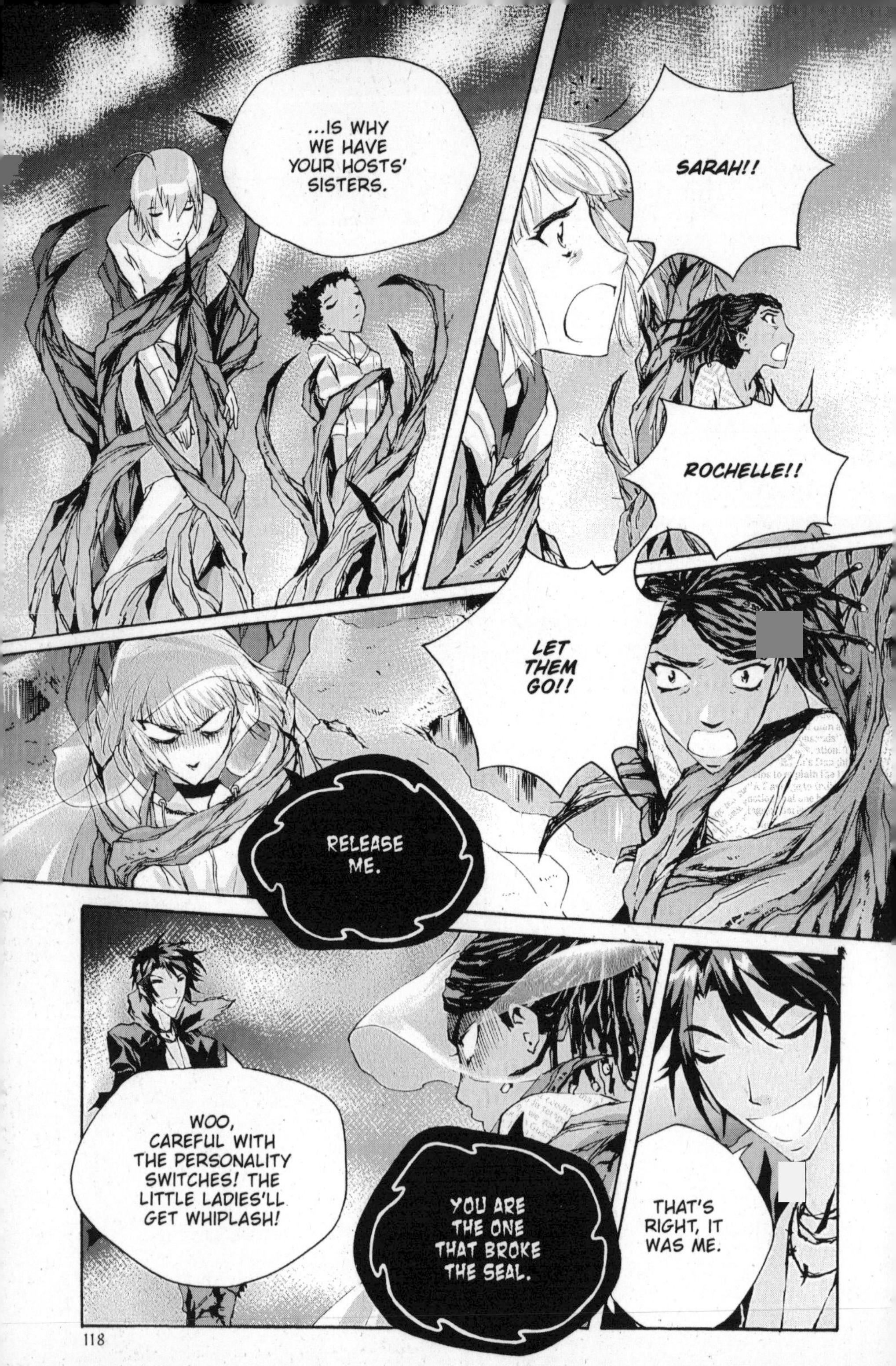
...IS WHY WE HAVE YOUR HOSTS' SISTERS.
SARAH!!
ROCHELLE!!
LET THEM GO!!
RELEASE ME.
WOO, CAREFUL WITH THE PERSONALITY SWITCHES! THE LITTLE LADIES'LL GET WHIPLASH!
YOU ARE THE ONE THAT BROKE THE SEAL.
THAT'S RIGHT, IT WAS ME.

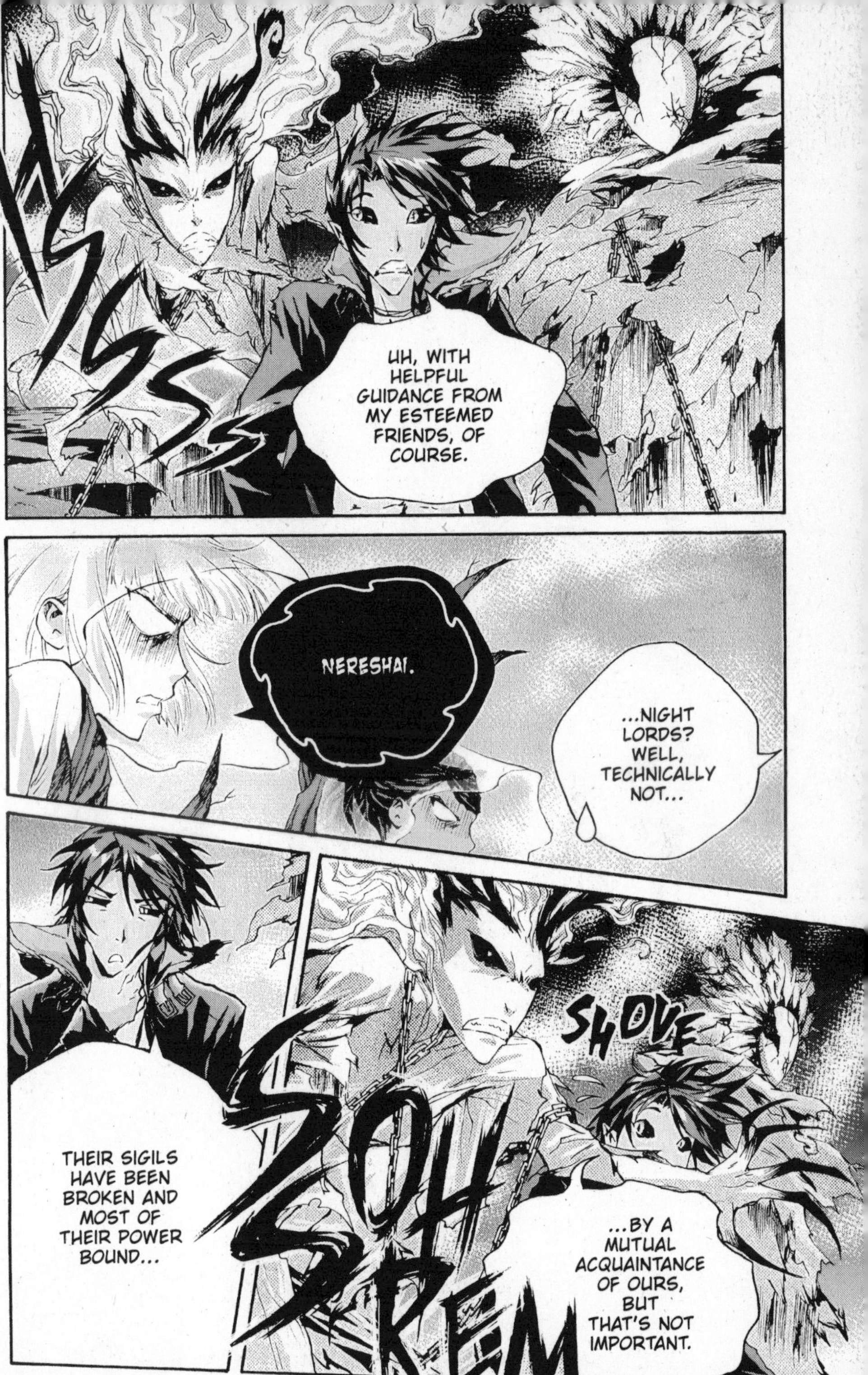
HSSSS
UH, WITH HELPFUL GUIDANCE FROM MY ESTEEMED FRIENDS, OF COURSE.
NERESHAI.
...NIGHT LORDS? WELL, TECHNICALLY NOT...
THEIR SIGILS HAVE BEEN BROKEN AND MOST OF THEIR POWER BOUND...
SHOVE
...BY A MUTUAL ACQUAINTANCE OF OURS, BUT THAT'S NOT IMPORTANT.

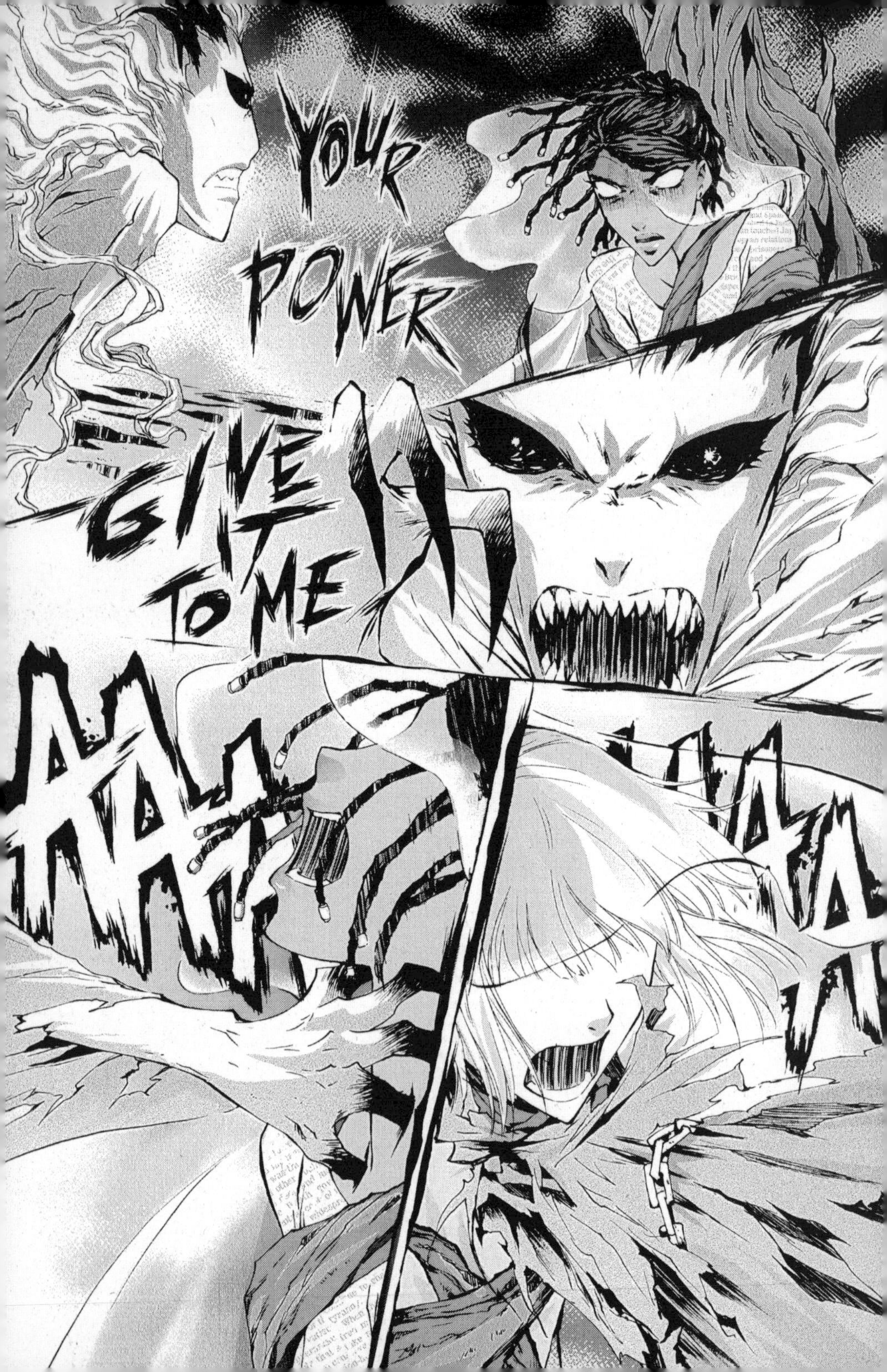
YOUR POWER
GIVE IT TO ME
AAAAAAAA

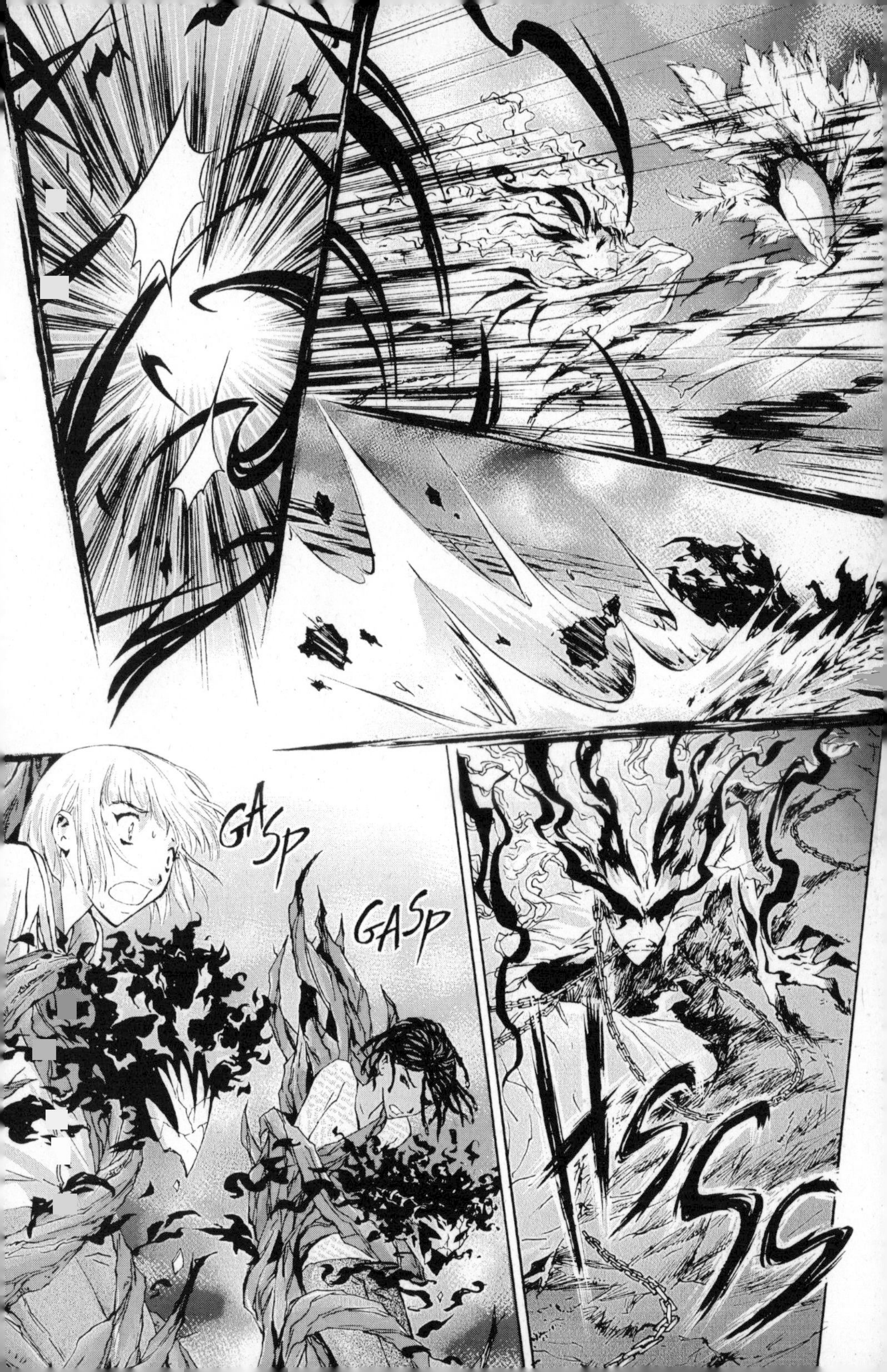
GASP
GASP
HSSS

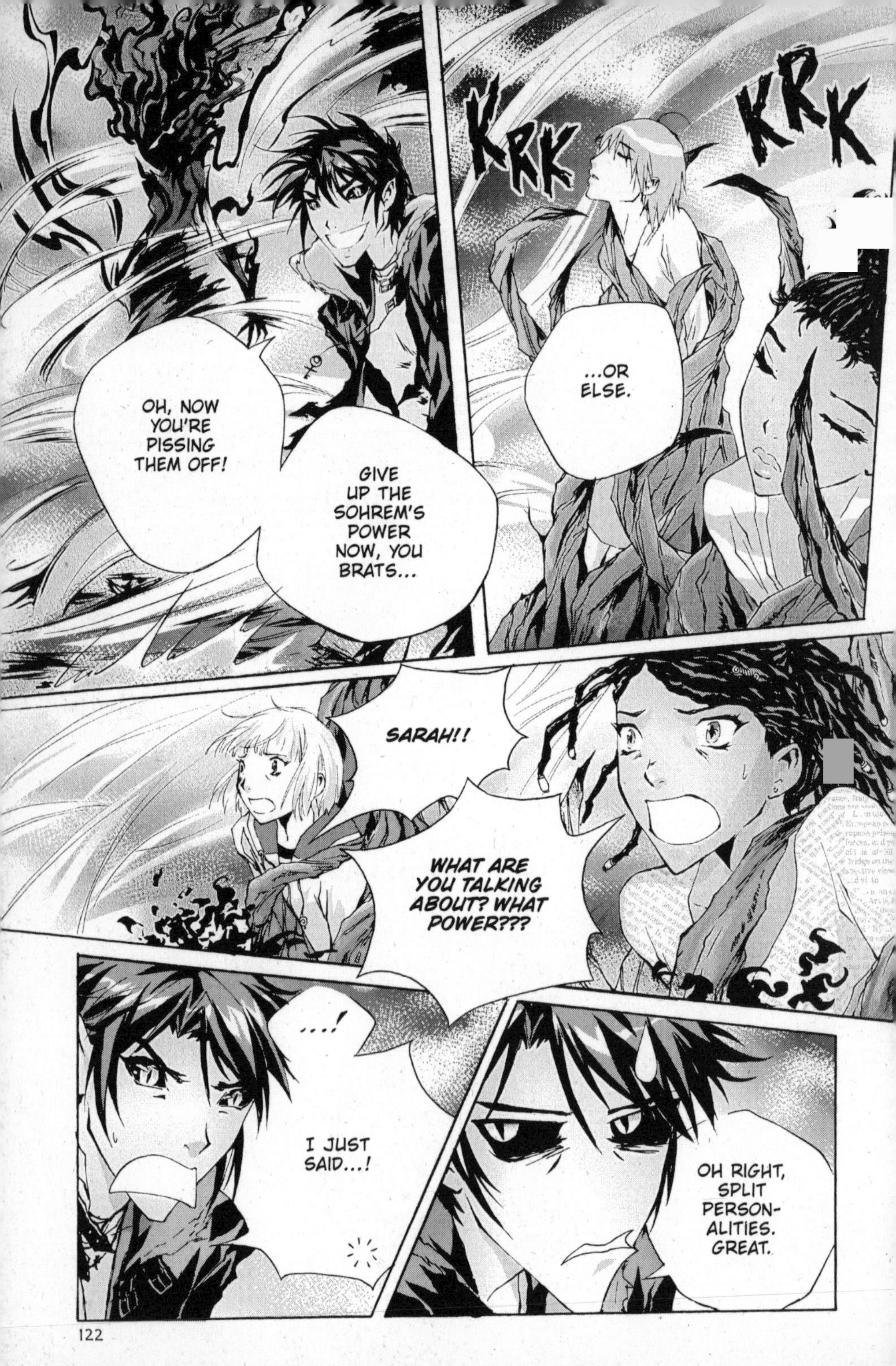
OH, NOW YOU'RE PISSING THEM OFF!
GIVE UP THE SOHREM'S POWER NOW, YOU BRATS...
KRK
KRK
...OR ELSE.
SARAH!!
WHAT ARE YOU TALKING ABOUT? WHAT POWER???
...!
I JUST SAID...!
OH RIGHT, SPLIT PERSON-ALITIES. GREAT.

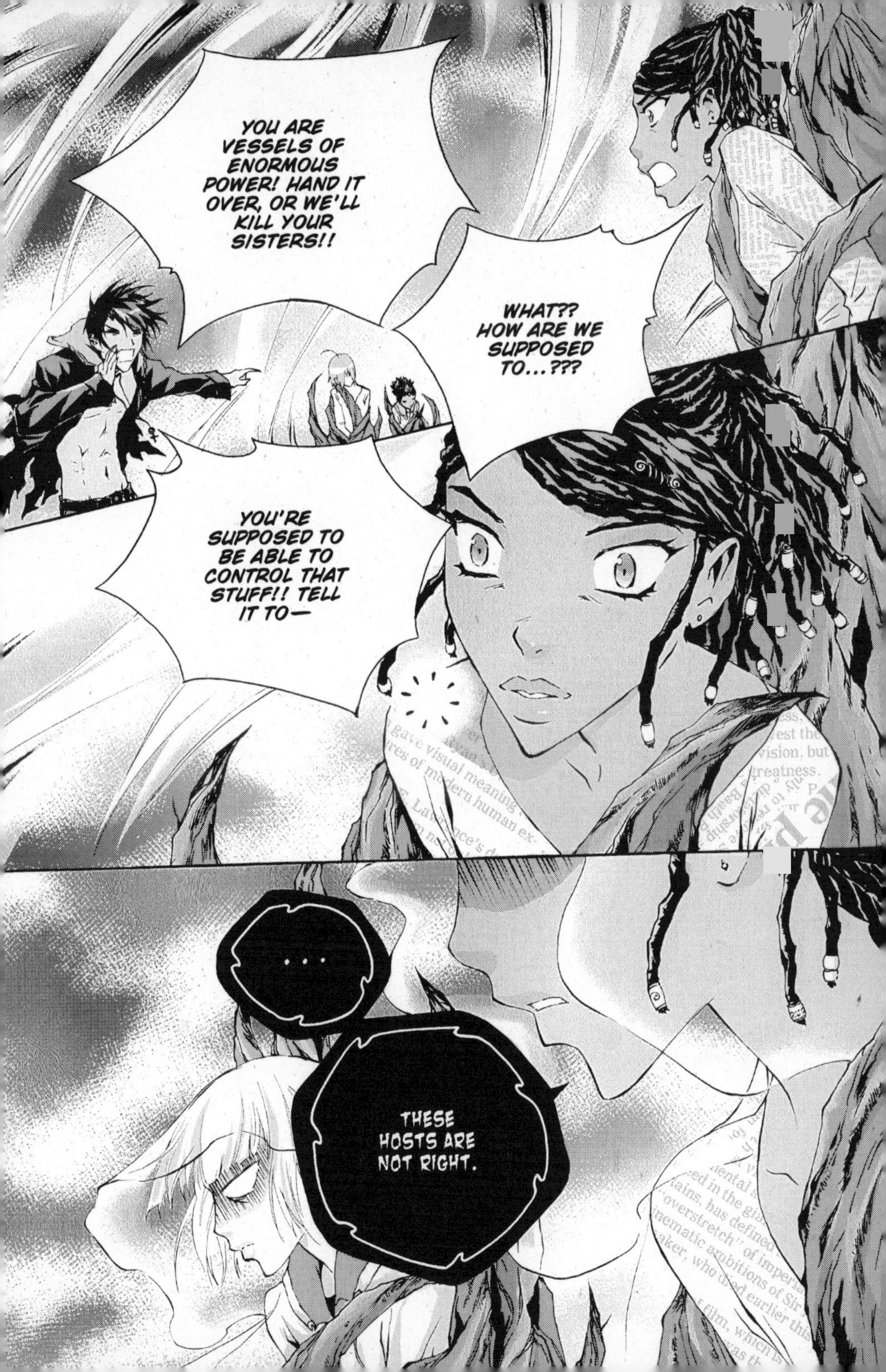
YOU ARE VESSELS OF ENORMOUS POWER! HAND IT OVER, OR WE'LL KILL YOUR SISTERS!!
WHAT?? HOW ARE WE SUPPOSED TO...???
YOU'RE SUPPOSED TO BE ABLE TO CONTROL THAT STUFF!! TELL IT TO—
...
THESE HOSTS ARE NOT RIGHT.

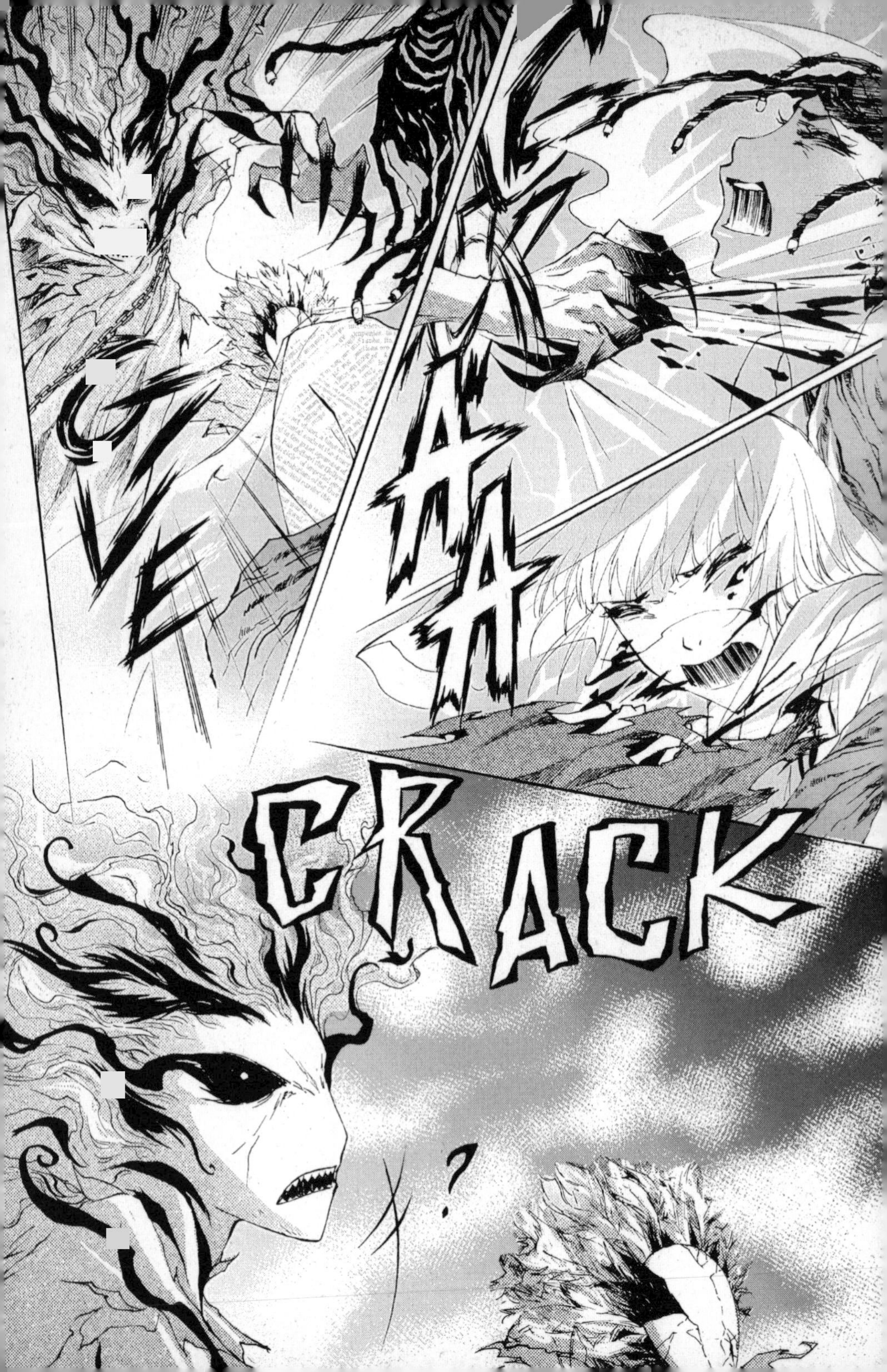
AAA
CRACK
?

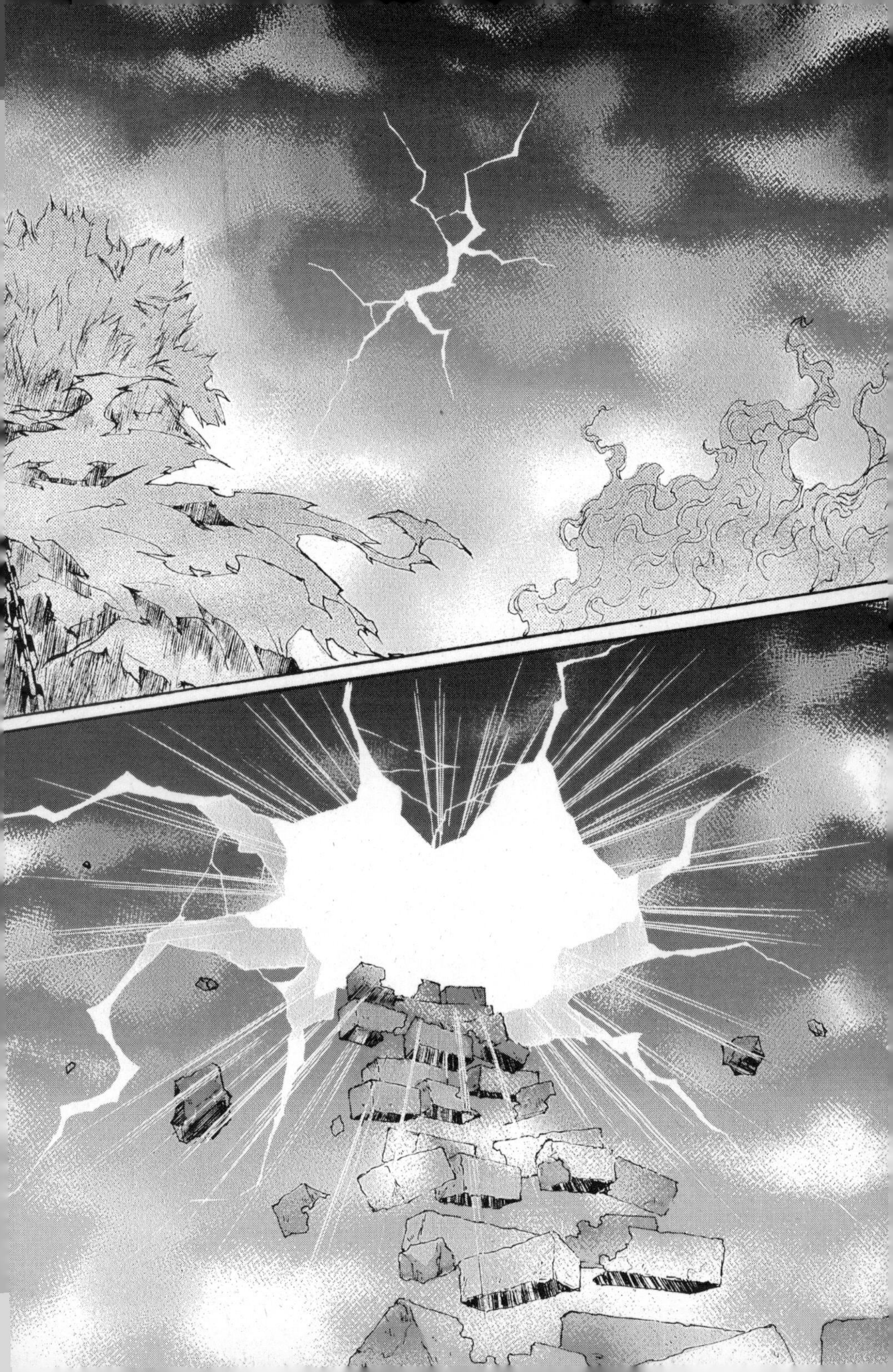

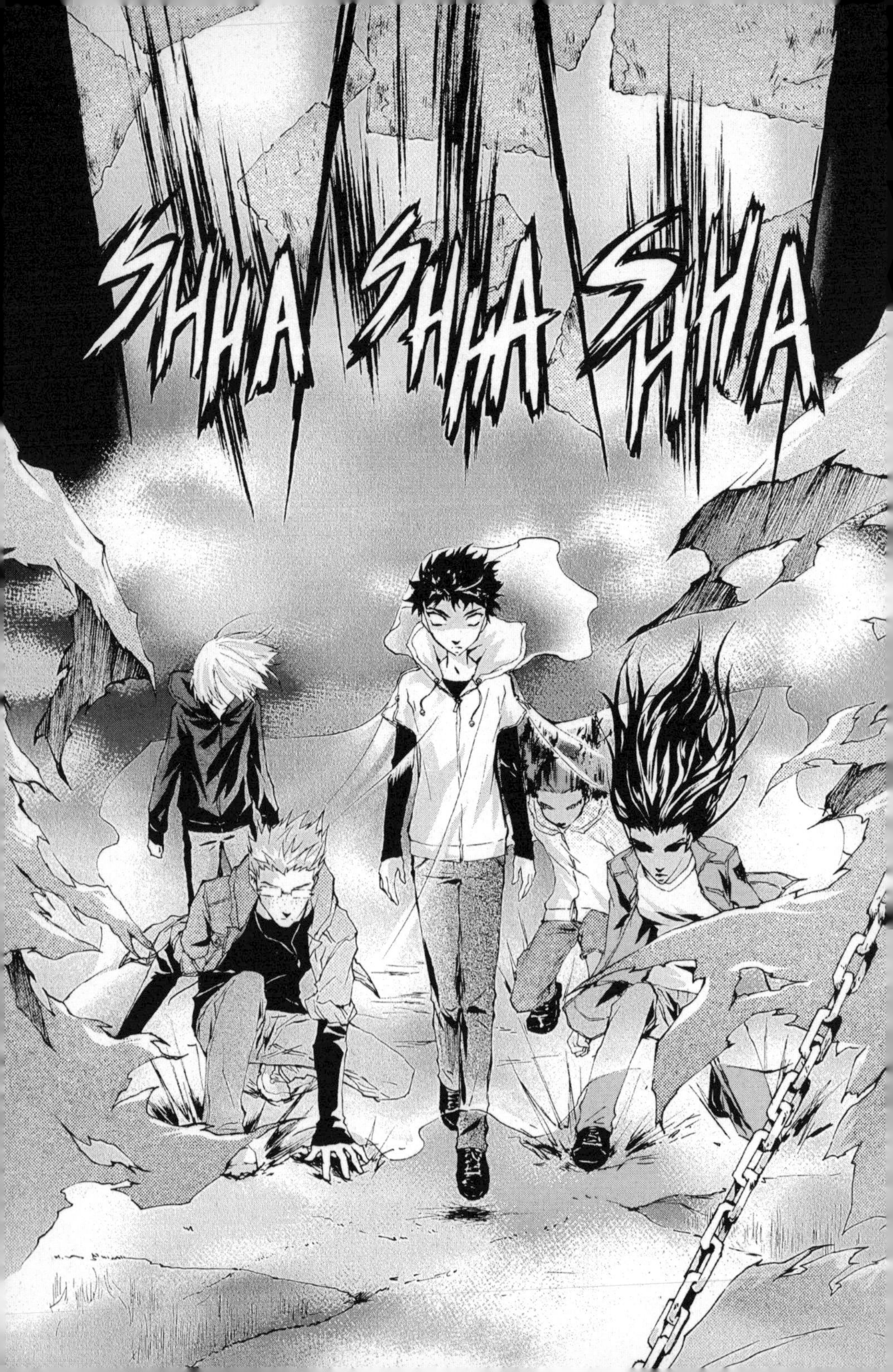
SHHA SHHA SHHA

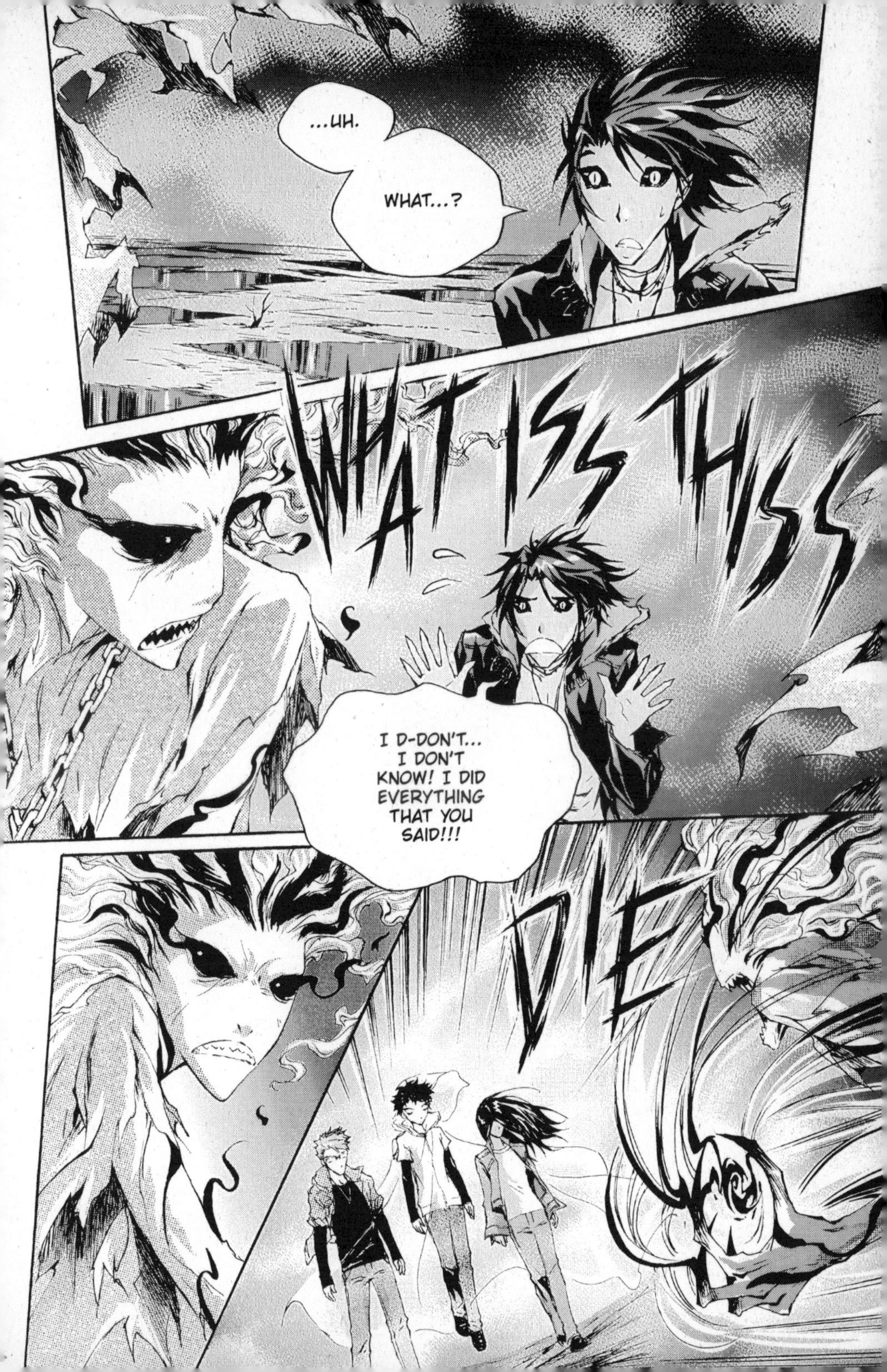
...UH.
WHAT...?
WHAT IS THIS
I D-DON'T... I DON'T KNOW! I DID EVERYTHING THAT YOU SAID!!!
DIE

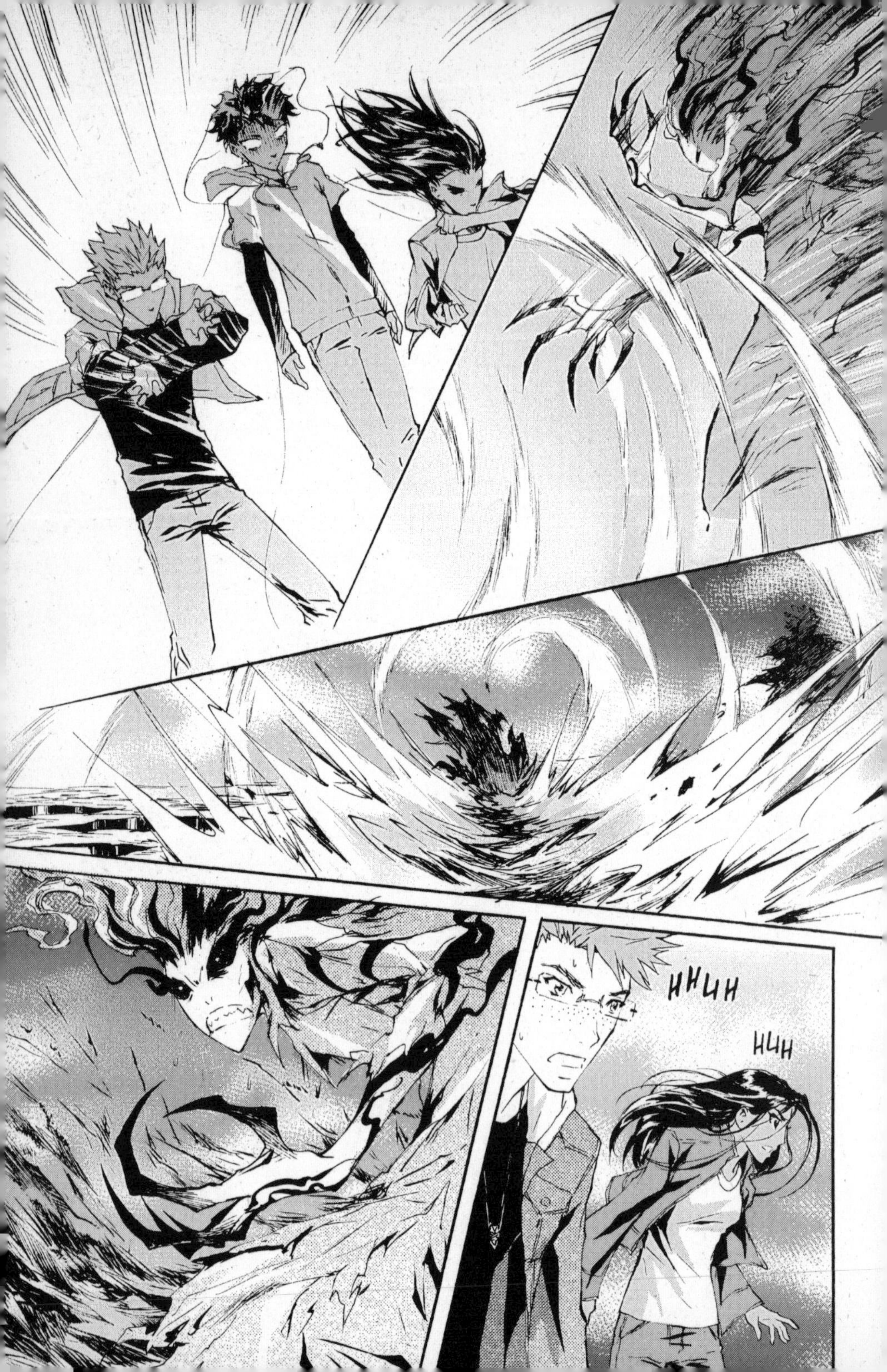
HHUH
HUH

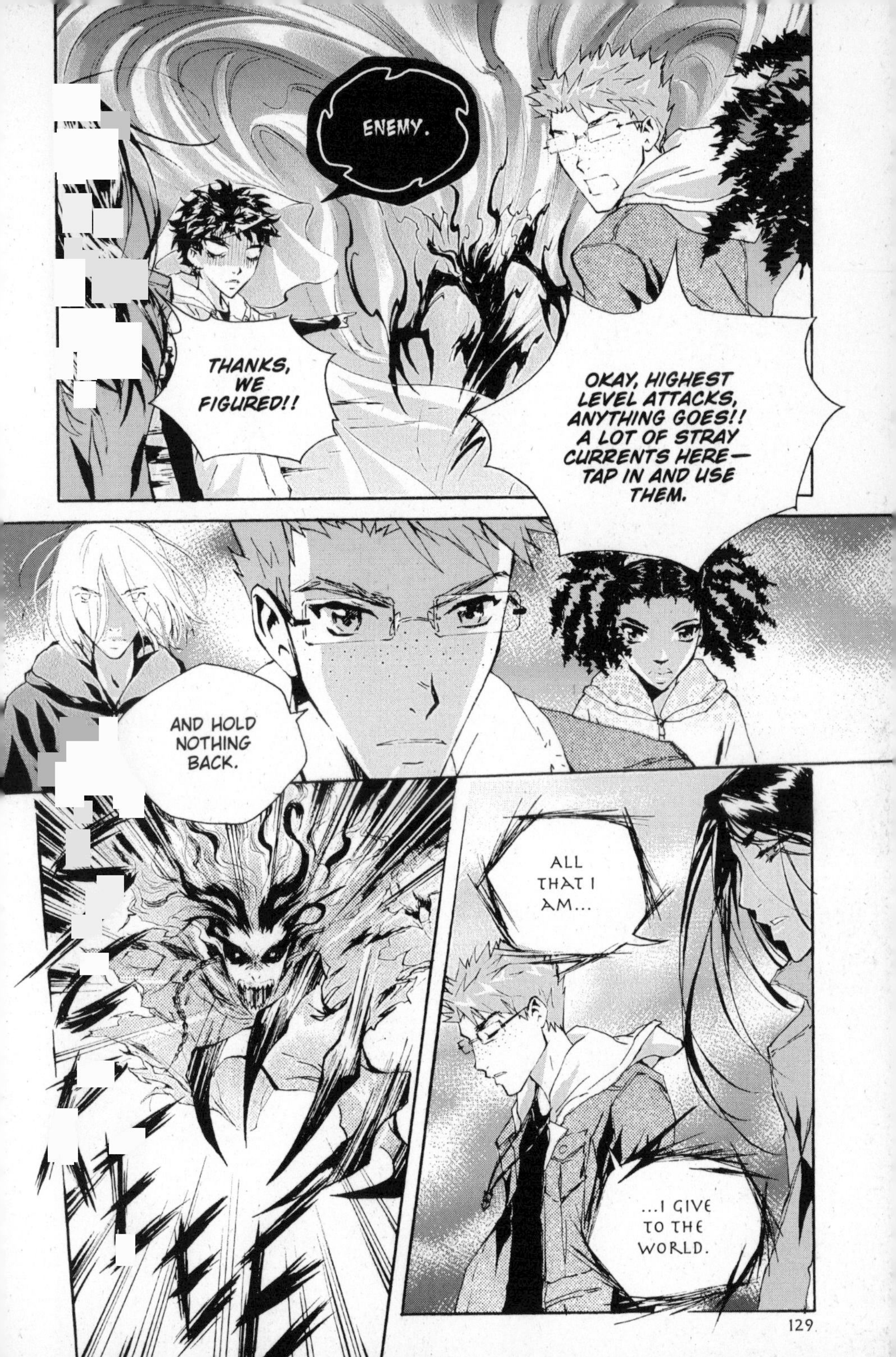
ENEMY.
THANKS, WE FIGURED!!
OKAY, HIGHEST LEVEL ATTACKS, ANYTHING GOES!! A LOT OF STRAY CURRENTS HERE—TAP IN AND USE THEM.
AND HOLD NOTHING BACK.
ALL THAT I AM...
...I GIVE TO THE WORLD.

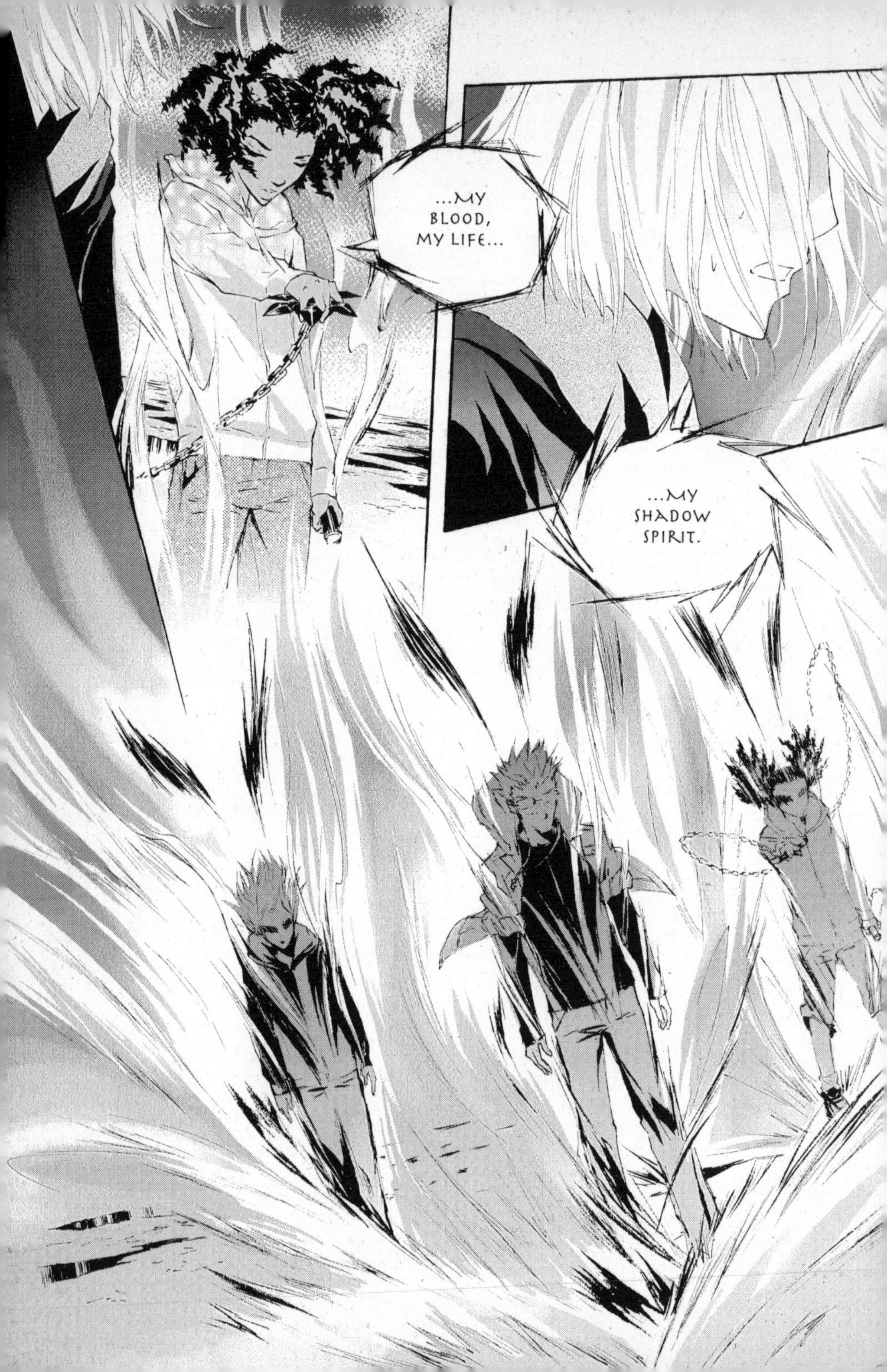
...MY BLOOD, MY LIFE...
...MY SHADOW SPIRIT.

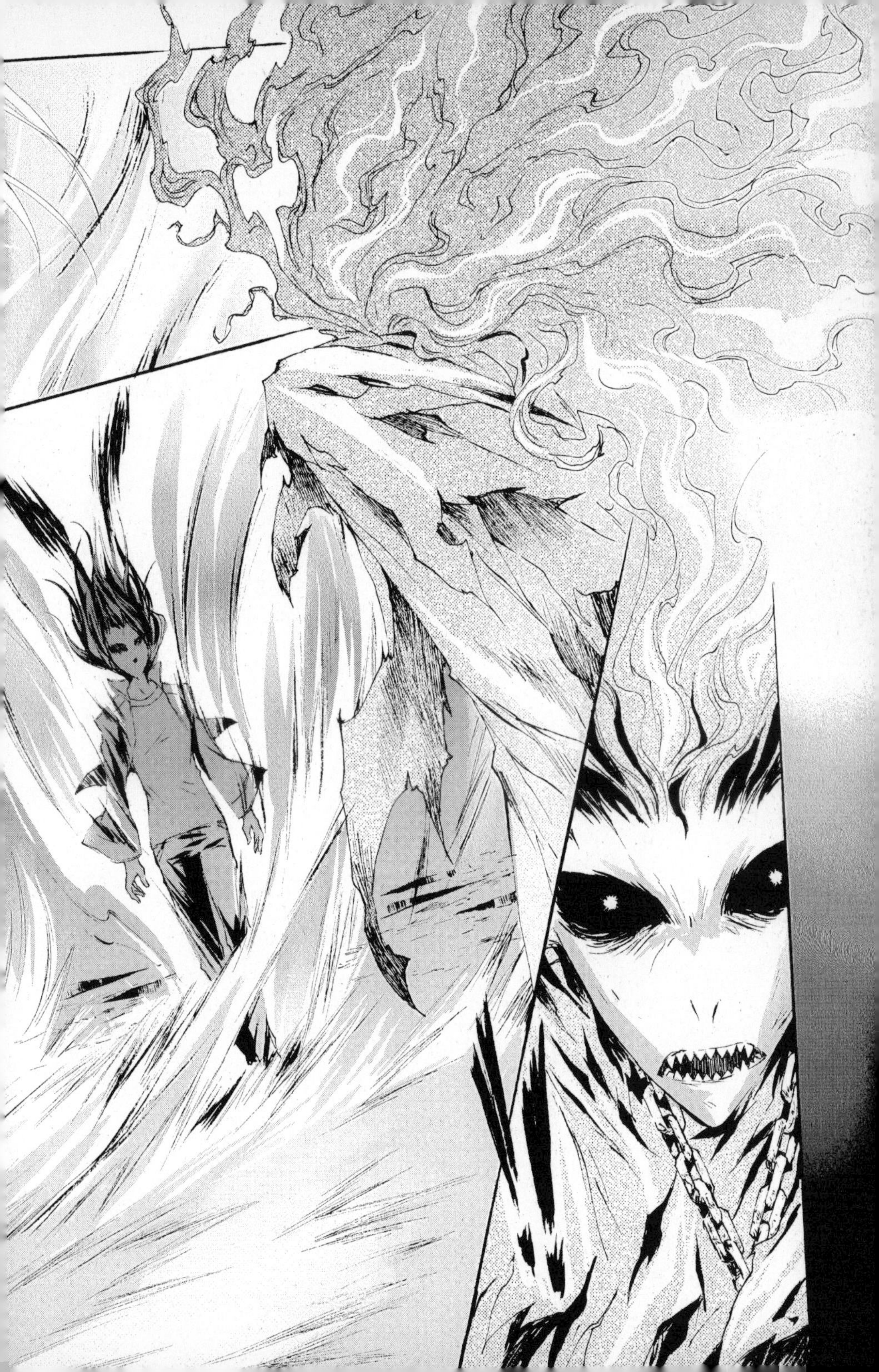

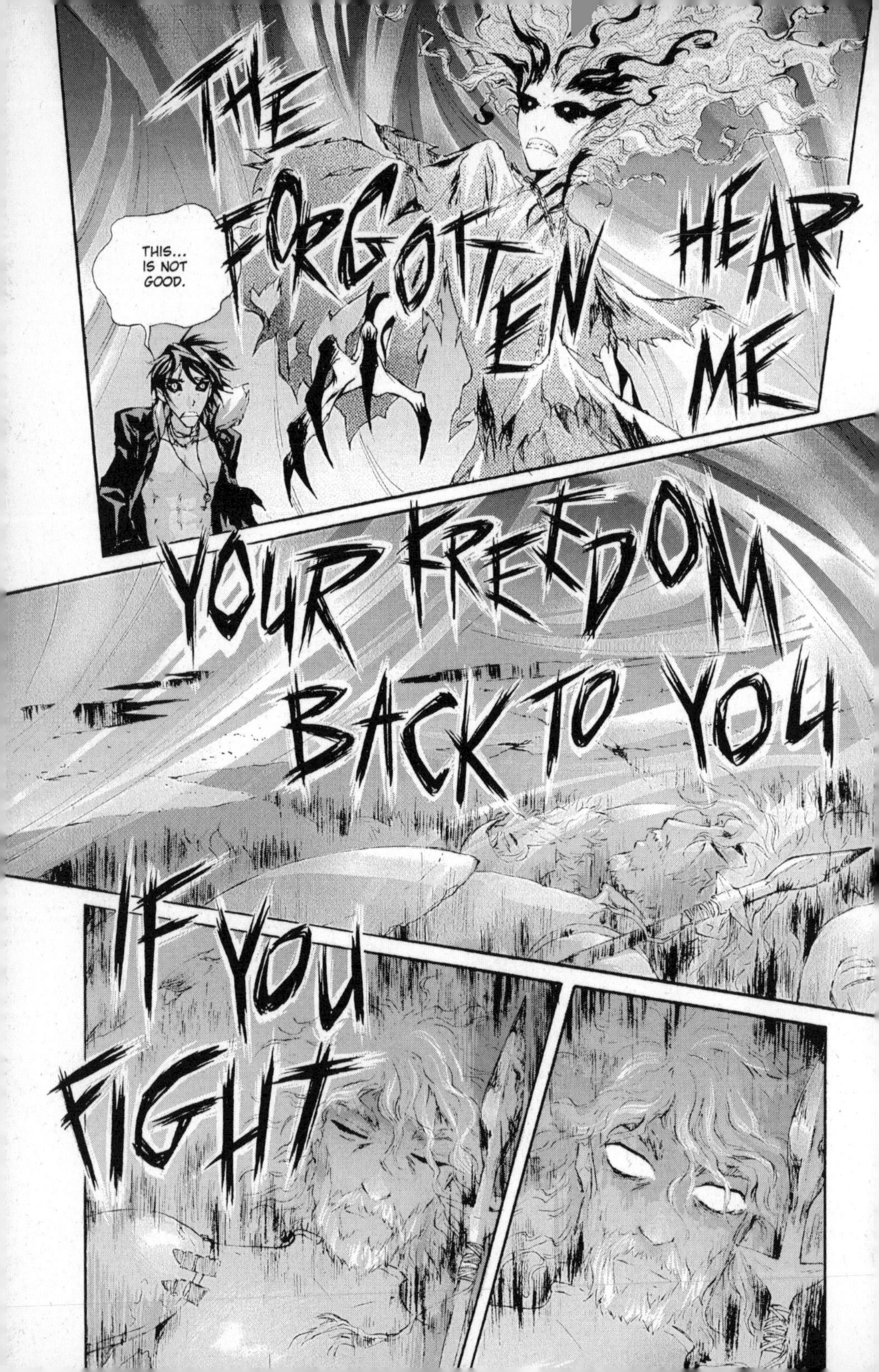
THE FORGOTTEN HEAR ME
THIS... IS NOT GOOD.
YOUR FREEDOM BACK TO YOU
IF YOU FIGHT

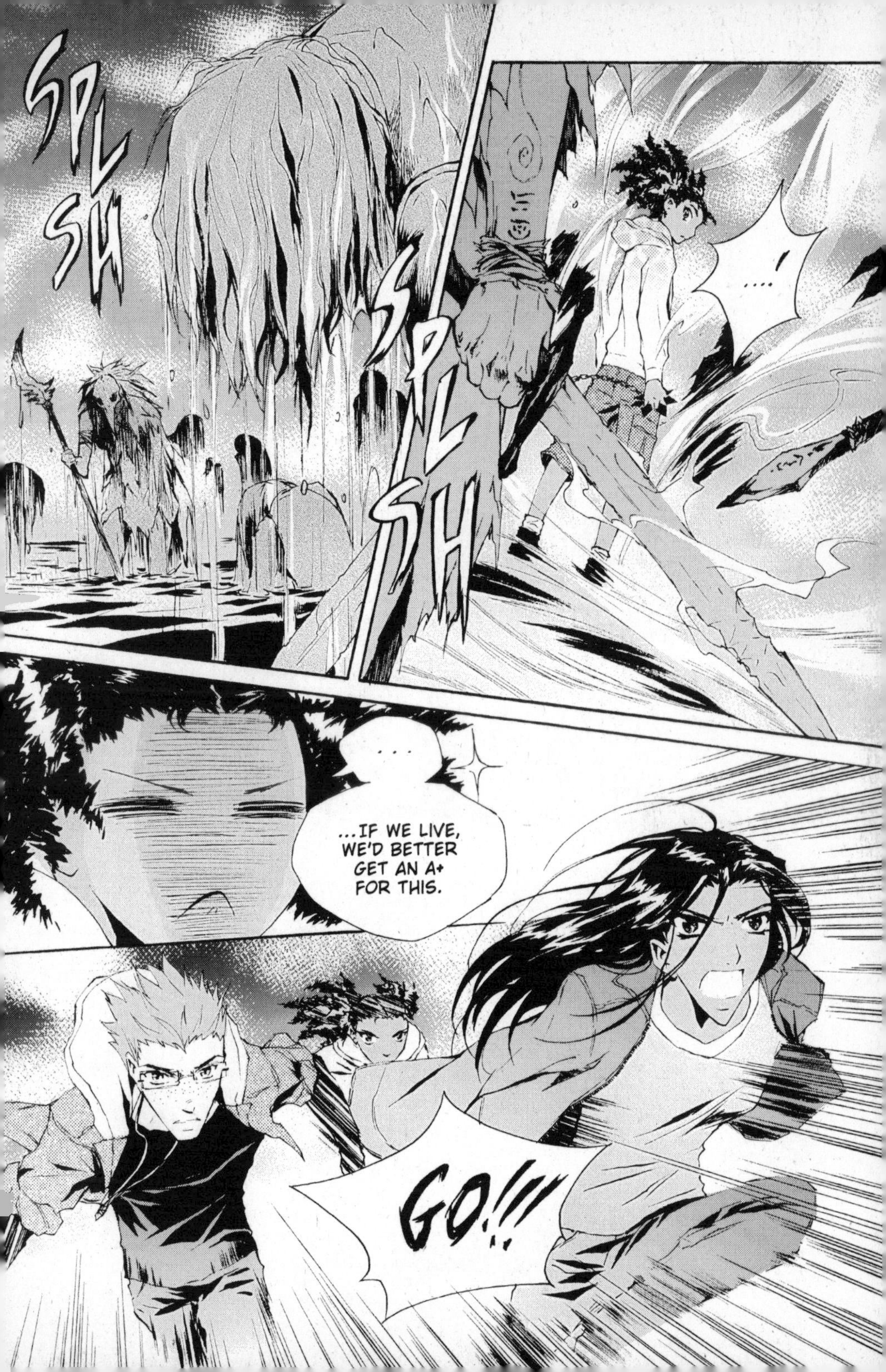
SPLSH
SPLSH
....!
...
...IF WE LIVE, WE'D BETTER GET AN A+ FOR THIS.
GO!!!

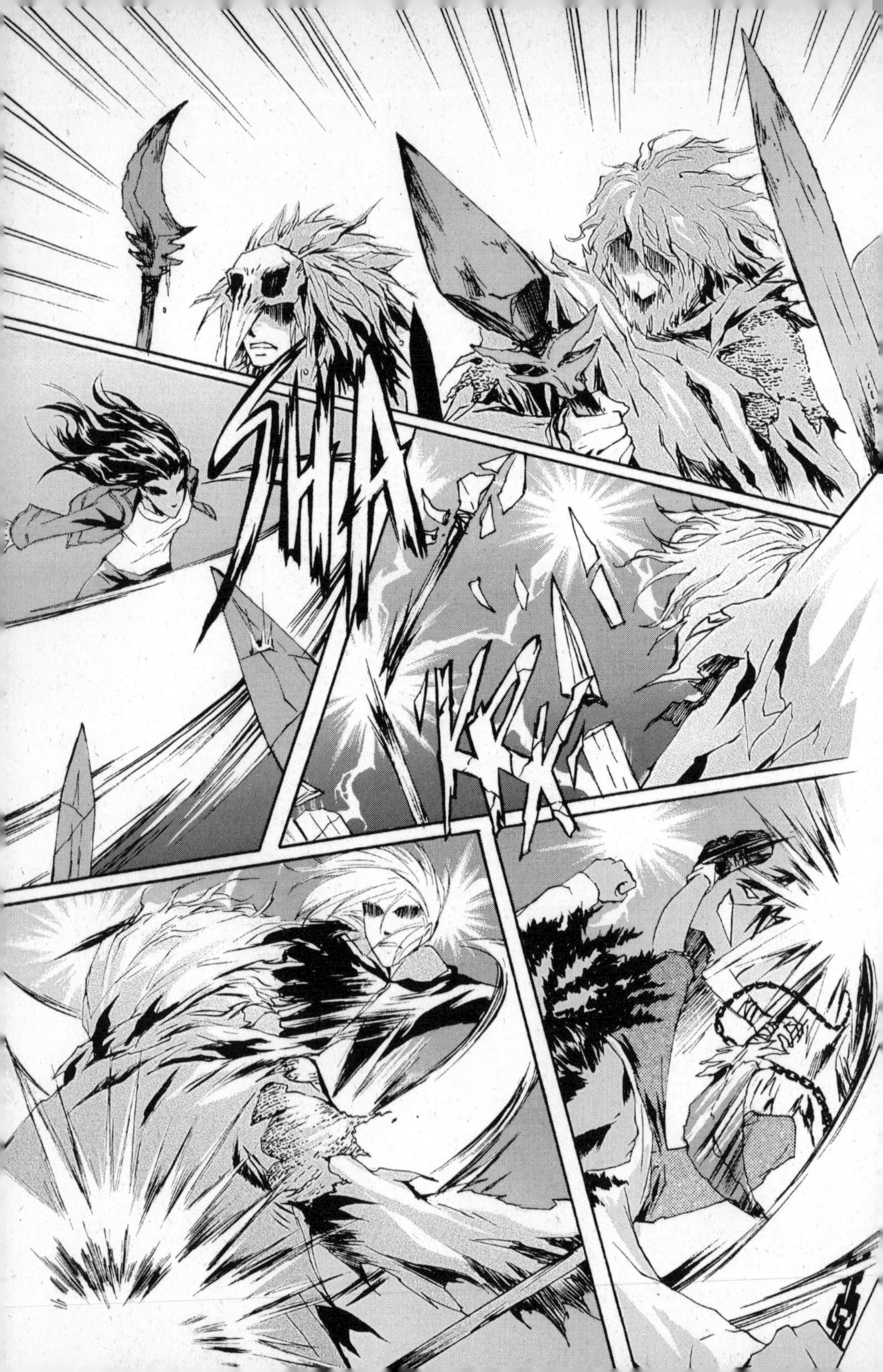
SHA
VKK

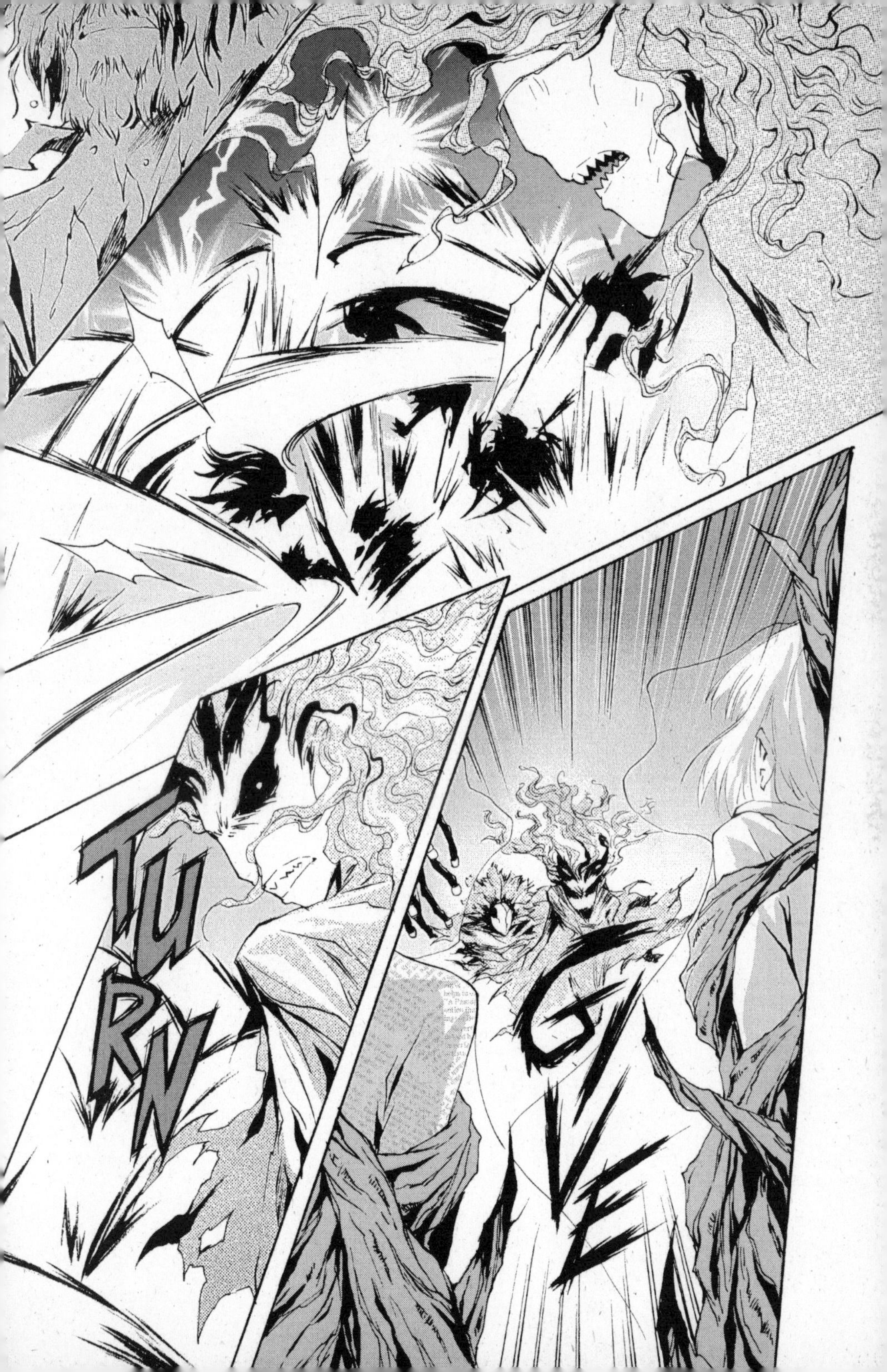
TURN
GIVE

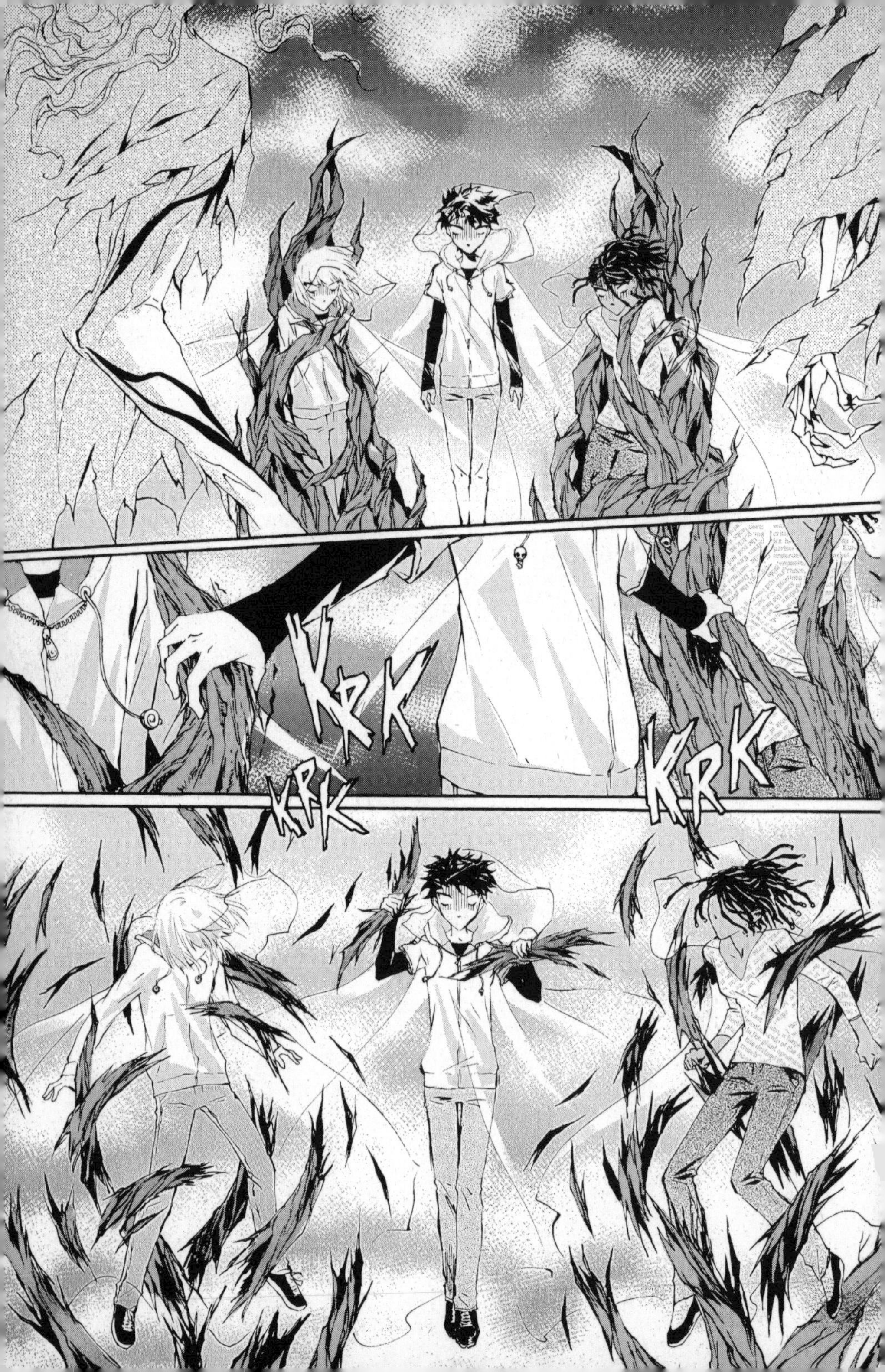
KRK
KRK
KRK

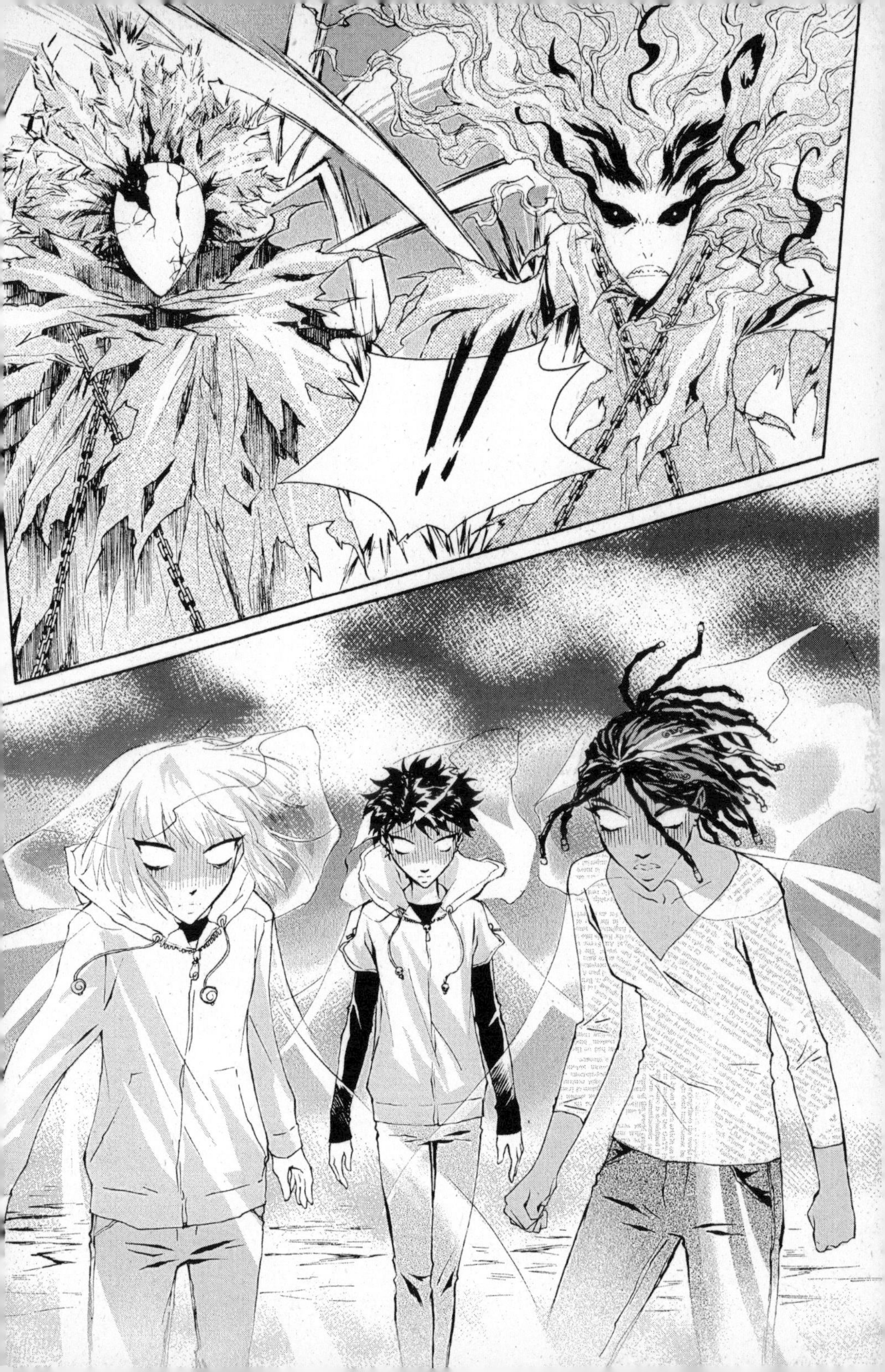

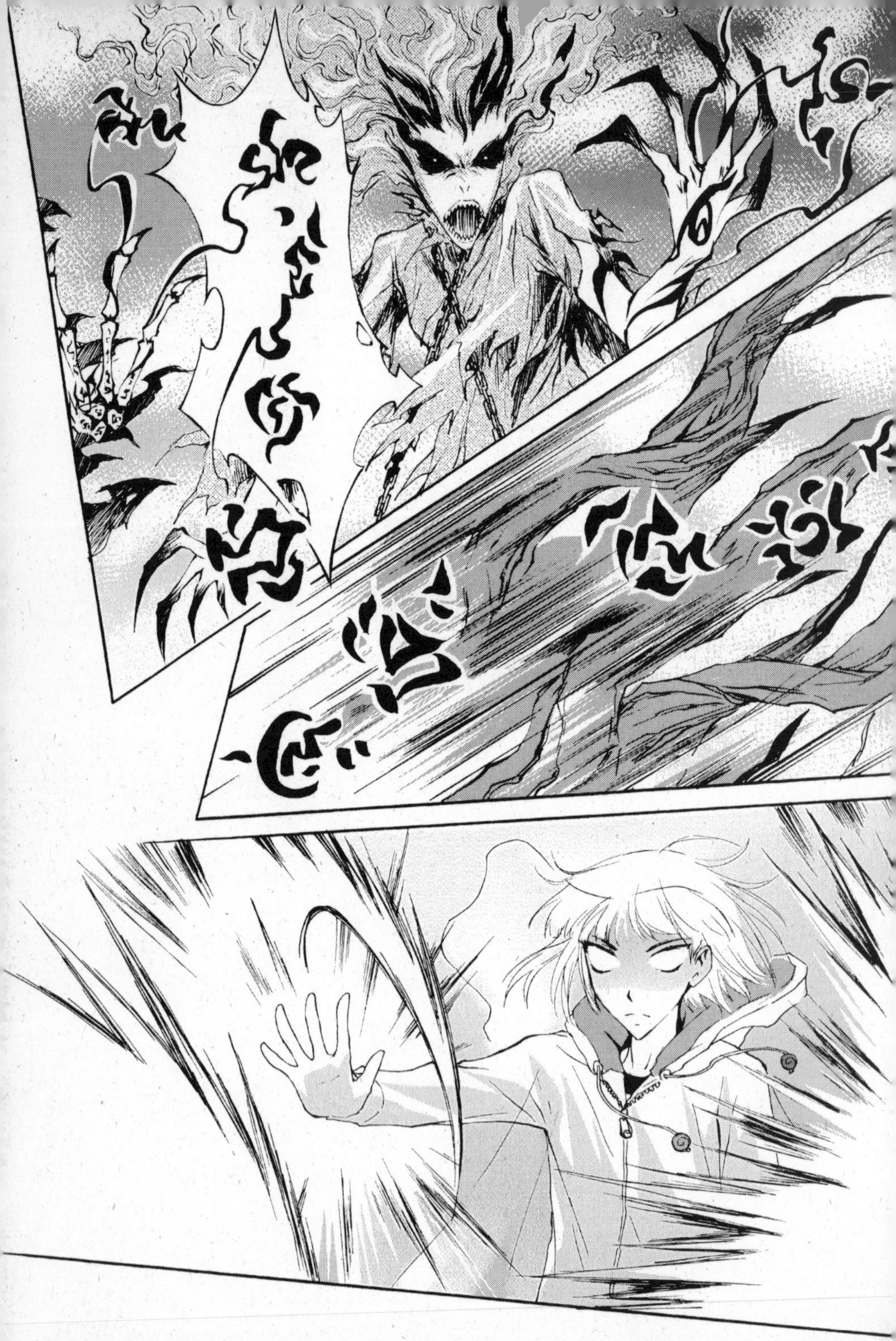

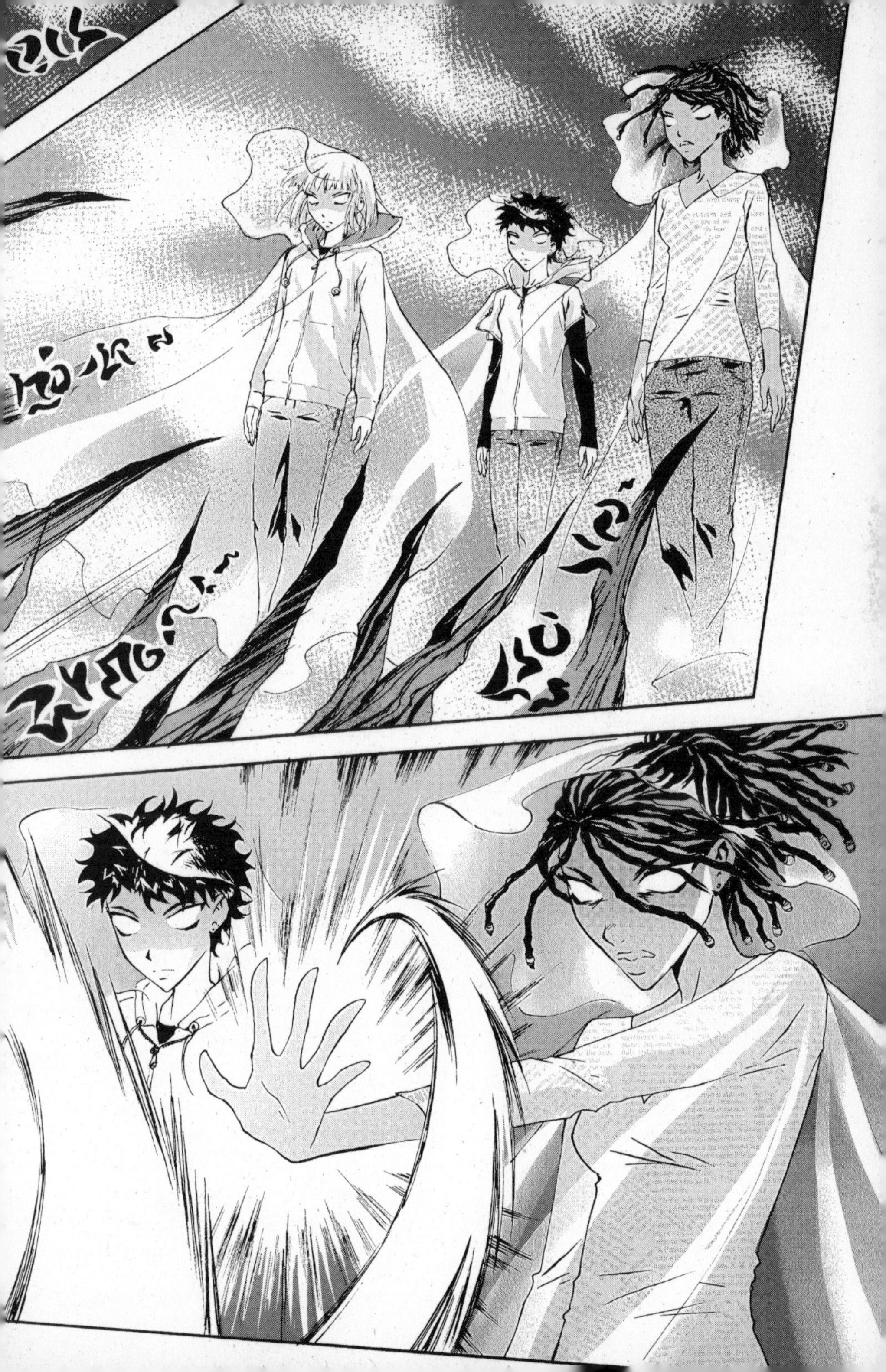

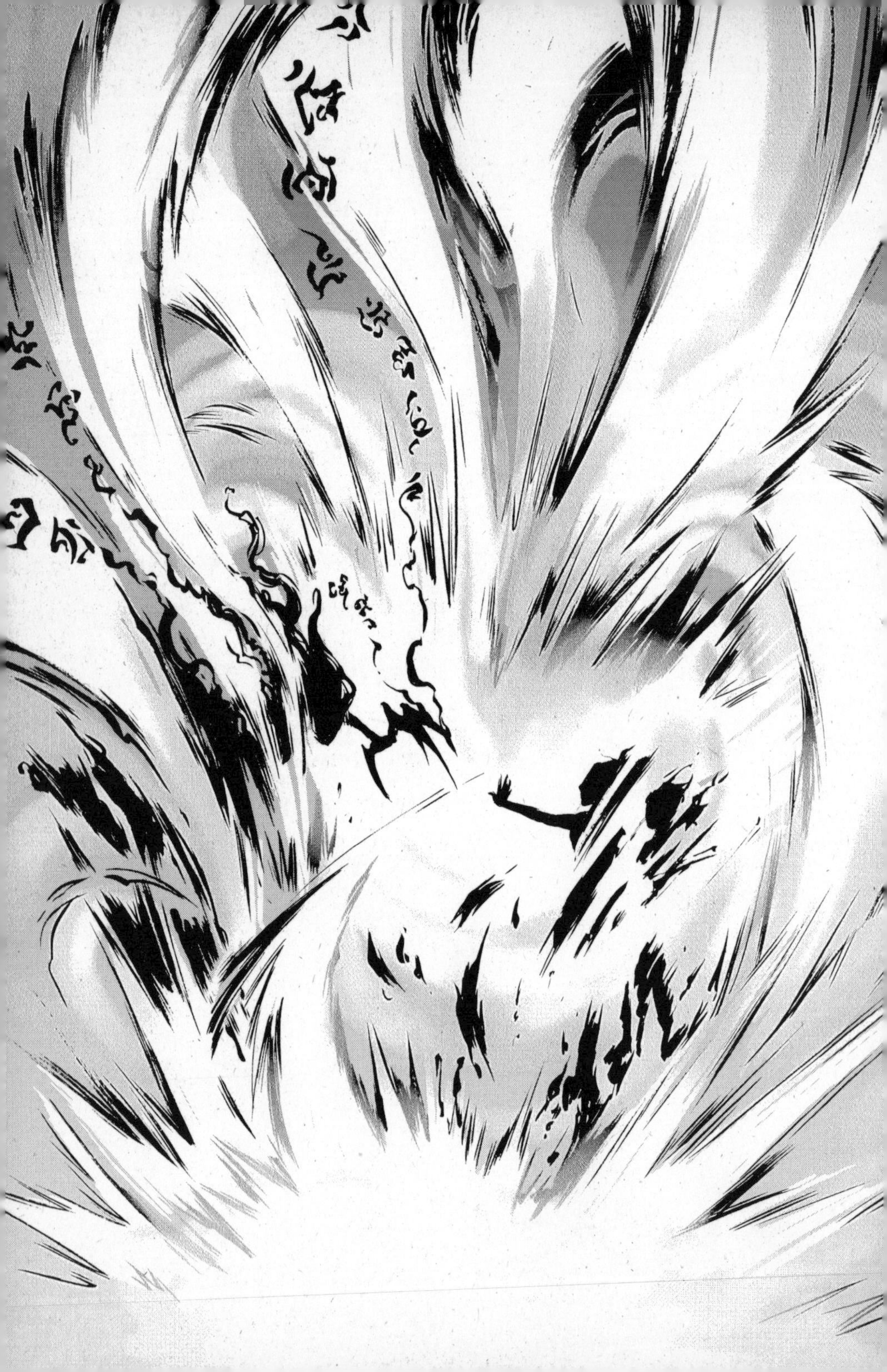

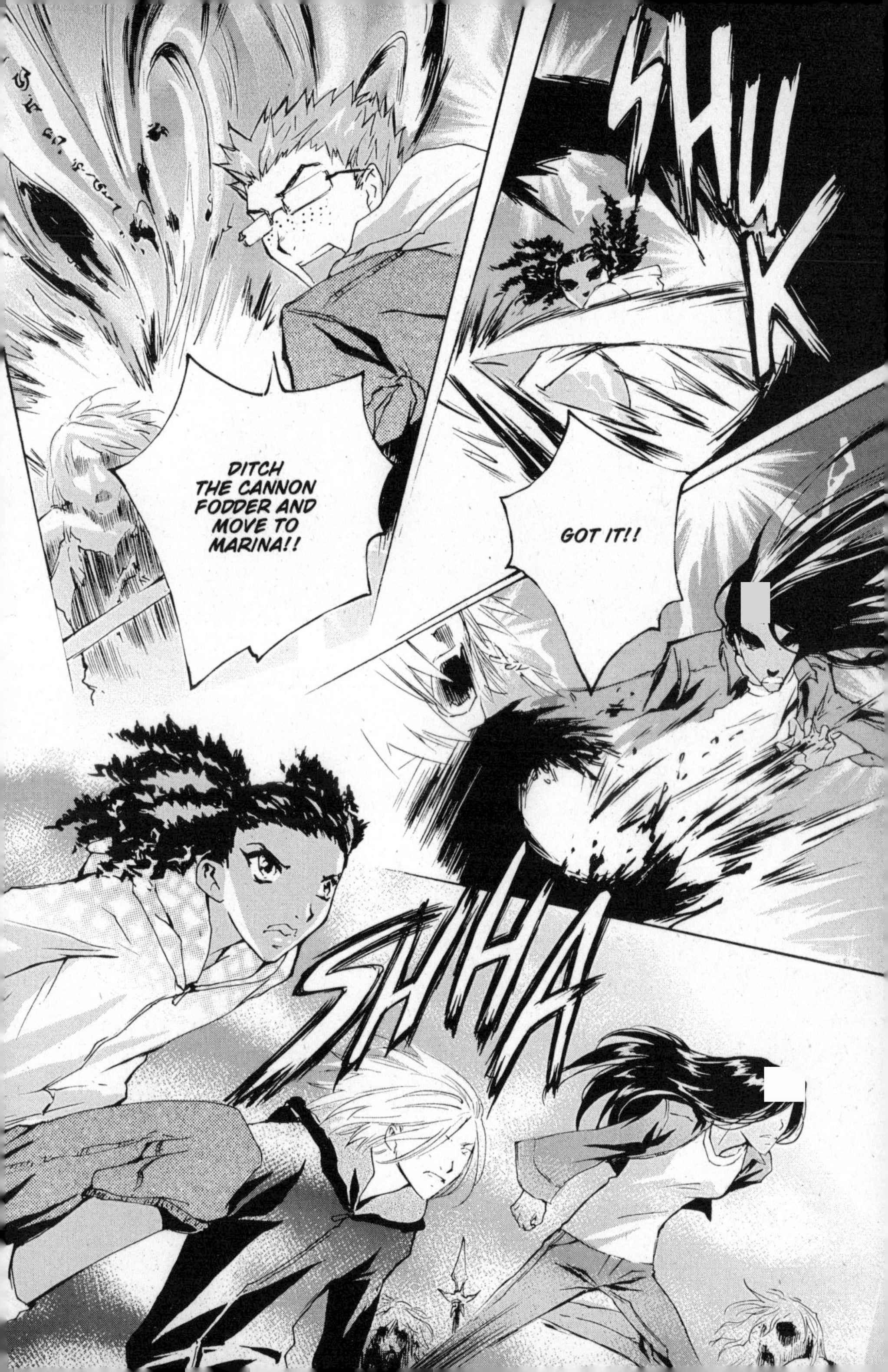
DITCH THE CANNON FODDER AND MOVE TO MARINA!!
SHUK
GOT IT!!
SHHA

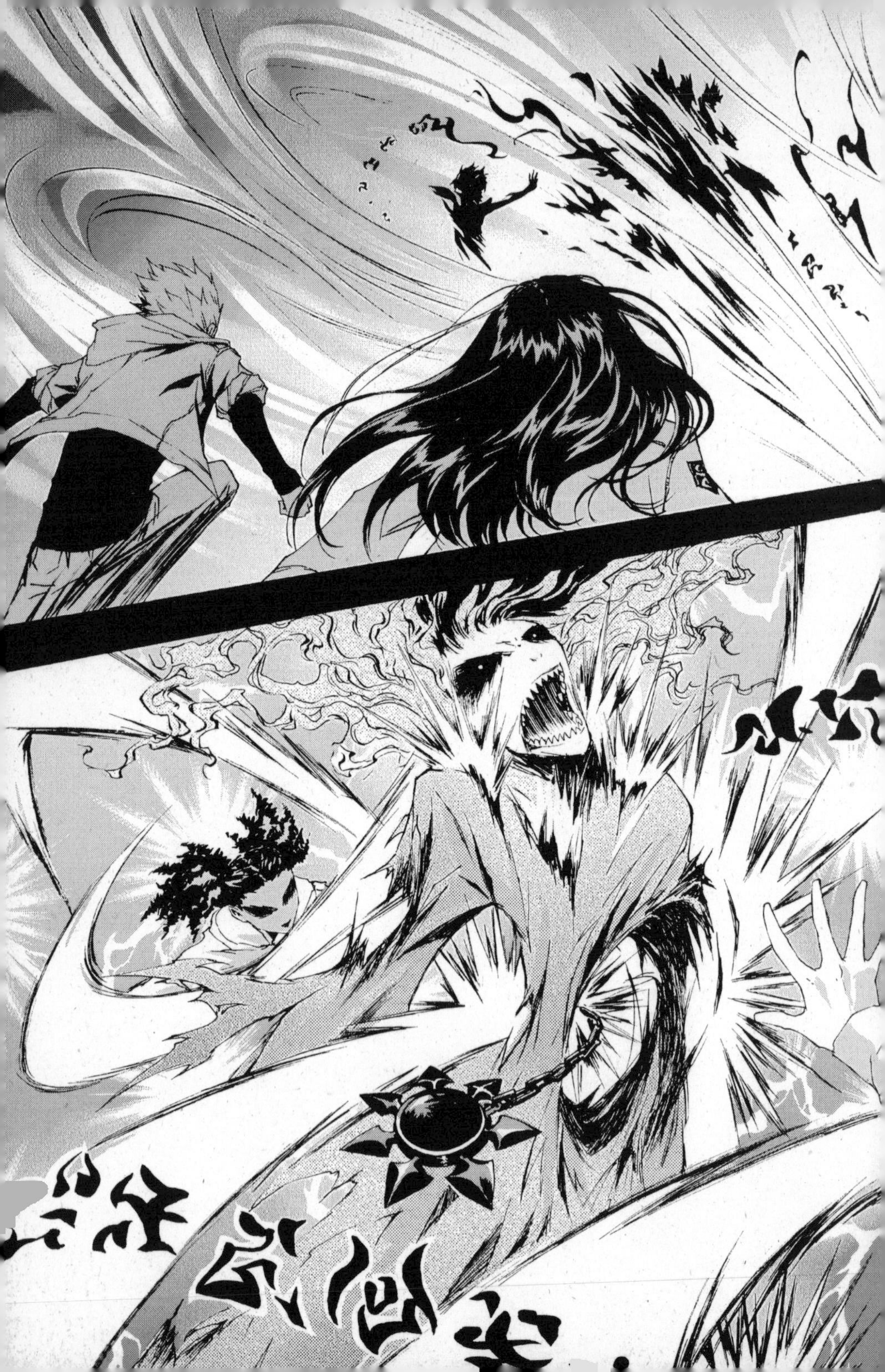

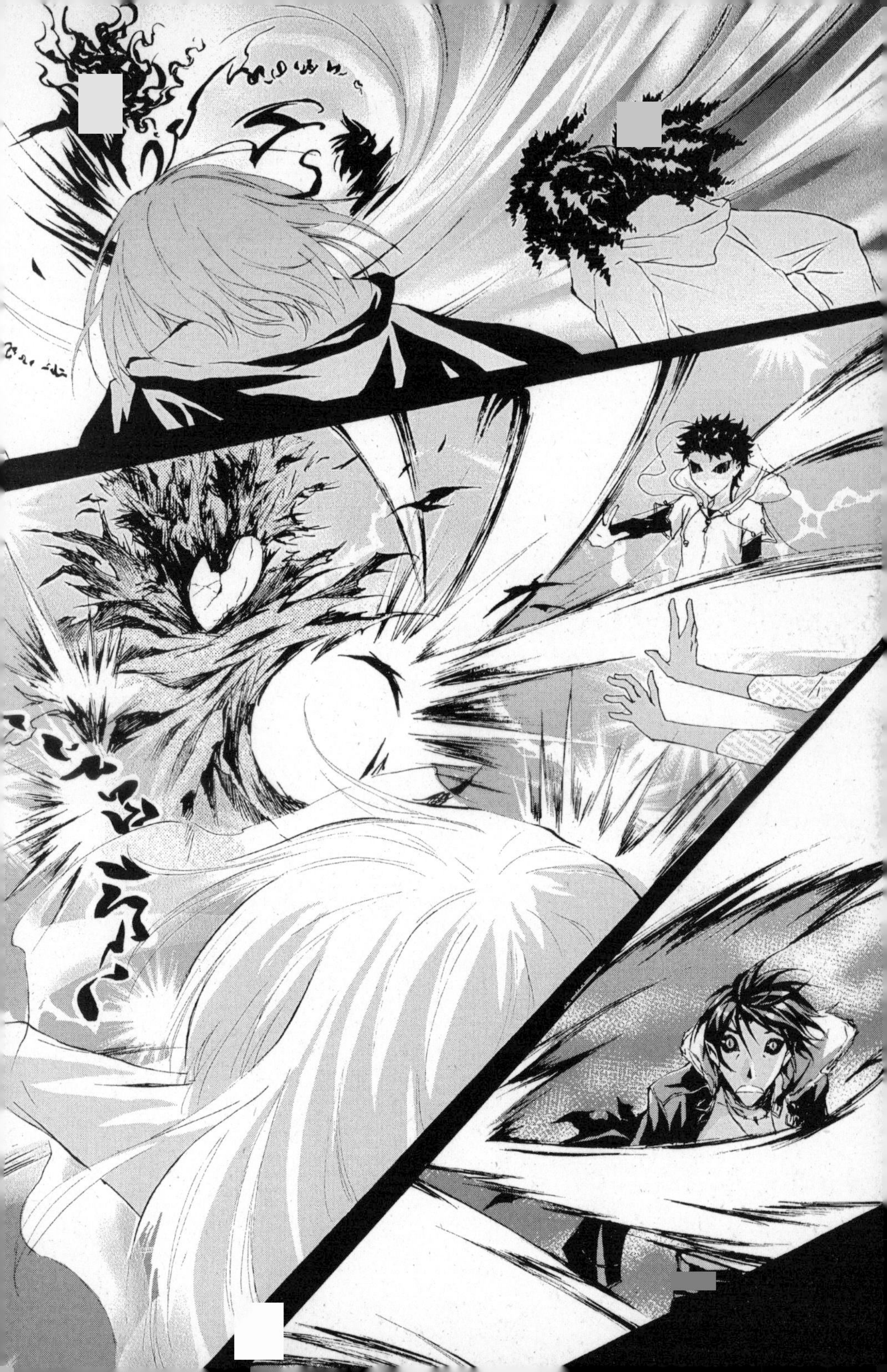

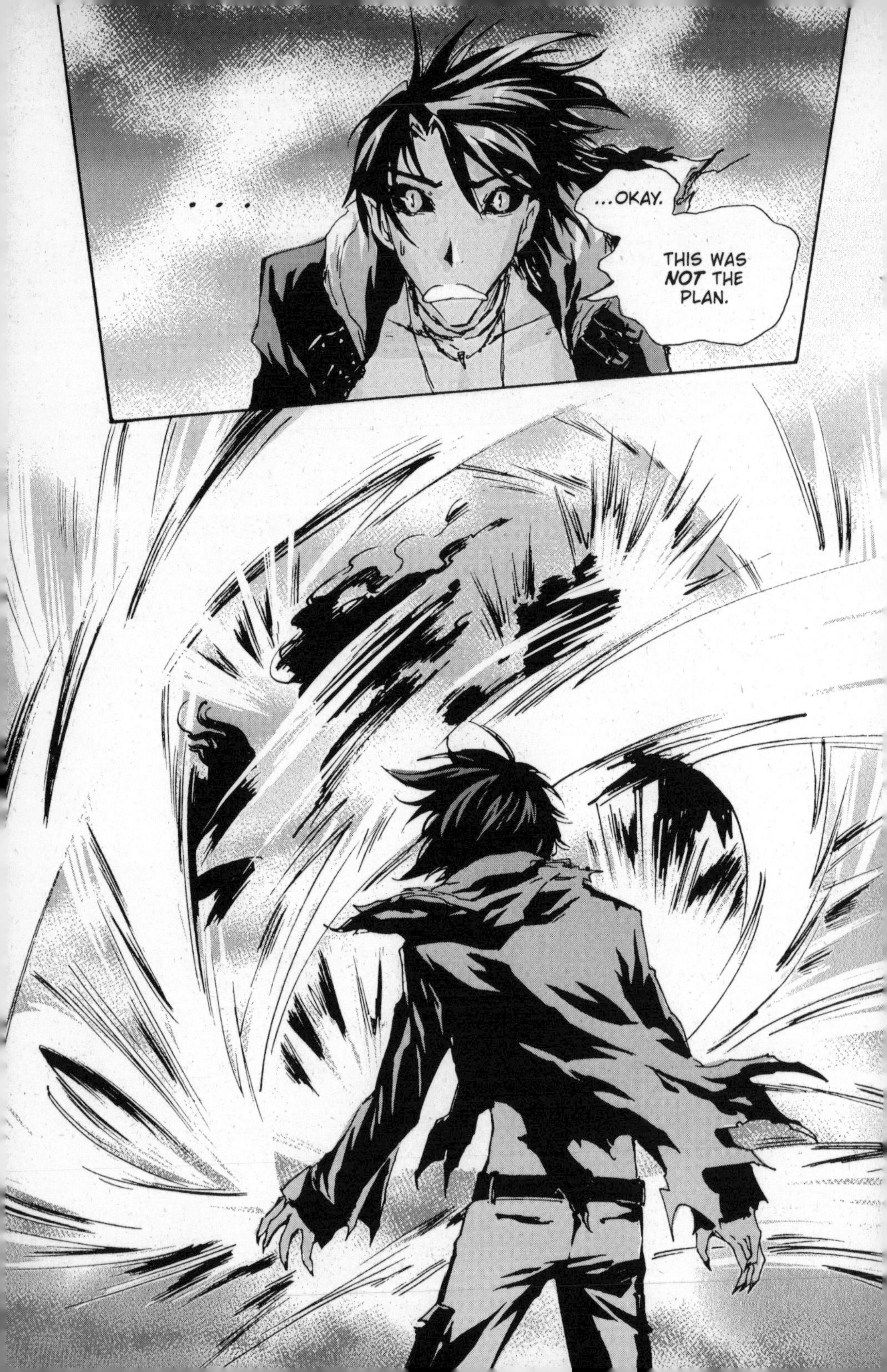
. . .
...OKAY.
THIS WAS *NOT* THE PLAN.

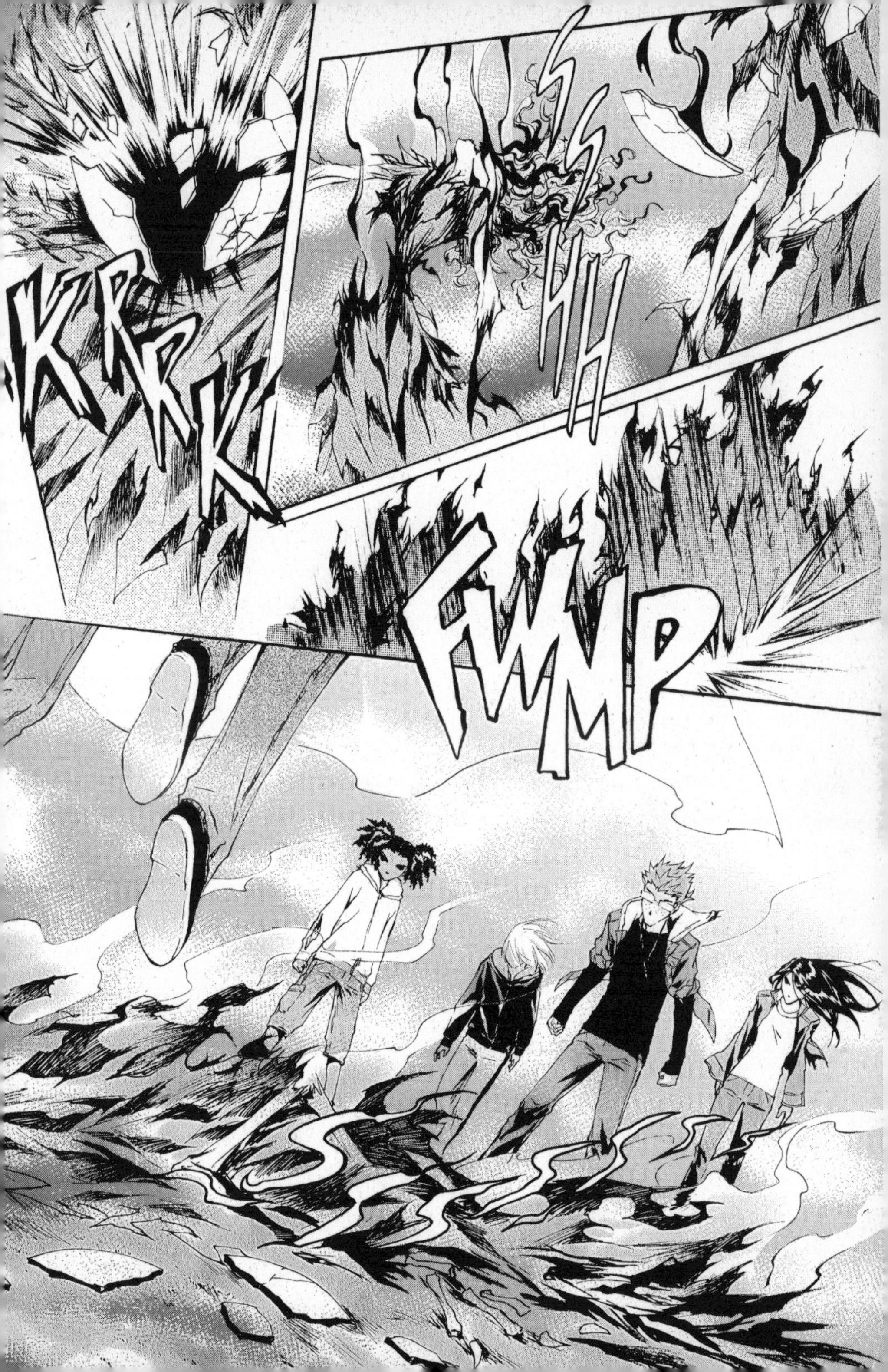
KRRK
SSHH
FWMP

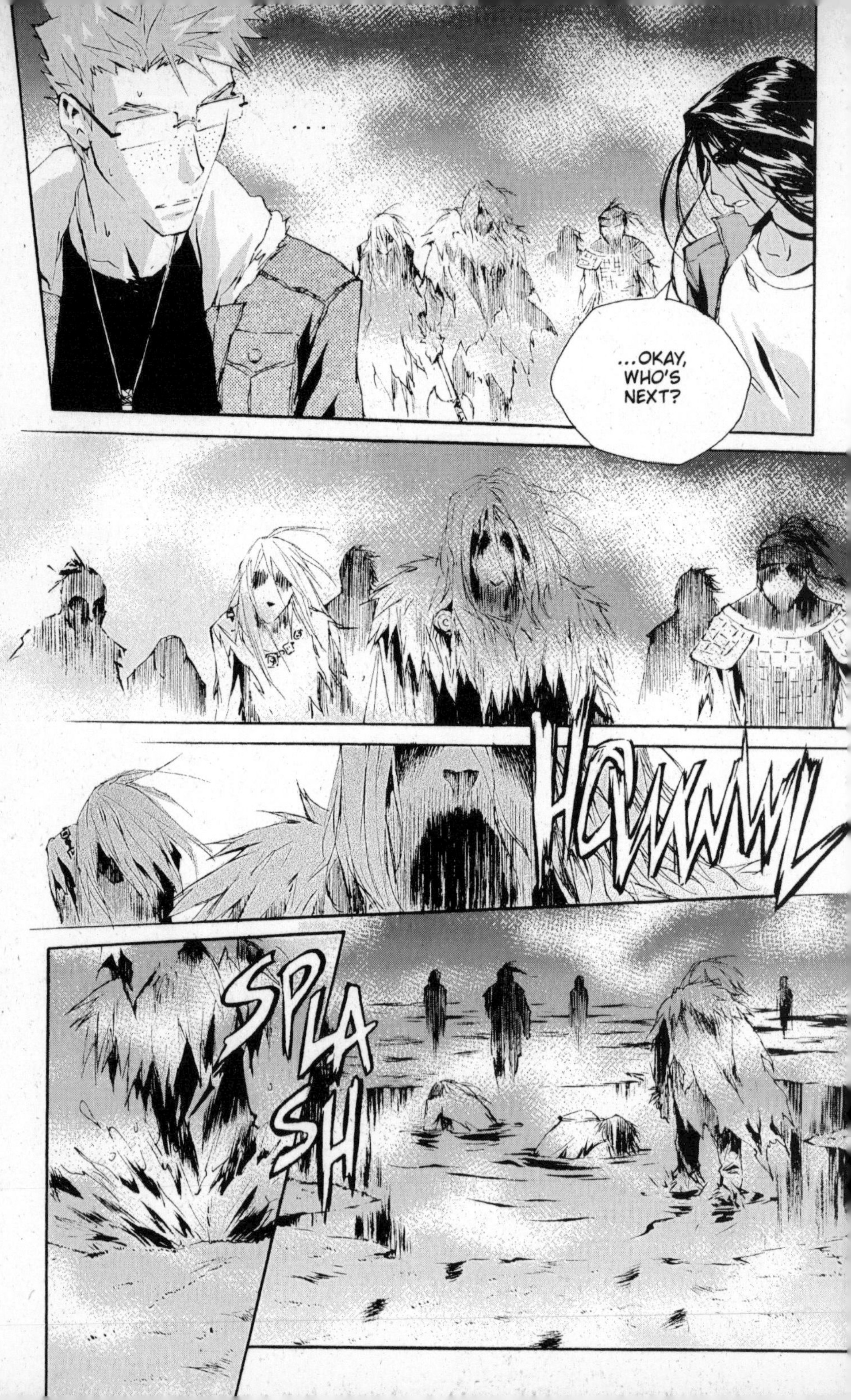
...
...OKAY, WHO'S NEXT?
HOWWWL
SPLASH

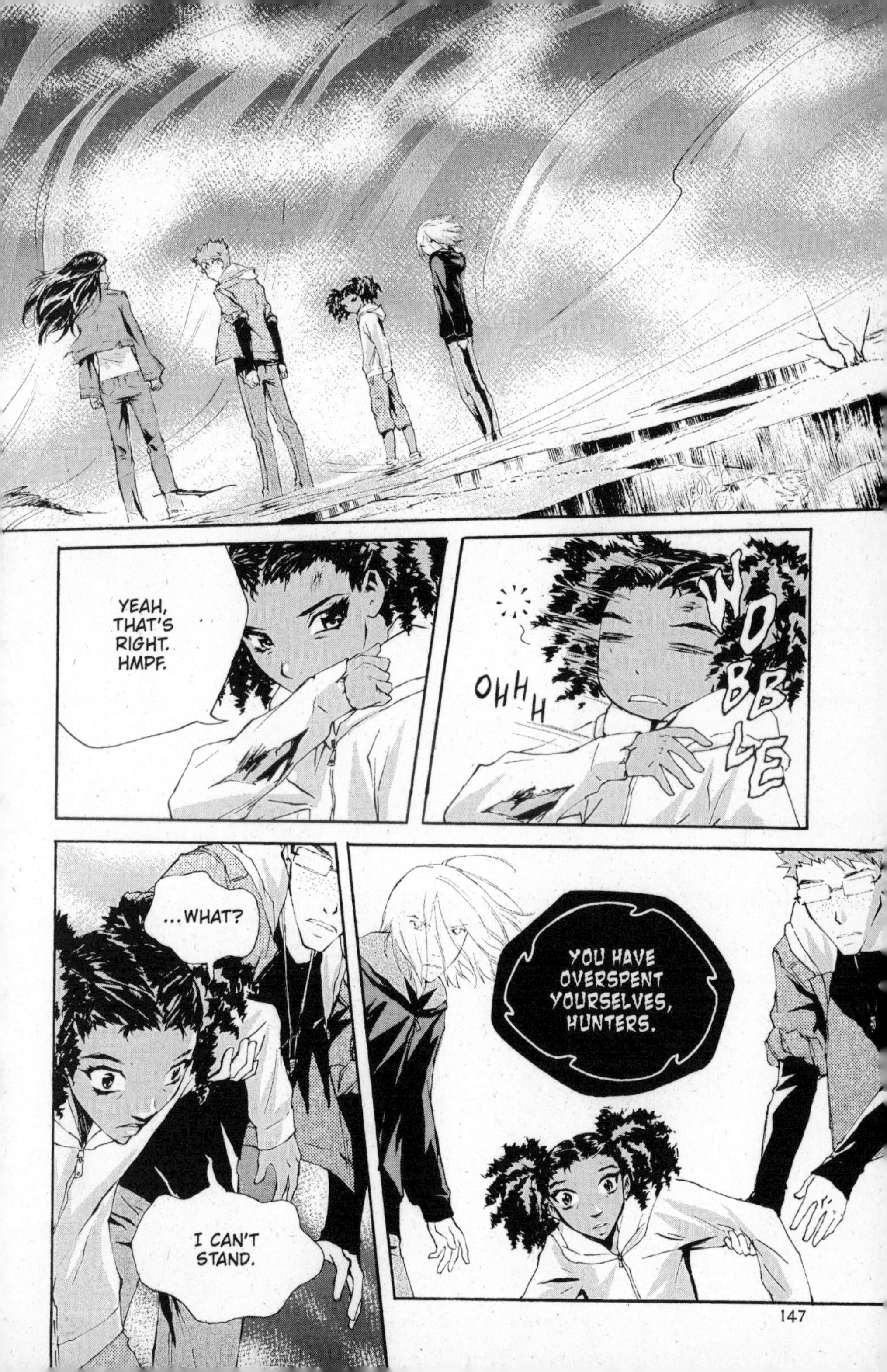
YEAH, THAT'S RIGHT. HMPF.
OHHH
WOBBLE
...WHAT?
I CAN'T STAND.
YOU HAVE OVERSPENT YOURSELVES, HUNTERS.

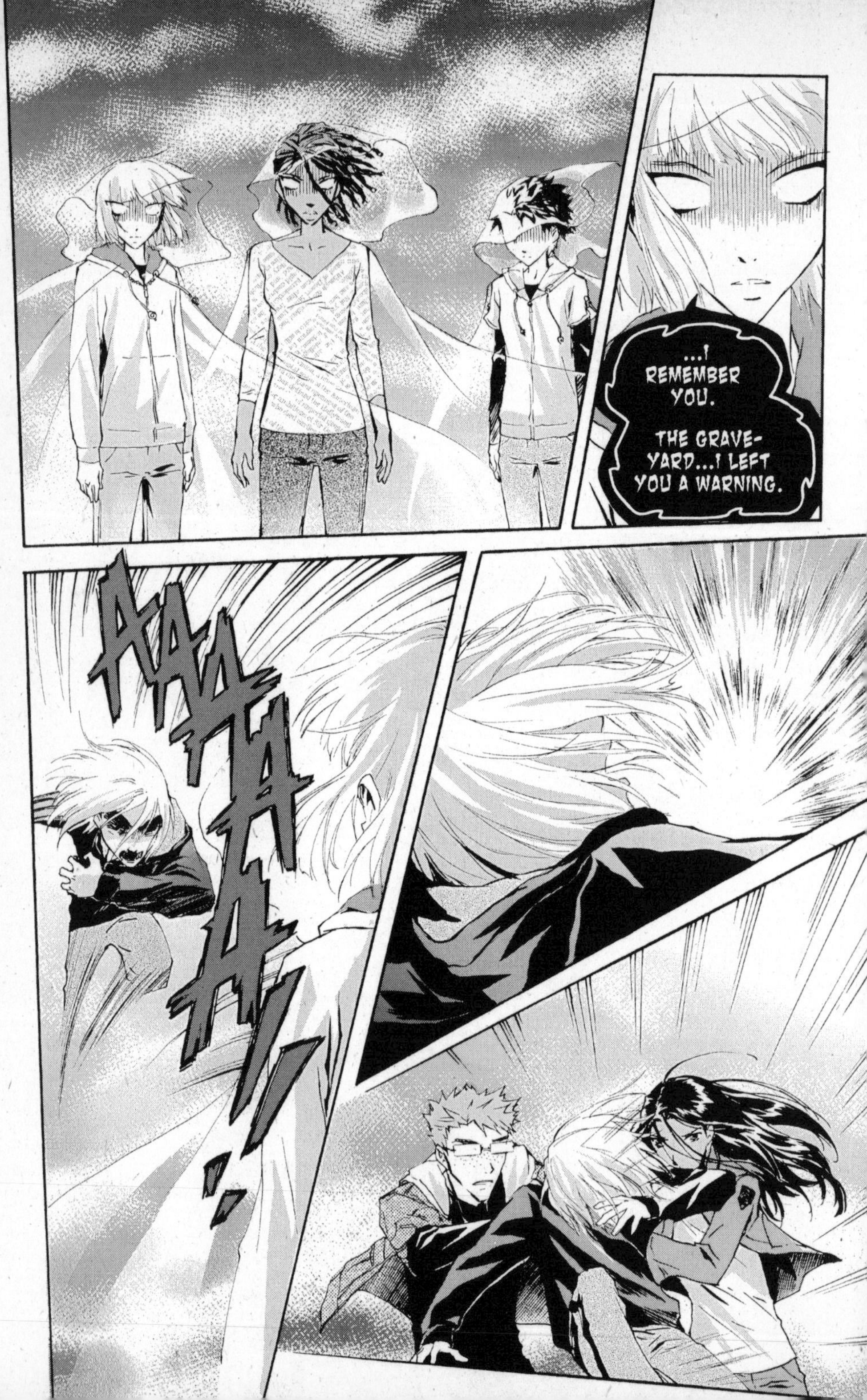
...I REMEMBER YOU.
THE GRAVE-YARD...I LEFT YOU A WARNING.
AAAAAA!!

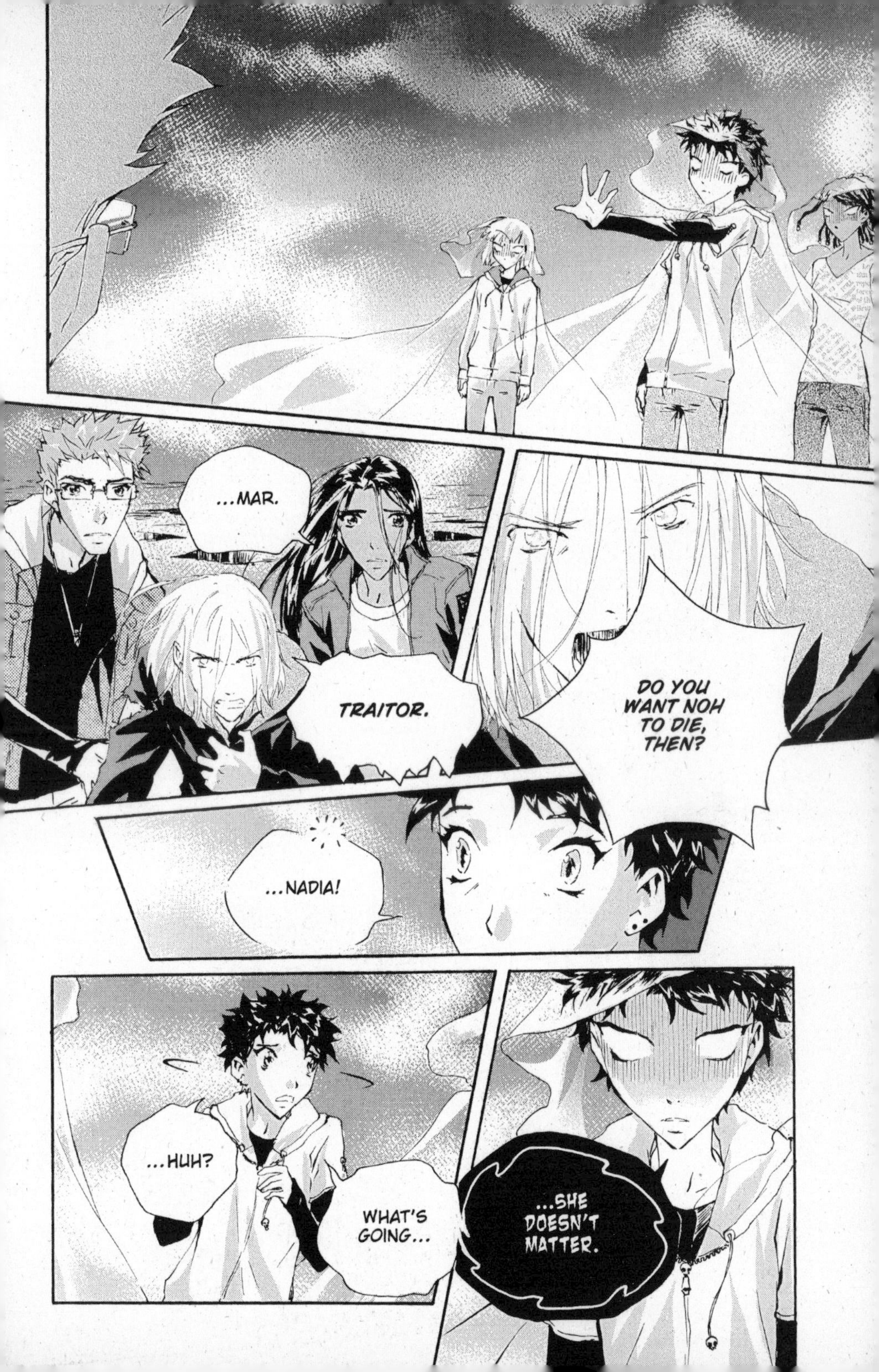
...MAR.
TRAITOR.
DO YOU WANT NOH TO DIE, THEN?
...NADIA!
...HUH?
WHAT'S GOING...
...SHE DOESN'T MATTER.

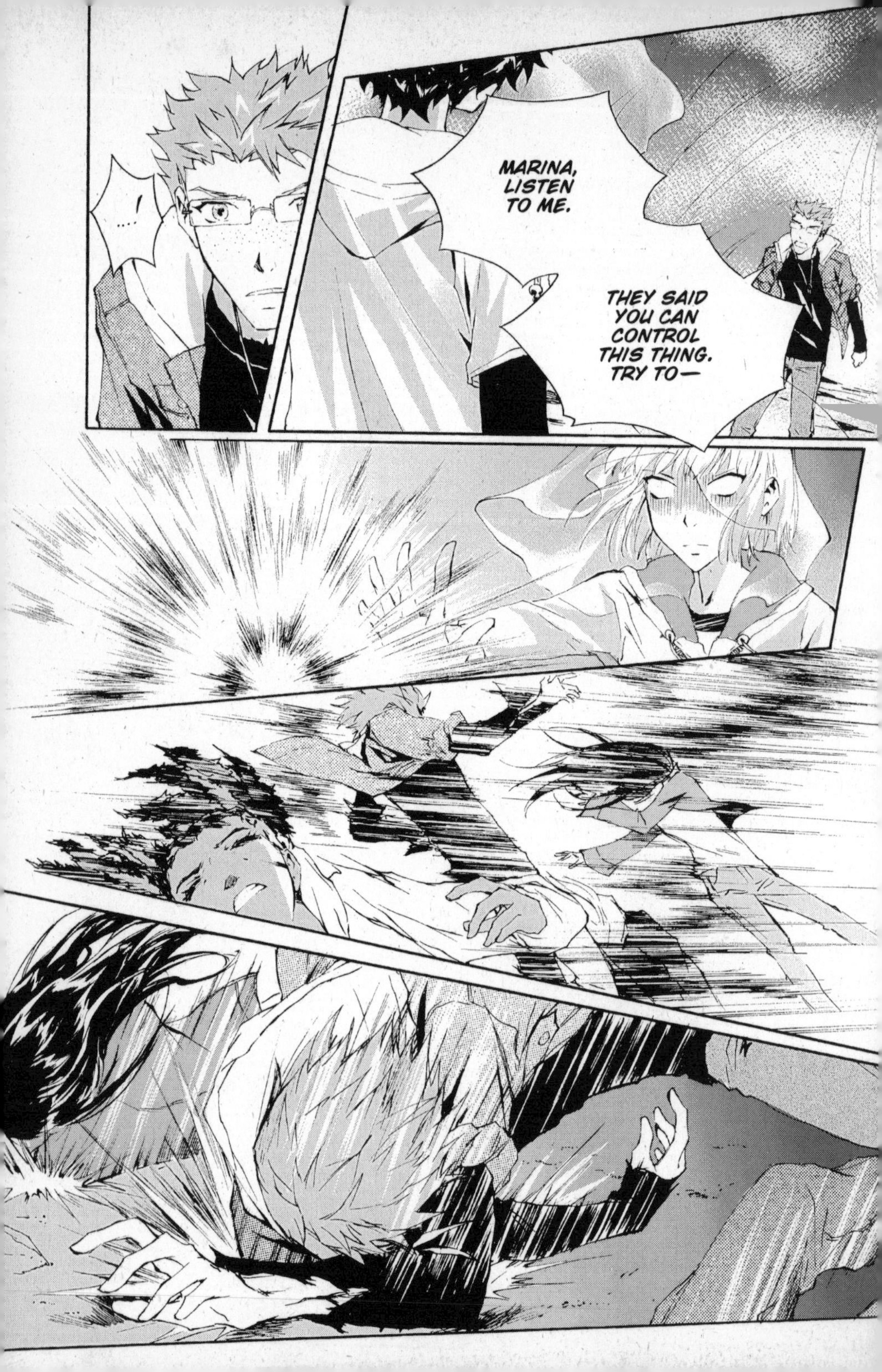
!
....
MARINA, LISTEN TO ME.
THEY SAID YOU CAN CONTROL THIS THING. TRY TO—

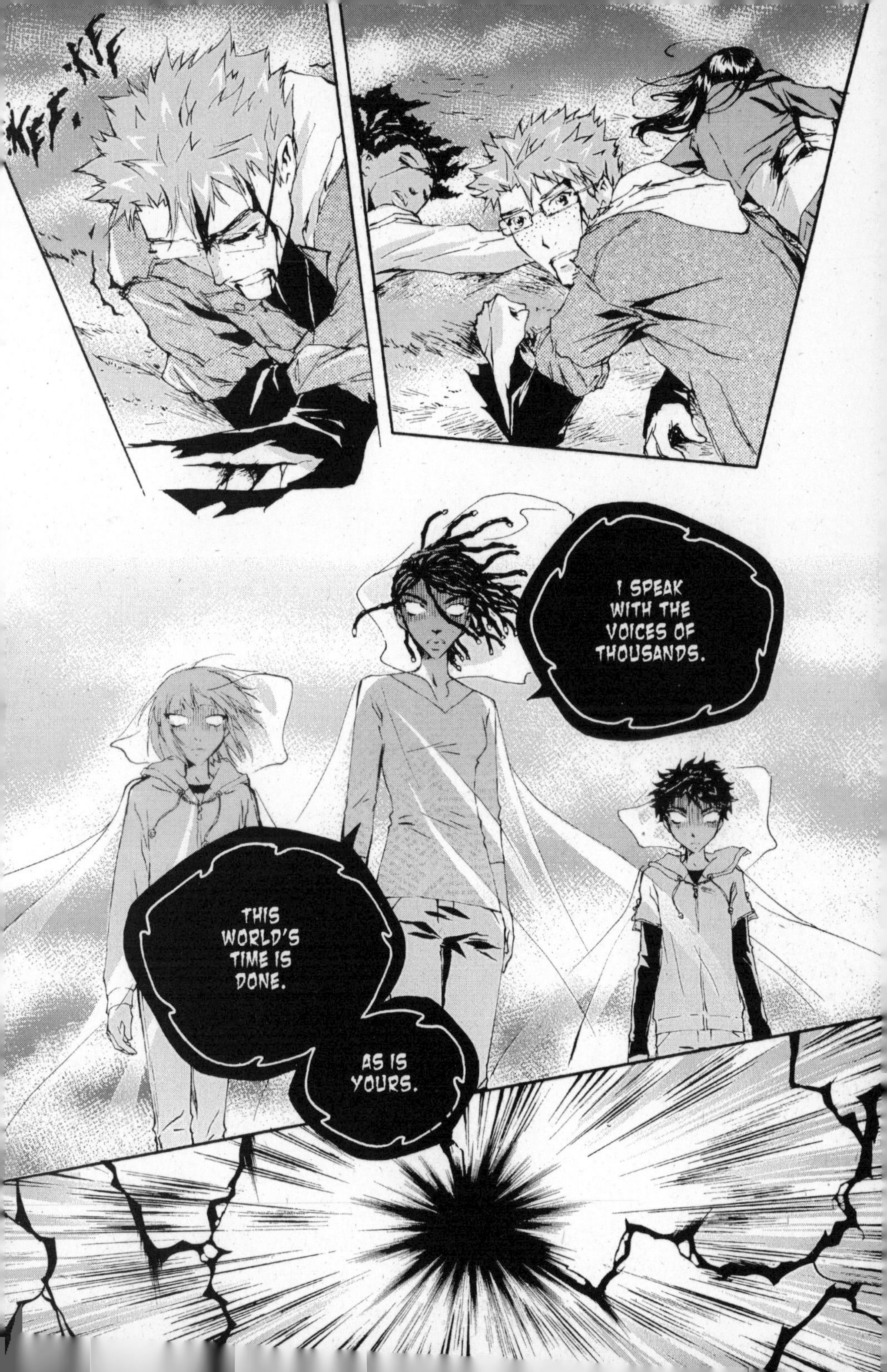
KFF. KFF
I SPEAK WITH THE VOICES OF THOUSANDS.
THIS WORLD'S TIME IS DONE.
AS IS YOURS.

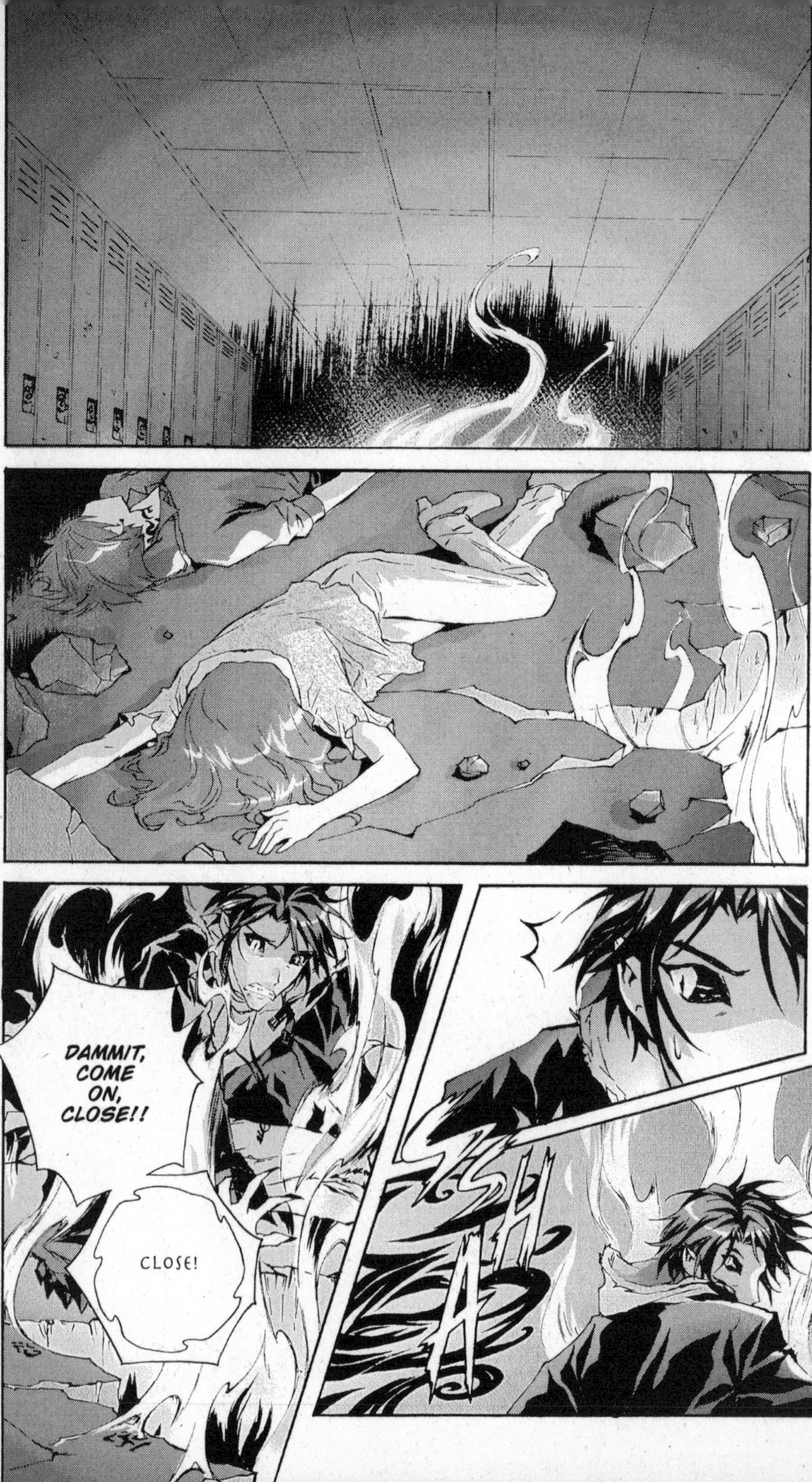
DAMMIT, COME ON, CLOSE!!
CLOSE!
SSHAH

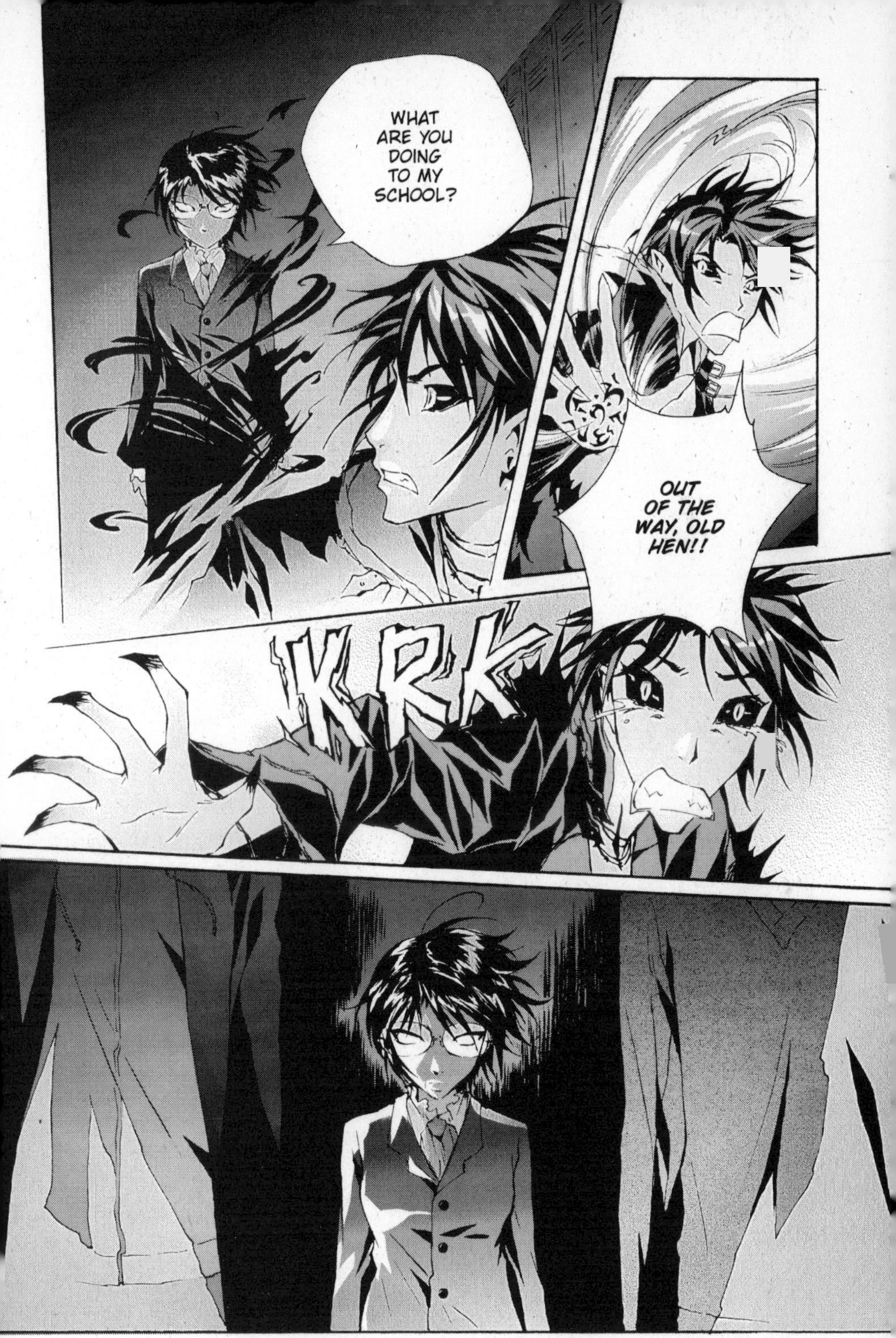
WHAT ARE YOU DOING TO MY SCHOOL?
OUT OF THE WAY, OLD HEN!!
KRK

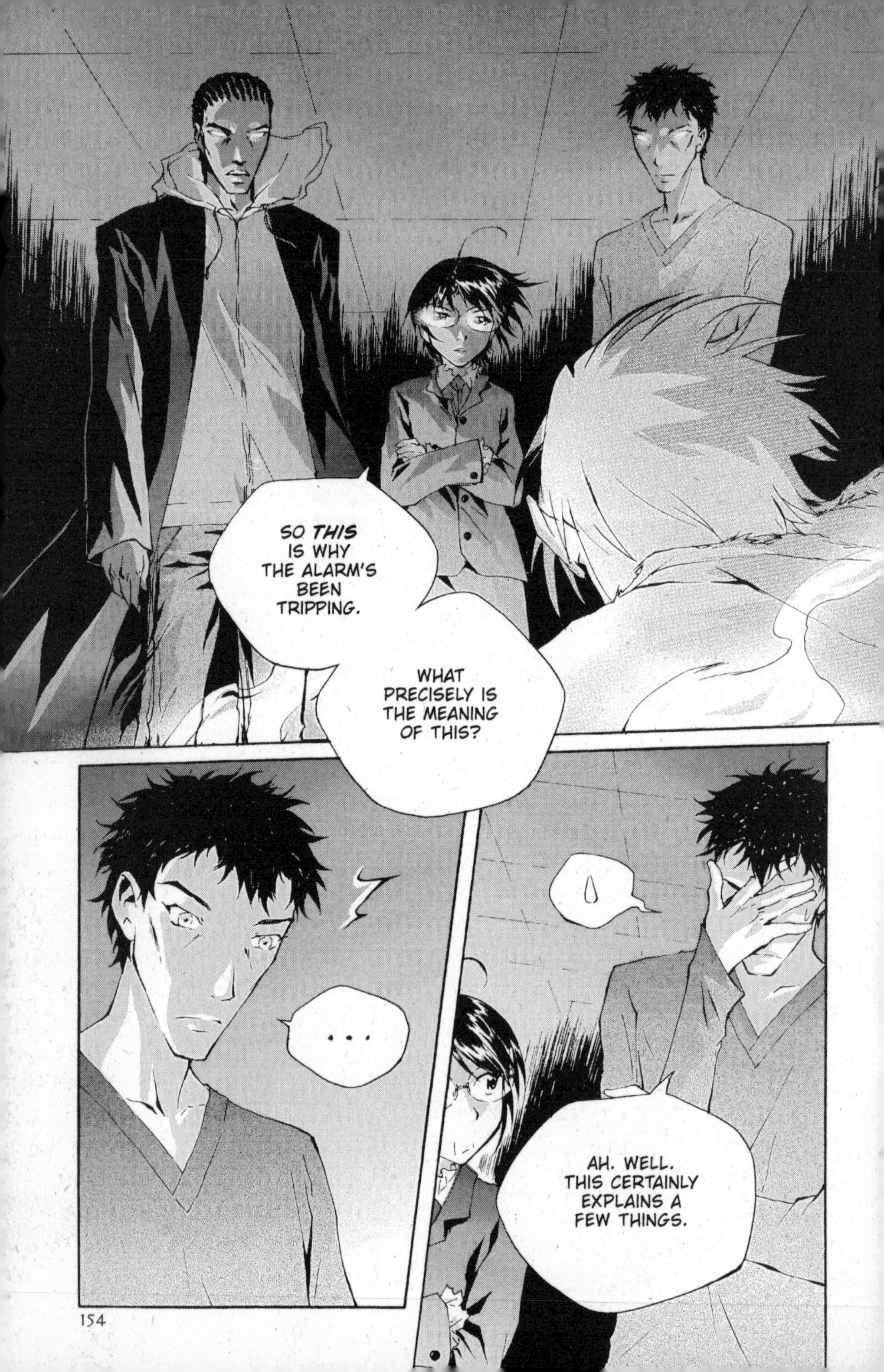
SO *THIS* IS WHY THE ALARM'S BEEN TRIPPING.
WHAT PRECISELY IS THE MEANING OF THIS?
. . .
AH. WELL. THIS CERTAINLY EXPLAINS A FEW THINGS.

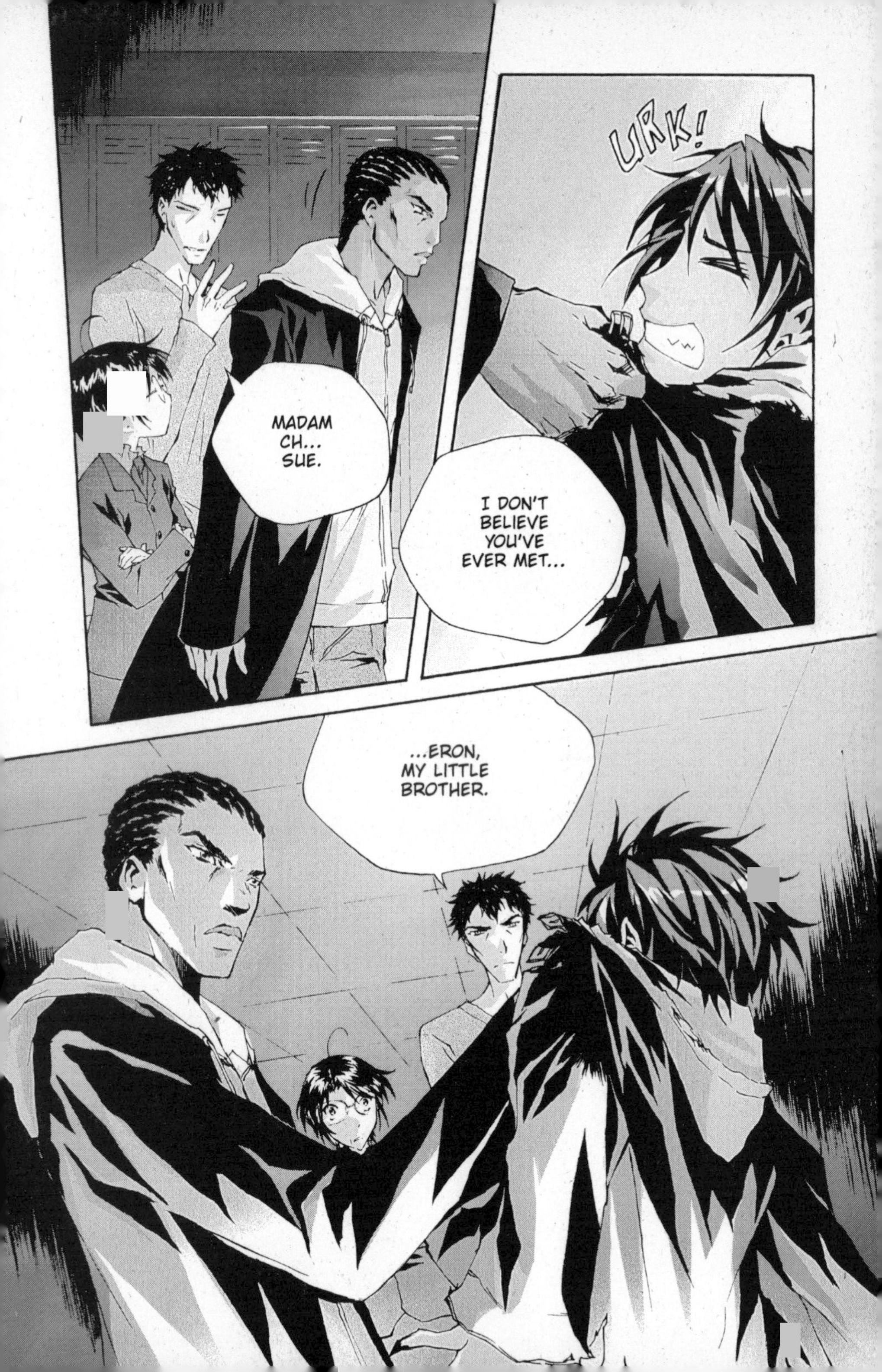
MADAM CH... SUE.
URK!
I DON'T BELIEVE YOU'VE EVER MET...
...ERON, MY LITTLE BROTHER.

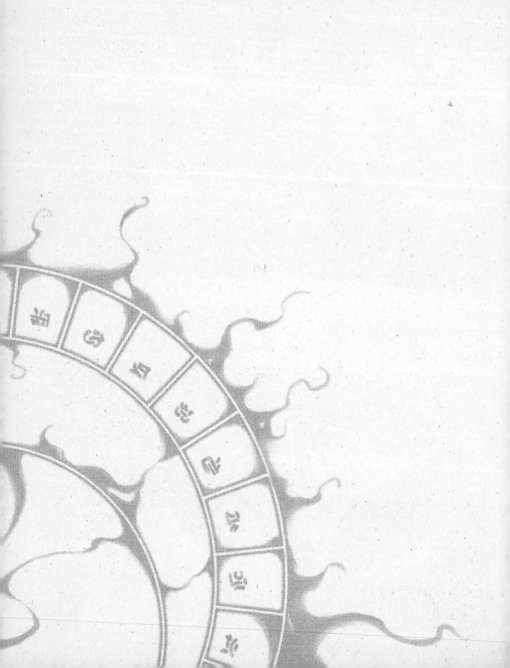

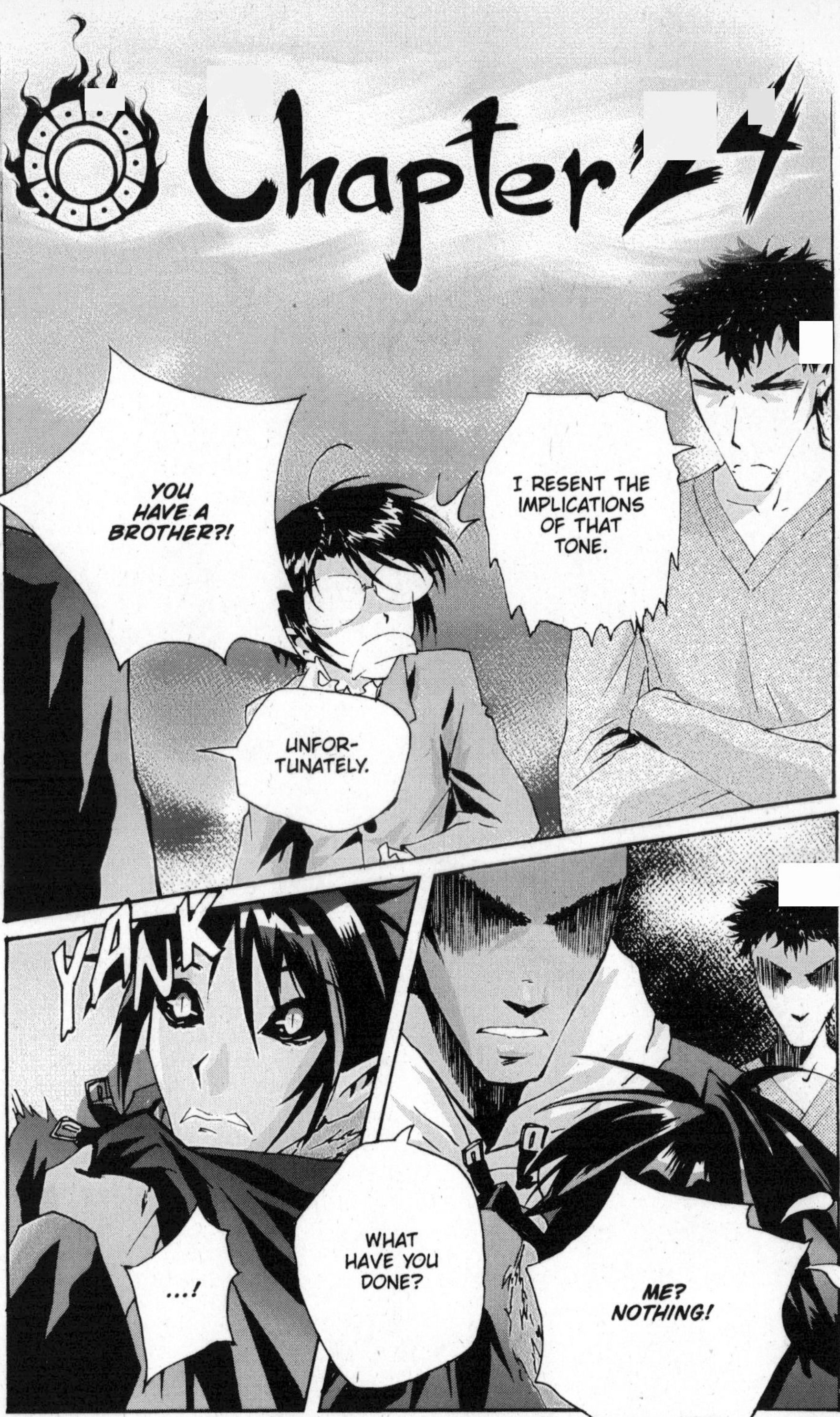
Chapter 4
YOU HAVE A BROTHER?!
UNFOR-TUNATELY.
I RESENT THE IMPLICATIONS OF THAT TONE.
YANK
...!
WHAT HAVE YOU DONE?
ME? NOTHING!

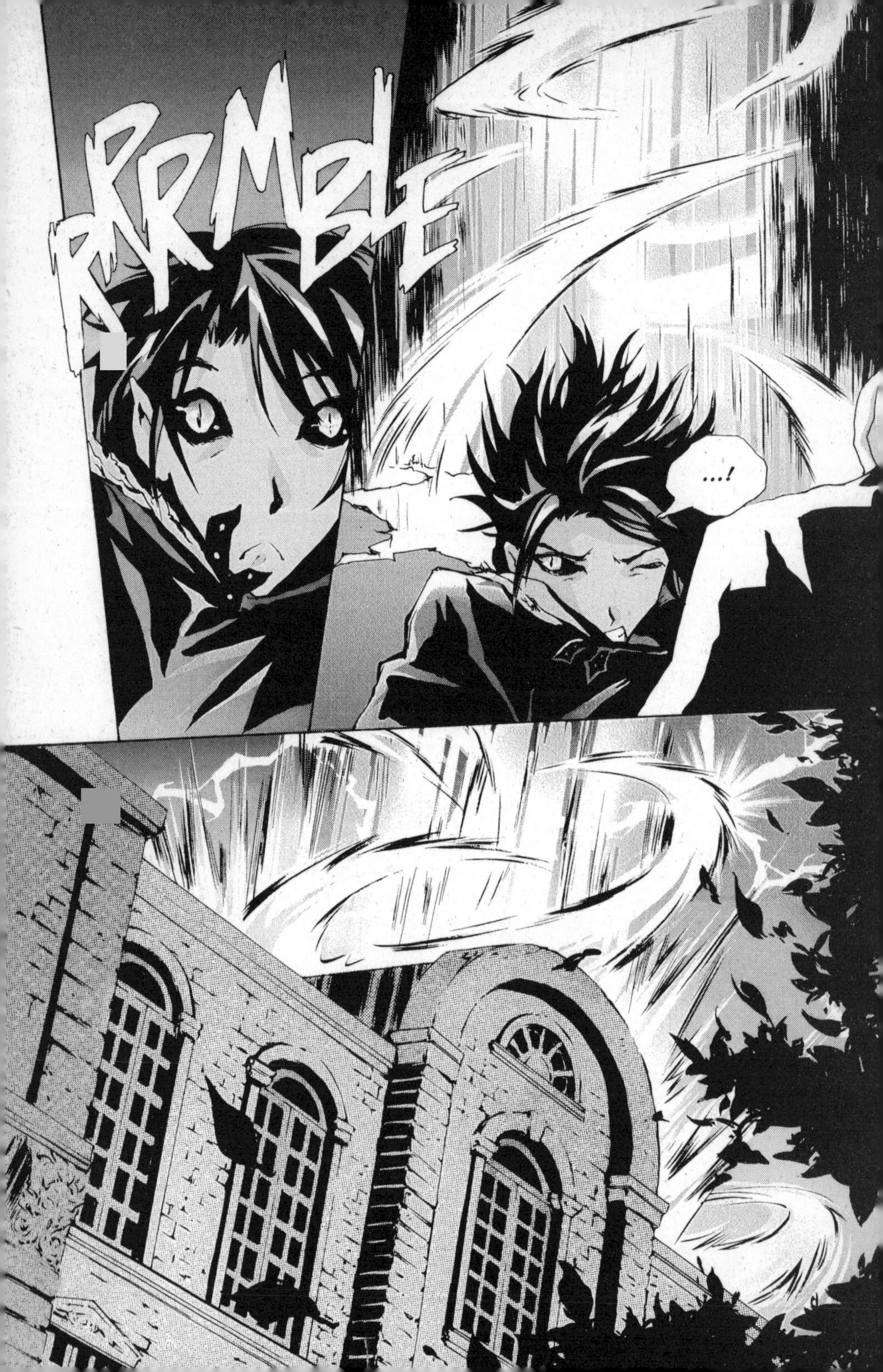
RRRMBLE
...!

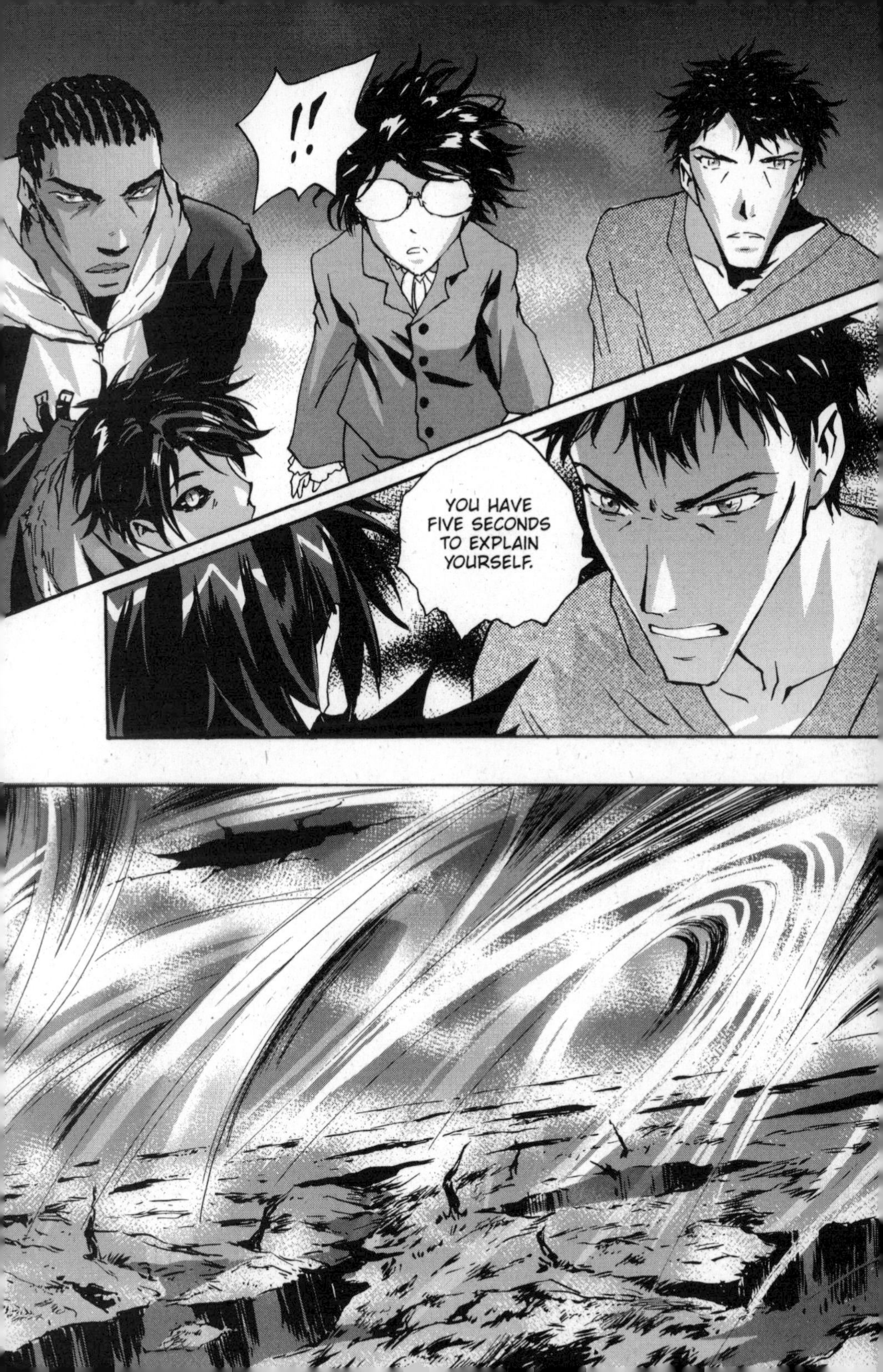
!!
YOU HAVE FIVE SECONDS TO EXPLAIN YOURSELF.

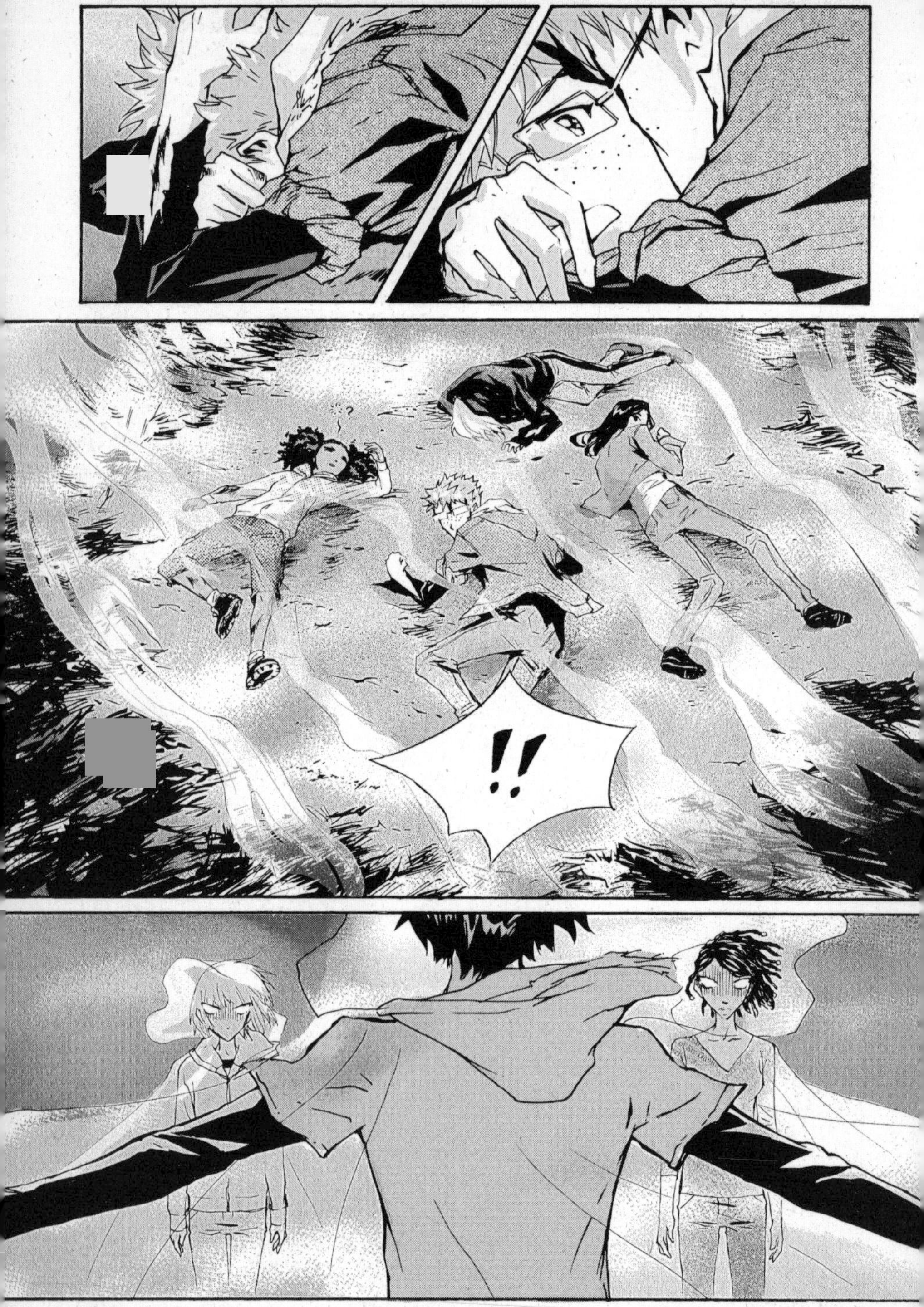
!!

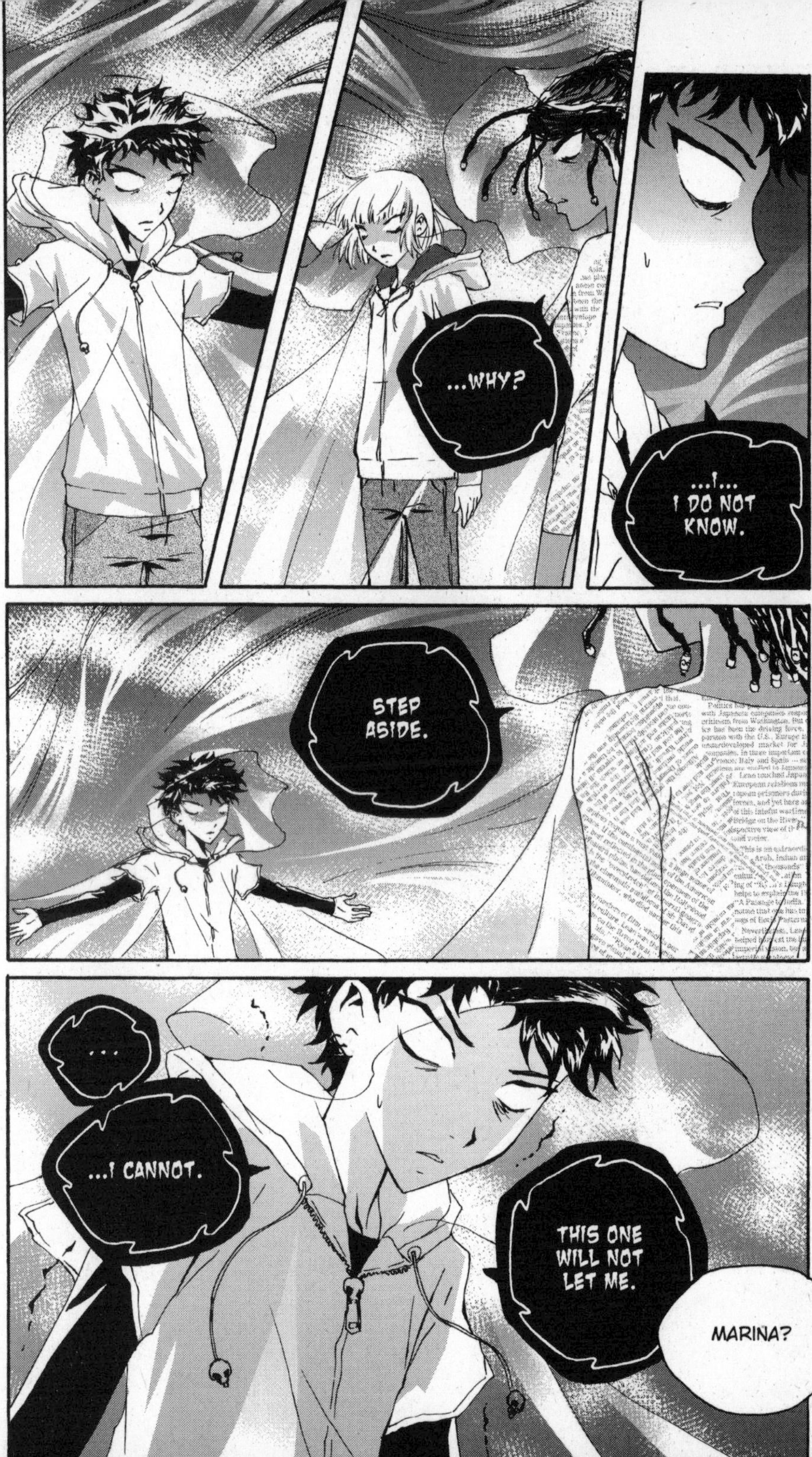
...WHY?
...I... I DO NOT KNOW.
STEP ASIDE.
...
...I CANNOT.
THIS ONE WILL NOT LET ME.
MARINA?

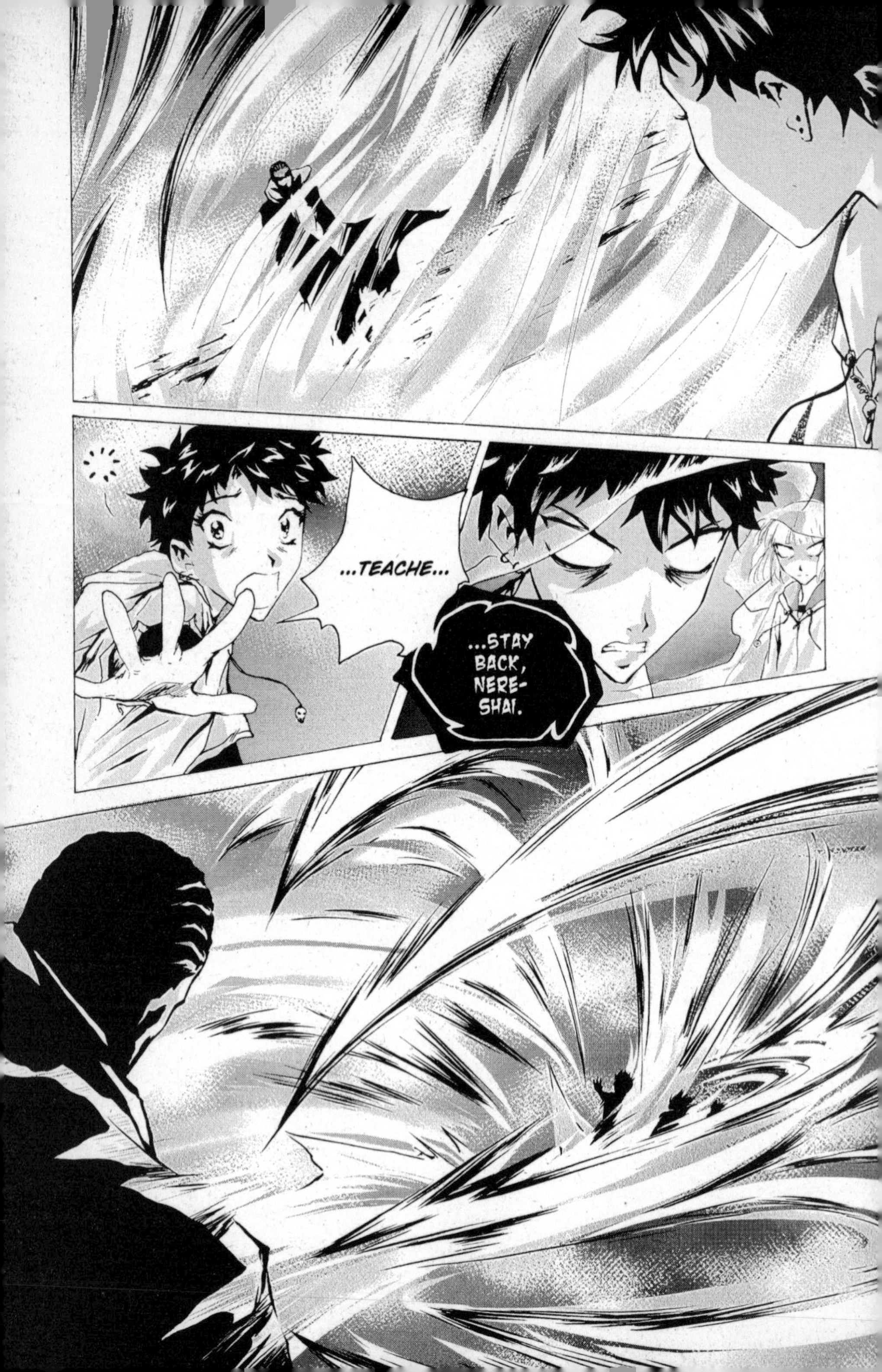
...TEACHE...
...STAY BACK, NERE-SHAI.

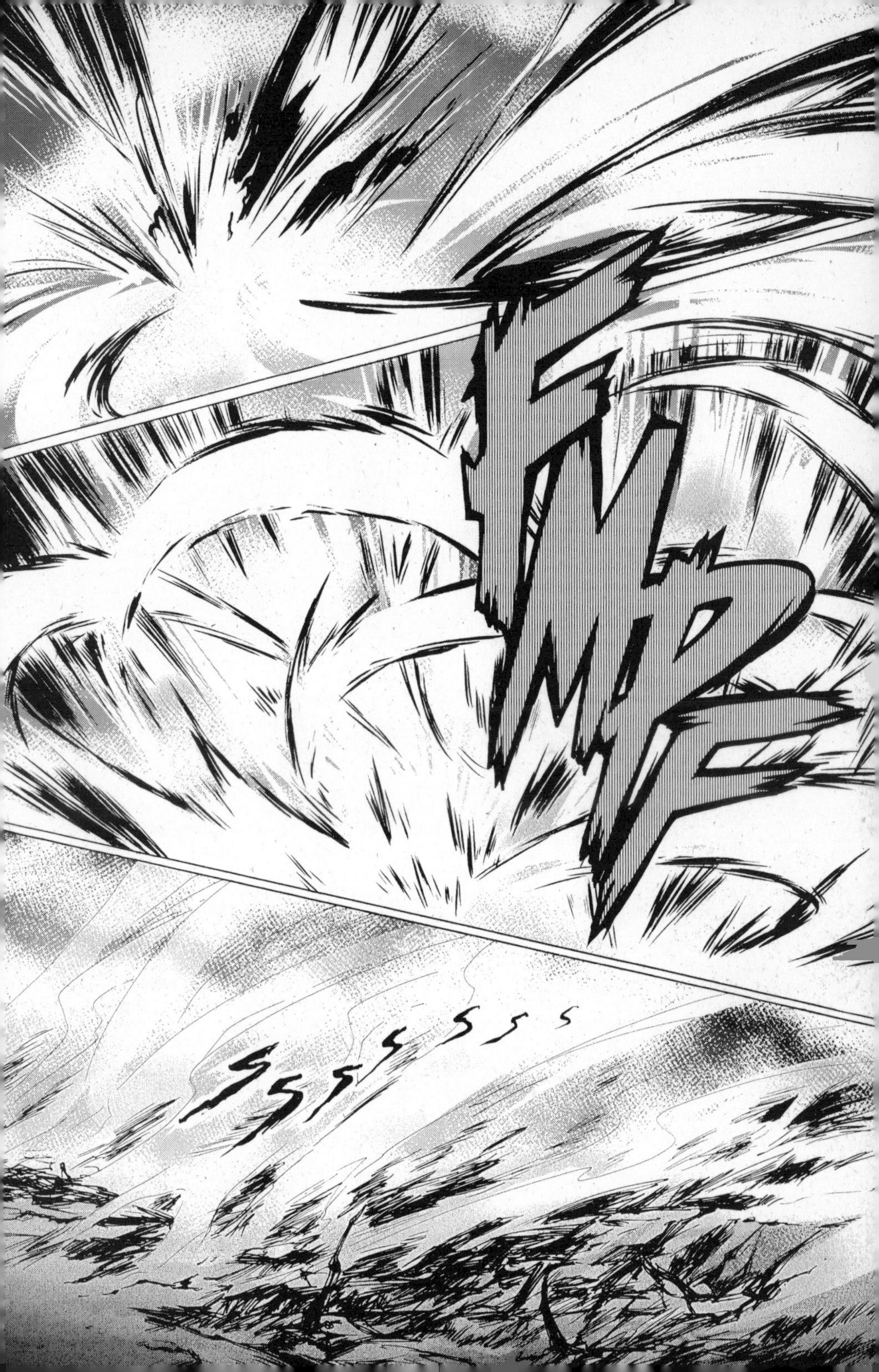
FWIP
SSSSSSSS

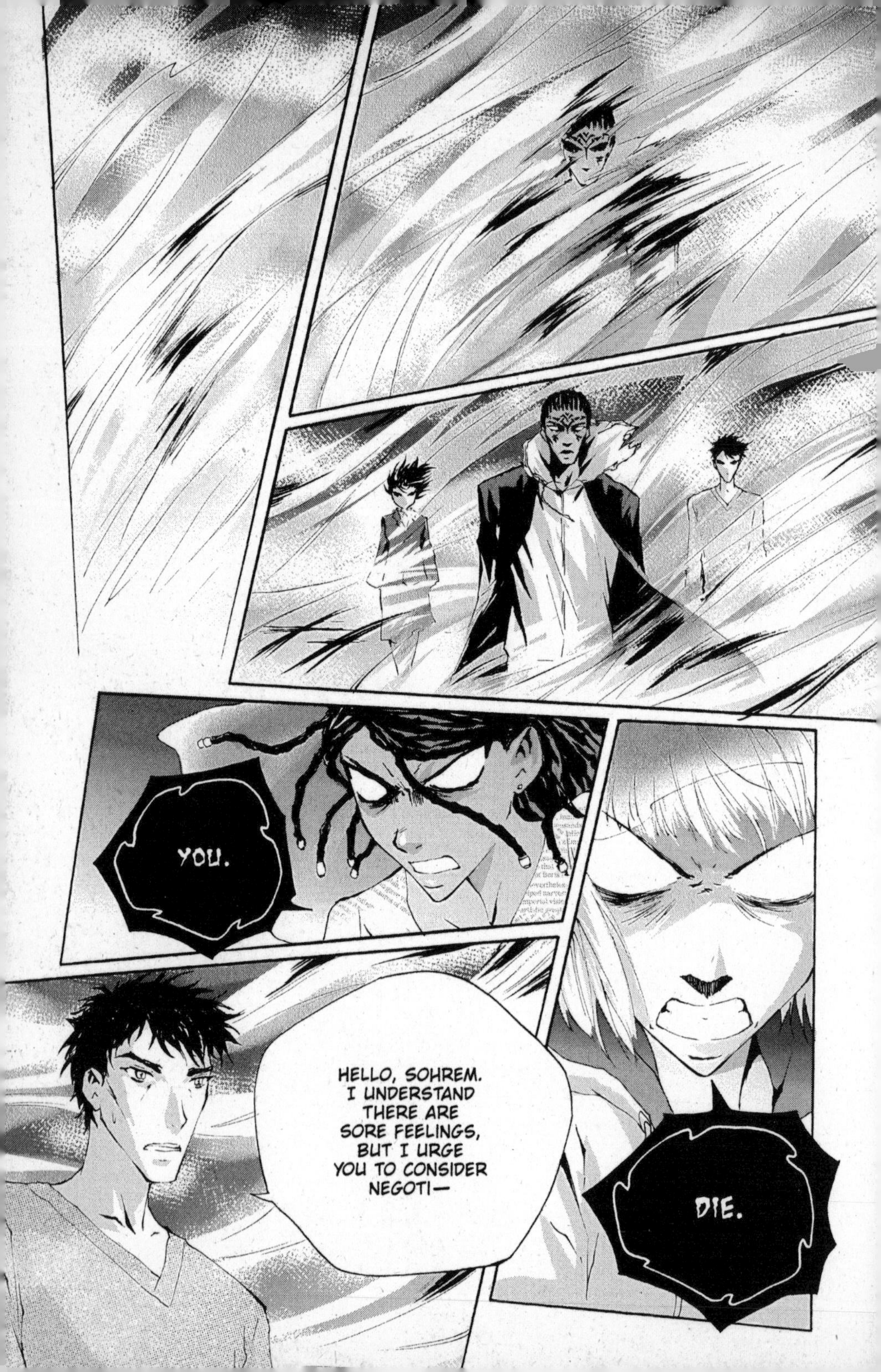
YOU.
HELLO, SOHREM. I UNDERSTAND THERE ARE SORE FEELINGS, BUT I URGE YOU TO CONSIDER NEGOTI—
DIE.

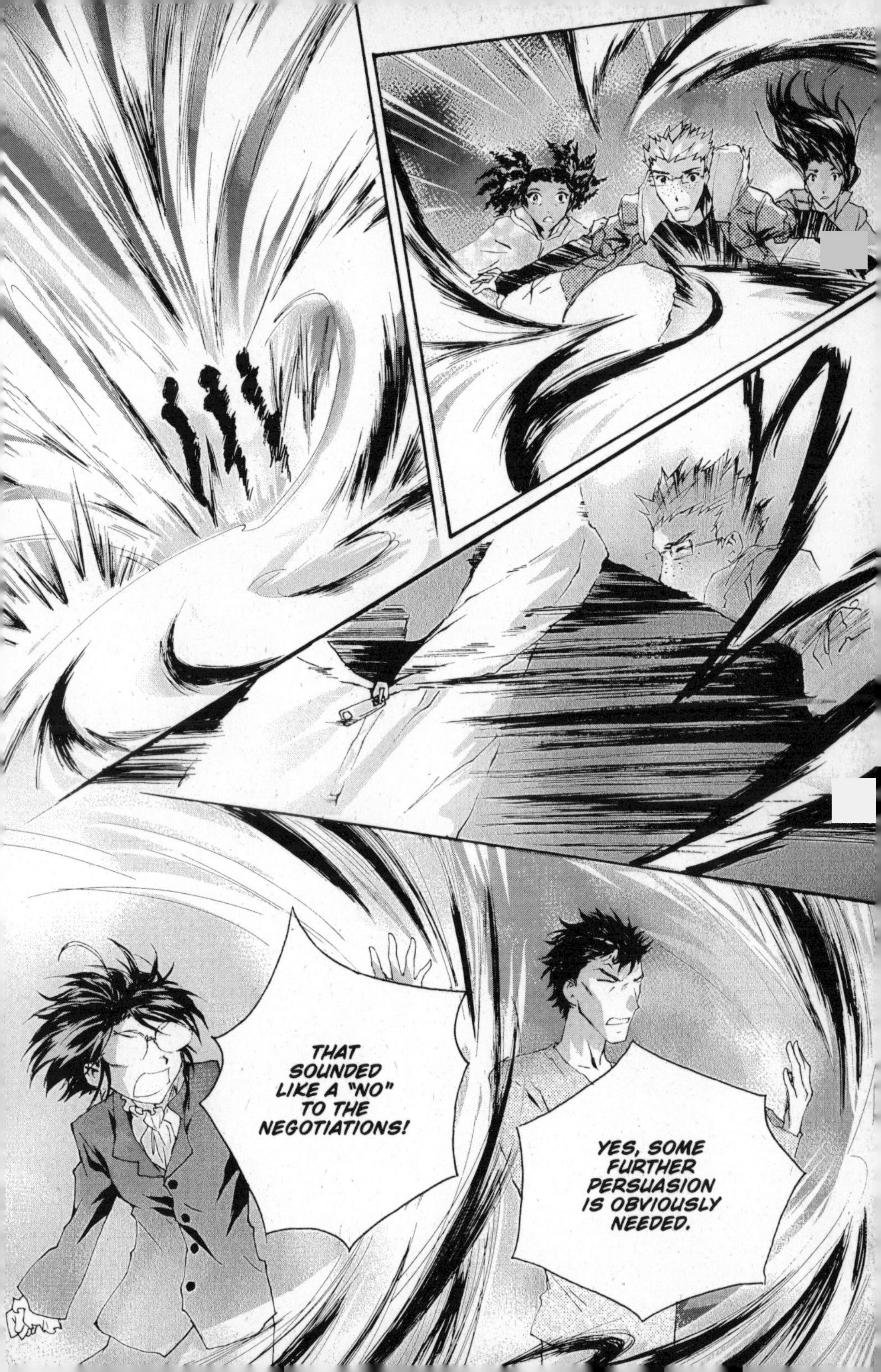
THAT SOUNDED LIKE A "NO" TO THE NEGOTIATIONS!
YES, SOME FURTHER PERSUASION IS OBVIOUSLY NEEDED.

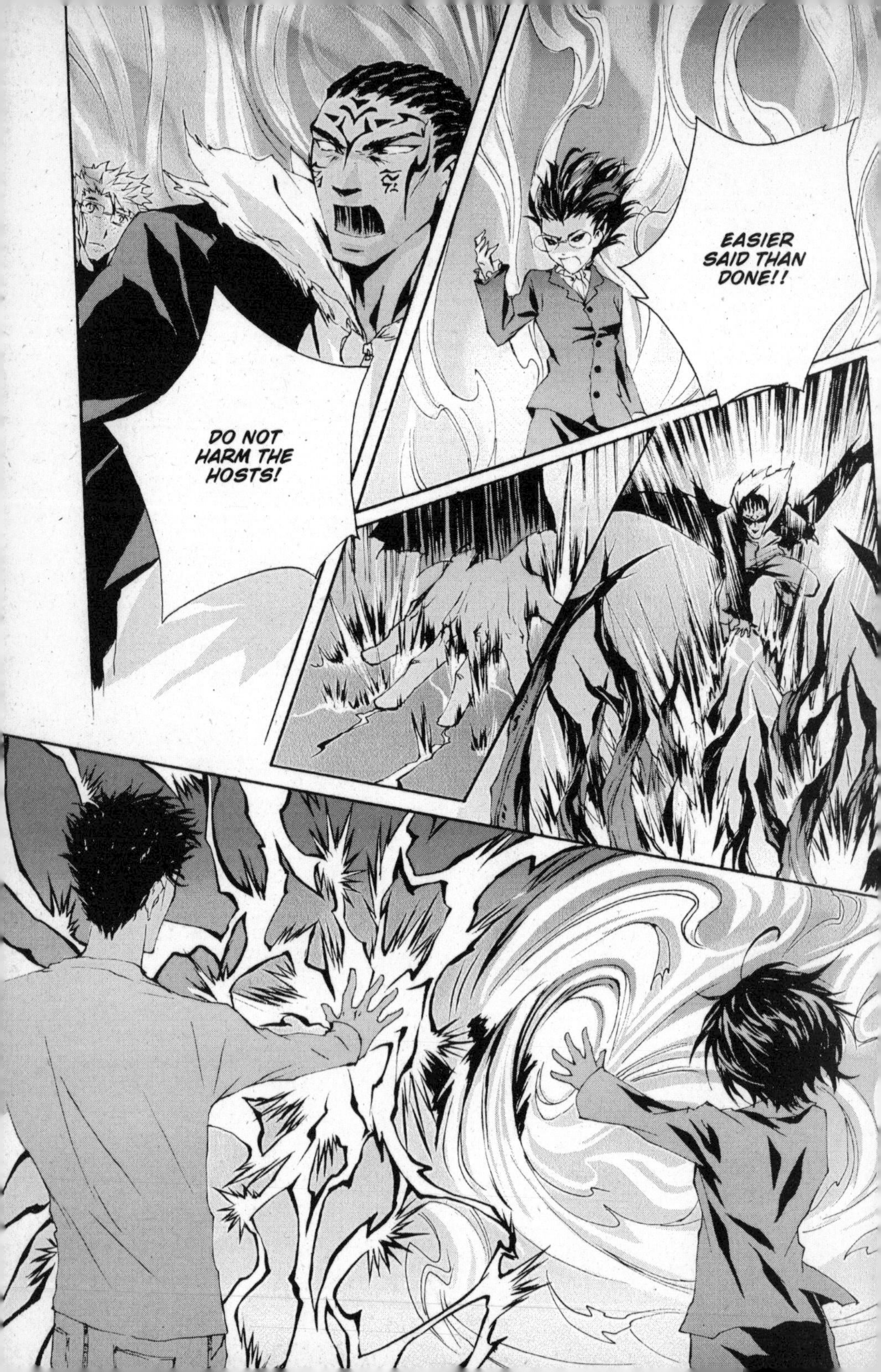
DO NOT HARM THE HOSTS!
EASIER SAID THAN DONE!!

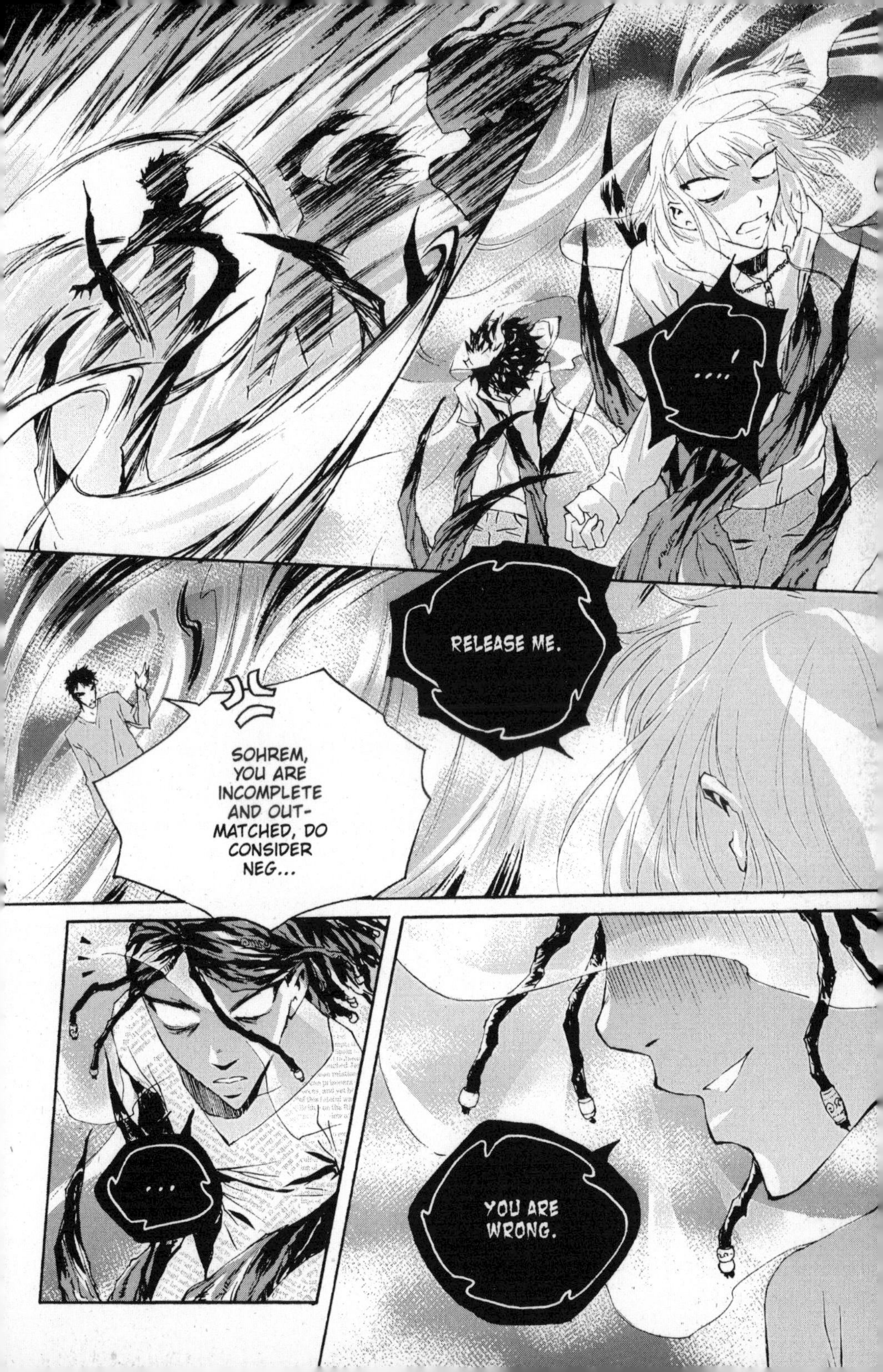
!
....
RELEASE ME.
SOHREM, YOU ARE INCOMPLETE AND OUT-MATCHED, DO CONSIDER NEG...
...
YOU ARE WRONG.

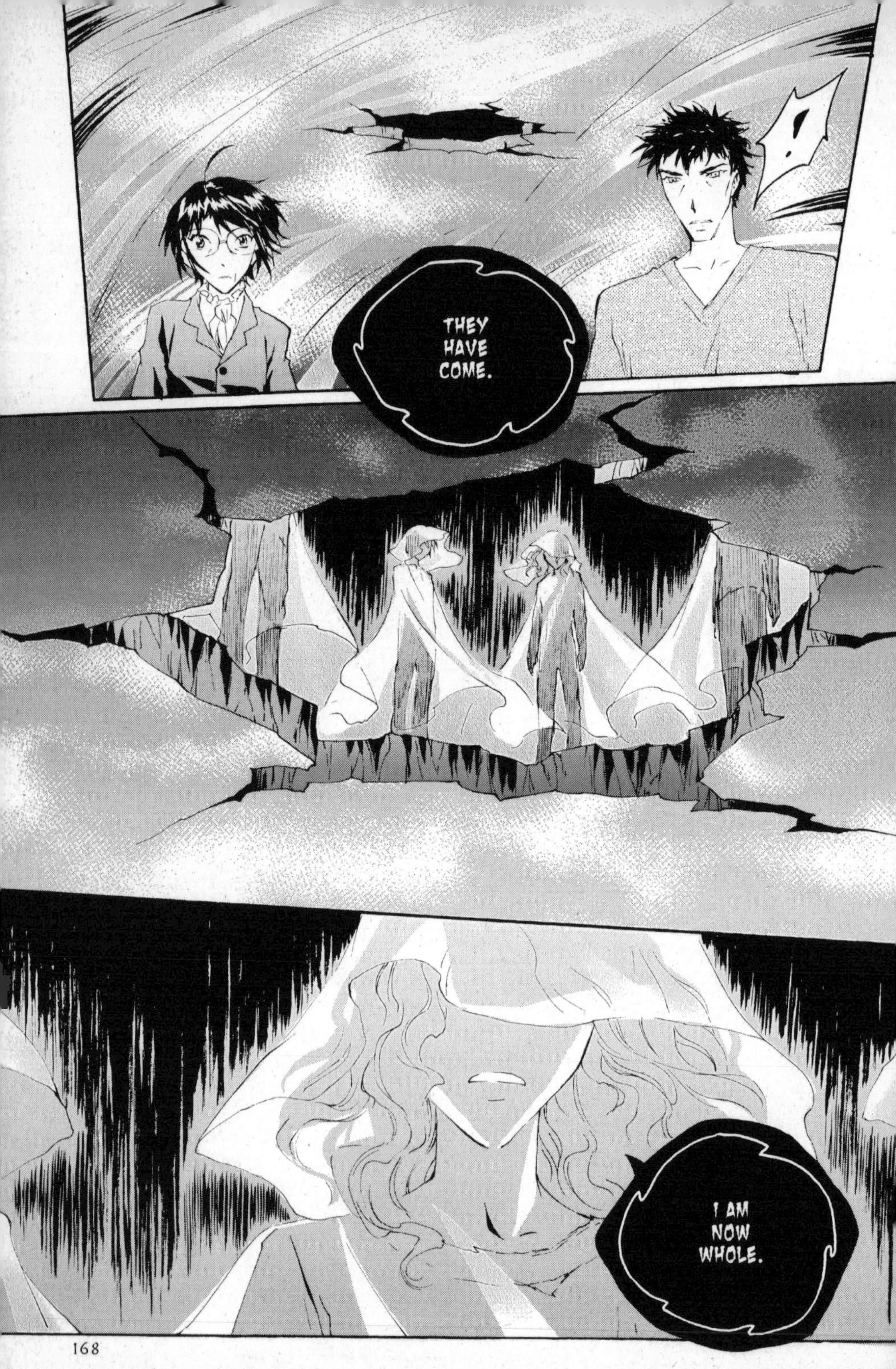
!
THEY HAVE COME.
I AM NOW WHOLE.

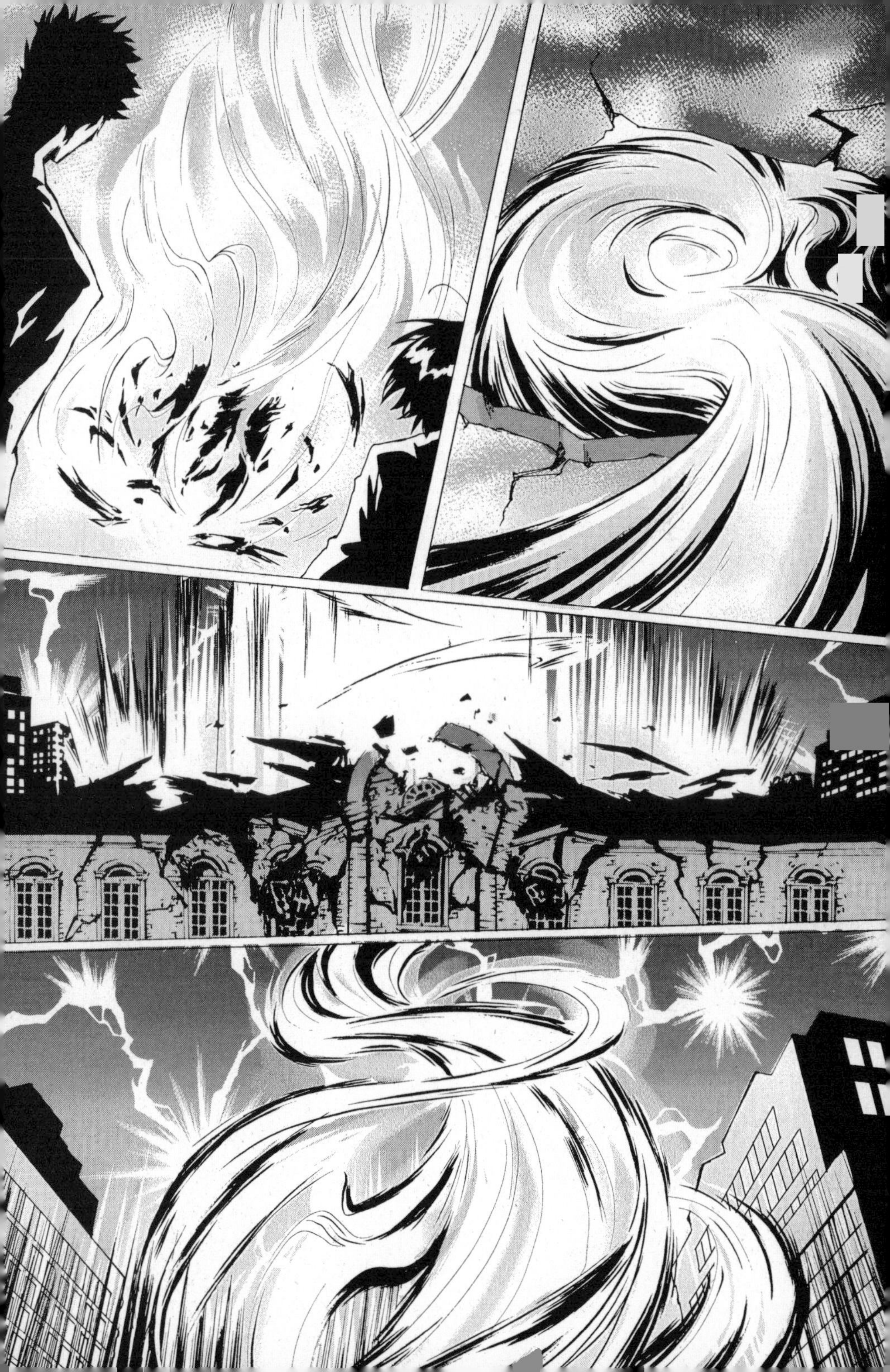

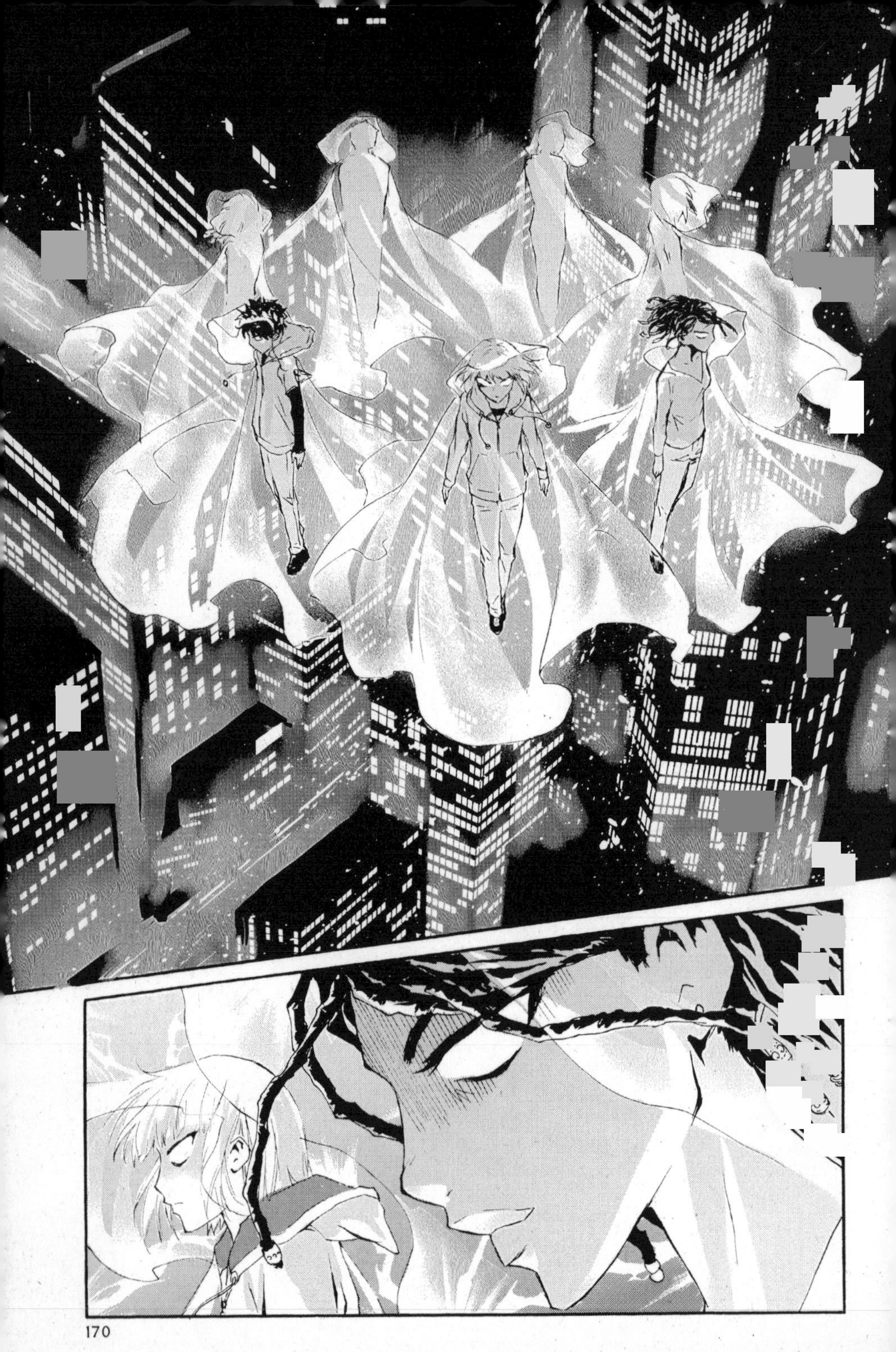

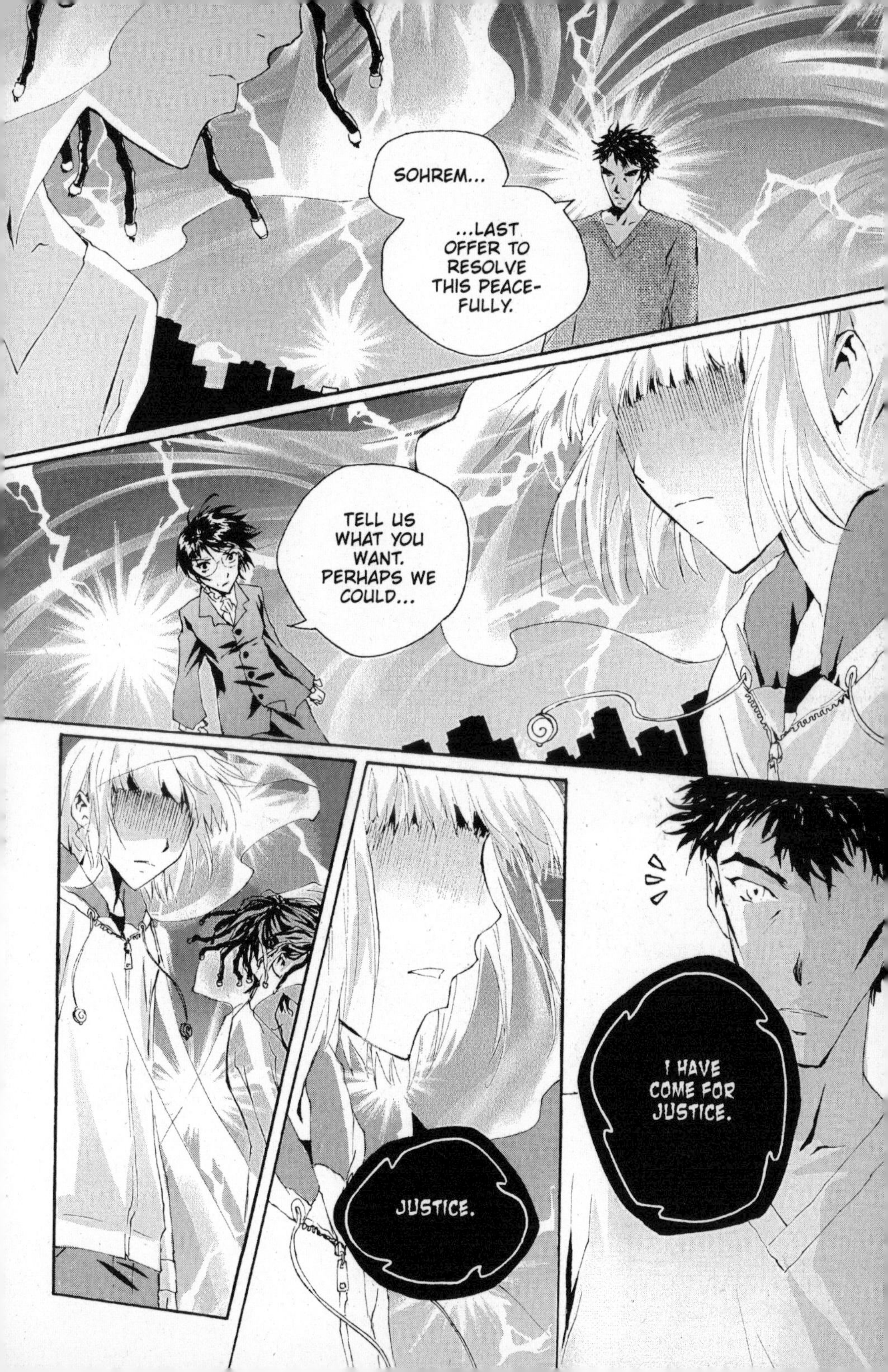
SOHREM...
...LAST OFFER TO RESOLVE THIS PEACE-FULLY.
TELL US WHAT YOU WANT. PERHAPS WE COULD...
JUSTICE.
I HAVE COME FOR JUSTICE.

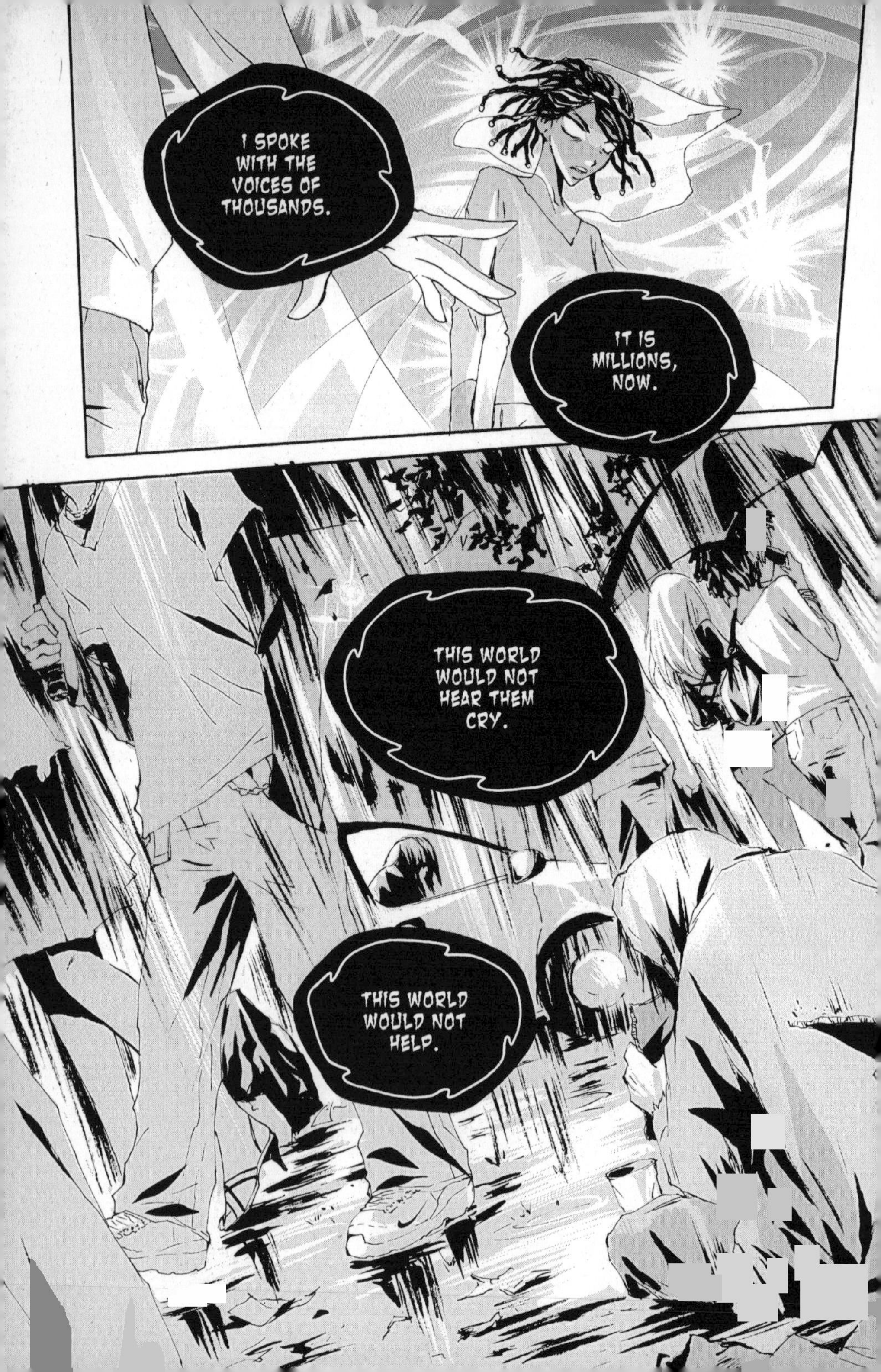
I SPOKE WITH THE VOICES OF THOUSANDS.
IT IS MILLIONS, NOW.
THIS WORLD WOULD NOT HEAR THEM CRY.
THIS WORLD WOULD NOT HELP.

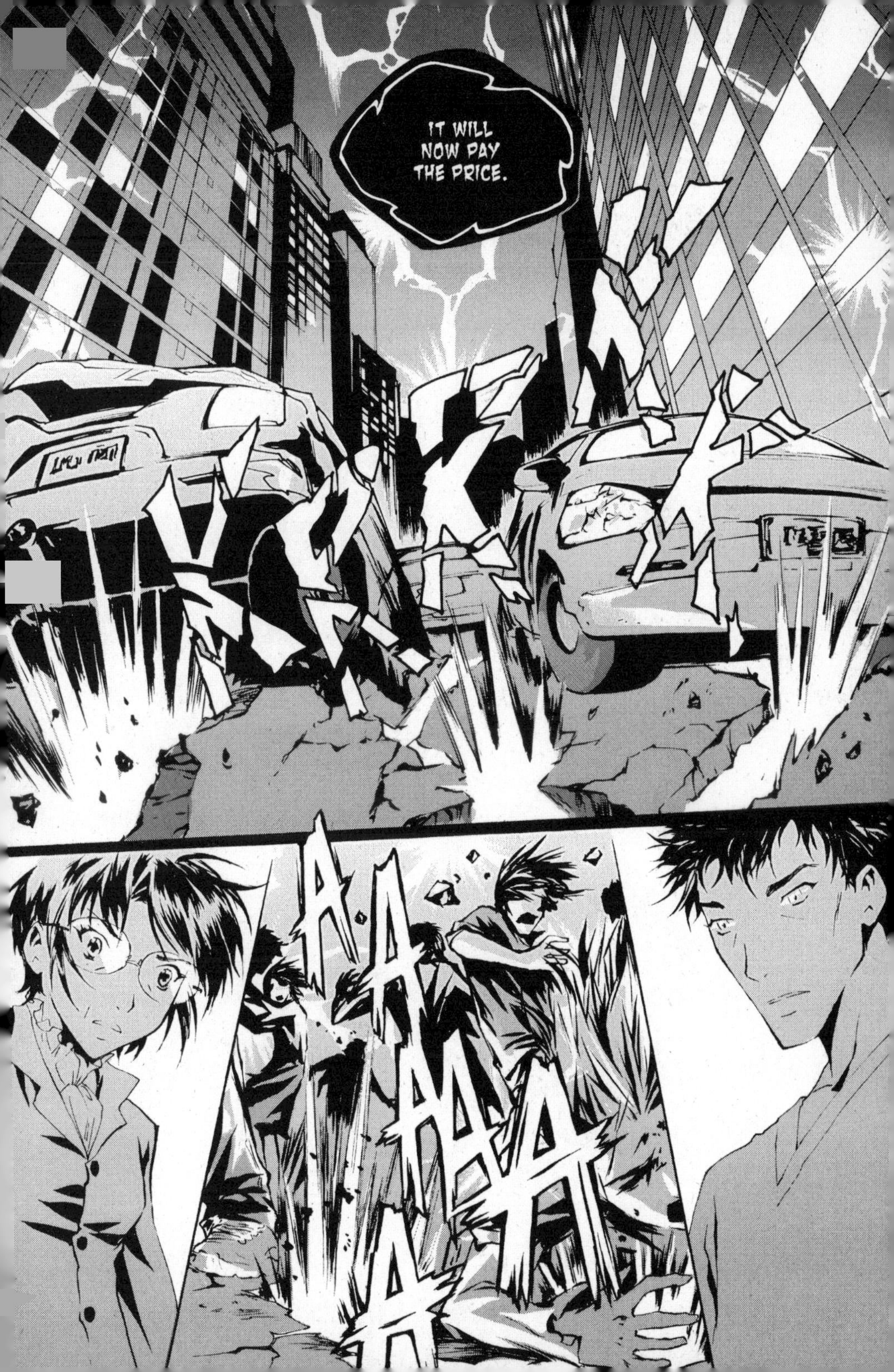
IT WILL NOW PAY THE PRICE.

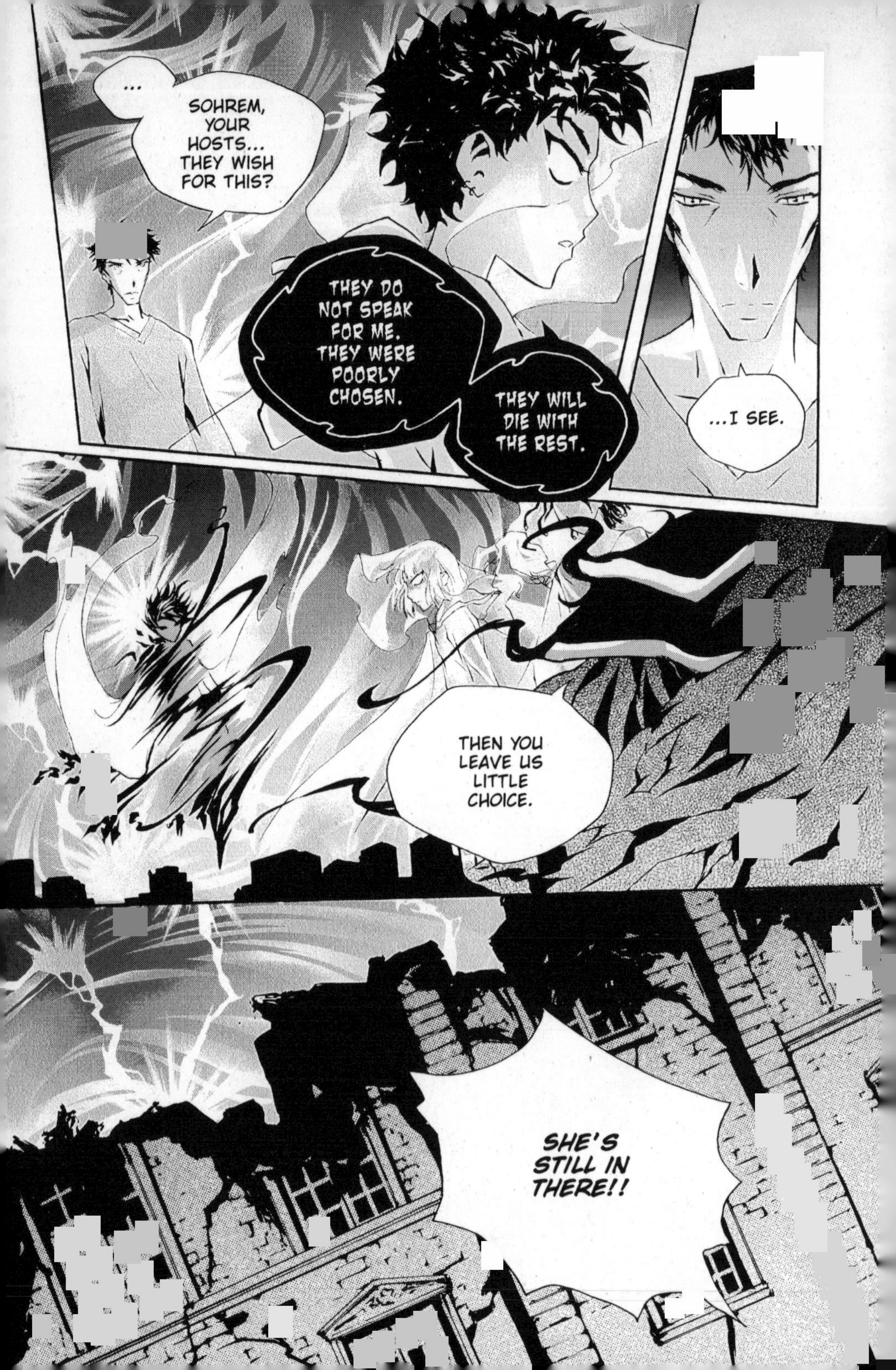
...
SOHREM, YOUR HOSTS... THEY WISH FOR THIS?
THEY DO NOT SPEAK FOR ME. THEY WERE POORLY CHOSEN.
THEY WILL DIE WITH THE REST.
...I SEE.
THEN YOU LEAVE US LITTLE CHOICE.
SHE'S STILL IN THERE!!

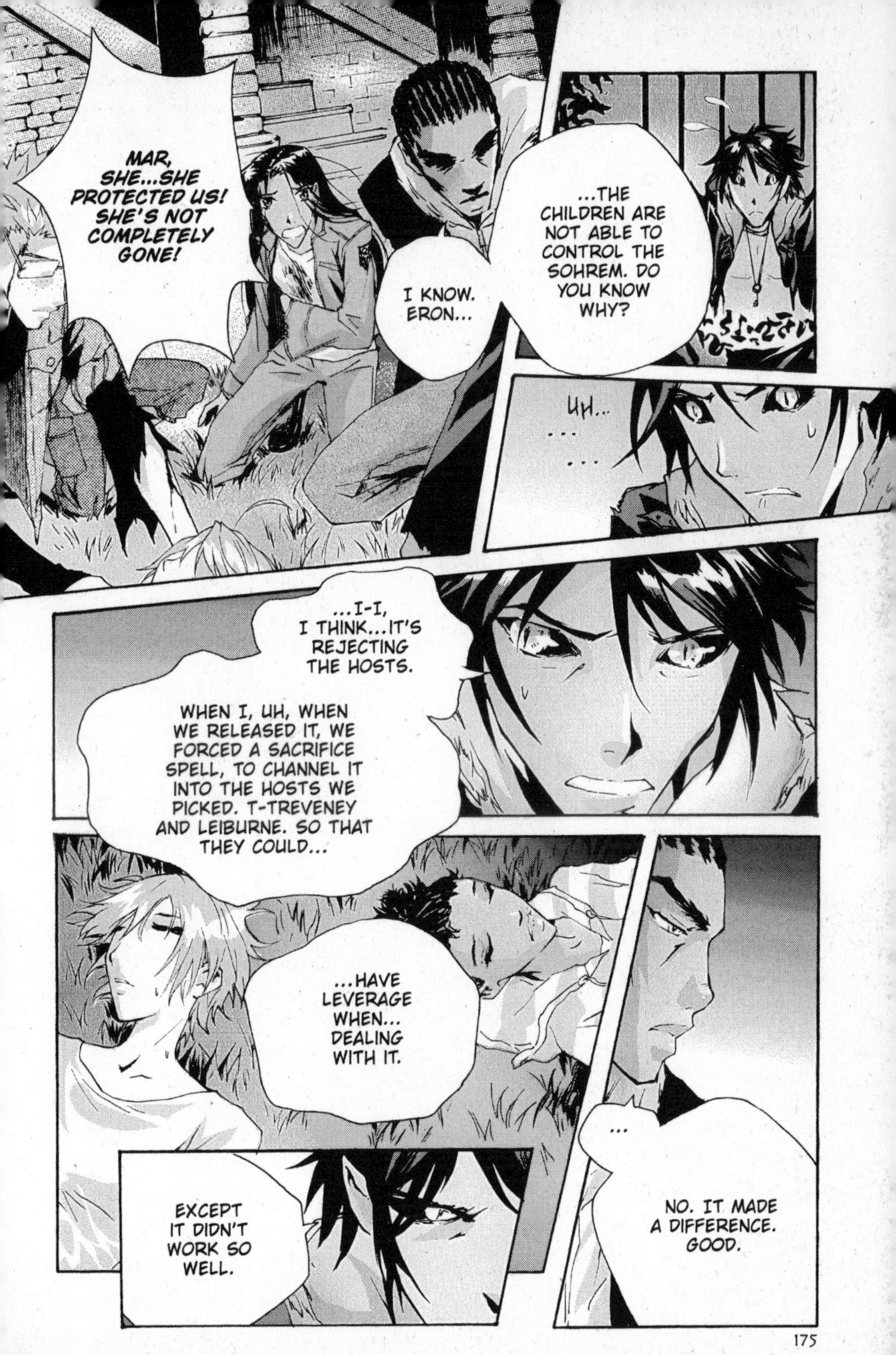

MAR, SHE...SHE PROTECTED US! SHE'S NOT COMPLETELY GONE!
I KNOW. ERON...
...THE CHILDREN ARE NOT ABLE TO CONTROL THE SOHREM. DO YOU KNOW WHY?
UH... ... ...
...I-I, I THINK...IT'S REJECTING THE HOSTS.
WHEN I, UH, WHEN WE RELEASED IT, WE FORCED A SACRIFICE SPELL, TO CHANNEL IT INTO THE HOSTS WE PICKED. T-TREVENEY AND LEIBURNE. SO THAT THEY COULD...
...HAVE LEVERAGE WHEN... DEALING WITH IT.
EXCEPT IT DIDN'T WORK SO WELL.
...
NO. IT MADE A DIFFERENCE. GOOD.

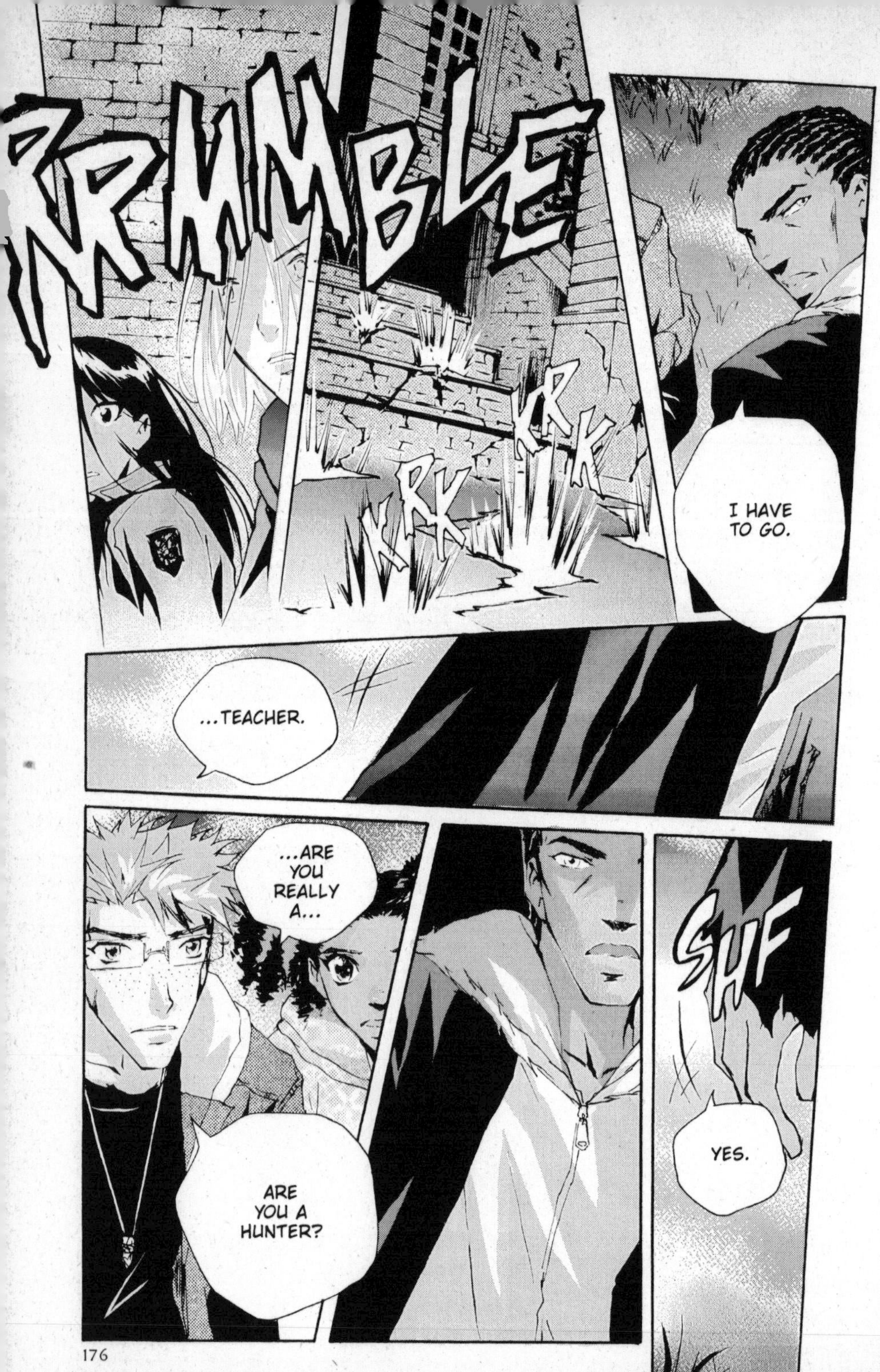
RUMBLE
KRK
KRK
I HAVE TO GO.
...TEACHER.
...ARE YOU REALLY A...
ARE YOU A HUNTER?
SHF
YES.

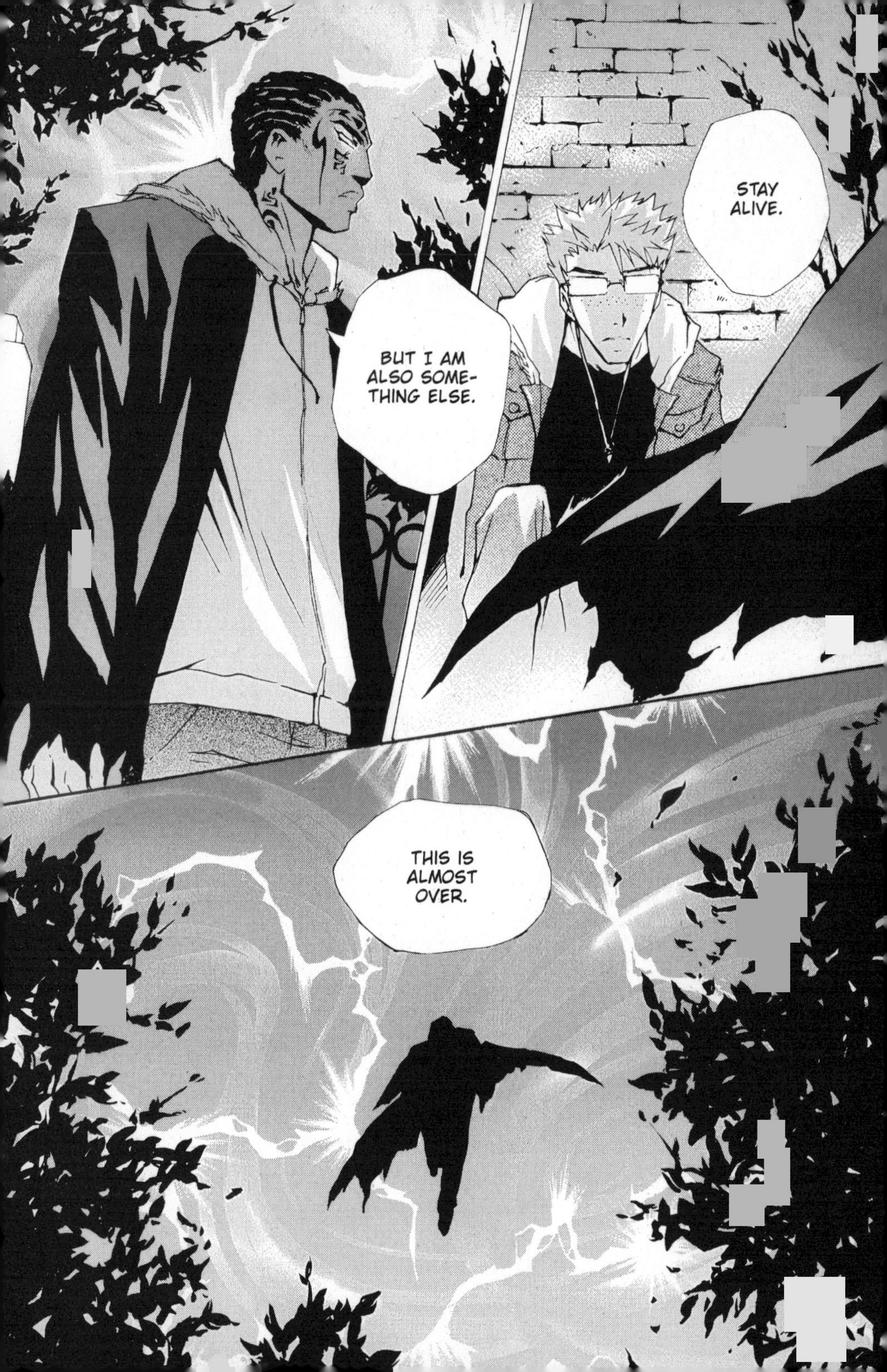
BUT I AM ALSO SOME-THING ELSE.
STAY ALIVE.
THIS IS ALMOST OVER.

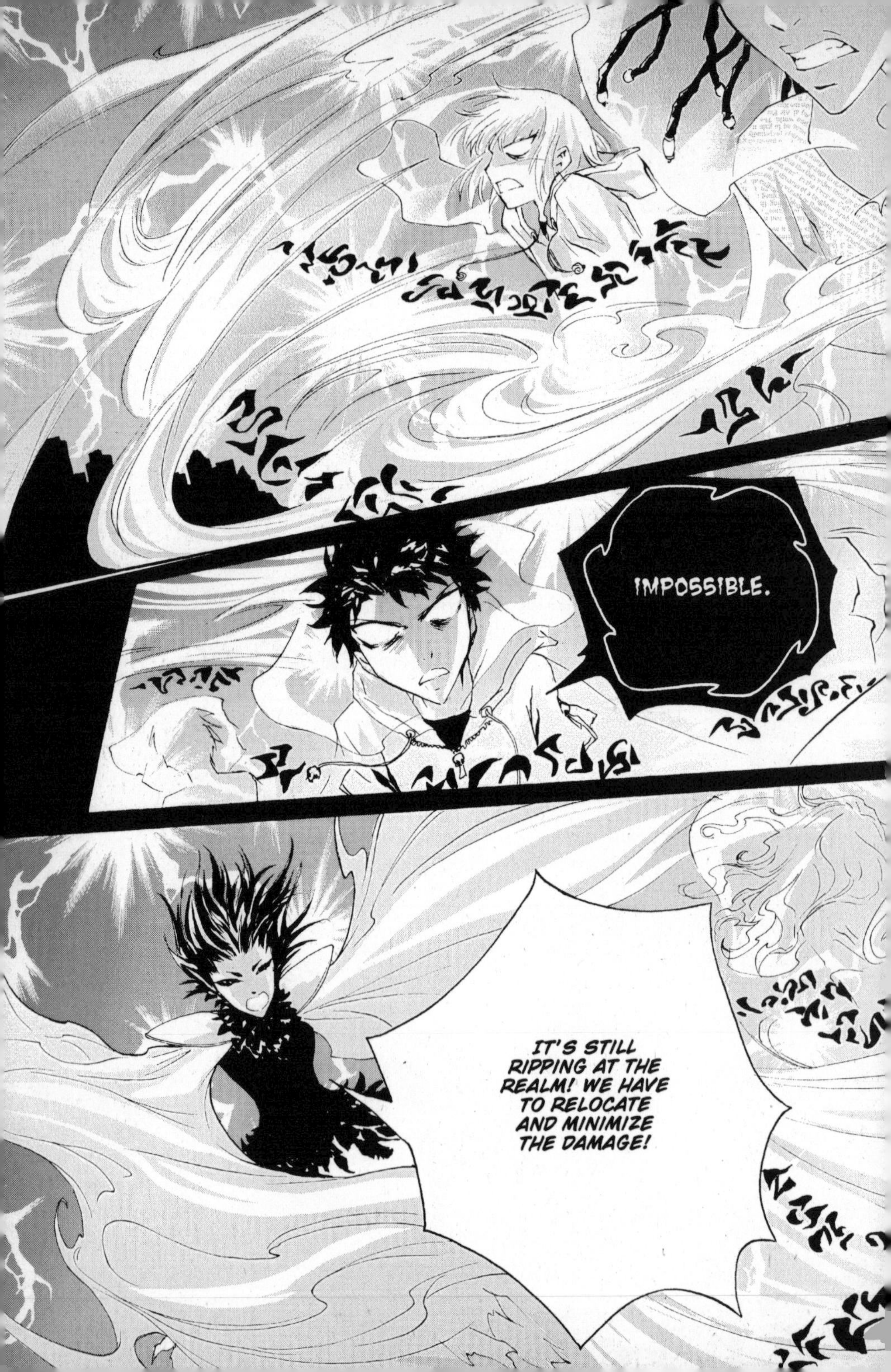
IMPOSSIBLE.
IT'S STILL RIPPING AT THE REALM! WE HAVE TO RELOCATE AND MINIMIZE THE DAMAGE!

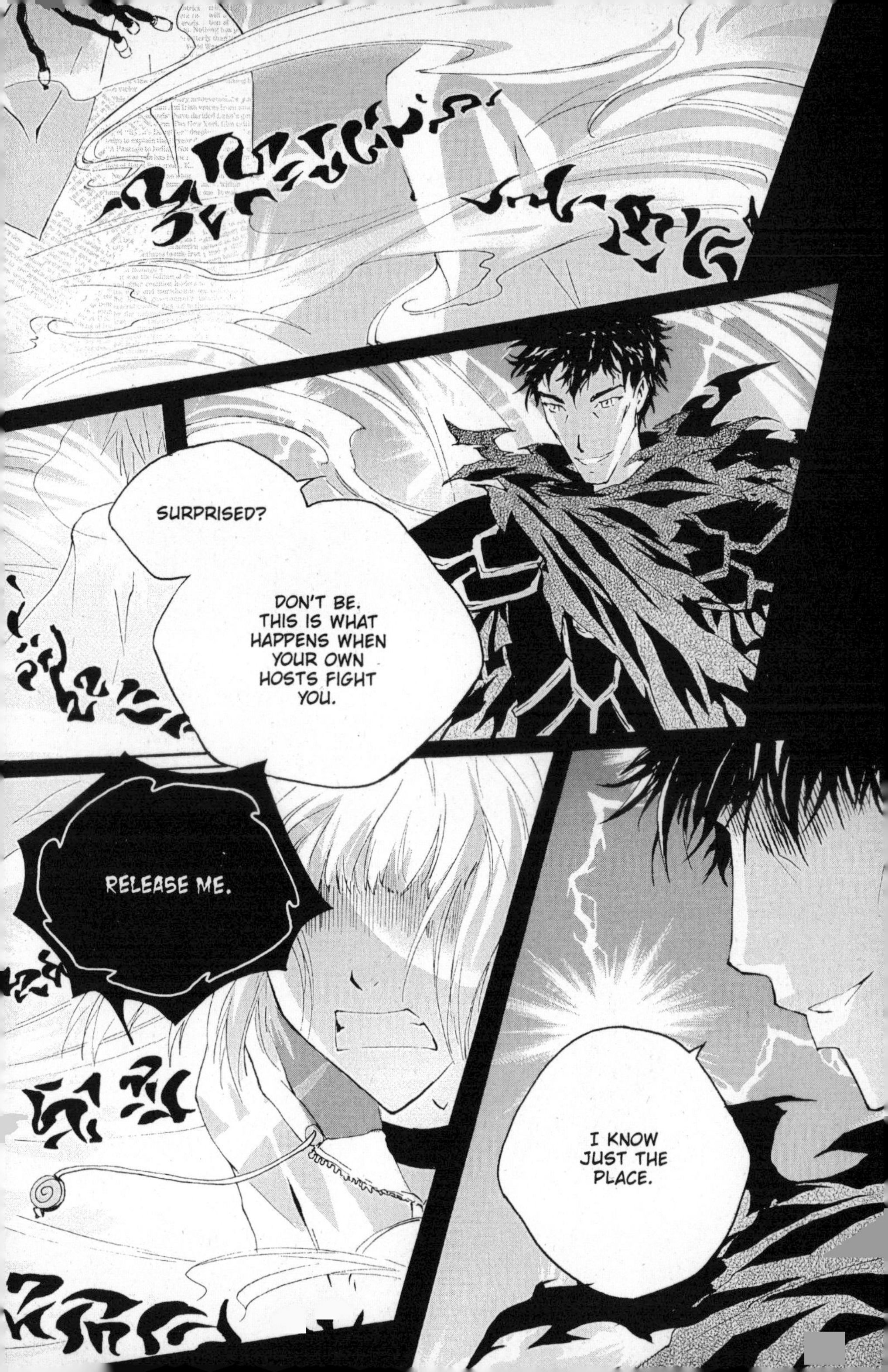
SURPRISED?
DON'T BE. THIS IS WHAT HAPPENS WHEN YOUR OWN HOSTS FIGHT YOU.
RELEASE ME.
I KNOW JUST THE PLACE.

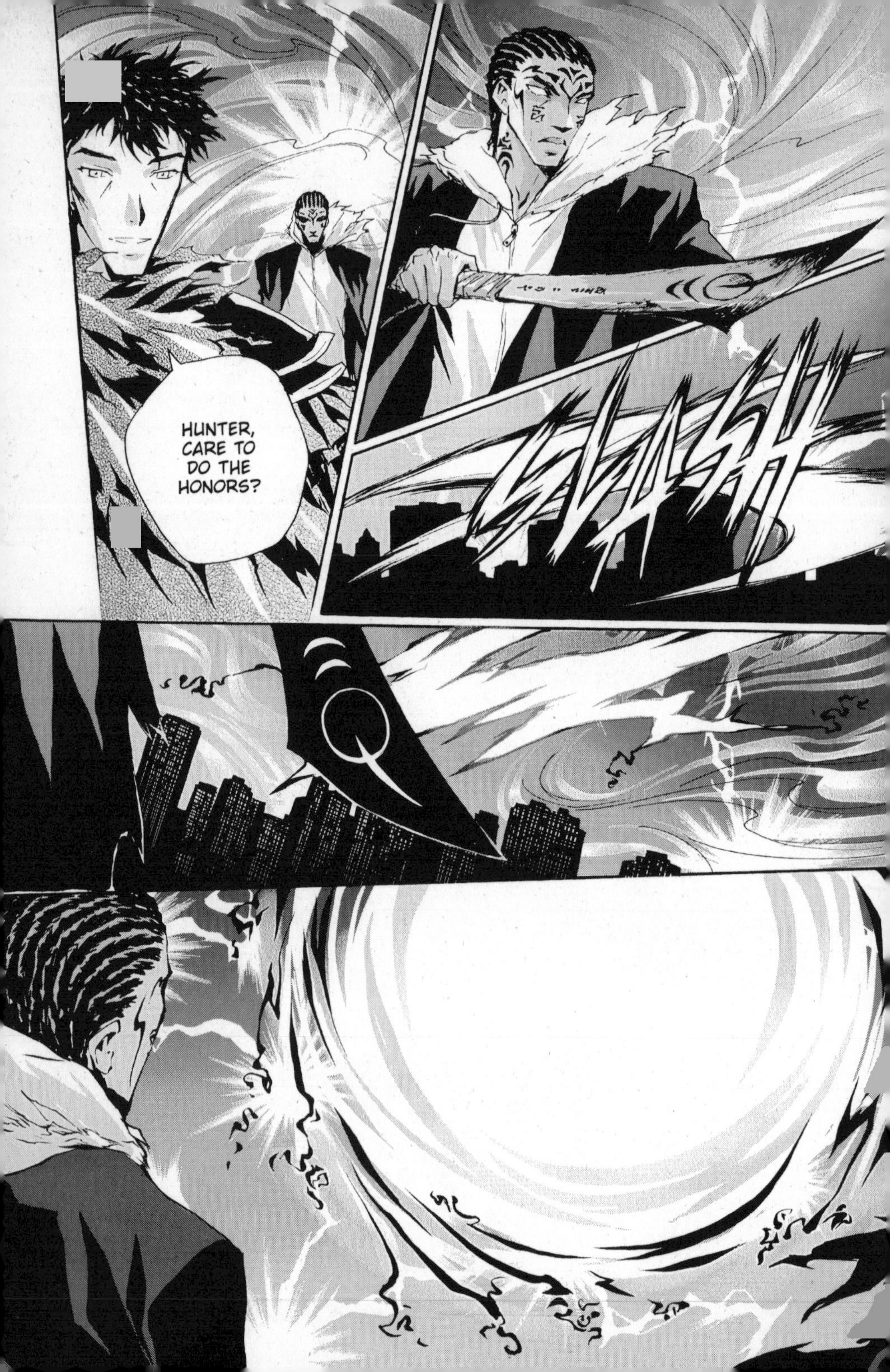
HUNTER, CARE TO DO THE HONORS?
SHASH

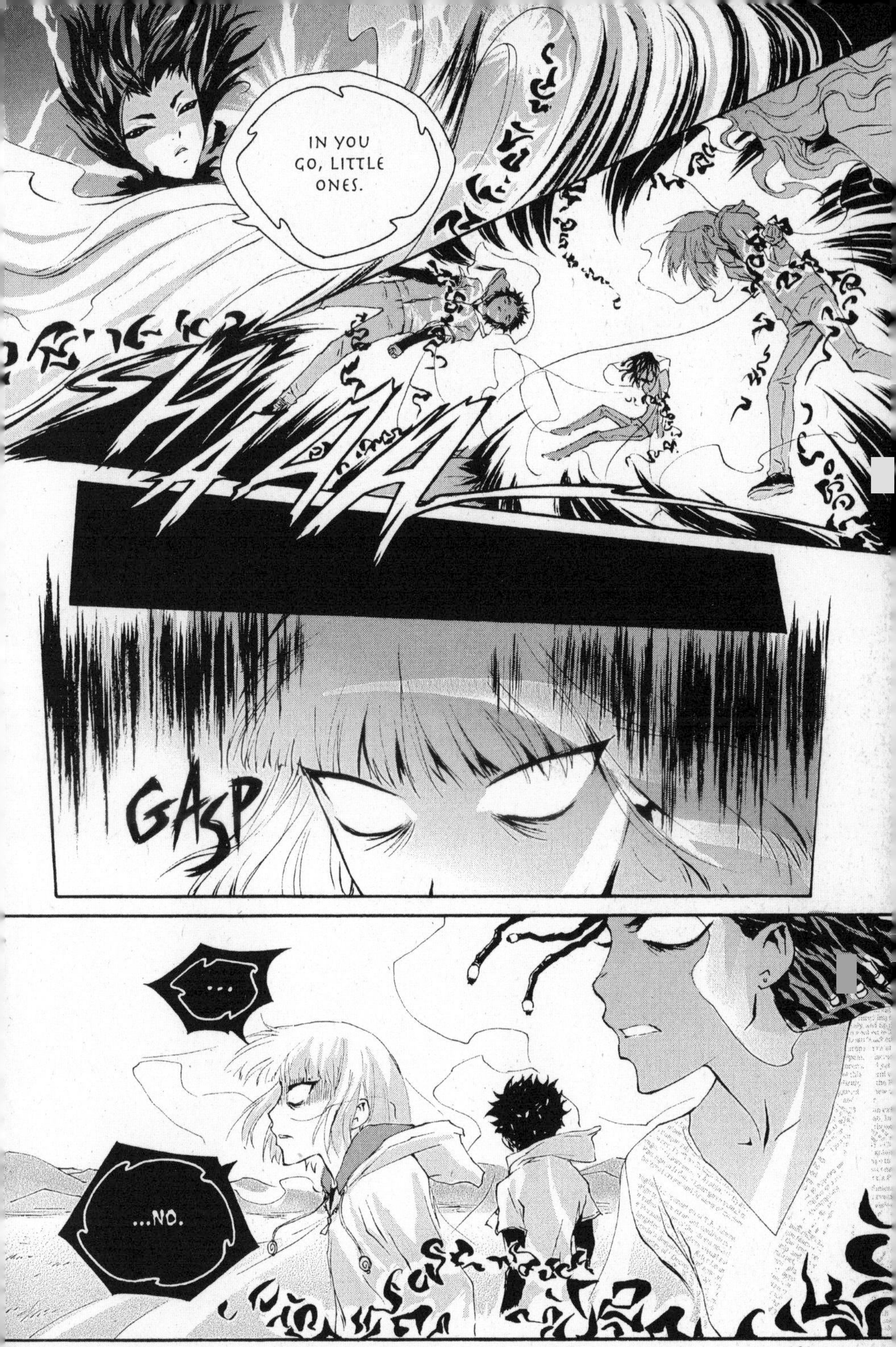
IN YOU GO, LITTLE ONES.
SHAAA
GASP
...
...NO.

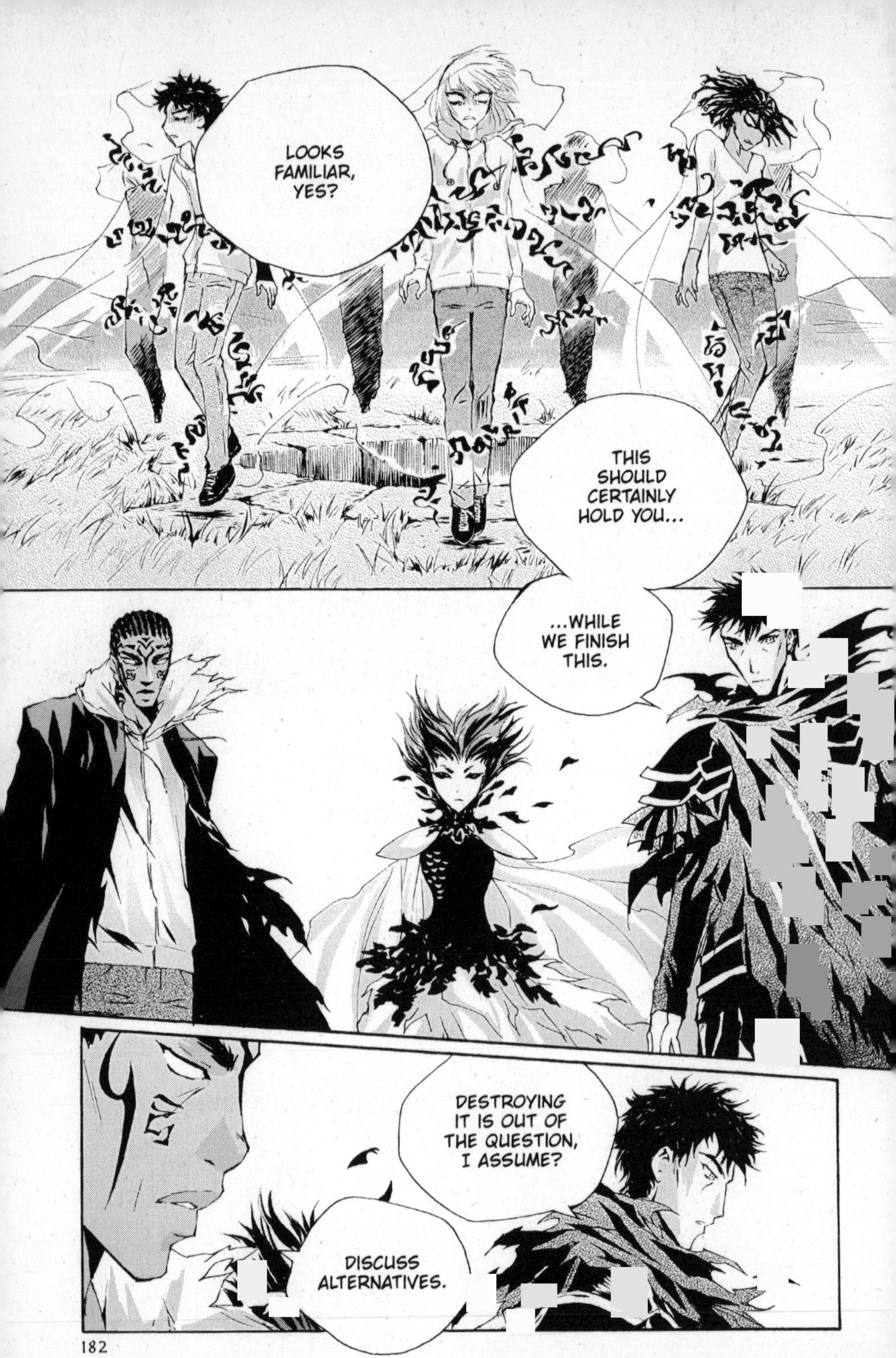
LOOKS FAMILIAR, YES?
THIS SHOULD CERTAINLY HOLD YOU...
...WHILE WE FINISH THIS.
DESTROYING IT IS OUT OF THE QUESTION, I ASSUME?
DISCUSS ALTERNATIVES.

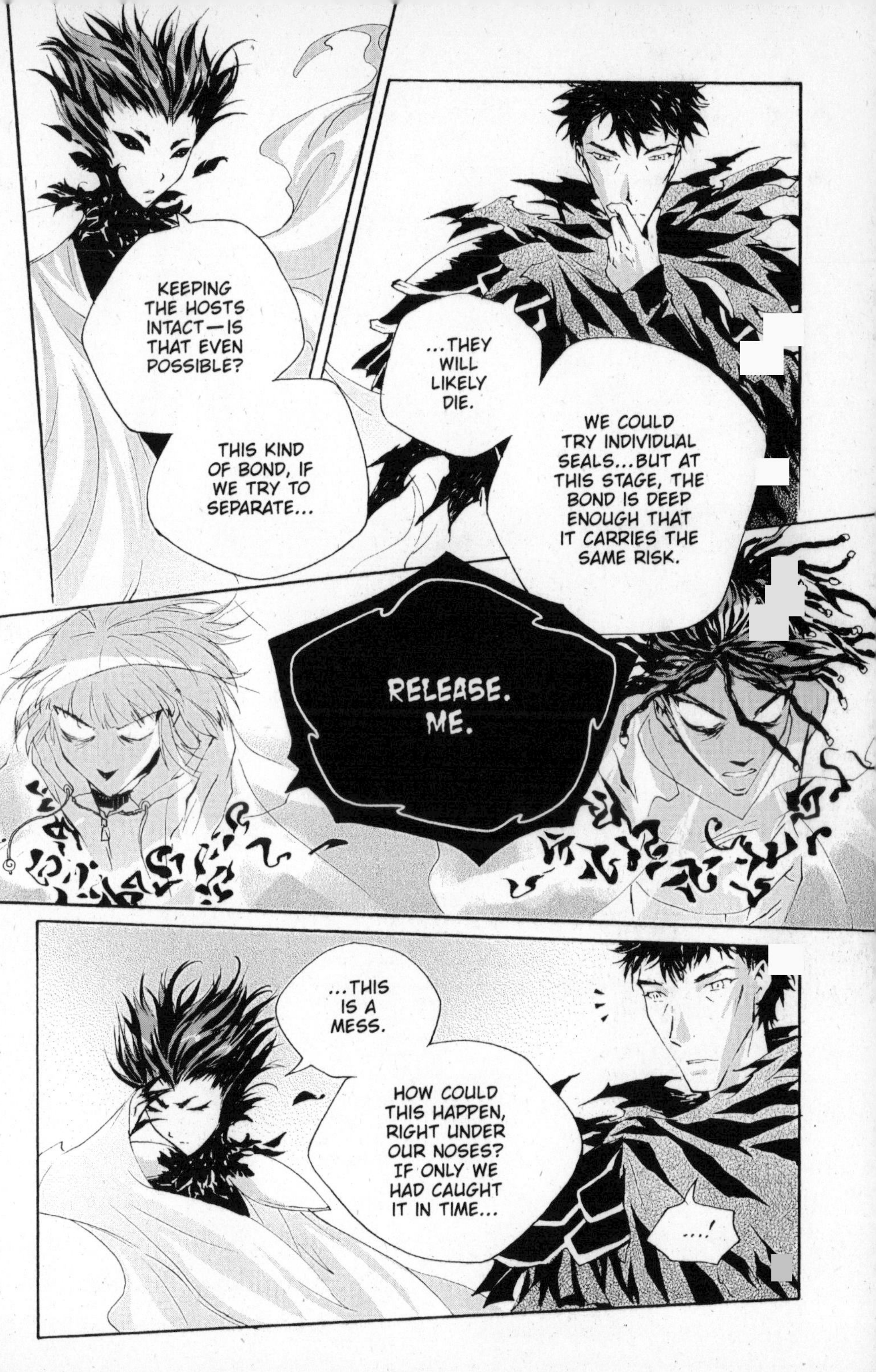
KEEPING THE HOSTS INTACT—IS THAT EVEN POSSIBLE?
THIS KIND OF BOND, IF WE TRY TO SEPARATE...
...THEY WILL LIKELY DIE.
WE COULD TRY INDIVIDUAL SEALS...BUT AT THIS STAGE, THE BOND IS DEEP ENOUGH THAT IT CARRIES THE SAME RISK.
RELEASE. ME.
...THIS IS A MESS.
HOW COULD THIS HAPPEN, RIGHT UNDER OUR NOSES? IF ONLY WE HAD CAUGHT IT IN TIME...
....!

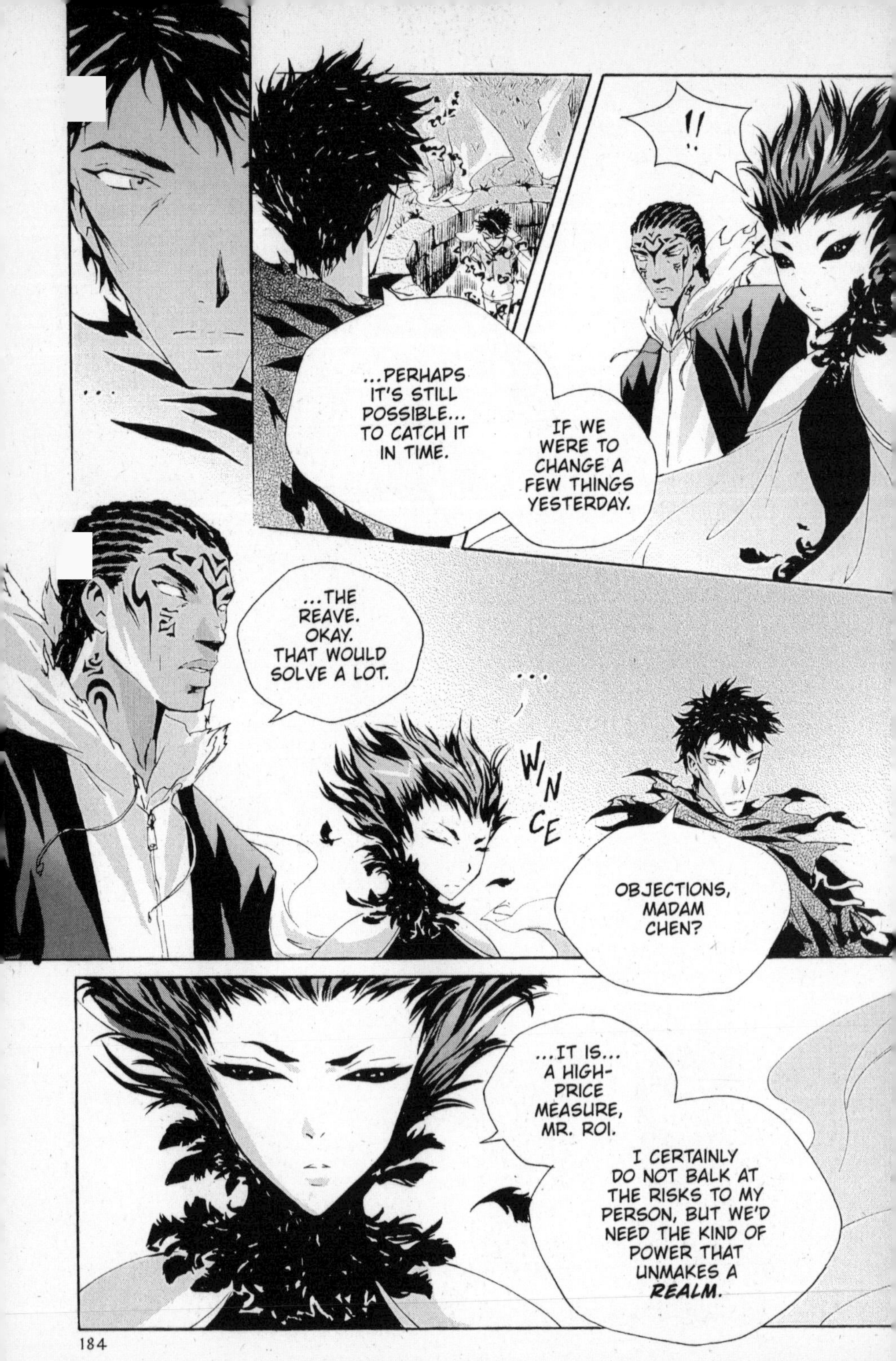
...
...PERHAPS IT'S STILL POSSIBLE... TO CATCH IT IN TIME.
IF WE WERE TO CHANGE A FEW THINGS YESTERDAY.
!!
...THE REAVE. OKAY. THAT WOULD SOLVE A LOT.
...
WINCE
OBJECTIONS, MADAM CHEN?
...IT IS... A HIGH-PRICE MEASURE, MR. ROI.
I CERTAINLY DO NOT BALK AT THE RISKS TO MY PERSON, BUT WE'D NEED THE KIND OF POWER THAT UNMAKES A ***REALM***.

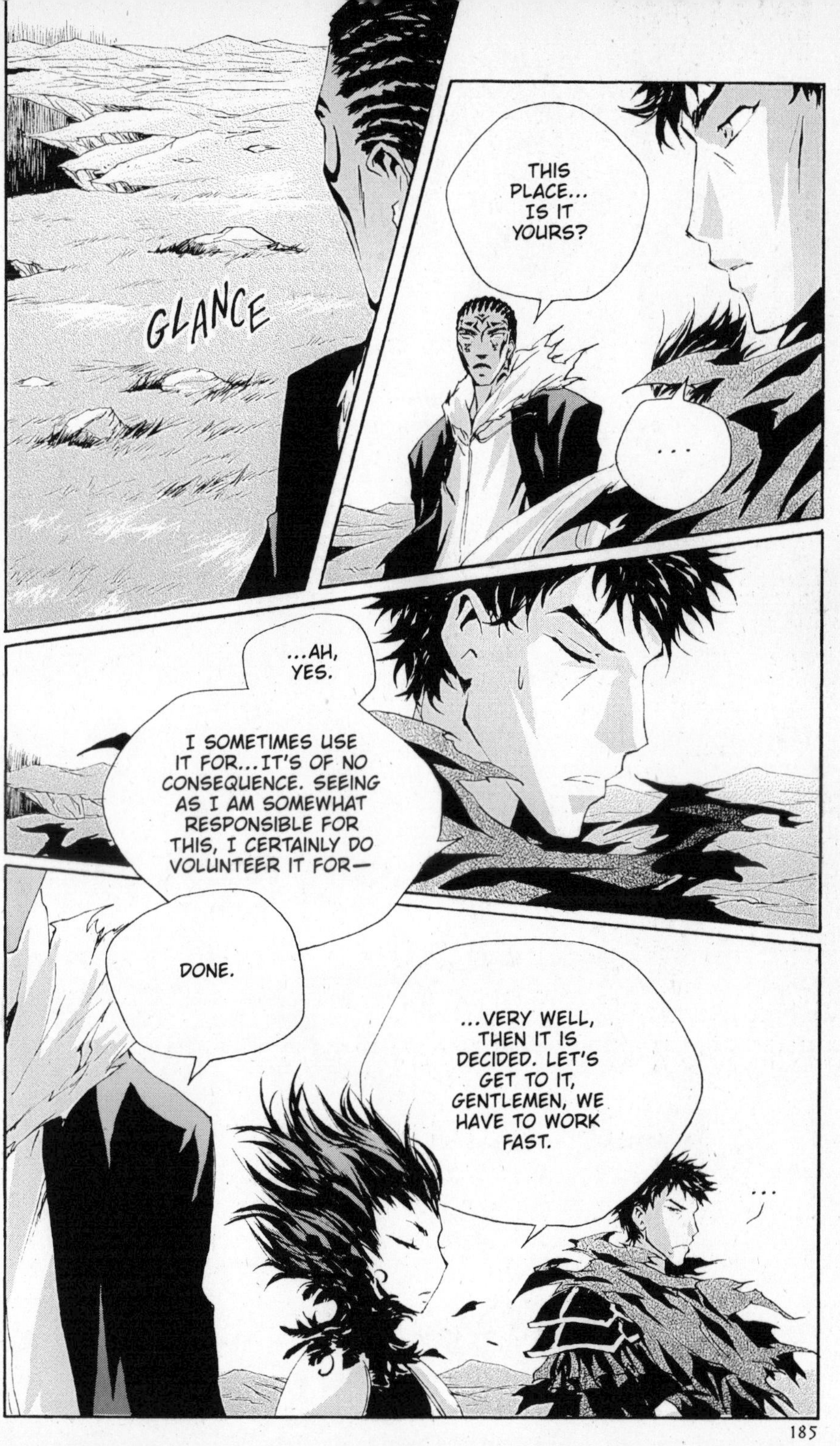
GLANCE
THIS PLACE... IS IT YOURS?
...
...AH, YES.
I SOMETIMES USE IT FOR...IT'S OF NO CONSEQUENCE. SEEING AS I AM SOMEWHAT RESPONSIBLE FOR THIS, I CERTAINLY DO VOLUNTEER IT FOR—
DONE.
...VERY WELL, THEN IT IS DECIDED. LET'S GET TO IT, GENTLEMEN, WE HAVE TO WORK FAST.
...

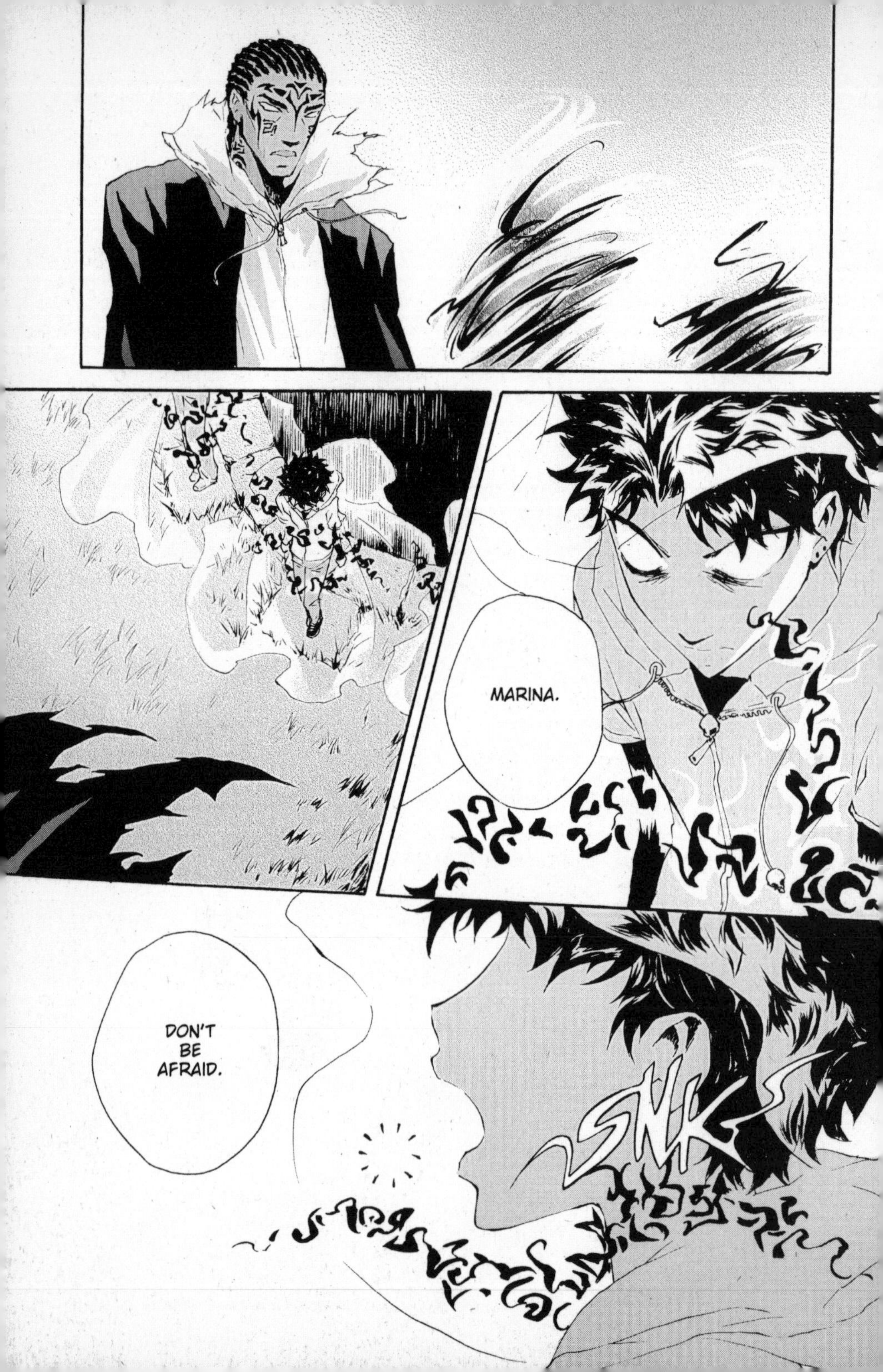
MARINA.
DON'T BE AFRAID.
SNK

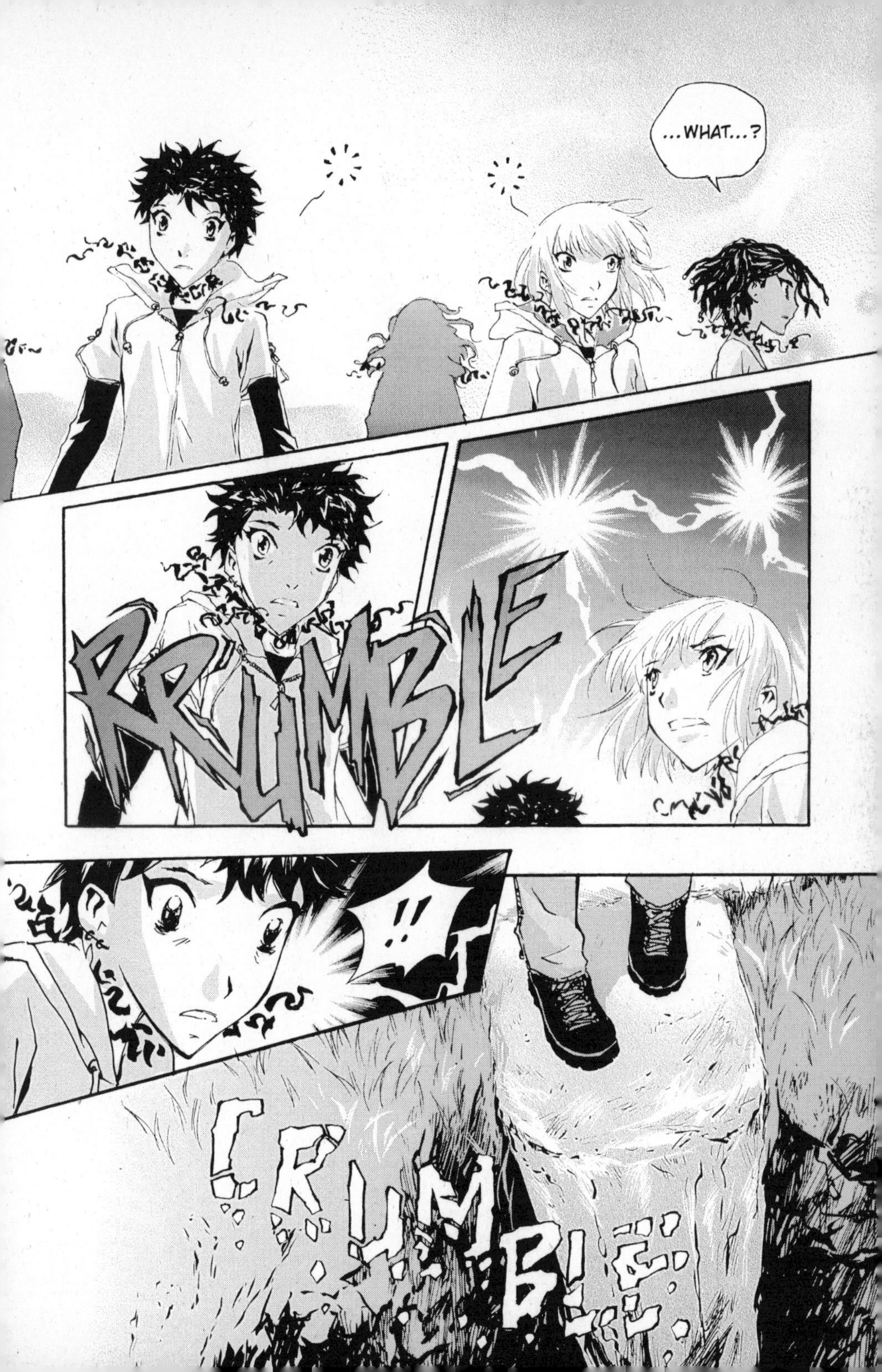
...WHAT...?
RUMBLE
!!
CRUMBLE

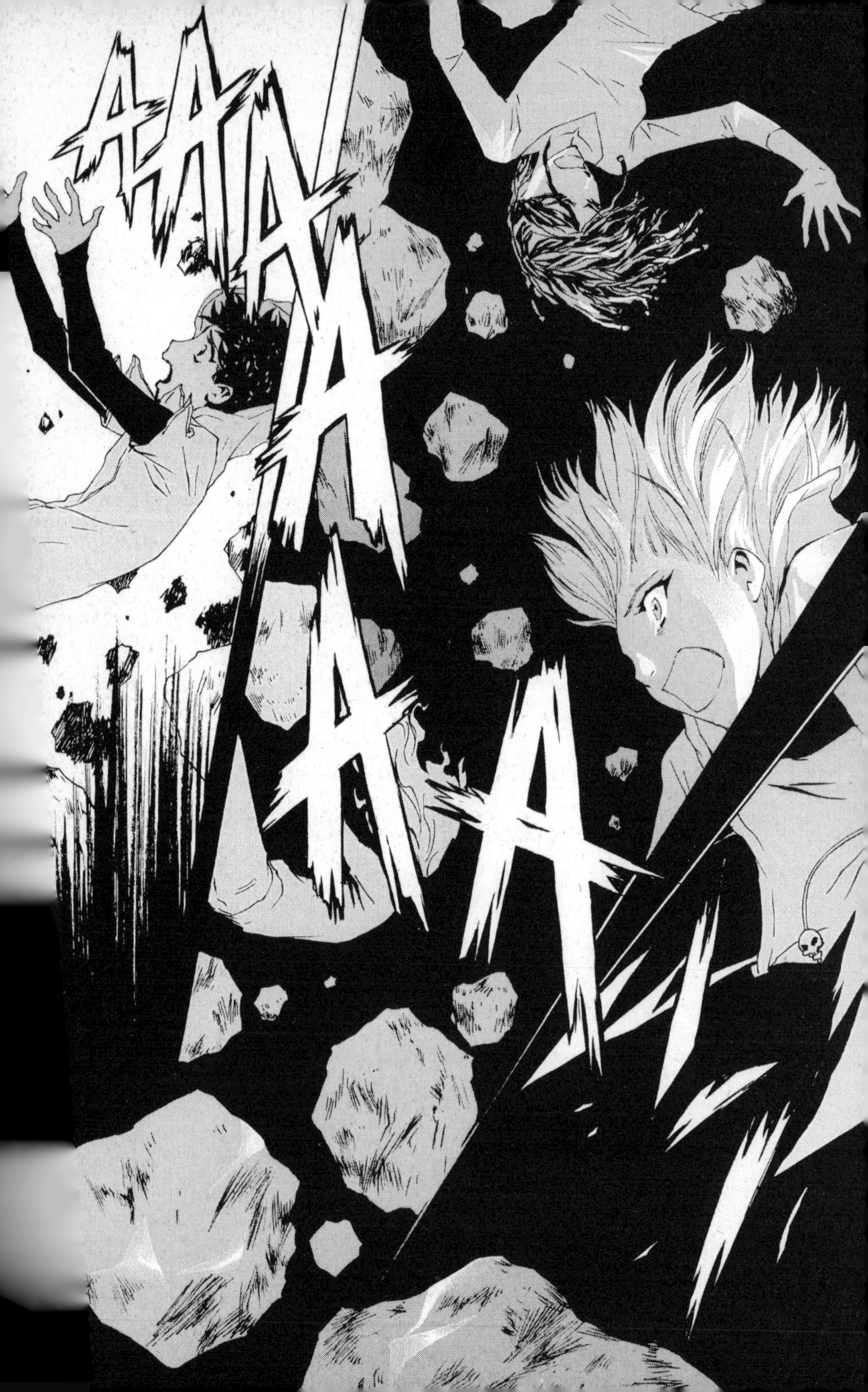
AAAAAA

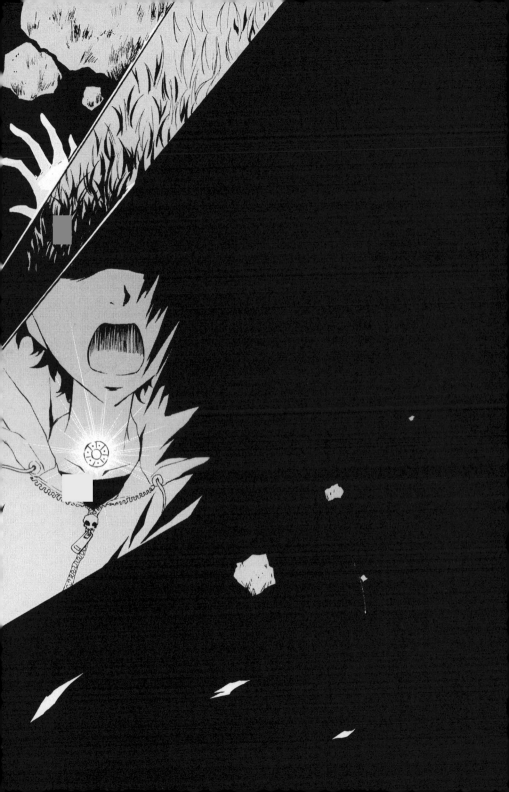

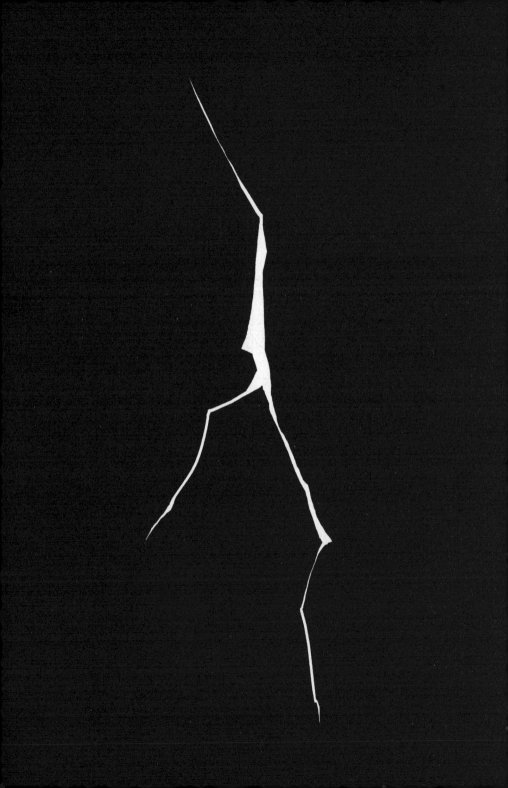

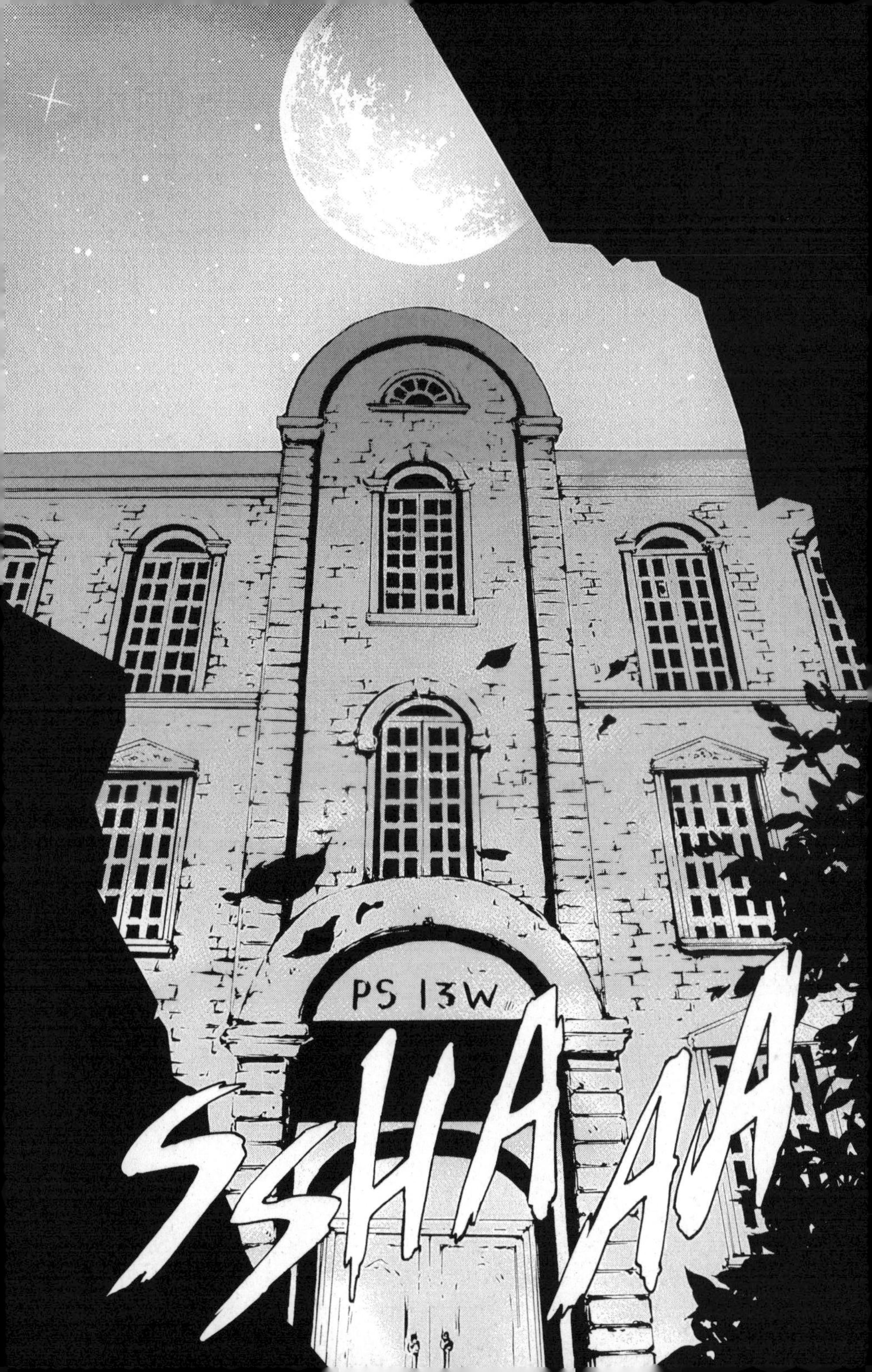
PS 13W
SSHAAA

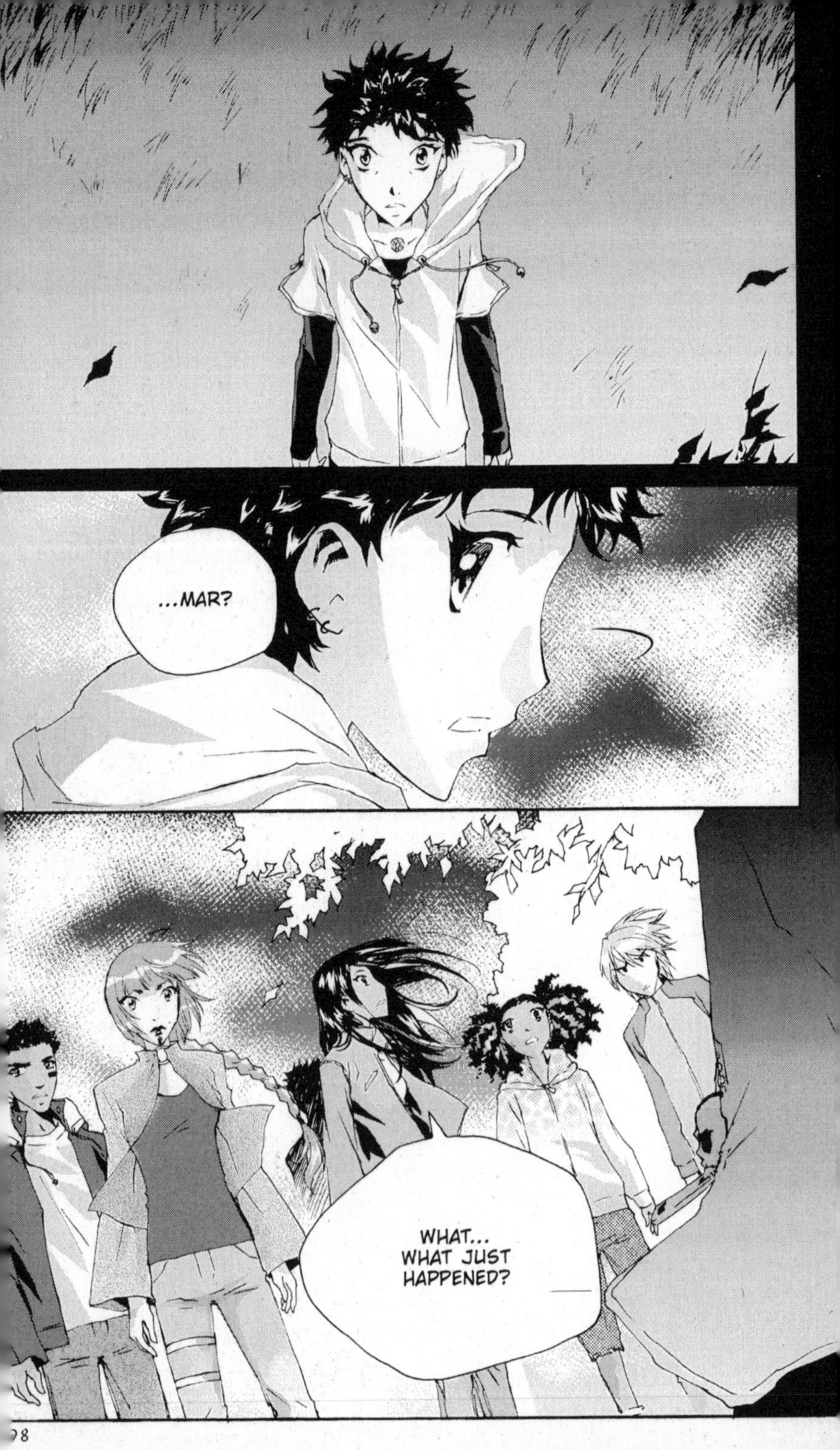
...MAR?
WHAT... WHAT JUST HAPPENED?

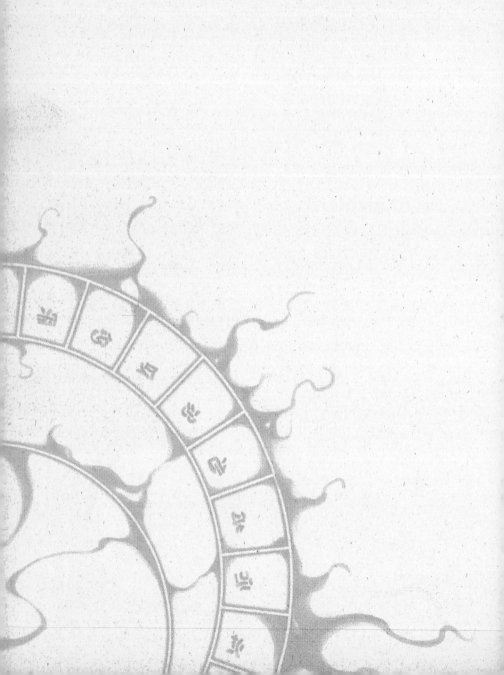

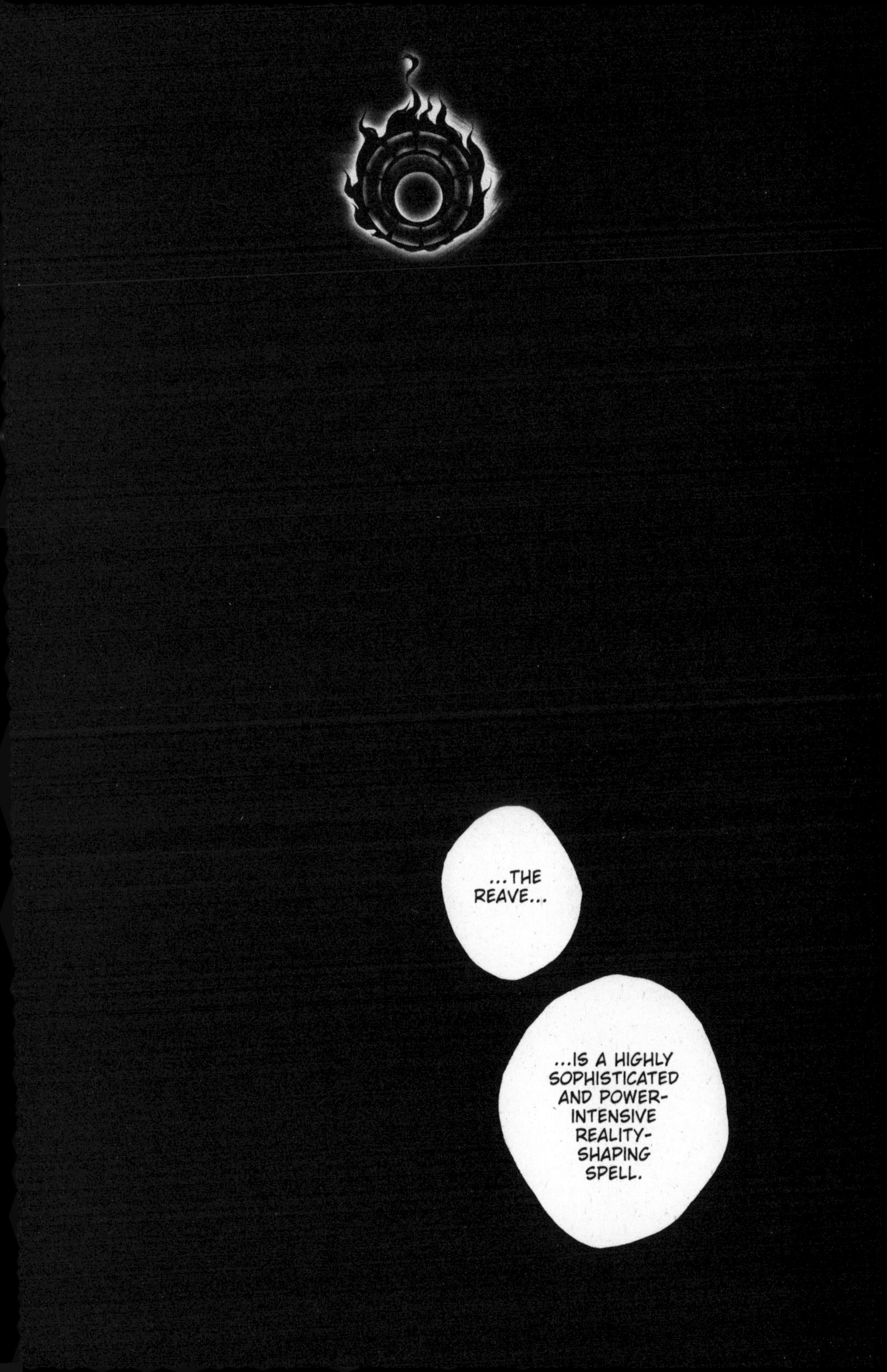
...THE REAVE...
...IS A HIGHLY SOPHISTICATED AND POWER-INTENSIVE REALITY-SHAPING SPELL.

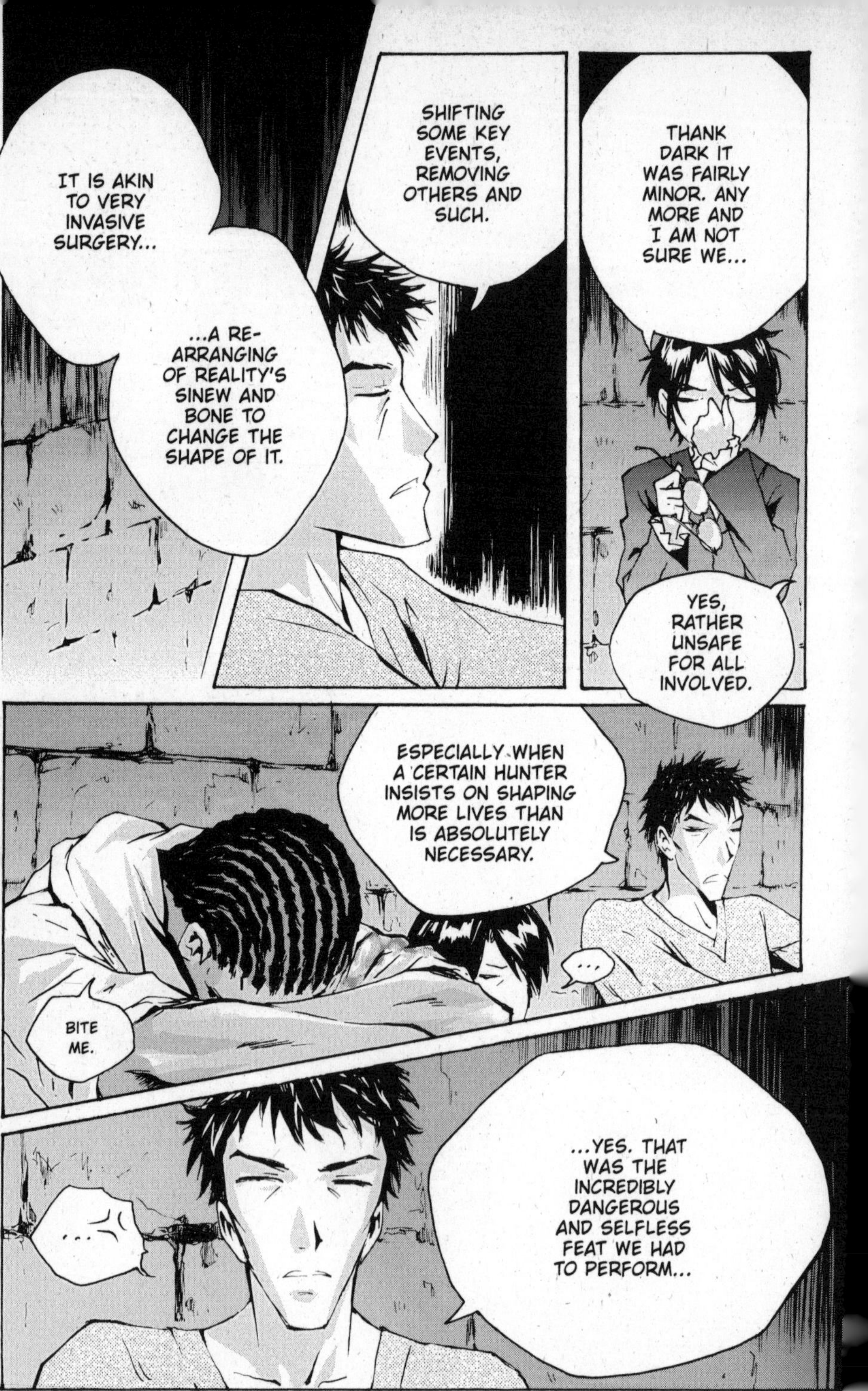
IT IS AKIN TO VERY INVASIVE SURGERY...
...A RE-ARRANGING OF REALITY'S SINEW AND BONE TO CHANGE THE SHAPE OF IT.
SHIFTING SOME KEY EVENTS, REMOVING OTHERS AND SUCH.
THANK DARK IT WAS FAIRLY MINOR. ANY MORE AND I AM NOT SURE WE...
YES, RATHER UNSAFE FOR ALL INVOLVED.
ESPECIALLY WHEN A CERTAIN HUNTER INSISTS ON SHAPING MORE LIVES THAN IS ABSOLUTELY NECESSARY.
BITE ME.
...
...
...YES. THAT WAS THE INCREDIBLY DANGEROUS AND SELFLESS FEAT WE HAD TO PERFORM...

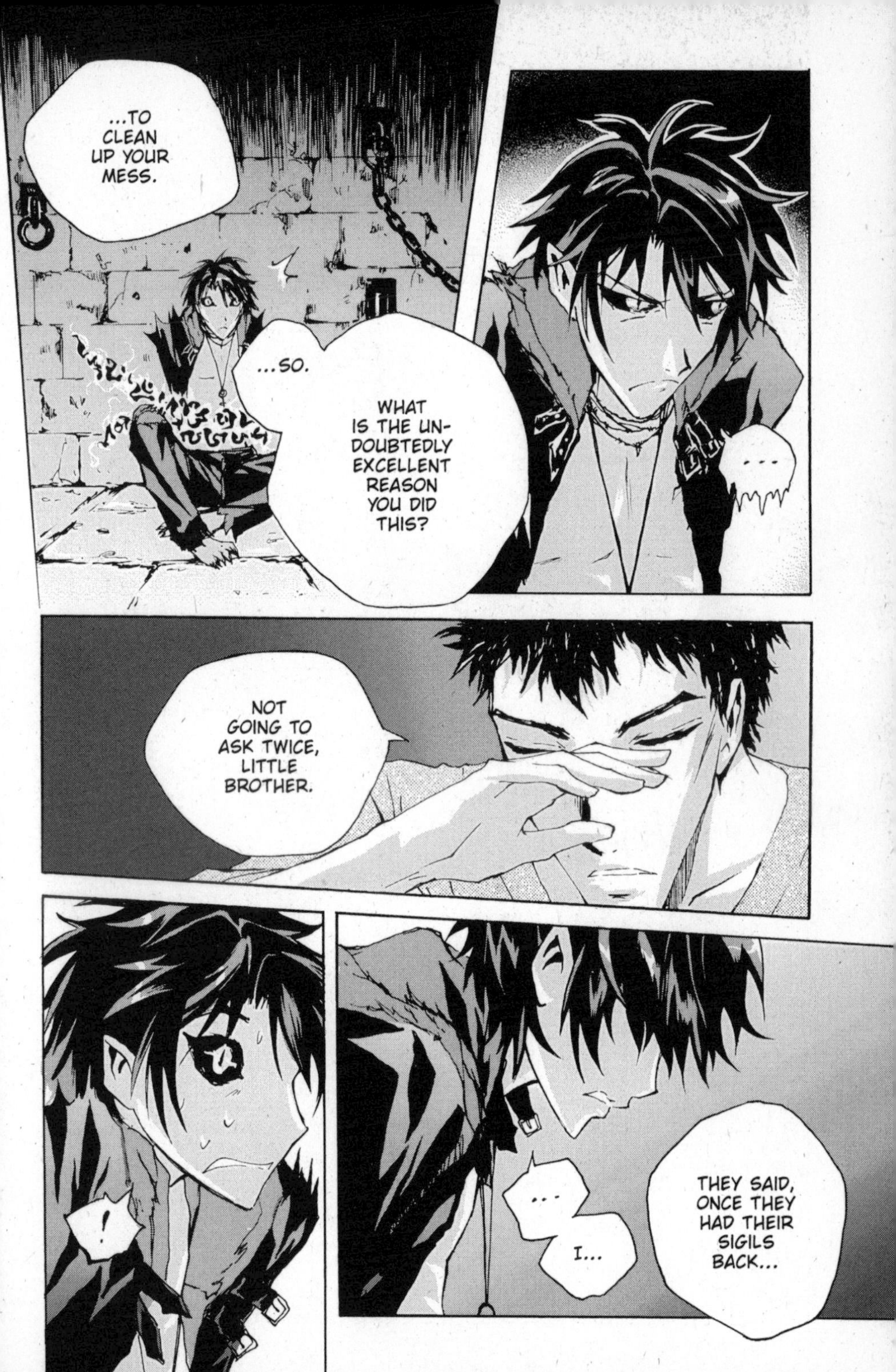
...TO CLEAN UP YOUR MESS.
...SO.
WHAT IS THE UN-DOUBTEDLY EXCELLENT REASON YOU DID THIS?
...
NOT GOING TO ASK TWICE, LITTLE BROTHER.
!
...
I...
THEY SAID, ONCE THEY HAD THEIR SIGILS BACK...

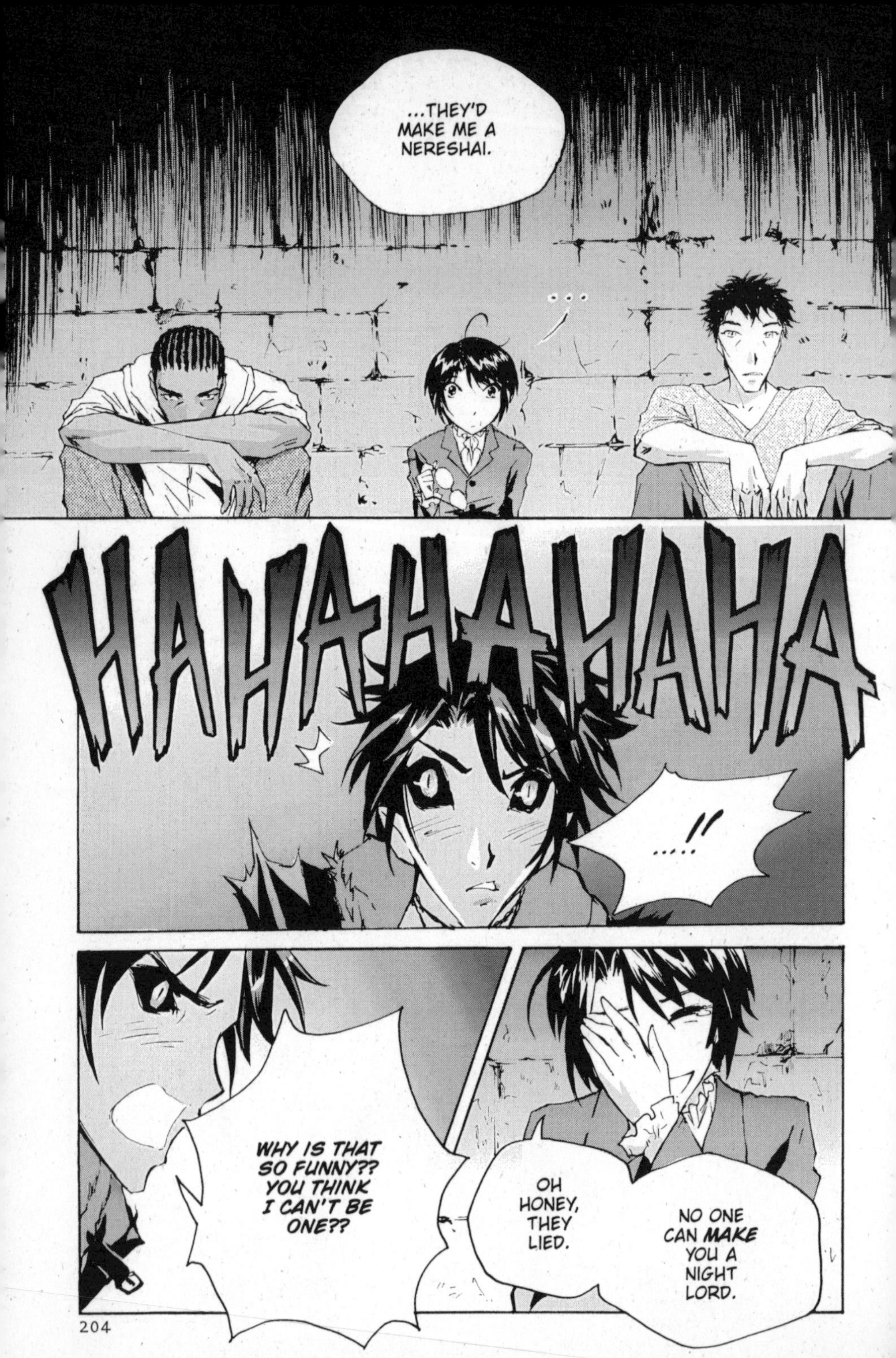
...THEY'D MAKE ME A NERESHAI.
HAHAHAHAHAHA
...!!
WHY IS THAT SO FUNNY?? YOU THINK I CAN'T BE ONE??
OH HONEY, THEY LIED.
NO ONE CAN *MAKE* YOU A NIGHT LORD.

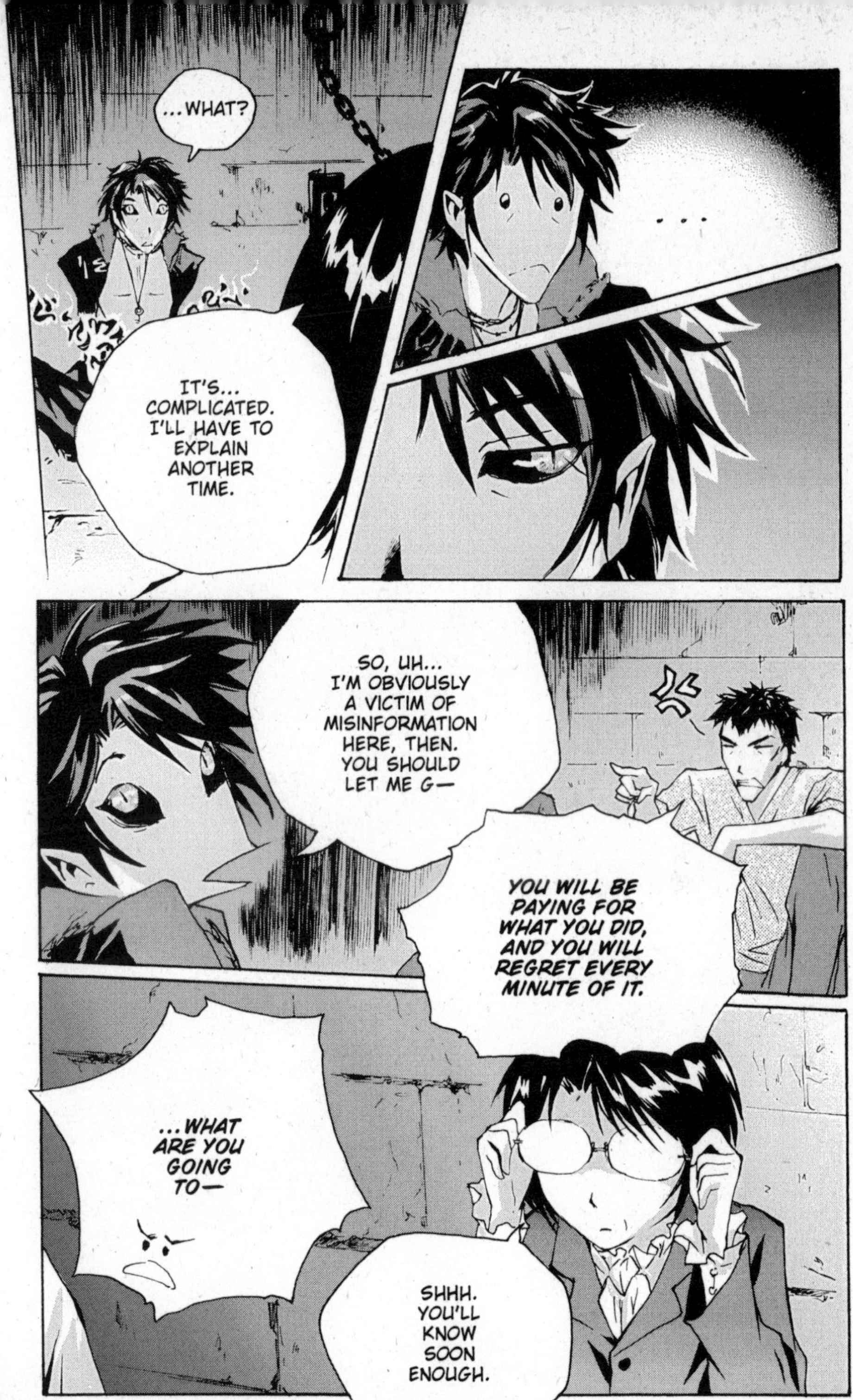
...WHAT?
...
IT'S... COMPLICATED. I'LL HAVE TO EXPLAIN ANOTHER TIME.
SO, UH... I'M OBVIOUSLY A VICTIM OF MISINFORMATION HERE, THEN. YOU SHOULD LET ME G—
YOU WILL BE PAYING FOR WHAT YOU DID, AND YOU WILL REGRET EVERY MINUTE OF IT.
...WHAT ARE YOU GOING TO—
SHHH. YOU'LL KNOW SOON ENOUGH.

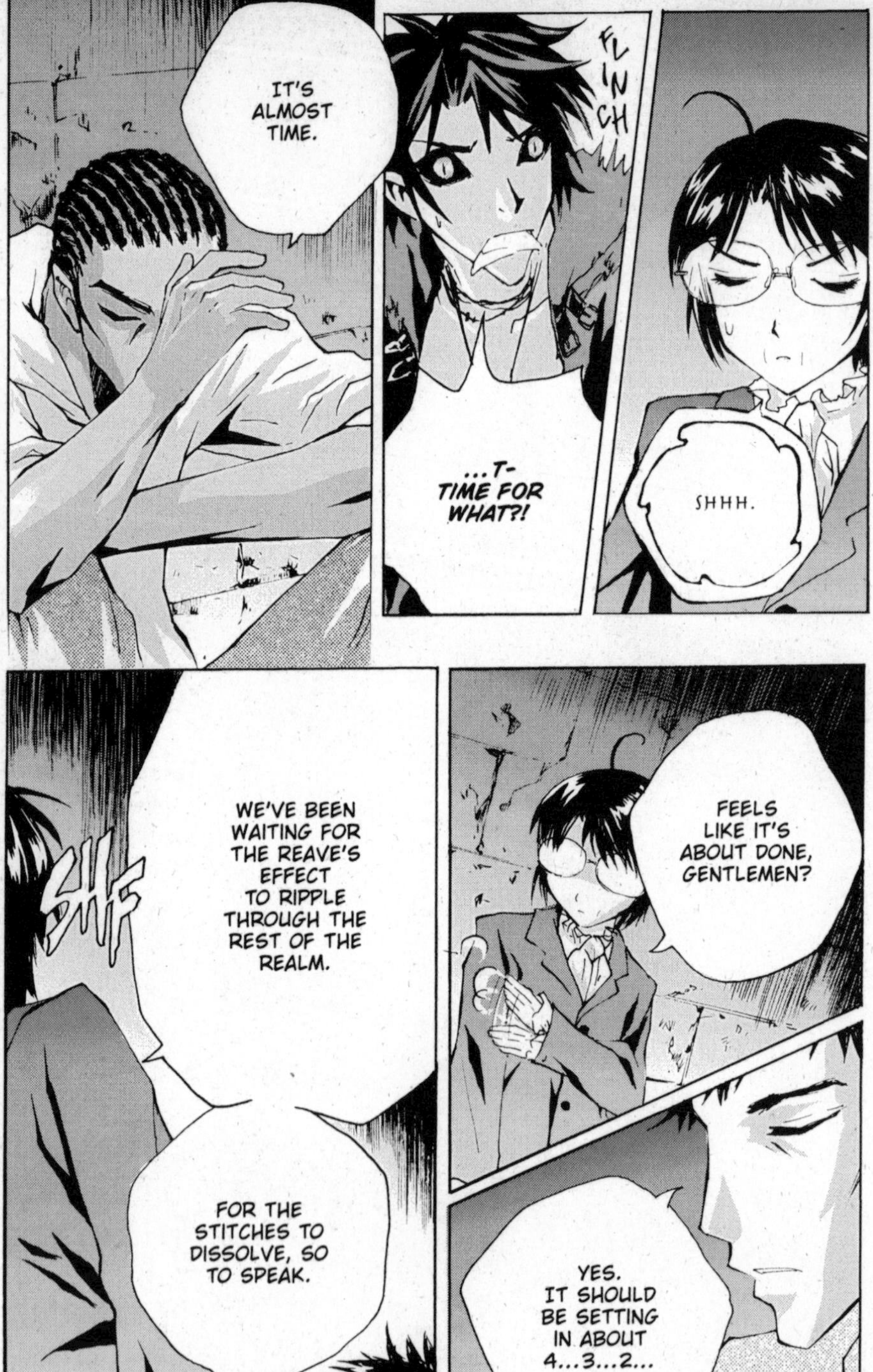
IT'S ALMOST TIME.
FLINCH
...T-TIME FOR WHAT?!
SHHH.
WE'VE BEEN WAITING FOR THE REAVE'S EFFECT TO RIPPLE THROUGH THE REST OF THE REALM.
SHF
FOR THE STITCHES TO DISSOLVE, SO TO SPEAK.
FEELS LIKE IT'S ABOUT DONE, GENTLEMEN?
YES. IT SHOULD BE SETTING IN ABOUT 4...3...2...

1.

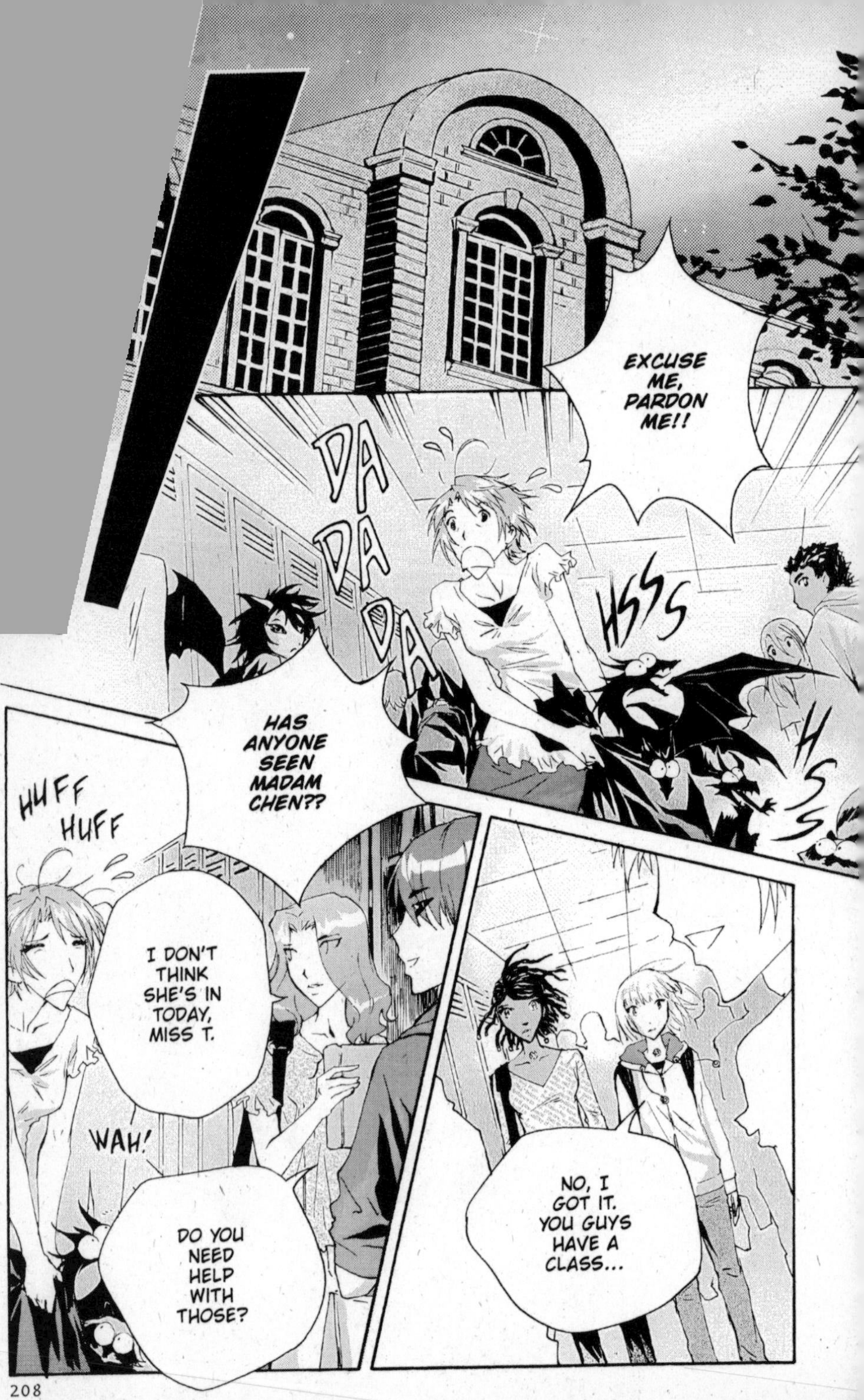
DA DA DA
EXCUSE ME, PARDON ME!!
HSSS
HAS ANYONE SEEN MADAM CHEN??
HSS
HUFF HUFF
I DON'T THINK SHE'S IN TODAY, MISS T.
WAH!
DO YOU NEED HELP WITH THOSE?
NO, I GOT IT. YOU GUYS HAVE A CLASS...

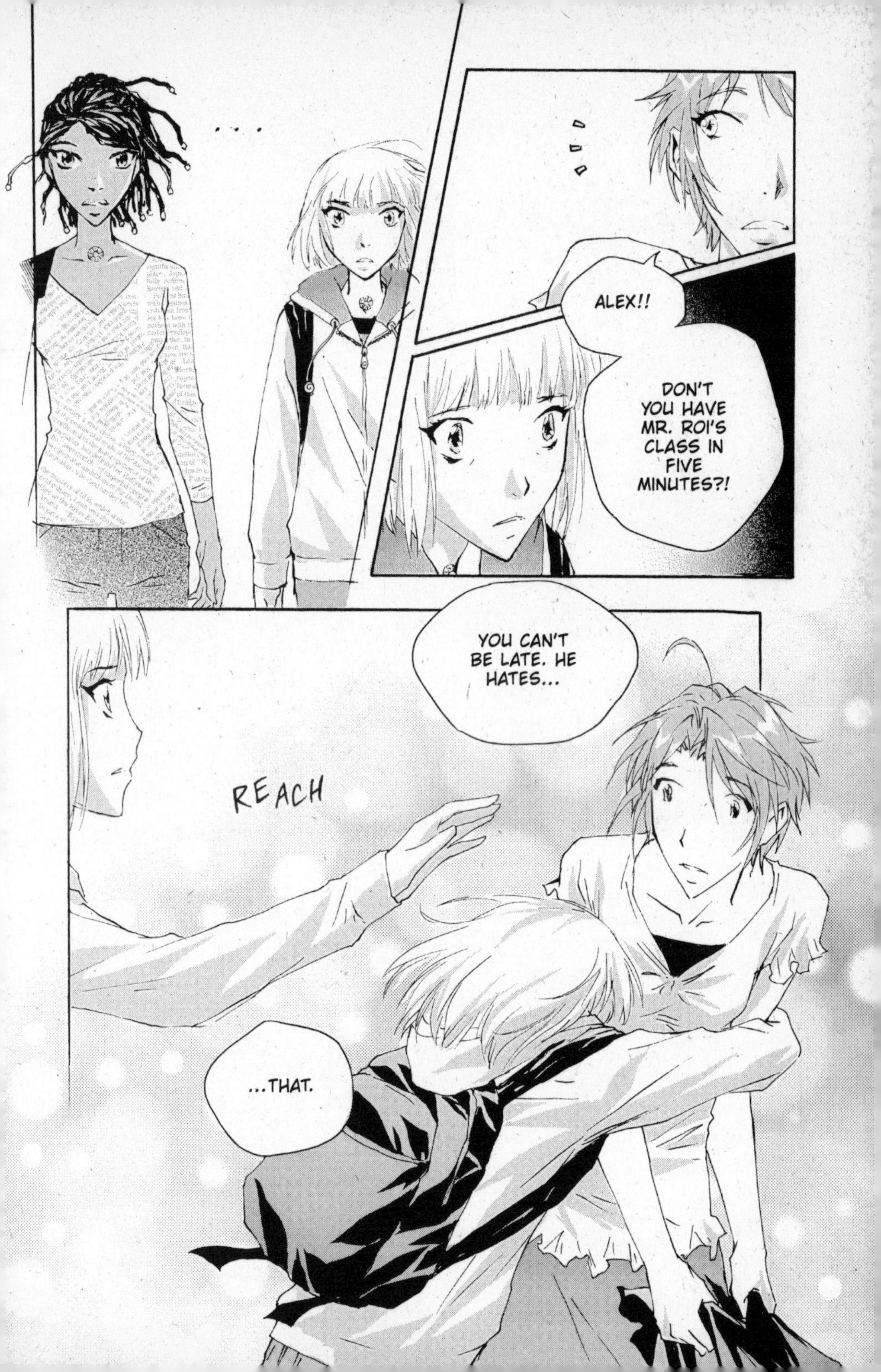
. . .
ALEX!!
DON'T YOU HAVE MR. ROI'S CLASS IN FIVE MINUTES?!
YOU CAN'T BE LATE. HE HATES...
REACH
...THAT.

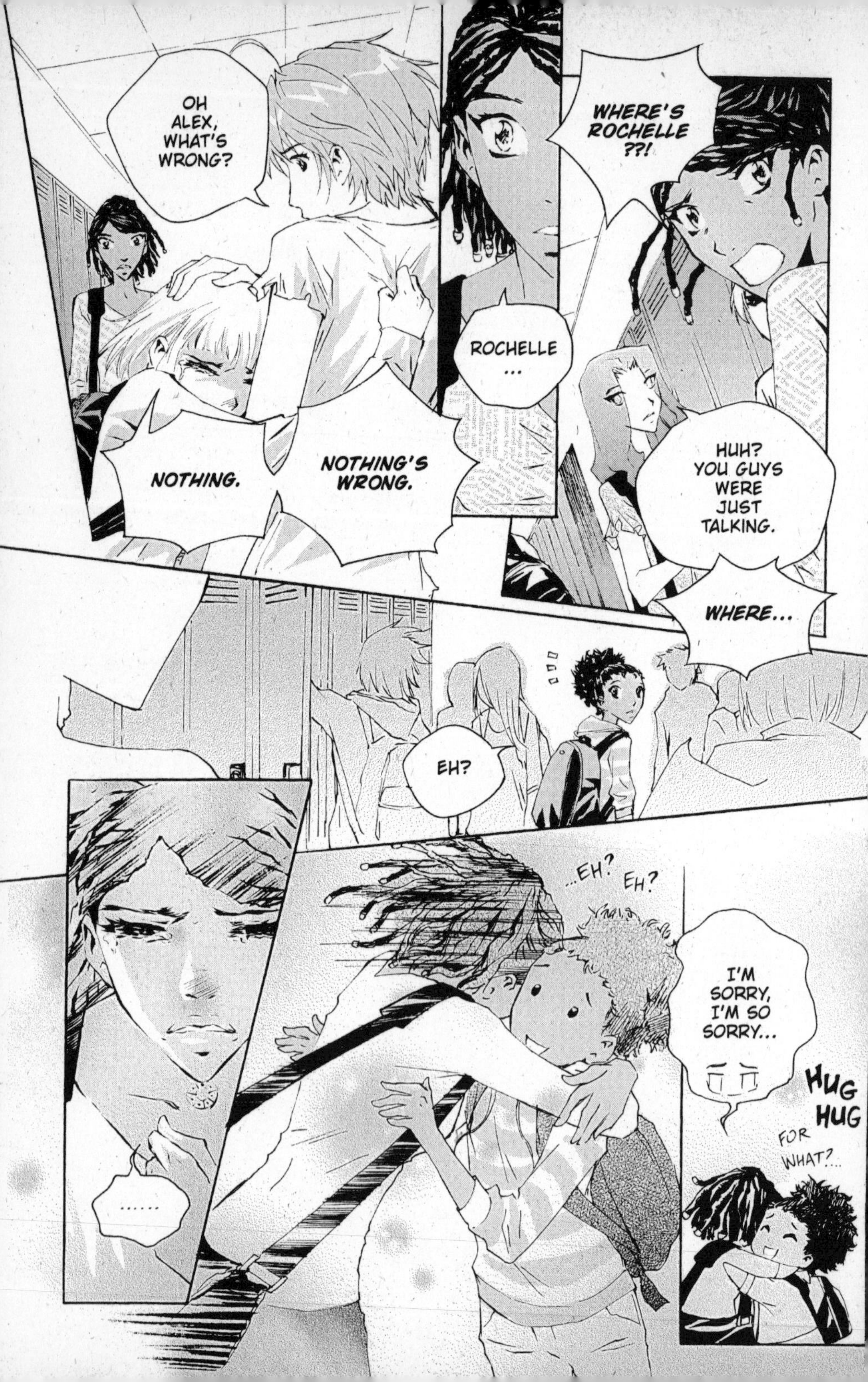
OH ALEX, WHAT'S WRONG?
NOTHING.
NOTHING'S WRONG.
WHERE'S ROCHELLE ??!
ROCHELLE ...
HUH? YOU GUYS WERE JUST TALKING.
WHERE...
EH?
......
...EH?
EH?
I'M SORRY, I'M SO SORRY...
HUG HUG
FOR WHAT?...

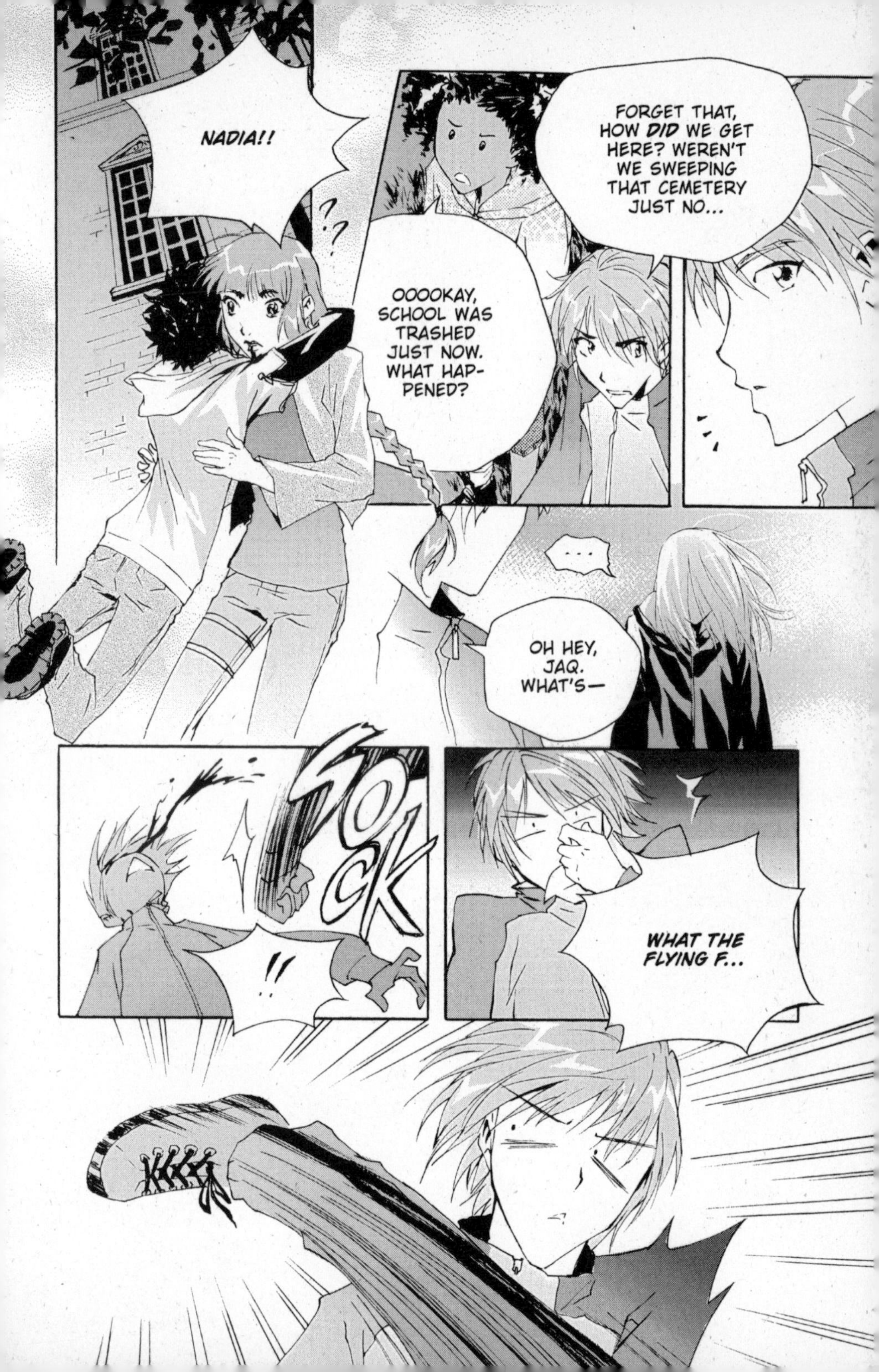
NADIA!!
??
OOOOKAY, SCHOOL WAS TRASHED JUST NOW. WHAT HAPPENED?
FORGET THAT, HOW *DID* WE GET HERE? WEREN'T WE SWEEPING THAT CEMETERY JUST NO...
...
OH HEY, JAQ. WHAT'S—
SOCK
!!
WHAT THE FLYING F...

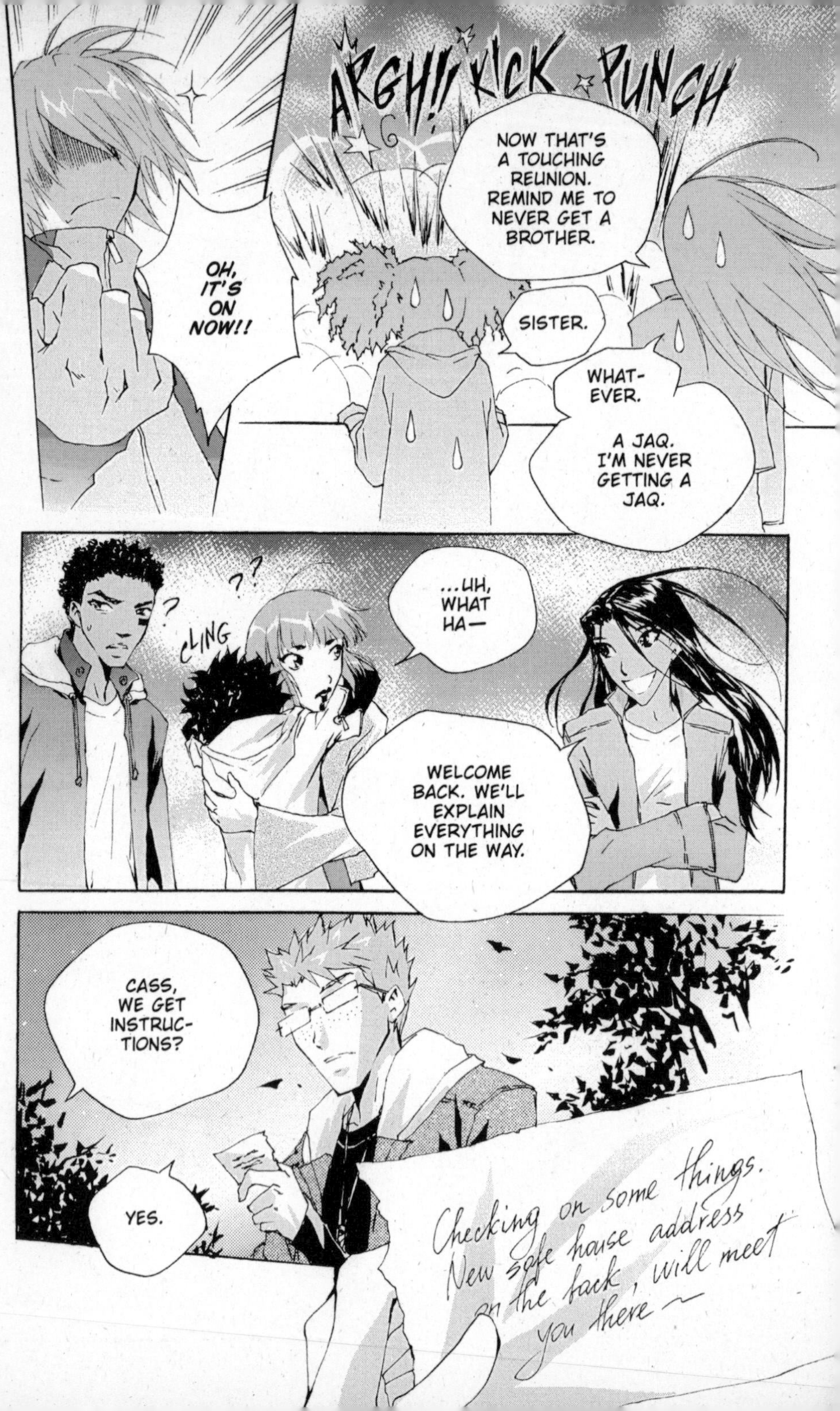
OH, IT'S ON NOW!!
ARGH!! KICK PUNCH
NOW THAT'S A TOUCHING REUNION. REMIND ME TO NEVER GET A BROTHER.
SISTER.
WHAT-EVER.
A JAQ. I'M NEVER GETTING A JAQ.
? ?
?
CLING
...UH, WHAT HA—
WELCOME BACK. WE'LL EXPLAIN EVERYTHING ON THE WAY.
CASS, WE GET INSTRUC-TIONS?
YES.
Checking on some things. New safe house address on the back, will meet you there ~

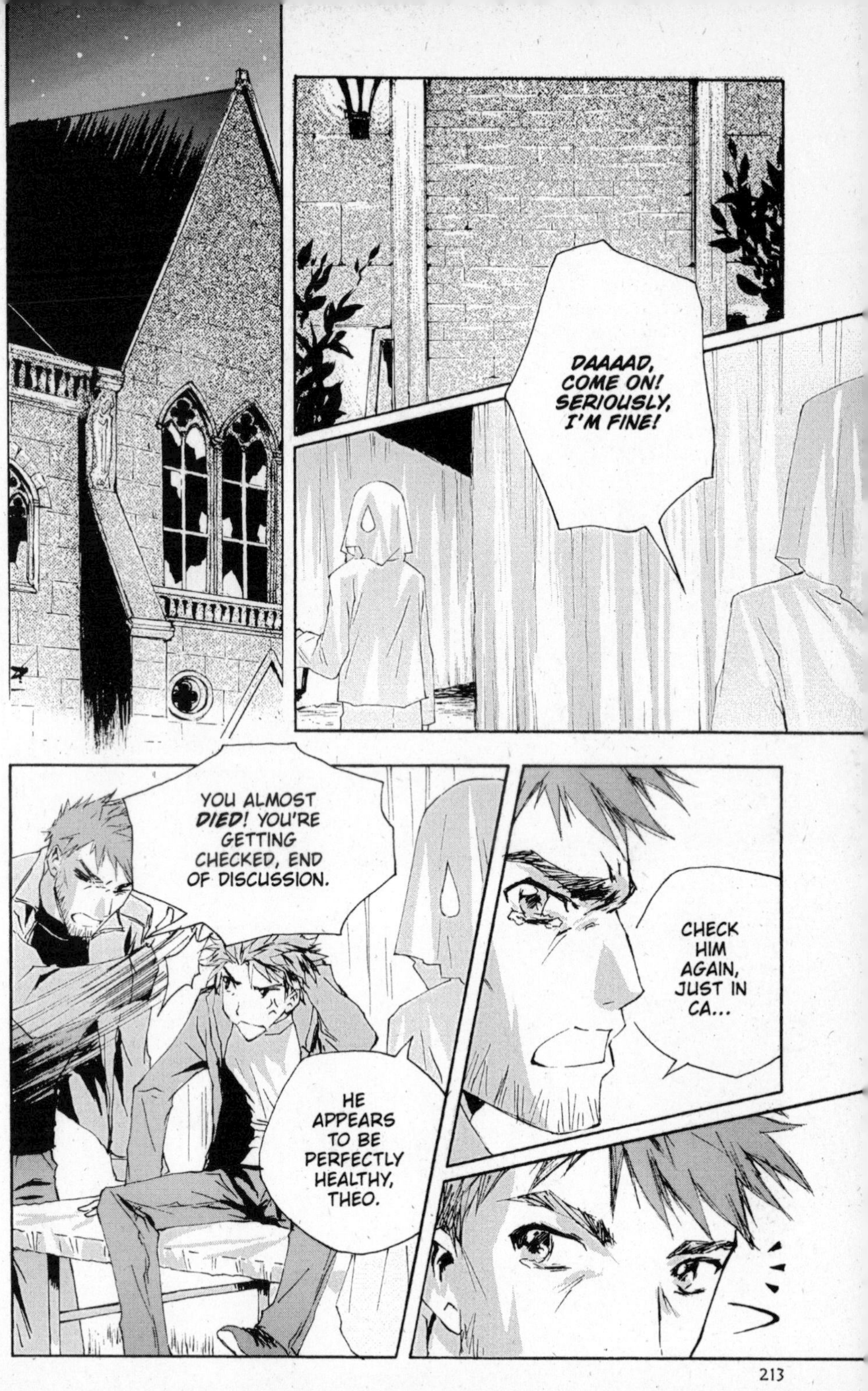
DAAAAD, COME ON! SERIOUSLY, I'M FINE!
YOU ALMOST DIED! YOU'RE GETTING CHECKED, END OF DISCUSSION.
HE APPEARS TO BE PERFECTLY HEALTHY, THEO.
CHECK HIM AGAIN, JUST IN CA...

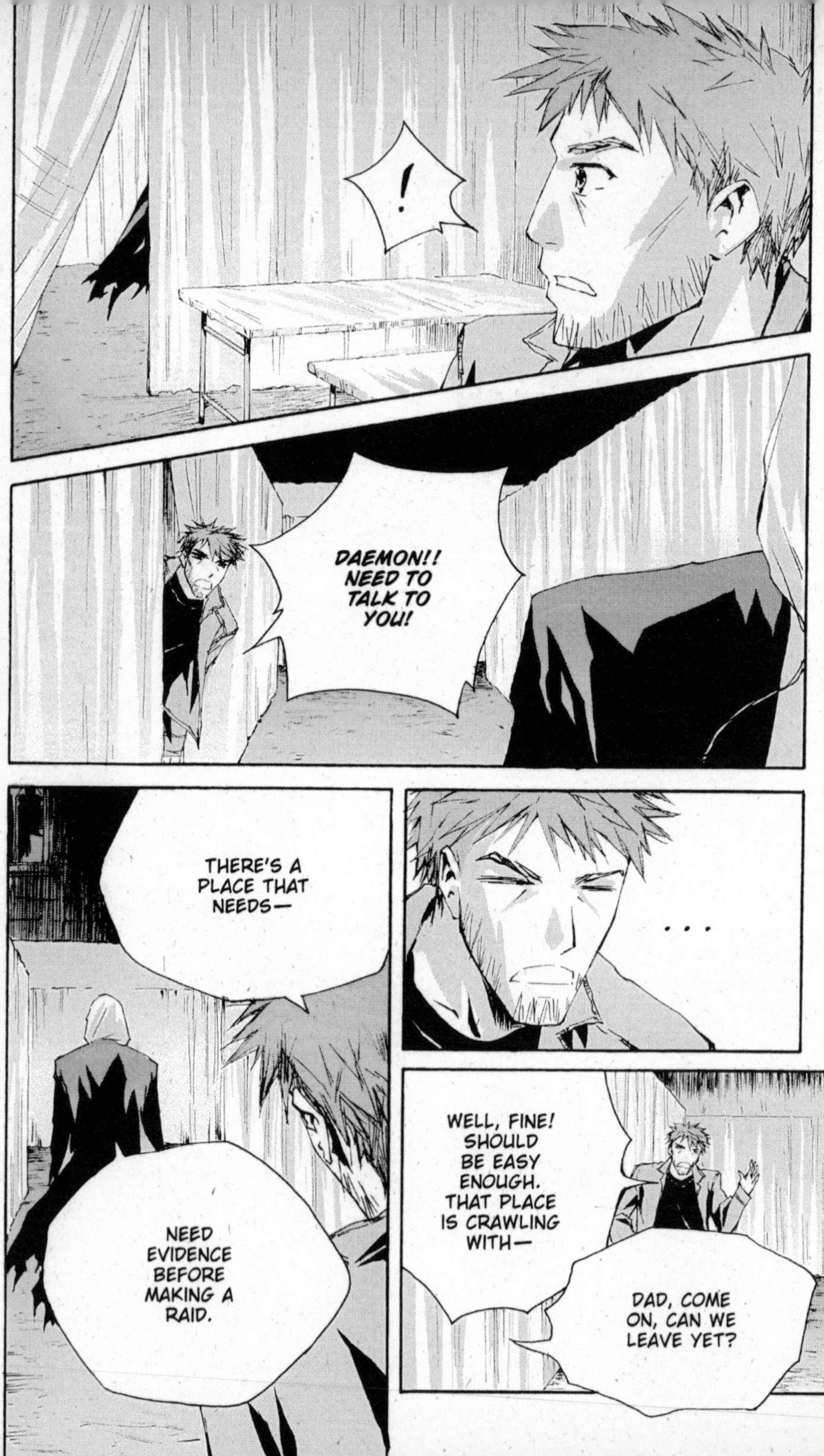
!
DAEMON!! NEED TO TALK TO YOU!
THERE'S A PLACE THAT NEEDS—
NEED EVIDENCE BEFORE MAKING A RAID.
...
WELL, FINE! SHOULD BE EASY ENOUGH. THAT PLACE IS CRAWLING WITH—
DAD, COME ON, CAN WE LEAVE YET?

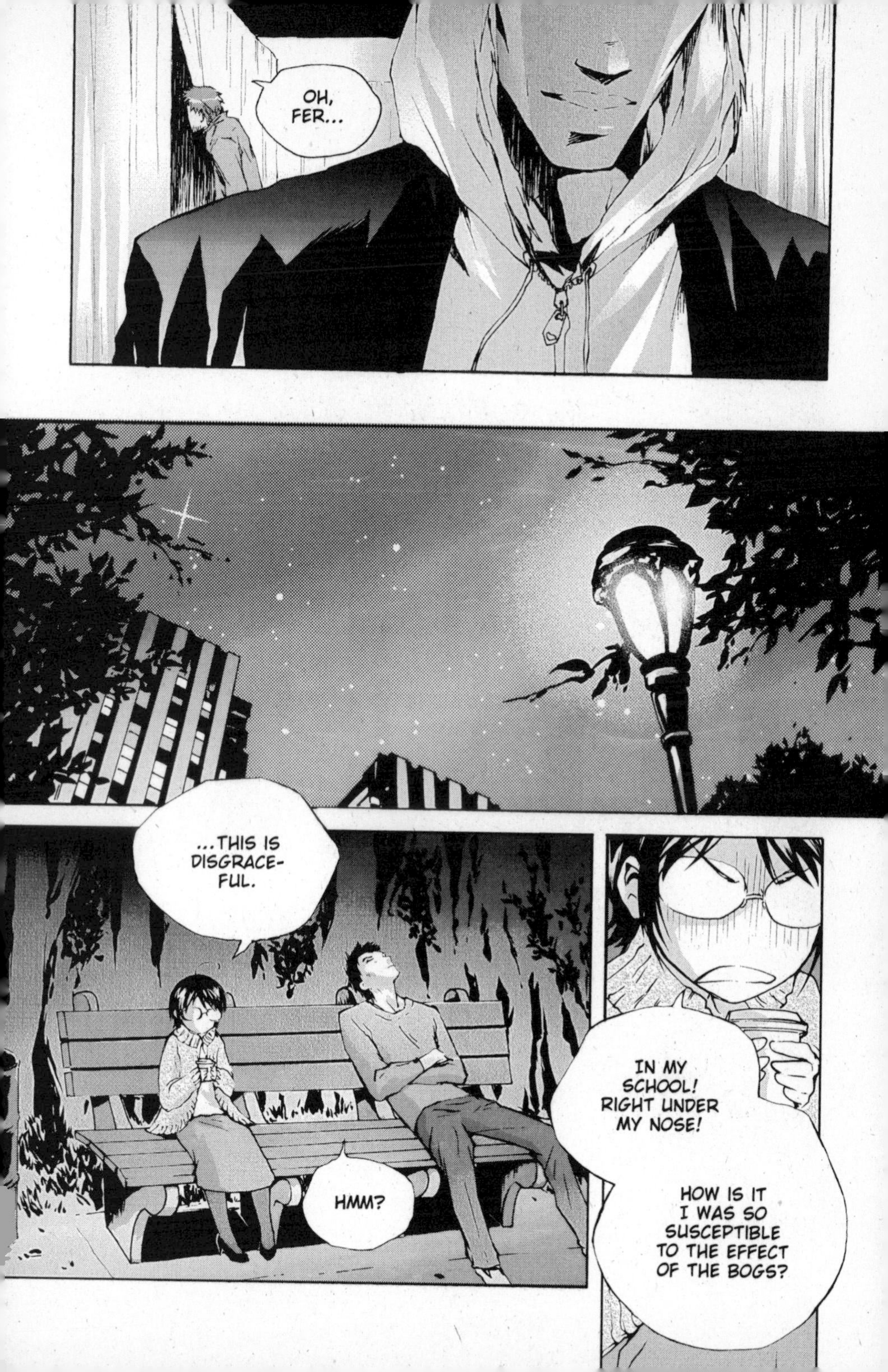
OH, FER...
...THIS IS DISGRACE-FUL.
HMM?
IN MY SCHOOL! RIGHT UNDER MY NOSE!
HOW IS IT I WAS SO SUSCEPTIBLE TO THE EFFECT OF THE BOGS?

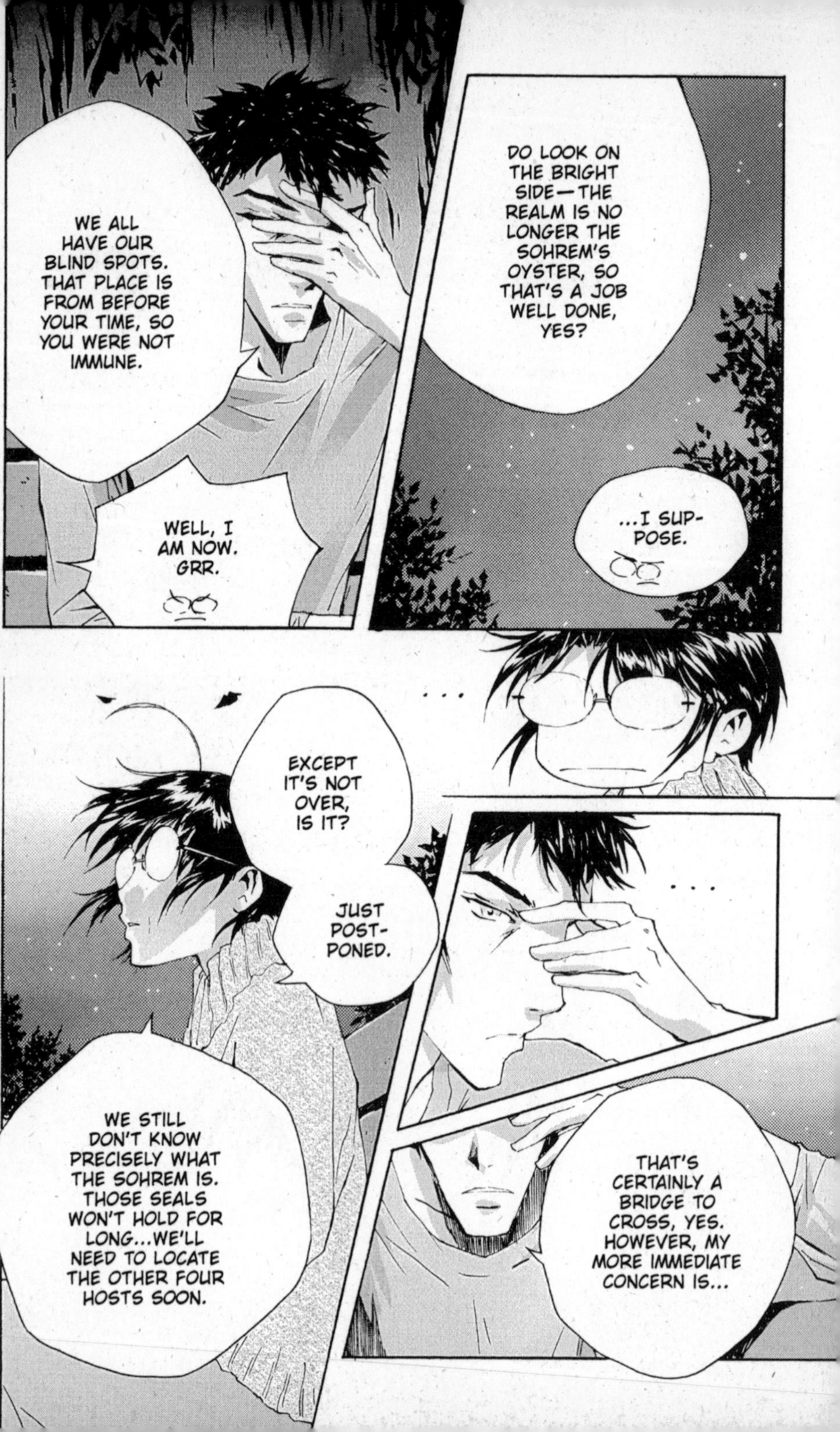
WE ALL HAVE OUR BLIND SPOTS. THAT PLACE IS FROM BEFORE YOUR TIME, SO YOU WERE NOT IMMUNE.
WELL, I AM NOW. GRR.
DO LOOK ON THE BRIGHT SIDE—THE REALM IS NO LONGER THE SOHREM'S OYSTER, SO THAT'S A JOB WELL DONE, YES?
...I SUP-POSE.
EXCEPT IT'S NOT OVER, IS IT?
JUST POST-PONED.
WE STILL DON'T KNOW PRECISELY WHAT THE SOHREM IS. THOSE SEALS WON'T HOLD FOR LONG...WE'LL NEED TO LOCATE THE OTHER FOUR HOSTS SOON.
...
...
THAT'S CERTAINLY A BRIDGE TO CROSS, YES. HOWEVER, MY MORE IMMEDIATE CONCERN IS...

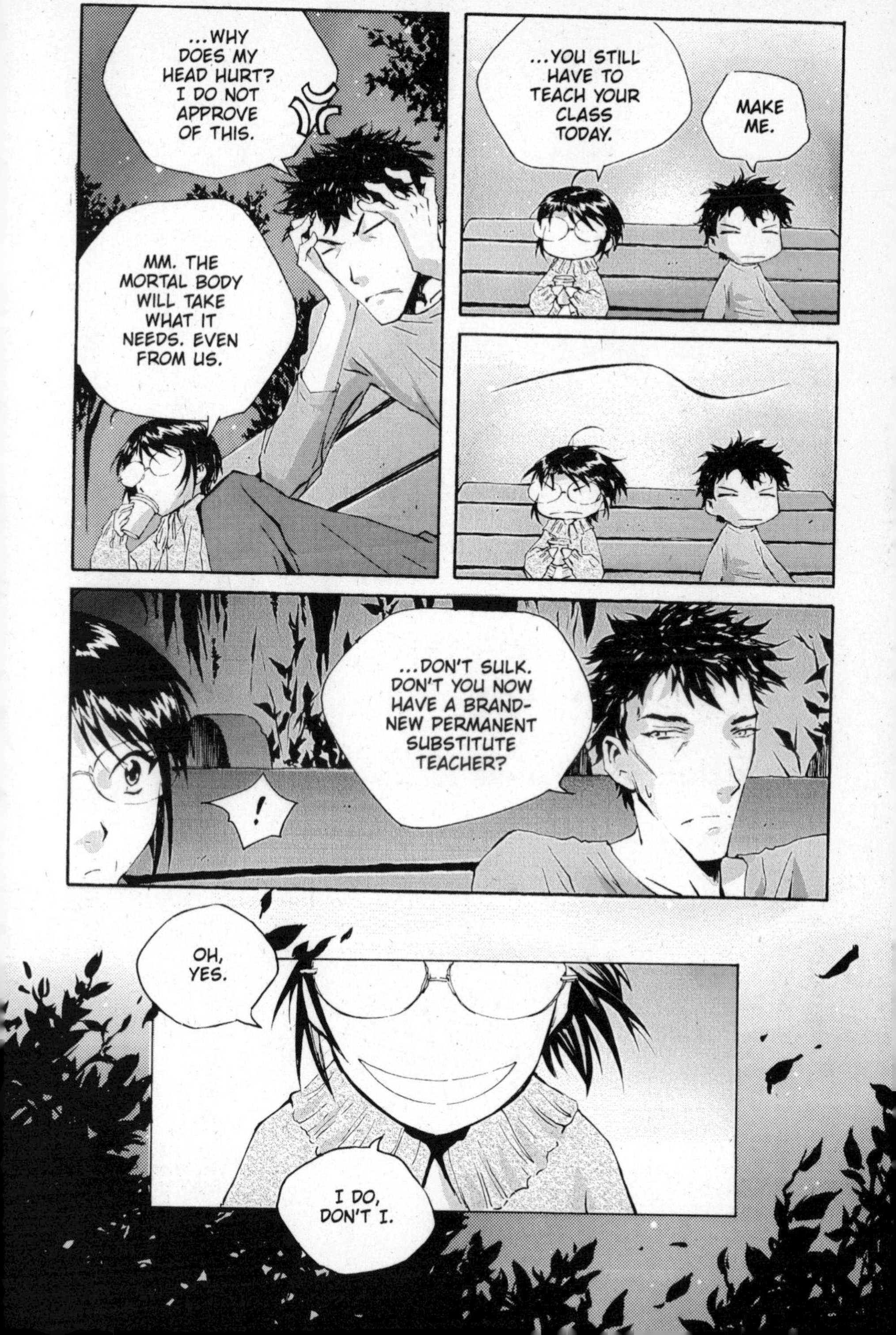
...WHY DOES MY HEAD HURT? I DO NOT APPROVE OF THIS.
MM. THE MORTAL BODY WILL TAKE WHAT IT NEEDS. EVEN FROM US.
...YOU STILL HAVE TO TEACH YOUR CLASS TODAY.
MAKE ME.
...DON'T SULK. DON'T YOU NOW HAVE A BRAND-NEW PERMANENT SUBSTITUTE TEACHER?
!
OH, YES.
I DO, DON'T I.

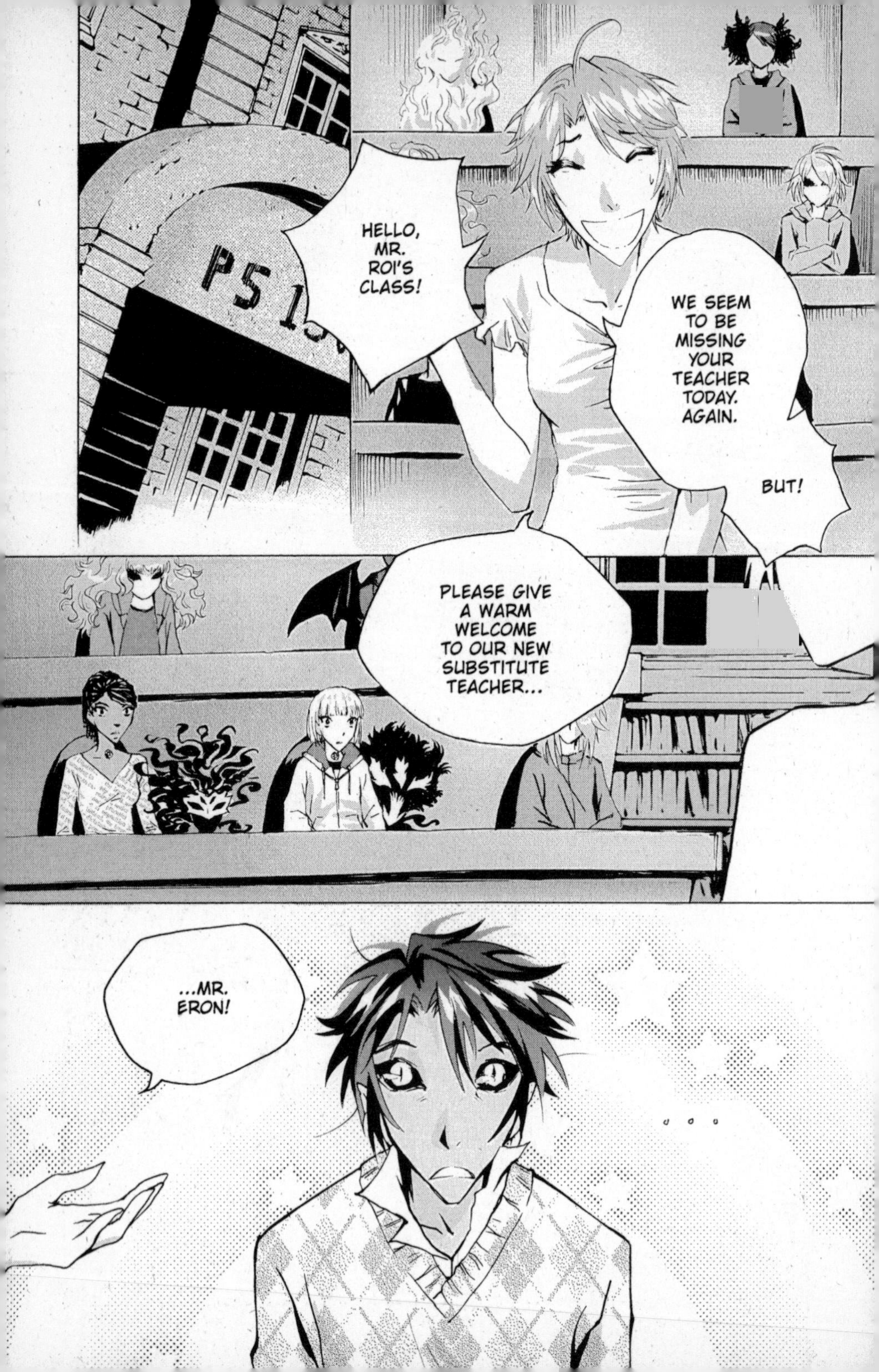
HELLO, MR. ROI'S CLASS!
WE SEEM TO BE MISSING YOUR TEACHER TODAY. AGAIN.
BUT!
PLEASE GIVE A WARM WELCOME TO OUR NEW SUBSTITUTE TEACHER...
...MR. ERON!

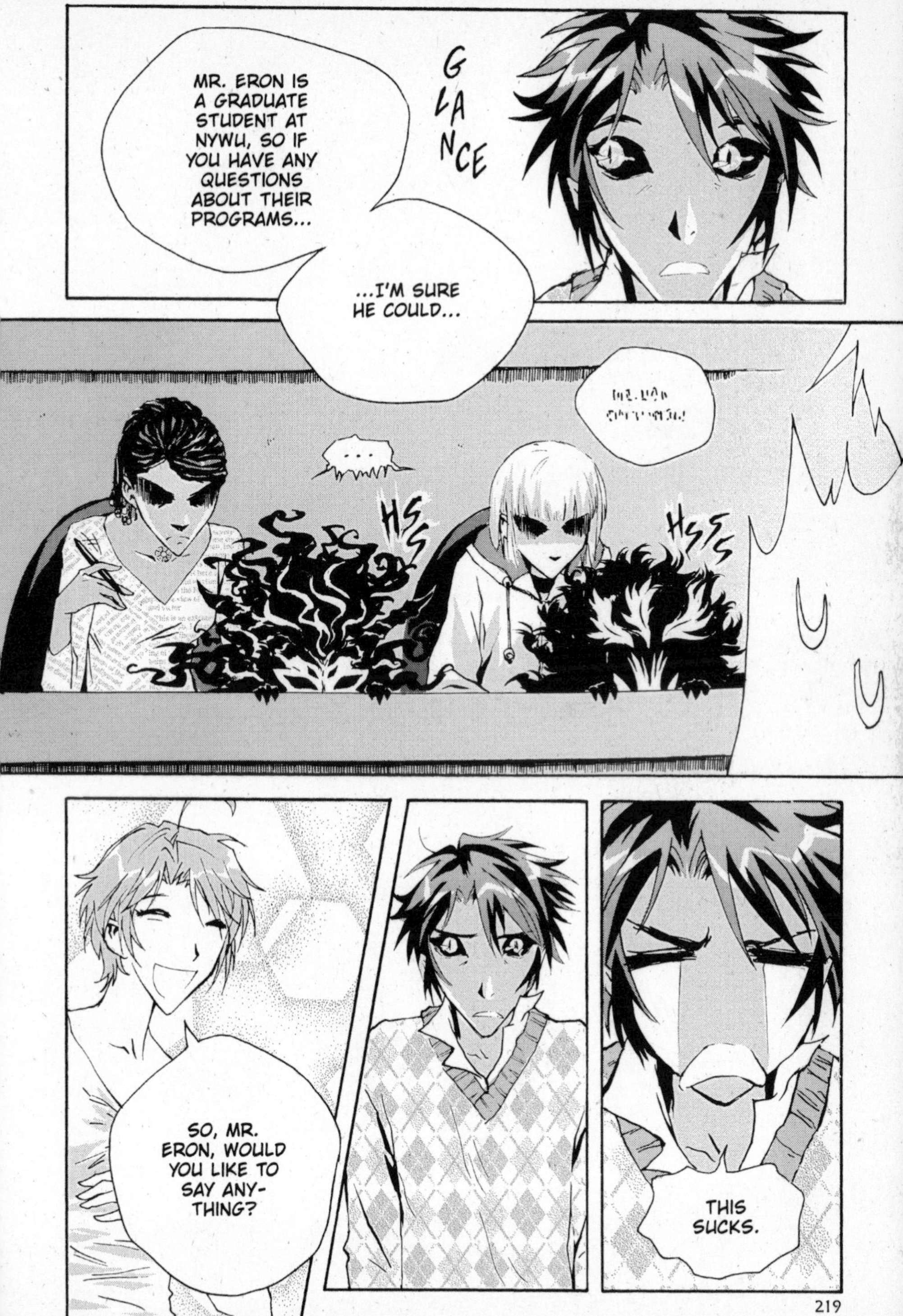
MR. ERON IS A GRADUATE STUDENT AT NYWU, SO IF YOU HAVE ANY QUESTIONS ABOUT THEIR PROGRAMS...
GLANCE
...I'M SURE HE COULD...
...
HSS
HSS
SO, MR. ERON, WOULD YOU LIKE TO SAY ANY-THING?
THIS SUCKS.

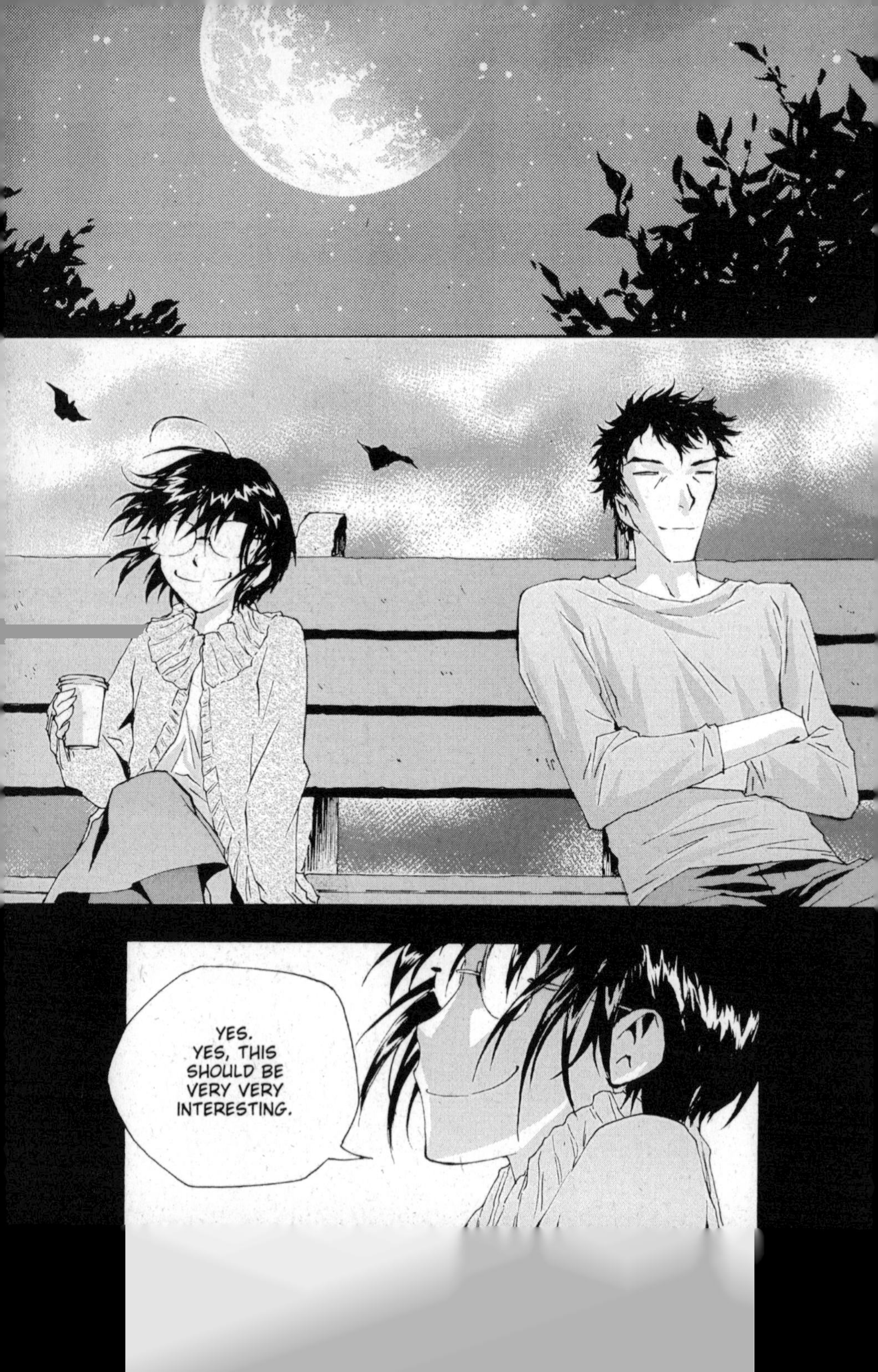
YES. YES, THIS SHOULD BE VERY VERY INTERESTING.

THE END!

(... for now :‑))

BWAH HA HA
HA HA
H......

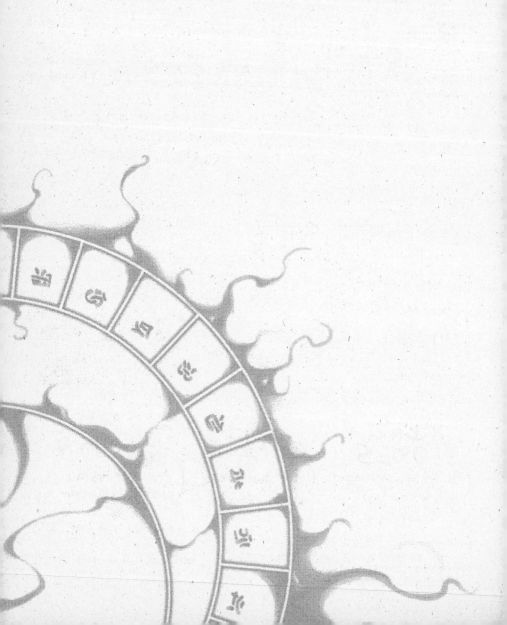

...SORRY, I HAD TO DO THE HAPPY FLINGING AND THE SCREAM, BECAUSE WOW, THE MARATHON TO FINISH THIS BOOK WAS EPIC!! EVEN MORE EPIC THAN USUAL, I DIDN'T THINK THINGS COULD GET THAT INTENSE, I THINK MY HAND FELL OFF SOMEWHERE IN CHAPTER 24 (IF YOU FIND IT, PLEASE RETURN TO OWNER, EVEN IT RESISTS AND TRIES TO RUN AWAY 8D!)
AND HOW ABOUT THAT ENDING, HUH?! BEFORE I AM PELTED WITH PRODUCE AND OTHER TOKENS OF, UH, APPRECIATION, I HASTEN TO SAY THAT NO! THIS IS NOT THE END OF THE SERIES! THIS STORY ARC IS DONE, BUT WE ARE PLANNING MORE BOOKS IN THE FUTURE*.

TO DISTRACT YOU FROM READING THE FOOTNOTE, I QUICKLY OFFER YOU VAGUELY AMUSING HIGHLIGHTS FROM THIS LAST MAD DEADLINE DASH! SOME OF THINGS I DID WHILE FINISHING:

ATTEMPT TO DRAW WITH THE WRONG END OF THE PEN:	TRY ENERGY DRINKS TO ACHIEVE "MENTAL ALERTNESS."	STAND ON THE BALCONY AND LOOK AT THE CITY STREETS, SMILING IN AN UNHINGED MANNER:

BUT I WAS NOT ALONE!! BIG THANKS AND HUGS GO OUT TO THESE KIND PEOPLE FOR HELPING ME OUT IN THE FINAL CRUNCH:

IRENE FLORES
(for gorgeous inking help in the last 2 chapters ♥)

DEE!
(for awesome tones, as always!)

JUYOUN!
(for getting me every extension imaginable and cheering me on ╥﹏╥)

* ...H-HOWEVER, FIRST I HAVE TO TAKE A BREAK TO DO ANOTHER PROJECT *DUCKS AIRBORNE PRODUCE* WHICH IS SECRET AT THE TIME OF MY WRITING THIS, BUT SHOULD ALREADY BE ANNOUNCED AT THE TIME THIS BOOK HITS THE SHELVES!! FOR DETAILS, PLEASE CHECK MY WEBSITE: www.svetlania.com

...SPEAKING OF JUYOUN

I SOMETIMES GET QUESTIONS ABOUT WHAT IT'S LIKE TO WORK WITH AN EDITOR ON *NIGHTSCHOOL*; IS IT BETTER THAN WORKING ON MY OWN? MY ANSWER TO SAID QUESTION IS ALWAYS A RESOUNDING "YES." IT WOULD'VE BEEN HELL(!!) TO WRITE THIS SPRAWLING BEAST OF A STORYLINE IF I DIDN'T HAVE JUYOUN TO RUN TO WHEN I'VE STARED AT A SCRIPT FOR SO LONG IT NO LONGER LOOKS LIKE IT'S IN ENGLISH AND I CAN'T EVEN TELL IF IT WORKS OR NOT. @_@;; WHEN TIMES GET TOUGH LIKE THIS? THE TOUGH GO CRYING TO JUYOUN AND SPEND AN HOUR ON THE PHONE WITH HER UNTIL THINGS MAKE SENSE AGAIN!!

NOW, BESIDES BEING A BADASS EDITOR ALWAYS RESCUING CREATORS FROM DIRE PERIL, JUYOUN IS ALSO A REALLY COOL PERSON AND A FRIEND, SO I DECIDED IT IS MY DUTY TO THOROUGHLY EMBARRASS HER WITH A GUSHY INTERVIEW :3 SO HERE SHE IS, GENTLE READERS (AND THANK YOU FOR DOING THIS, EDITOR-SAN!!):

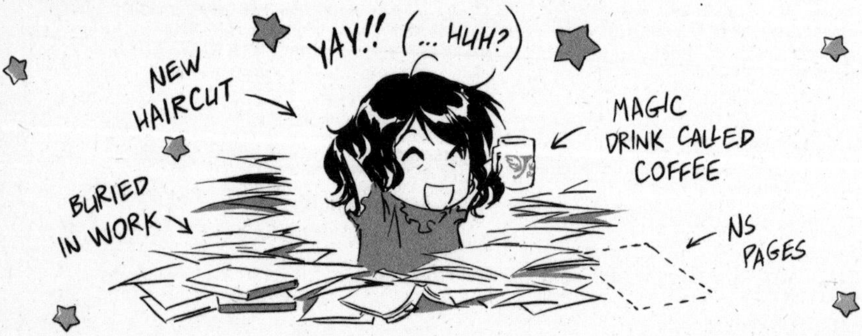
YAY!! (...HUH?)
NEW HAIRCUT
MAGIC DRINK CALLED COFFEE
BURIED IN WORK
NS PAGES

Svet: You are originally from Korea, where you edited and managed an impressive lineup of original books from Korean creators. Now you live in the US and oversee original books from North American (and Russian-Canadian :D) creators as well! Has it been a difficult switch? What are some of the differences? (I know sometimes you wish Canada was next door...Like, when there is a deadline and the latest chapter pages are MIA...)

JuYoun: Oh, I do so wish Canada was next door! LOL The switch itself was not as difficult as some might think, but to me, I guess the biggest difference is indeed the face time. It's not just when the deadline is close, but even at the earlier stages, I was used to sitting down and discussing things with creators, which I don't get to do a lot in the US. I still miss those times, but I wonder if I'm just reminiscing about the good old days, since technology has allowed many to work without actually having to be in the same room.

Svet: You fluently speak roughly a billion languages (...well, at least three that I know of). Is there any language you would really love to learn?

JuYoun: I feel like I'm fluent in none these days. LOL The motivation for learning a language (for me, of course) is my interest in the culture. These days, I really want to learn Chinese and French, since I feel like those two have a lot of influence on English, Japanese, and Korean, and I would love to learn more about those cultures.

Svet: How is it that you became an editor? Do you have a favorite part of the job? (That's not the weekend :3?)

JuYoun: Hmm. As anyone who works in publishing would say, I've always loved books, but the direct reason probably is that I worked for the school magazine while I was in college, and I found that I loved it. Comics, or manga, have always been my passion, so it felt only natural to get into this area of publishing. As far as favorite parts, while everything from finding talent to actually getting the books in my hand is exciting, I used to love getting to work on the artists' original pages, which felt like a privilege. But these days, I don't get that satisfaction, since everything's digital. :(

Svet: I found out you were an architecture major when I was working on the floor plans for Nightschool 13W in book 2. You helped me work out some of the problems with that (thank you!!), so now I wonder—if you could design any building in the world, fictional or real, what would it be?

JuYoun: What help are you talking about? It was already perfect! :D Yes, I was an architecture major, which was lots of fun, and it also involved a lot of art classes and whatnot. At the moment, I don't have any ambitions in that regard. (I hardly remember anything!) I do hope that someday, though, I'll design my dream house! Well, if I can't, I do still have many friends in that field that I could hire. LOL

Svet: I know quite a few aspiring mangaka read *Nightschool.* Would you like to say anything to any future Svetlanas out there? :D

JuYoun: An image of a little, chibi Svet popped into my head! LOL Hmmm. Well, there's a lot to be said, like...practice a lot, always remember that the art and the text has to work together, etc. But I guess the one thing would be to always have passion and to always think about what's in your heart, what story you want to tell. That will give you the strength to try hard, to let you get to where you need to be in order to be a professional!

CHIBI SVET RIGHT HERE!! AGREEING! ♥

YOU REALLY DO HAVE TO LOVE THIS TO DO IT!!

...WELL, AND HAVE A GOOD EDITOR ☺

THANK YOU, JUYOUN!! ♥ *HUGS*

SVET   JUYOUN

SDCC '08

(Nightschool launch celebration ☺)

AND FOR MY NEXT VICTIM...

DEE!!

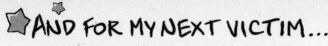

FOR THOSE WHO ARE UNAWARE, DEE IS TEN KINDS OF AWESOME AND ALSO THE TONE ARTIST ON *NIGHTSCHOOL*. WE'VE BEEN WORKING TOGETHER SINCE MY *DRAMACON* DAYS, AND IT'S A WORK RELATIONSHIP THAT STARTED ABOUT SIX YEARS AGO, APPROXIMATELY THUS... DEE: SAY, SVET, YOU SOUND STRESSED. DO YOU NEED HELP WITH YOUR BOOK DEADLINE? SVET: YEEEEEES ;___; ...AND SINCE NO GOOD DEED GOES UNPUNISHED, I ENDED UP DRAGGING HER THROUGH ALL MY BOOK DEADLINES EVER SINCE :D;;; WE'VE BECOME GOOD FRIENDS ALONG THE WAY, DESPITE LIVING IN DIFFERENT PARTS OF THE WORLD, THUS I OWE HER AN EMBARRASSINGLY GUSHY INTERVIEW AS WELL! :D HEEEEEEERE IT IS:

Svet: You've been the long-suffering and patient tone artist for *Nightschool* for over two years now, on top of a full-time job, a move halfway across the world, and other miscellaneous things like life and stuff. Would you like to share any insights about working with an author who has a "durr" chip where her deadline sense should be? (...Er, besides a resounding "DON'T" XD;; ?)

Dee: I'm not sure people really understand just how crazy the amount of work is that it takes to make a comic book. And how crazy the deadlines are. You have to be insane to do this job. We both have a "durr" chip. :D I watched a truly remarkable series grow and a gifted creator make magic against all odds. I'm not complaining.

Svet: You are also an independent manga creator (more *OniKimono* chapters plz *begs* ;o;). How did you start creating your own stories? Was there a "spark" moment, a book or an event that pushed you down that dark and winding path?

Dee: I remember sitting on the floor of my mom's house with a ballpoint pen and a stack of used printer paper. I remember drawing a horse. And then, without knowing why, drawing a vertical line. And then I drew what the horse did next. I think all the comics creators I know independently "invented" comics out of some place deep within themselves.

Svet: What tools did you use then, and what do you use now? Did anything change/evolve in your creative outlook?

Dee: From a ballpoint pen to Bristol board with a dip-pen to a Cintiq. The important evolution is your vision, not your tools, I think. And as for evolution of my toning technique, I fail, 'cause I'm still using the same battered copy of Deleter ComicWorks 1 on the same piece of crap PC I've been hauling all over the planet for eight years.

Svet: One of the many things I really love about *OniKimono* and *Shatterstone* (besides the fact that they are excellent stories) is that they both have hot, wisecracking detectives as main characters. You've mentioned that you are influenced by film noir; what are some must-watch titles that you would recommend?

Dee: If you watch *Casablanca* so many times that you can close your eyes and replay the entire thing in your head, read everything Dashiell Hammett ever wrote, spend your '80s watching *Miami Vice*, have the ANNOTATED Sherlock Holmes on your shelf, and listen to swing in your off hours, you will find yourself writing a hard-boiled detective into all of your comics. The hard part becomes keeping him out of them.

Svet: The obligatory desert island question: If you could only take three things, etc., what would they be? :D

Dee: A ballpoint pen, a stack of printer paper, and...does "the Internet" count as one thing?

Svet: Where could people go to find your work (besides my shelf, heh-heh-heh)?

Dee: If you drop by jdeedupuy.com, please say hello ^__^

NOH
HUNTER

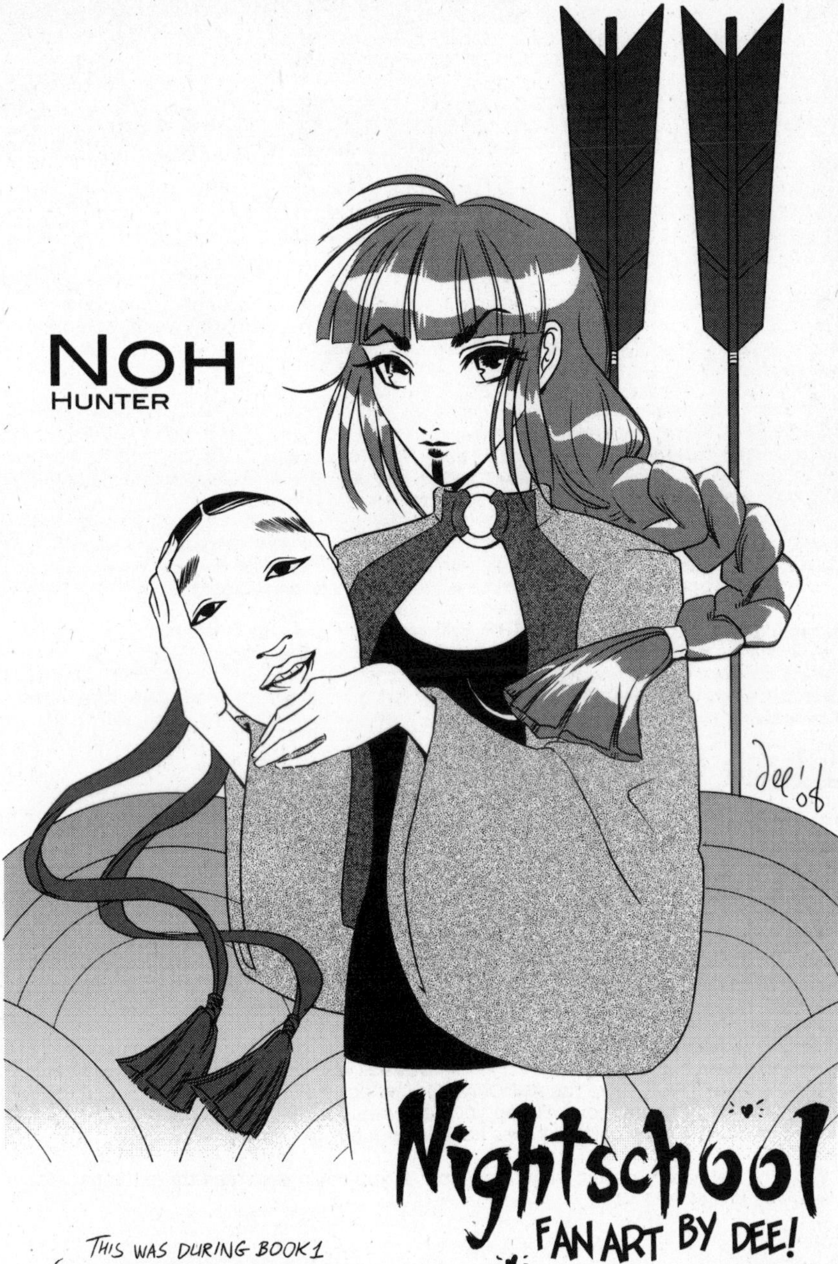
dee'08

Nightschool
FAN ART BY DEE!

^^

THIS WAS DURING BOOK 1
(BEFORE NOH GOT KNOCKED OUT
AND MISSED ALL THE ACTION ≥≤)
SUCH A GORGEOUS PIECE,
THANK YOU FOR EVERYTHING, DEE!!

AND LAST BUT NOT LEAST...

THE WORLD IN *NIGHTSCHOOL* IS VERY COMPLEX, AND I'VE ONLY BARELY SCRATCHED THE SURFACE IN THESE FOUR BOOKS... SO I LEAVE YOU WITH A VAIN ATTEMPT TO CLARIFY A FEW THINGS ABOUT SOME OF THE KEY GROUPS IN IT! BEHOLD THE...

NIGHTSCHOOL COMPANION!

(the really really short version)

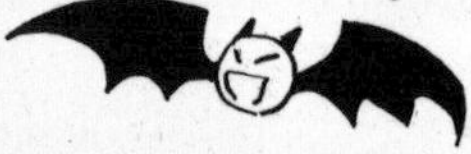

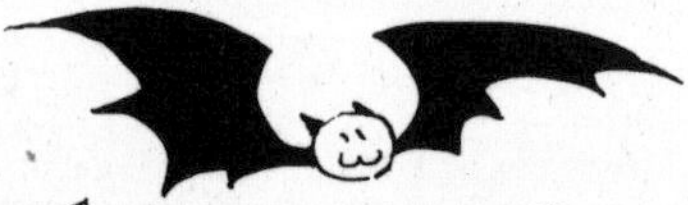

HUNTERS

HUNTERS—supernatural beings who are neither human nor of the Night World. They are very strong, fast, and can live a long time (but often die early in their line of work). Hunter bodies heal very rapidly, which makes it impossible for them to have tattoos or piercings (much to the chagrin of Hunters like Teresa, who really wants a salamander tattoo on her left leg.) The Hunters' initial natural function is to protect humans from Night Things, but things get complicated beyond that.

CLAVE—Hunters are brutally self-sufficient starting at an early age and don't really have families per se (many of them start out as abandoned children or orphans), so they have Claves instead. A Clave is a small group of young Hunters headed by an adult (or two or three, depending on the size of the Clave), who is usually referred to as "Teacher." Here they are homeschooled to know everything about the Hunter trade, the Night World, and the world in general (so math, chemistry, languages, etc.—there's no escape from those!) NOTE: Dating within a Clave is forbidden (though sometimes Teachers turn a blind eye, even if they know something's going on).

THE SCORING—a yearly event where many claves meet and Hunters-in-training proceed to beat one another to a bloody pulp in moderated fights, with the purpose of furthering their battle skills. Those who repeatedly lose at The Scoring are most likely to die first back in the real world.

WEIRNS

WEIRNS—a special breed of witch who are born with demon guardian spirits (Astrals) bound to them. Each Weirn has a spellbook which only they can open. (Alex carries hers around in the story.)

ASTRALS—demon guardian spirits (usually of limited intelligence, but nonetheless quite perceptive and clever in certain ways—like, cookie-stealing ways). Astrals are irrevocably bound to their Weirn hosts and have often been known to take on hidden traits of their hosts' personalities, sometimes even acting on the hosts' suppressed desires. Adult Astrals look very different from their younger incarnations. (Sarah has one, but it hasn't made an appearance yet.)

VAMPIRES

TURNING—to become a vampire in the *Nightschool* world you need to a.) get bitten, and b.) lose a lot of blood, but not enough to die. The Turning is a gradual process that takes a few days, during which time your mortal body is actually still around, but slowly being devoured by the vampire persona. If you look in the mirror, you will see your reflection—but even if your vampire self is smiling, your mortal reflection will still look lost and terrified, as you are effectively dying. During these few days, you can still turn back into a human by subjecting yourself to a heavy dose of sunlight to burn out the vampire. (However, it's very painful.) After that, it's too late, and no mirror in the world will ever see you again.

RIPPERS—the future of any vampire—no exceptions—though many "live" a long time before they finally succumb. Rippers are vampires who've forgotten what it's like to be alive and can no longer maintain the illusion, which causes them to physically change into the dry, mindless, and perpetually hungry creatures portrayed in chapter 3 of book 1. If you want to scare a *Nightschool* vampire, tell them their skin is looking a little dry. None of them want to go that way anytime soon...

SHIFTERS ☆

THE SHAPESHIFTER community is incredibly diverse—there are wolves, foxes, ravens, and count-less other species. Even anacondas, I kid you not! These are all creatures of both the Night World and the wild—either people who turn into animals or animals who turn into people—who have claimed the city as their new dark and dangerous woods. Many of them are very urbane and have carved out new occupations for themselves in all areas of business. (For example, Gray and his buddies are basically muscle for hire... Too bad they didn't quite understand who they were messing with. 8D)

THE NERESHAI ☆

....are basically the resident badasses of the Night World who keep an eye on things. They are immensely powerful to the point where they don't posture or brag, they simply Take Care Of Business and move on. (...Well, unless they are Mr. Roi, who does like to indulge in a bit of posturing and self-congratulating. :D) Their job is largely thankless, incredibly demanding, and they'd all really love to quit, except that they can't for reasons that will be revealed later! Their individual histories are fasci-nating, especially for Daemon and Mr. Roi, who in fact are technically the same age and go way back. ...Did I mention that the Nereshai are my best, favorite people in this book? I could just draw them all day. I wish I could hang out with them. Madam Chen and I would have coffee, and Daemon and Mr. Roi would just sit there looking good and trying to not kill each other, and then I'd be all "Hey, I know, let's go fight bad guys, lemme just get my astral, brb! 8D"
/sad fantasy life...OTZ

THE WORLD ☆

LEYLINES—Jaq mentions these briefly in this volume. They are a net of energy lines weaving through the world and can be used for (barely reliable) communication. What you do is you give a piece of your voice to a Leyline in the form of a message as well as the name of the person you wish for it to reach. Such messages sometimes take the long way and may arrive a century later instead of, well, sooner. Giving a message to a Leyline will leave you hoarse for a couple of hours.
VOICES—voice messages that got lost on Leynet (and sometimes acquired a life of their own, or merged with others). If a person with a good feel for it were to stand in the middle of a Leysite (a place where a bunch of Leylines cross), they could hear all kinds of things from different times and places.
OLD WORLD VESTIGES—the Bogs of Lethe are one of them. They are very dangerous artifacts of a time past that lie in wait and only grow in power as the centuries roll on. Many try to use them for their own ends... When someone actually succeeds instead of becoming their sacrifice, well, that's when the Nereshai cancel all their meetings and wipe the floor with everyone involved.

... AAAAND THAT'S IT FOR NOW! ♥ THANK YOU EVERYONE FOR READING AND FOR YOUR SUPPORT, IT REALLY MAKES ALL THE DIFFERENCE WHEN I'M FACING OFF WITH THE BOOK PAGES IN THE STUDIO ALL BY MYSELF...
(... IT ALSO HELPS WHEN I FIGHT EVIL, SO IT'S JUST AN ALL-AROUND AWESOME BOON TO HAVE SUPPORTIVE READERS ♥ b)
SEE YOU IN THE NEXT BOOK!!!
crawls off to sleep Svet ♥

NIGHTSCHOOL
THE WEIRN BOOKS ④

SVETLANA CHMAKOVA

Toning Artist: Dee DuPuy

Lettering: JuYoun Lee

NIGHTSCHOOL: The Weirn Books, Vol. 4 © 2010 Svetlana Chmakova.

Yen Press
Hachette Book Group
237 Park Avenue, New York, NY 10017

www.HachetteBookGroup.com
www.YenPress.com

Yen Press is an imprint of Hachette Book Group, Inc. The Yen Press name and logo are trademarks of Hachette Book Group, Inc.

First Yen Press Edition: October 2010

ISBN: 978-0-316-09126-8

10 9 8 7 6 5 4 3 2

BVG

Printed in the United States of America